The Forum of Federations Handbook of Fiscal Federalism

Jean-François Tremblay
Editor

The Forum of Federations Handbook of Fiscal Federalism

Forum of Federations
The Global Network on Federalism and Devolved Governance

palgrave
macmillan

Editor
Jean-François Tremblay
Department of Economics
University of Ottawa
Ottawa, ON, Canada

ISBN 978-3-030-97257-8 ISBN 978-3-030-97258-5 (eBook)
https://doi.org/10.1007/978-3-030-97258-5

This Palgrave Macmillan imprint is published by the registered company Springer Nature Switzerland AG
The registered company address is: Gewerbestrasse 11, 6330 Cham, Switzerland

Foreword

This volume, *The Forum of Federations Handbook on Fiscal Federalism*, we consider to be an important contribution to the study of federalism. Bringing together scholars and practitioners from across the globe, it seeks to broaden and update current understandings of the state of fiscal federalism within 11 country case studies, and by so doing attempts to tease out some extrapolatory lessons that might be learned from the Forum of Federation's signature comparative analysis.

The importance of the work that this volume sets out to do, is in broadening and in some cases updating the Forum's work on fiscal federalism. This includes the book *The Practice of Fiscal Federalism: Comparative Perspectives* (*Global Dialogue on Fiscal Federalism* volume 4), edited by Anwar Shah, almost 15 years ago, which in a similar fashion sought to examine a variety of country case studies. It also seeks to continue the work of the Forum of Federations in building on past scholarship and offering key insights that will be of use to both academics and practitioners.

In this latest overview of the state of fiscal federalism in different countries, we changed some of the country case studies, looking to incorporate more countries from Africa (Ethiopia, where the Forum has worked on many Development Assistance Projects over the years, and South Africa) as well as interesting new case studies, such as Italy (a unitary state albeit one that is highly decentralized). New authors were chosen in many instances, owing to retirements, work schedules, or a desire to incorporate new scholars in the field of fiscal federalism.

The Forum acknowledges all the work of the previous authors of the *Global Dialogue* volume, without whom we would not have the foundations upon which we are building, including Anwar Shah; Alan Morris; Fernando Rezende; Robin Boadway; Jürgen Von Hagen; Govinda Rao; Shankaran Nambiar; Akpan Ekpo; Alexander Derugyin and Galina Kurlyandskaya; Bongani Khumalo and Renosi Mokate; Julio Lopez-Laborda, Jorge Martinez-Vasquez and Carlos Monasterio; Gebhard Kirchgassner; and William Fox.

Finally, we would like to thank our colleagues Asma Zribi and John Light for helping to finalize the manuscript and to ensure a successful publication.

Ottawa, Canada

Felix Knüpling
George A. Stairs

Felix Knüpling is Vice President of the Forum of Federations. He has co-edited several books on federalism, among them *Federalism and the Response to the Covid 19 Pandemic: A Comparative Analysis* (with Rupak Chattopadhyay and others; Taylor and Francis 2021); *Reformbaustelle Bundesstaat* ('Reforming German Federalism'; with Mario Kölling and others, Springer 2020) and *Das Teilen beherrschen* ('Managing fiscal federalism'; with Sabine Kropp and others, Nomos 2015).

George A. Stairs is a Project Officer at the Forum of Federations. He completed his M.A. in International Affairs: Conflict Analysis and Conflict Resolution at the Norman Paterson School of International Affairs in 2016 through a master's Research Project on Tunisia's democratization process post-Arab Spring. During his graduate studies, he wrote for the student-run website iAffairsCanada.ca, as their Associate Editor for Peace and Security producing a number of articles that are still findable today. His chapter 'The Amplification of the Sunni-Shia Divide through Contemporary Communications Technology: Fear and Loathing in the Modern Middle East', was published in IGI Global's 2016 volume *Impact of Communication and the Media on Ethnic Conflict*.

Introduction

Taxation, government expenditures and income, and regulatory responsibilities, all are components of a state's toolbox for dealing with fiscal matters. For those countries with a federal arrangement, an added layer of complexity is taken into account, being what is called fiscal federalism. What is meant by fiscal federalism is that area of policy concerned with economic policymaking in federal systems of government in which public sector decisions can be taken at various orders of government. The overriding issue in fiscal federalism is referred to as the assignment problem, that is, the assignment of different relevant fiscal responsibilities to different orders of government. What institutions do these countries use at different levels of government, how do they resolve tensions between those levels? What are the historical components that have led countries to adopt the systems and mechanisms that they have? Countries with multi-level governance structures have a range of key components to consider, taxation responsibilities, responsibility for service provision (and the commensurate expenditures), fiscal equalization transfers to different levels of governance, and so on. The manner in which all these components are managed differs from federal country to federal country, for a wide range of reasons. Countries may have more centralized federal systems, with more powers and responsibilities accrued by the national government, or more heavily decentralized systems, where the bulk of responsibility lies with the constituent units of the federation. These are some of the issues this volume is concerned with.

Fiscal federalism is a critical area of study as it underpins almost all other facets of federal governance. Through a country's ability to manage its own service provision and revenue generation, all government actions flow from the basic requirement of funding. How the different orders of government determine who gets what, who manages what, and how things get to change if at all, are all key topics discussed in this book.

This volume seeks to explore the myriad approaches to fiscal federalism in different countries around the globe using a consistent framework to examine what challenges and what opportunities there are for different countries to learn from one another. This book covers the diverse cases of Australia, Brazil, Canada, Ethiopia, Germany, India, Italy, South Africa, Spain, Switzerland, and the United States of America. These 11 country case studies all follow a similar structure which covers key questions on the structure of government and allocation of expenditure responsibilities, taxation responsibilities, intergovernmental fiscal transfers and revenue sharing, macroeconomic management, and ongoing challenges to their structure of fiscal federalism. Further, these chapters provide an outlook on how the ongoing COVID-19 global pandemic has affected their systems of fiscal federalism, and how they have adapted to the crisis. From this, it may be possible to extrapolate some broader lessons learned and look for policy solutions for ongoing concerns. Each country chapter will explore how current fiscal federalism arrangements exist in theory and in practice in their respective country, as well as examine the achievements and ongoing challenges these systems face, whether there are current or past efforts at reform, whether there has been any success with reform and from where these reforms are being driven.

Throughout the following chapters, our authors will explore their case studies by looking first at each country's unique situation, their population, what system of government they have, what sorts of institutions are present and in use, as well as the economic indicators that shape a country's capacity for revenue generation. They will delve deeper into the structure of government and look at exactly how fiscal responsibilities are divided and assigned in these countries, who has regulatory and taxation powers, and are there tensions between different levels of government or more cooperative federalism? Do these countries have equalization programs in place for subnational governments' programs, and how are they administered? And of course, what are the current challenges facing these countries' fiscal arrangements, are there calls for reform, and what efforts at reform are currently being undertaken?

The volume concludes with a chapter offering a comparative analysis on this subject, tying together recurring themes from each of the chapters, and offering some summary thoughts and analysis that might serve as guiding lessons to future work that the Forum or others might be doing in this field.

It is hoped that the lessons included within this volume, about the challenges and opportunities faced by these countries in their various forms of fiscal federalism, will be of key use to both academics in the field of governance studies, and policymakers and practitioners working in these fields to navigate a complex and yet wholly important field.

Felix Knüpling
Jean-François Tremblay
George A. Stairs

Contents

Notes on Contributors

Elisabeth Alber is Senior Researcher and Program Head (Federal Scholar in Residence) at Eurac Research Institute for Comparative Federalism. She examines intergovernmental relations in federal and regional States, multinational federalism, institutional innovations, and participatory democracy. Elisabeth holds a Ph.D. in Comparative Politics from the University of Innsbruck, where she is an external lecturer. She acts as co-convenor of the IACL Research Group Constitutionalism and Societal Pluralism and holds external associate positions at the Centre for Deliberative Democracy and Global Governance at the University of Canberra, the Centre for Multilevel Federalism of the Institute of Social Sciences in New Delhi and the Vienna based KDZ-Centre for public administration research.

V. N. Alok has been associated with the Indian Institute of Public Administration (IIPA) as professor for more than two decades. He has been a member of the Fifth Delhi Finance Commission and contributed to nearly all successive union (federal) and state finance commissions in different capacities since 1995. He has contributed many public policy research studies to the union and state governments in India including the yearly construction of the 'devolution index'. He has organized, with key participation, many consultations of policymakers in parts of Asia, Africa, and Latin America in spheres of public finance including fiscal federalism, tax reform, fiscal decentralization, etc.

Yannick Bury studied Economics at the University of Freiburg. During his studies, he attained practical experience at the foreign offices of Konrad Adenauer Foundation in Shanghai and Singapore, in the Economists Team of Berenberg Bank in London as well as the German Federal Ministry of Finance in Berlin. From 2017 until 2021 he has been Research Associate at the Walter Eucken Institute in Freiburg. His research focuses on different topics of (local) public finance, especially Germany's fiscal federalism. In 2021, Yannick Bury was elected as a Member of the German Bundestag.

Alexandre Cialdini holds a Ph.D. in Public Administration from the Higher Institute of Social and Political Sciences (ISCSP), University of Lisbon, a master's degree in Economics from the Federal University of Ceará (1997), a master's in Territorial Planning and Regional Development from the University of Barcelona, having completed the credits of the doctorate (2005). He graduated in Economic Sciences from the University of Fortaleza (1985) and completed postgraduate studies in Advanced Public Finance Management, at the Brazilian School of Public and Business Administration, Fundação Getulio Vargas-Rio de Janeiro (2001). He is Assistant Tax Auditor of the Secretariat of Finance of Ceará and Secretary of Finance of the Municipality of Eusébio-Ceará.

Lars P. Feld has been holding a chair of Economics, in particular Economic Policy, at Albert-Ludwigs-University of Freiburg since 2010 and is the current Director of the Walter Eucken Institute. He is a member of Leopoldina (the German National Academy of Sciences) and the Mont Pelerin Society. From 2007 to 2009, he was president of the European Public Choice Society. Since 2003, Lars P. Feld has been a member of the Scientific Advisory Council of the Federal Ministry of Finance and, from 2011 to 2021, a member and during the last year of his second term the chairman of the German Council of Economic Experts (GCEE). From 2013 to 2021, he represented the GCEE in the Independent Advisory Council of the Stability Council, Germany's construction of a fiscal council. Since 2020, he is also a member of the German minimum wage commission. In 2017, he received an honorary doctorate from the University of Lucerne in Switzerland.

Teresa Garcia-Milà is Professor of Economics at Universitat Pompeu Fabra (UPF) and Director of the Barcelona School of Economics. She received her Ph.D. in Economics from the University of Minnesota. She has been Dean of Economics and Deputy-Provost for Scientific Policy at UPF. Her research focuses on the impact of public investment on economic growth and on how different tax structures and fiscal federalism models influence economic growth, the distribution of resources, and economic wellbeing.

Yakob Bekele Hundie is a Senior Program Manager at the Forum of Federations, Ethiopia office. He holds a bachelor's degree in Economics and a master's degree in Federalism. He worked for various federal government institutions including the Secretariat of the House of Federation (HOF), and the Ministry of Federal Affairs (currently renamed as Ministry of Peace) of the FDRE. He has more than 12 years of experience in the areas of intergovernmental relations (IGR) and intergovernmental fiscal transfers (IGFT). At the Secretariat of the HOF, he directed the department of intergovernmental fiscal transfer.

Julio López-Laborda is Professor of Public Economics at the University of Zaragoza, Spain, and associate research at the Fundación de Estudios de Economía Aplicada, FEDEA. His areas of interest include fiscal federalism, income distribution and redistribution, and the economics of taxation. He has published his research in academic journals, such as *International Tax and Public Finance*, *National Tax Journal*, *Fiscal Studies*, *Energy Economics*, and *Constitutional Political Economy*. He has participated in numerous projects and committees involved in the evaluation of tax policies and tax reform.

Ramos Emmanuel Mabugu is Professor in Economics at Sol Plaatje University in South Africa. He is also Research Fellow at Stellenbosch University and the Partnership for Economic Policy. He earned his Ph.D. from Gothenburg University in Sweden. He has published widely on topics related to applied economics, public finance, tax policy, and intergovernmental fiscal relations. Prior to joining Sol Plaatje University, he was head of the research and policy division (Deputy Director General Level) at South Africa's Financial and Fiscal Commission, taught, and supervised at the postgraduate level at the University of Zimbabwe and the University of Pretoria in South Africa. He has consulted widely on internationally funded projects.

Jorge Martínez-Vázquez is Regents Professor of Economics Emeritus at Georgia State University. He has published over 25 books and numerous articles in academic journals, such as *Econometrica* and the *Journal of*

Political Economy. He has advised federal and state agencies in fiscal policy in the US and over 90 countries including China, Russia, Pakistan, Indonesia, and Mexico, and directed numerous fiscal reform projects, including the GSU $20 million USAID Fiscal Reform Project in Russia (1997-2000). He is the recipient of numerous prizes and awards, and he has directed or participated in over one-hundred doctoral dissertations.

Therese J. McGuire is Professor of Strategy at the Kellogg School of Management at Northwestern University. She has held various administrative positions at Kellogg, including Senior Associate Dean for Curriculum and Teaching. McGuire was President of the National Tax Association and the editor of the NTA's academic journal, the *National Tax Journal*. Her research centers on state and local public finance, fiscal federalism, property tax limitations, and regional economic development. McGuire received her Ph.D. in Economics from Princeton University.

Carlos Monasterio-Escudero is Professor of Public Finance at the Oviedo University (Economics Department). He has published 8 books and numerous articles in academic journals in the areas of Fiscal Federalism, the Economics of Social Security, and Fiscal Reforms. He has advised the Senate of Spain and several Autonomous Parliaments in the reform of the Spanish regional finance.

Bernardo Motta works as a researcher at the Public Sector Economics Center at FGV/IBRE and as a private consultant. Has technical and academic publications on public sector economics, public finance, and taxation. Holds a degree in economics from UFRJ and is a master's student at the Lisbon School of Economics and Management—ISEG.

Eddie M. Rakabe holds a master's degree in economic development from the University of Johannesburg and is currently a Ph.D. candidate at the University of Witwatersrand in South Africa. Rakabe has vast experience and has written extensively on South Africa's system of intergovernmental relations having worked at the National Treasury in a policy analysis role and the Financial Fiscal Commission in a senior research capacity. He has contributed immensely to the design of intergovernmental relations in South Africa through a number of policy papers focusing on intergovernmental transfers, education, health and housing policy financing, and horizontal and fiscal gap issues. His other research interests are in the area of low-income markets, informal sector, rural markets, and industrial value chains where he has published many working papers and book chapters.

Fernando Rezende works as a consultant in matters related to public finance, tax policy, and fiscal federalism. He is Ex-President of the Brazilian Institute of Applied Economic Research and Professor at the Getulio Vargas Foundation. He was a member of the Editorial Board of the Forum of Federations from 2003 to 2010. Presently, he is engaged in discussions of proposals for tax reform in Brazil that ignores the need for reconstructing the Brazilian fiscal federalism regime.

Christoph A. Schaltegger is Professor of Political Economy at the University of Lucerne, Switzerland, and the dean of its Faculty of Economics and Management. Previously, as a member of the Executive Board of economie suisse, he headed the Finance and Tax Policy Division and worked as an advisor to the Swiss Finance Minister.

Lukas A. Schmid is a fellow at the Zurich-based think tank Avenir Suisse where he primarily works on fiscal policy and institutional topics. After studying economics at the University of St. Gallen he first worked at Swiss Federal Railways (SBB) before spending several years as a research assistant at the Chair of Political Economics at the University of Lucerne.

Sisay Regassa Senbeta holds a Ph.D. in applied economics from Antwerp University, Belgium, and is Assistant Professor of economics at Addis Ababa University, Ethiopia. For the last 6 years, he has led various projects on intergovernmental fiscal relations in the Ethiopian federal system. Some of the studies are the general-purpose grant distribution formula, the revenue sharing mechanism, and the effectiveness of Ethiopian intergovernmental fiscal transfer systems in reducing interregional disparity. His most recent works are on income tax reforms in Ethiopia.

Miranda Stewart is Professor of Law at the University of Melbourne Law School and an Honorary Professor at the Tax and Transfer Policy Institute, Crawford School of Public Policy, The Australian National University. Miranda carries out research, teaching, and consulting on a wide range of tax and public finance law and policy topics, and has an enduring interest in the resilience, legitimacy, and fairness of tax systems to support good government. Books include *Death and Taxes* (2021, latest edition with Michael Flynn), *Tax, Social Policy and Gender* (ANU

Press, 2017, ed.) and *Tax, Law and Development* (Edward Elgar, 2013, ed. with Yariv Brauner).

Jean-François Tremblay is Professor in the Department of Economics at the University of Ottawa where he teaches public finance and macroeconomics. Since 2018, he is the Editor of *FinanzArchiv/Public Finance Analysis*. His main field of specialization in public finance and his main areas of expertise include fiscal federalism, taxation theory and policy, and economic growth. He has published journal articles and produced reports and consulting assignments for various government agencies, non-governmental organizations, research institutes, and foreign governments on various dimensions of fiscal federalism from both a theoretical perspective and an applied policy perspective.

Alice Valdesalici is Senior Researcher at the Institute for Comparative Federalism of Eurac Research. She got her Ph.D. in Italian and European Constitutional Law at the Graduate School of Law of the University of Verona in May 2016. For her research, she has been awarded the 'Ronald Watts Young Researcher Award 2016', by the International Association of Centres for Federal Studies (IACFS), and the 'Award for Federal and Regional studies 2016', by the Austrian *Landtagspräsidentenkonferenz* and the Institute for Federalism (IFÖ—Innsbruck). Her studies and publications focus on fiscal federalism and comparative federalism, constitutional asymmetries, and decision-making processes in federal systems, and local governments in federal systems.

List of Figures

Australia

Brazil

Fiscal Federalism in Germany

South Africa

Spain

Switzerland

United States

Comparative Perspectives on Fiscal Federalism Systems

List of Tables

Fiscal Federalism in Germany

Republic of India

Italy

South Africa

Spain

Switzerland

United States

Comparative Perspectives on Fiscal Federalism Systems

Australia

Miranda Stewart

1 Overview of Australia's Federal System

Australia's federation, established in 1901, is now more than 120 years old. After 50 years of the federation, one analyst commented: "Australians are not federalists except momentarily half a century ago" (Butlin 1954: 461). Yet the Australian federation has survived in its original form with 6 (originally 5) sovereign states and 2 territories, weathering a petition for secession from Western Australia in 1933. The federation has survived with only a few changes to the constitutional framework in the written Australian *Constitution* (Commonwealth of Australia Constitution Act 1900 (Imp.).

The Australian Constitution is modelled in part on the Constitution of the United States of America and in part on British constitutional and parliamentary structures and practices. The Constitution establishes the federal (Commonwealth) government and recognises the sovereignty of State governments which were self-governing colonies of the British

M. Stewart (✉)
Melbourne Law School, The University of Melbourne, Melbourne, VIC, Australia
e-mail: m.stewart@unimelb.edu.au

J.-F. Tremblay (ed.), *The Forum of Federations Handbook of Fiscal Federalism*, https://doi.org/10.1007/978-3-030-97258-5_1

Empire before federation (New South Wales, Queensland, Victoria, South Australia, Tasmania and Western Australia). The Australian Capital Territory and the Northern Territory are subject to federal legislative control with delegated tax and administrative powers. Australia is a dual federation, as local government is not recognised in the Constitution. However, in practice Australia has three tiers of government: federal, state and local. The Constitution is entrenched and can only be amended by a referendum supported by a majority of votes in a majority of States. This threshold is rarely reached in practice and therefore it is difficult to achieve reform of Australia's fiscal federal system (or other aspects of the federation) by Constitutional amendment.

Despite strong "nationalist" feeling and a centrist system of economic governance and tax system in Australia, State and Territory governments play an important role in democratic law making and delivery of services. The importance of State governments has been highlighted in the response of the federation to the COVID-19 pandemic, which revealed the importance of State leadership this is discussed further below. State governance is likely to become more, not less, important in the future and some differences between States including population and wealth are becoming more marked as time goes on.

Australia is one of the most multicultural nations in the world, with a population of more than 25 million. Its population growth rate of about 1.5% or close to 400,000 people each year has slowed temporarily because of the COVID-19 pandemic (ABS 2019b). Australia's population lives on a vast land territory of 7.692 million km^2, the world's sixth-largest country and largest island. Australia's land mass is close to the size of the United States of America (excluding Alaska), which has 10 times the Australian population; or of the European continent, which has 30 times the Australian population. In 1901, the population of 3.8 million people were mostly from the United Kingdom and Ireland, with a small number of Indigenous peoples who had survived the invasion of 1788, frontier wars and disease. Today, nearly 30% of the population are born overseas, with the top ten foreign countries of birth being England, China, India, New Zealand, Philippines, Vietnam, South Africa, Italy, Malaysia and Scotland. More than 300 languages are spoken and more than 20% of Australians speak a language other than English at home, most commonly Mandarin, Arabic, Cantonese and Vietnamese. Just over 50% of the population identify as Christian (including 22.6% Catholic, 13.3% Anglican,

3.7% Uniting Church and 2.6% other), 30% stating no religion, 2.6% Islam and 2.4% Buddhism.

A century prior to federation, Australia was established as a series of British colonies commencing with the convict colony of New South Wales in 1788, described as "settlement" but in reality an invasion. The legal fiction of "terra nullius" that was the basis of settlement by the British and the concomitant denial of Aboriginal sovereignty meant that there was never a formal treaty process, unlike in comparable countries including Canada and New Zealand. This legal fiction was overturned by the High Court of Australia in the historic decision in *Mabo* (1992) 175 CLR 1, which recognized Indigenous native title over land. The existence and continuation of native title was subsequently acknowledged in the *Native Title Act 1993* (Cth) and in subsequent cases. Today, about 3% of the population identifies as Aboriginal and Torres Strait islander, a growing population compared to the time of federation (ABS 2019a). Aboriginal and Torres Strait Islander land title and some elements of Indigenous self-government extends over nearly half of the Australian land mass through native title agreements, land rights and various claims and negotiations. There is a growing movement for treaties with State governments and in support of formal recognition of Aboriginal and Torres Strait islander first nations in the Constitution (Davis and Langton 2016). The implications for reform of Australian fiscal federalism are addressed in Sect. 7 of this chapter.

The Australian population is spread unevenly across the States and territories (ABS 2019a). The largest state by population is New South Wales, with a population of 8 million. Victoria has 6.5 million (and has recently been the fastest-growing state), while Queensland has 5 million people. At the other end of the spectrum, Tasmania has about 530,000 people and the Northern Territory about 246,000 people. Australia's population is highly urbanized in large cities including Sydney (5.2 million), Melbourne (4.9 million), Brisbane (2.4 million) and Perth (2 million). The dominance of these cities, which are engines of Australian economic growth, creates significant tensions in the federal system.

Australia had GDP of USD $1.39 trillion in 2019, ranked in the top 20 wealthiest countries globally (World Bank 2019). Australia experienced nearly three decades of economic growth to 2019 but, like the rest of the world, faced a significant economic contraction as a result of the COVID-19 pandemic. Prior to the pandemic, growth had slowed to about 2.5% of GDP in the years since the Global Financial Crisis of 2009, half the average of the previous two decades. Australia is an open trading and investment economy and a net capital importer, with an inbound investment of about $3.5 trillion, and outbound investment of $2.5 trillion in 2018 (DFAT 2020). Investment in the resources sector, and the benefits of the resource industry, is unevenly distributed across the States and Territories. The States of Western Australia, New South Wales and Queensland depend heavily on extractive industries of iron ore, coal and gas. This contributes to difficult federal politics around benefits and costs of the resources sector (see, e.g., Eccelston and Krever 2017). The uneven benefit and impact of resource extraction also contribute to difficult environmental politics that Australia has not been able to resolve. Australia has previously enacted, and repealed, a carbon emissions trading scheme. Australia has an average per capita footprint of 17 tonnes of carbon emissions, above the United States and Canada and exceeded only by the middle eastern oil-producing states.[1]

The Commonwealth government and all State governments operate a system of parliamentary democracy. The Head of State is the Queen of Australia (who is currently also the Queen of the United Kingdom), represented in Australia by the Governor General.[2] The Commonwealth Parliament has a lower House (the House of Representatives) and an upper House (the Senate) which was established as a states' house (as in the United States), as well as a house of review. Elections are held every 3 to 4 years at federal, state and local government levels. The major parties of the Liberal/National Coalition and the Australian Labor Party operate at all levels of government. Typically, the party that has a majority in the House of Representatives establishes the government of the day. Voting is compulsory and generally, a preferential system is applied, resulting in a "two-party preferred" outcome for the House of Representatives. Different voting approaches and minimum numbers of Senators for each State and Territory in the Senate mean that the party which governs, by majority in the House of Representatives, usually will not control the Senate. As a result of Australia's strong party-based democracy, Senators

[1] Our World in Data, https://ourworldindata.org/per-capita-co2 (October 4, 2019), University of Oxford.

[2] By constitutional convention (i.e. practice), the Governor-General acts on advice of elected Ministers of State. The exceptions, known as the 'reserve powers', are controversial and are not discussed here.

generally act along party lines and not as representatives of State interests, reducing the role of the Parliament as a site of federal negotiation. Minor parties including the Green party and some Independents usually hold the balance of power in the Senate. The current Labor government led by Prime Minister Anthony Albanese and Treasurer Jim Chalmers was elected at the 2022 federal election with a slim majority.

2 The Structure of Government and Expenditure Responsibilities

The Constitution establishes the Commonwealth government's power to enact laws with respect to taxation, to appropriate funds and to grant money to the States. It limits the legislative power of the Commonwealth Parliament to a list of enumerated matters, including defence, external affairs, taxation, social security and pensions, corporations, interstate trade and commerce, an executive power and other matters (section 51). The State governments retain primary for core functions including education, health and hospitals, police and criminal justice, city and town planning, sport and recreation, roads and other transport infrastructure (apart from national rail), although funding is often shared with the Commonwealth under national partnership agreements. The States retain sovereign power to legislate on any subject matter, subject only to constraints imposed by the federal Constitution.

2.1 *Commonwealth Power of Expenditure*

All federal taxes and other revenues must go into consolidated revenue and the Commonwealth government must appropriate funds by a law of the Commonwealth Parliament to be spent "for purposes of the Commonwealth" (sections 81 and 83 of the Constitution). This is, as noted by French C.J. of the High Court in *Pape v. FCT* (2009) 238 CLR 1 (p. 37), "central to the idea of responsible government". However, the extent of this federal spending power has long been unsettled (Saunders 2009). The issue can be stated as follows: if the Commonwealth Parliament is not free to spend the taxes that it has raised in the manner that it sees fit (we return to its almost unlimited power to tax, below), this contradicts a basic principle of political and legal accountability by the federal government. On the other hand, if the Commonwealth Parliament had unlimited power to spend the taxes it raised, this would permit it to spend on a wide range of matters that would otherwise be solely within the legislative power of the States and would enable the federal government to encroach significantly on state government functions. Consequently, this breaches the Constitution and sovereignty of several States.

High Court cases including *Pape v. Cth* (2009) 238 CLR 1 and *Williams v Cth* [2012] HCA 23 have indicated that sections 81 and 83 of the Constitution do not themselves confer a substantive "spending" power on the Commonwealth Parliament. This suggests that the power of expenditure relies on the legislative and other powers of the Commonwealth set out in the Constitution. As it is relevant to governing in a crisis, and therefore to the COVID-19 pandemic, this chapter will briefly discuss the *Pape* case. Mr. Pape challenged the Rudd government stimulus package in response to the Global Financial Crisis of 2008, in which the government handed out a "cash bonus" on a means-tested basis to about 8.7 million taxpayers. The High Court held that the monies for the cash bonus were validly appropriated and the majority upheld the expenditure on the cash bonus, based in part on the taxation power (as some of the bonuses were paid by tax refund) and in part on the executive power under section 61 of the Constitution to respond to the "large scale adverse effects of the circumstances affecting the national economy" (per French C.J., [8]). The executive power is supported by the power of the Parliament to legislate applying its "incidental" power in section 51(xxxix) and this was relied on as the Parliament passed the law to pay the cash bonus. The High Court appears to have accepted that the Global Financial Crisis and the potential damage to the Australian economy satisfied the requirement of a crisi triggering the exercise of executive power (see, e.g., Appleby 2009; Appleby and McDonald 2011). The very much larger federal fiscal package in response to the COVID-19 pandemic in 2020, including JobKeeper and JobSeeker payments to businesses and individuals, has not been challenged but would undoubtedly be upheld and is supported by other powers for example relating to borders and quarantine.

Despite this recent line of authority, control of the federal expenditure power remains a weakness in the Australian federal system, and the ability to spend revenues it raises is a constant temptation to federal governments. An example is the use of the expenditure power by Commonwealth ministers to make financial grants to organisations, businesses and regions that fall outside Commonwealth regulatory power, exercised bypassing State governments, often with implications of political influence or "porkbarrelling". During the 1970s, the issue arose in relation to Commonwealth grants to local and regional agencies. These grants were upheld by a bare majority of the High Court in *AAP case*, *Victoria v. Cth* (1975) 134 CLR 338. In 2019, a scandal arose about federal ministerial grants to sporting organisations that ignored independent assessments and benefited marginal electorates in the months before the federal election (e.g. Grattan 2020). These "sports rorts" were strongly criticized in a report of the Australian National Audit Office (ANAO 2020) and were the subject of Senate inquiry.[3]

2.2 Commonwealth Power to Grant Funds to States

The main way in which Commonwealth Parliament controls policy and expenditures across the federation is by relying on its power to grant monies to the States under. Section 96 of the Constitution states that "until Parliament otherwise provides, the Parliament may grant financial assistance to any State on such terms and conditions as the Parliament thinks fit". The grants power is a key element in shaping Australia's particular form of fiscal federalism. Grants have been used dramatically by the Commonwealth government to influence policy in areas over which the States have nearly exclusive legislative power. Payments to the States of general revenue assistance from GST revenue (see Sect. 5) are special appropriations of the federal Parliament under section 22 of the Federal Financial Relations Act; specific grants subject to conditions are appropriated under a variety of relevant legislation.

Historically, the Commonwealth paid surplus revenues back to the States and then began to make special grants to needy claimant states, primarily Western Australia, Tasmania and South Australia. These grants had the goal of enabling those states to operate at a standard "not appreciably below that of the other States" (Brown 1952). An attempt was made in a referendum in 1926 to entrench in the Constitution the approach of federal grants to the States on a *per capita* basis but this failed, perhaps because the *per capita* formula was already perceived to disadvantage some states (Saunders 1989).

[3] Australian Senate Select Committee on Administration of Sports Grants Final Report (March 2021); see https://www.aph.gov.au/Parliamentary_Business/Committees/Senate/Administration_of_Sports_Grants/AdminSportsGrants.

During World War II, the grants power was used to force States to stop levying income taxes, thereby centralising the income tax as a single national tax. As explained below, this cemented central fiscal supremacy. The Commonwealth Parliament cannot discriminate between States in imposing taxation but it *can* discriminate in respect of its power to make grants (*Moran (WR) Ltd v. DFCT* (1940) 63 CLR 338).

After World War II, both Liberal-National and Labor Commonwealth governments expanded the use of grants under section 96 for a range of purposes, from roads and infrastructure to drought relief, national fitness, and funding universities, in what appeared to be an inexorable process of centralisation of responsibilities and expenditure. State governments often contested this exercise of the Commonwealth grants power but on the whole, the High Court has affirmed the Commonwealth power to make conditional grants, and it has also upheld some important limits on State taxation (also discussed in Sect. 3). On the other hand, State governments have sometimes been willing to hand over expensive responsibilities to the Commonwealth, on the basis that they could not finance them adequately. For example, in the 1970s the States handed the financing and regulation of tertiary education entirely to the Commonwealth, "apparently with some relief" (CEDA 1975: 15).

In this unequal fiscal context, the management of federal financial relations has been a process of continual political bargaining, sometimes presented as the States having to "beg" or go "cap in hand" to the Commonwealth; and sometimes in a more positive light as a form of cooperative federalism balancing diversity and national standards through cooperative partnership agreements. The Commonwealth has from time to time sought to leverage conditional grants to support nationwide economic and competition reform. Today, financial responsibility for the expensive core functions of education and health is substantially shared between Commonwealth and State governments and there has been a trend for regulatory responsibilities also to be shared in these areas (e.g. Warren 2006). In this, Australia appears to be different from some other federations. This approach of shared funding and regulatory responsibility presents both opportunities and challenges for managing accountability and finances in the federation.

3 Taxation in the Australian Federation

The Constitution provides the foundation for the Commonwealth power to tax, establishes limits on State government taxing powers and sets up

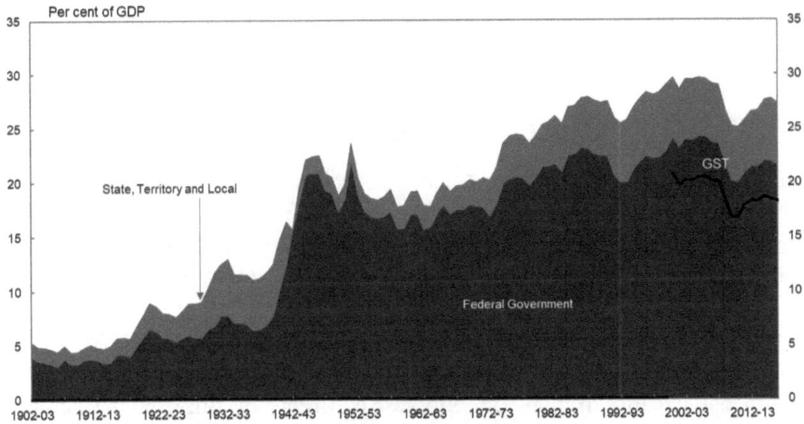

Fig. 1 History of tax revenue in Australia (*Source* Reinhardt and Steel [2006]. A brief history of Australia's tax system; updated with budget revenue figures and ABS Taxation Revenue Statistics to 2017–18)

a skeletal regime for intergovernmental financial relations. The issue of federal and state taxation, and the federal power to make grants, has been the subject of some of Australia's most heated federal-state disputes, which have played out in a context of overall growth in Australian governmental taxation and expenditures through the twentieth century. The growth of taxes to finance the public sector as a share of GDP from the beginning of the federation to today is shown in Fig. 1, which tells the story of Australia's growth as a nation in fiscal terms.

As Fig. 1 shows, from the start of the federation, when the Commonwealth government took over the customs and tariffs base, most tax revenues were raised at the Commonwealth level and this pattern has continued throughout the history of the federation. The expansion in the size of the government was similar to other member states of the Organisation for Economic Cooperation and Development (OECD), although Australia has had a smaller public sector than many other OECD countries. Total government revenue in Australia was 36% of GDP in 2018, among the lowest in the OECD.[4] Australia is a relatively low taxing country by OECD standards, raising 28.5% of GDP in taxes in 2018,

[4] OECD, Data: https://data.oecd.org/gga/general-government-revenue.htm#indicator-chart (2018).

below the OECD average of 34.3% and significantly lower the tax levels of countries such as France and Denmark which are above 40% of GDP.[5]

3.1 Commonwealth Taxing Power

The Commonwealth government has power to tax under section 51(ii) of the Constitution. The definition of a "tax" defines the boundaries of the power; this has been controversial from time to time, but is essentially defined as any compulsory exaction of monies under statutory power, for public purposes that are not a fee or penalty (*Matthews v Chicory Marketing Board* (1938) 60 CLR 263, per Latham CH at 276). It has been established since the early days of federation that a tax is not unconstitutional because it may be oppressive, unfair or imposed to achieve purposes other than taxation (*Osborne v. Cth* (1911) 12 CLR 321). The Commonwealth Parliament is prohibited from giving preference to one state or another in taxation by section 99 of the Constitution.[6] It cannot tax property of the States or State governments by section 114 of the Constitution and the principle of intergovernmental immunity.[7] Various Commonwealthj taxes have been challenged as unconstitutional because they apply to State functions or employees but most of these challenges have failed.[8] There are some procedural requirements for the passage of tax legislation including that tax bills must originate in the House of Representatives. By section 53 of the Constitution, the Senate (in form, but not in practice, a "States" house) does not have the power to amend tax bills (see, e.g., Cominos and Dwyer 1999).

[5] OECD, Data: https://www.oecd.org/tax/revenue-statistics-australia.pdf (2018).

[6] Some Commonwealth taxes have been struck down on this basis: e.g., the *Excise Tariff Act 1906* (Cth) was invalidated for discrimination between states in *R v Barger* (1908) 6 CLR 41 and see *Cameron v DFCT* (1923) 32 CLR 68; *Conroy v Carter* (1968) 118 CLR 90.

[7] A Commonwealth sales tax, in so far as it purported to tax the property of a State agency, was struck down under section 114 in *Deputy Commissioner of Taxation v. State Bank of New South Wales* (1991) 174 CLR 219. In *South Australia v. Commonwealth* (1991) 174 CLR 235, the Court held that a tax on the capital gain derived by a State on the disposal of an asset was unconstitutional. See further Stone and Waters (1992).

[8] *Davoren v. FCT* (1923) 29 ALR 129; *Victoria v. Cth (Payroll Tax Case)* (1971) 122 CLR 353; see Morabito (1997); however, the High Court upheld a challenge to a special tax levied on State judges in relation to their pensions: *Austin v. Commonwealth* (2003) 215 CLR 185, at 219.

Australia's most important taxes are imposed by the Commonwealth Parliament: the personal income tax on individuals and corporations, including capital gains tax; fringe benefits tax on employee benefits; Goods and Services Tax (GST); customs duties; excises on fuel, alcohol and tobacco; and petroleum resource rent tax. Australia's heavy reliance on personal and corporate income tax, and less heavy reliance on GST contrasts with the pattern of reliance on social security taxes and value-added taxes in many other OECD countries. Australia has no wealth, inheritance or gift taxes at Commonwealth or State level. All Commonwealth taxes, apart from customs and excise, are administered by the Australian Taxation Office (ATO). State and local governments raise less than 20% of taxes in Australia, as shown in Table 1. The states of NSW

Table 1 Commonwealth, State and local taxes, 2017–18

	Commonwealth		*State and local*		*All taxes*	
	$m	*%*	*$m*	*%*	*$m*	*%*
Taxes on income						
Personal	212,787	49.8	0	0	212,787	40.2
Company	86,764	20.3	0	0	86,764	16.4
Total[a]	312,474	73.1	0	0	312,474	59.0
Taxes on goods and services						
GST	64,062	15.0	0	0	64,062	12.1
Excise	23,561	5.5	113	0.1	23,674	4.5
Gambling	0	0	6,223	6.1	6,223	1.2
Motor vehicle	0	0	10,804	10.6	10,804	2.0
Insurance	0	0	6,054	5.9	6,054	1.1
Stamp duties, conveyances	0	0	21,700	21.2	21,700	4.1
Total[b]	106,492	24.9	47,490	46.5	153,982	29.1
Payroll	1,107	0	24,371	23.9	25,478	4.8
Property	0	0	30,293	29.7	30,293	5.7
Total[c]	427,237	80.7	102,154	19.3	529,391	

[a] In addition to taxes identified above, this includes income tax paid by superannuation funds and income taxes levied on non-residents

[b] In addition to taxes identified above, this also includes taxes on international trade, levies, franchise taxes and other state and local taxes on financial and capital transactions

[c] In addition to taxes identified above, this also includes other minor taxes

Source ABS (2019a). Compiled from ABS cat. no. 5506.0, *Taxation Revenue, Australia, 2017–18* (29 April 2019 release), Tables 1–10

and Victoria raise the most tax revenues, with NSW raising more than a third and Victoria nearly one-quarter of total State and local tax revenues.

The Commonwealth income tax was introduced in 1915 but became a "mass tax" after World War II (WWII). As indicated in Table 1, total income tax revenues on individuals, companies and superannuation funds were AUD 312.4 billion in 2017–18, comprising 73% of Commonwealth taxes and about 60% of total tax revenues. Corporate income tax comprises 20% of federal tax revenues. The Medicare Levy of 2% under the *Medicare Levy Act 1986* (Cth) is a surcharge on taxable income and is intended to contribute to support the Medicare and National Disability Insurance schemes; however, it is not legally hypothecated and is not sufficient to fund their cost, which is funded out of consolidated revenue.

The second-largest Commonwealth tax is the GST, introduced in 2000 to replace a wholesale sales tax on goods, after 30 years of political struggle (Eccleston 2005). The GST generated revenue of AUD 64 billion in 2017–18, comprising 15% of Commonwealth tax collections. It is a broad-based consumption tax imposed at a flat rate of 10%, structured as an invoice-credit value added tax. The GST has significant exemptions including basic foods, health, education, housing (except new housing), water and sewage, childcare and financial transactions which are input-taxed. The Commonwealth Parliament also imposes excises on fuel, tobacco and alcohol which raise about 9% of federal revenues; customs duties, which raise only a small percentage of revenues; and some other minor indirect taxes.

3.2 State Taxes

The Commonwealth power to tax in section 51(ii) is a "concurrent" power that does not remove the power of the States to legislate with respect to taxation. The source of the States' power to tax is in their nature as sovereign political entities having plenary legislative power, which includes the power to tax. This is implicitly protected by sections 106 and 107 of the Australian Constitution, which ensure the continued existence of the States. The process for enacting tax laws depends on the State constitution, but in general, such laws must originate in the lower house; pass both houses of parliament; and receive the assent of the Governor of the State. States cannot tax the property of the Commonwealth (section 114) and are prohibited from discriminating in tax or other laws on the basis of a person's State of residence under section 117 of the Constitution.[9] Table 1 summarised the taxes levied by states and territories. In spite of their broad legal power to tax, concurrent with the commonwealth, the States and Territories impose a limited range of taxes which are often said to be less than optimal.

The most important state tax in terms of revenue is the payroll tax, which raises much more revenue in populous and industrialised NSW and Victoria than in states that have smaller populations. In Australia, payroll taxes are not used to finance social security, and consequently are less important than such taxes in other countries. The NSW payroll tax raised 30% ($9.4 billion) of its tax revenue in 2018–19 (Government of NSW 2019: 74). The Commonwealth levied payroll tax concurrently with State governments from 1941 to 1971, when it left what has been described as its least favourite tax base to the states (Smith 2004). The payroll tax base has been reasonably well harmonised between the States on a largely similar base and rate, essentially total payments for employee wages of employers over specified thresholds (including wages, fringe benefits, bonuses and commissions). Most small businesses are exempt. The tax was described by the NSW Review of Federal Financial Relations (the *NSW Review*) as one of the "better" taxes on grounds of revenue and efficiency, but the Review expressed concern that it is being eroded by interstate tax competition (NSW Government 2020: 75–76). The NSW Review found that, all jurisdictions had raised their tax-free threshold for payroll tax, while three had cut headline tax rates, two introduced concessional rates and various states added concessions for regions, trainees or to attract investment. State governments have provided payroll tax relief in response to the COVID-19 crisis.

The second most important State tax is transfer or stamp duty on the conveyance of residential and commercial immovable (real) property, by sale or gift, and on the transfer of interests in land-rich entities such as trusts and companies. Duty is usually payable by the purchaser calculated on the sale price of the property. Duty rates are progressive, ranging in NSW from 1.25 to 5.5% (over AUD $1,013,000 in value) and in Victoria from 1.4 to 5.5% (on total value, if over AUD $960,000).[10] The base

[9] Exemptions under the *Income Tax Act 1932* (Qld) that were available to in-State residents on a discriminatory basis were struck down under this provision: *Commissioner of Taxes (Qld) v. Parks* (1933) St R Qd 306.

[10] For a discussion of State taxes, see Freebairn et a.l (2015); Stewart (2011).

includes the main residence of taxpayers. In states with growing populations and rising property prices, most importantly NSW, Victoria and Queensland, transfer duty has an increasingly important role in raising revenue. The reliance on transfer duty leaves states vulnerable to revenue volatility as house prices fluctuate.

Land tax is levied by all states and territories except the Northern Territory, on the aggregate holding of unimproved land value that is owned by a taxpayer in the jurisdiction. In the early years of the federation, the Commonwealth levied a land tax at steeply progressive tax rates but in 1952, the Commonwealth vacated land tax, leaving this tax base for the states; NSW re-entered the land tax base in 1955 (Smith 1992: 26). State land taxes are generally progressive. For example, in Victoria, rates range from 0.2% above a tax-free threshold of AUD $250,000 to 2.25% over a value of AUD 3 million. However, the base for land tax in all states is relatively narrow, as it excludes the principal place of residence of taxpayers—which comprises about half of the potentially taxable land value.

Economists generally agree that transfer duty is inefficient and inequitable and should be replaced with a broad-based land tax (NSW Government 2020; Freebairn et al. 2015). Property taxes (rates) are levied to a limited extent at the local government level but this comprises a relatively small share of the tax base. The Australian Capital Territory is the only state or territory to have commenced a process of transitioning away from transfer duty to land tax, and it therefore levies a land tax on the home. The case for the transition from transfer duty to land tax is discussed in detail in the NSW Review. There are significant disincentives for such reform by any State acting alone, or without the support of the Commonwealth government, including potentially being disadvantaged in the federal horizontal fiscal equalisation regime and financing the significant transition (NSW Government 2020: 52–53).

States (but not Territories) are sovereign owners of resources in their jurisdiction. Royalties are a price for access to a nonrenewable resource. States levy a range of royalties including a fixed rate per unit (e.g. tonne) of production; *ad valorem* royalties as a percentage of value or price of resources or profit-based royalties. Although not as big as most of the State tax bases, royalties are particularly important in Western Australia, Queensland and NSW. In Western Australia, royalty income in 2019–20 was $6.3 billion which comprised 20% of state revenues; in Queensland, royalties and land rents comprised $4.9 billion, or 8.3% of State revenues;

in NSW, royalties comprised only 2% of State revenue and in other States, the proportion is lower.[11] In some states and territories, royalties are also paid to Indigenous or native title land holders.

3.2.1 *Why No State Income Taxes?*

Prior to WW II, all States levied income taxes (some had done so since colonial times). Constitutional protection of the states' power to levy income tax did not prevent the Commonwealth from driving them out of this "concurrent" legislative area, using a combination of its own power to tax and the grants power described in Sect. 2. This unique Australian history provides a striking contrast with the Anglo-federations of Canada and the United States, where states held tightly to their income tax base.

Leading up to and during WWII, the Commonwealth took over the income tax to fund the war effort and to streamline collection. The Commonwealth and States concurrently enacted the *Uniform Income Tax Act* (1936) aimed at harmonising income taxes. In 1942, a Committee on Uniform Taxation recommended that the Commonwealth take over all income taxation (Mills et al. 1942). The Commonwealth Parliament enacted the "Uniform Tax Scheme", which took over the tax base and prevented the States from levying income taxes for the duration of the war. The Scheme was challenged by the States in the High Court. The challenge failed, in part due to the deference given to the Commonwealth Parliament during war time (*South Australia v. Cth*, First Uniform Tax Case (1942) 65 CLR 373). After the end of WWII, the so-called "temporary" scheme remained in place. A decade followed during which various reform proposals were made and negotiations conducted on returning the income tax base to the states, but these all failed. In 1957, Victoria and NSW again challenged the scheme , and again the High Court upheld its validity (*Victoria v. Cth, Second Uniform Tax Case* (1957) 99 CLR 575). The most important element of the *Second Uniform Tax Case* was the finding by the High Court that it was legitimate for the Commonwealth to use its power to make grants to the States under section 96 of the Constitution, so as to require the States not to impose an income tax. A State government could have rejected a grant and instead levied its own income tax, but none was prepared to do this.

[11] See https://www.ourstatebudget.wa.gov.au/ (Western Australia, 2019–20 budget); https://www.qtc.com.au/queensland/queenslands-finances/ (Queensland 2019–20 budget); www.budget.nsw.gov.au (NSW 2019–20 budget).

The Constitutional challenges show that the Commonwealth "takeover" of income tax was disliked by at least some of the states. It led to a significantly increased vertical fiscal imbalance, which is generally seen to be a major problem in the federation. However, the uniform federal income tax was popular with Australian taxpayers, especially businesses that increasingly operated across state borders; it was not opposed by the smaller states. The web of income taxes that had spread across Australia in the early decades of the twentieth century had become extraordinarily complex. Earlier attempts at harmonisation, culminating in the *Uniform Income Tax Act* (1936), apart from an administrative collection agreement of 1920, failed to ensure simplicity and stability (e.g., Laffer 1942). Most acknowledged the advantages of uniform taxation and there was "surprising hesitancy" of State governments and others in suggesting alternative schemes (e.g. Binns and Bellis 1956). In 1959, the Liberal government under Prime Minister Robert Menzies enacted the *States Grants Act* (Cth) to remove the condition that States had to restrain from imposing income taxes in order to receive grants, which had been a critical element in the Uniform Tax Scheme. No State took up the opportunity Menzies (1961: 12) expressed doubt that State governments would seek the return of income taxation:

> There has been no positive evidence that most of the State governments really want a return of taxing powers on terms which would be reasonably acceptable to the Commonwealth and still permit it to discharge its admittedly major responsibilities. Yet a return of taxing powers by unilateral Commonwealth action would be pregnant with disaster if a genuine agreement between Commonwealth and States were not arrived at.

It has been suggested that the reason that no State has yet enacted an income tax was "primarily because the Commonwealth did not 'make room' for a state income tax by reducing its own income tax rates to accommodate a State income tax without raising the overall level of income tax" (Warren, 2006: 19; Carling 2007). In 1964, the Victorian government proposed a State income tax but this failed after the Commonwealth refused to collect it (Smith 2004: 30). In 1976, the Fraser Liberal-National government elected on a platform of "new federalism" proposed, first, a new formula for grants based on a tax-sharing approach under the *States (Personal Income Tax-Sharing) Act 1976*, and second, a law to allow a State to enact a surcharge on the Commonwealth personal income tax, excluding company and international aspects under the *Income Tax (Arrangements with the States) Act 1978 (Cth).* No state took up the opportunity to levy an income tax surcharge, and the Commonwealth law was repealed in 1989. In 2015, during the last (brief) federation reform attempt, Liberal/National Prime Minister Turnbull announced that he would give the states the ability to raise a proportion of personal income tax, but the idea was described as a "caricature" of policy making that could not be taken seriously (Fenna 2017: 134).

3.2.2 Why No State Sales Taxes?

The main exclusion from State taxing power is the exclusive Commonwealth power to legislate with respect to excise and customs duties under section 90 of the Constitution.[12] This is the second main constitutional provision shaping Australian fiscal federalism. The High Court has held that a duty of excise is a tax on the production, manufacture, distribution or sale of goods up to the point of consumption. This broad definition denies the States jurisdiction to levy any tax on goods (*Parton v. Milk Board (Vic.)* (1949) 80 CLR 229).

State governments for many years levied "licence fees" on businesses selling tobacco, alcohol and petrol, calculated in a variety of ways on of the quantity or value of goods sold, initially at relatively low rates. Early High Court authority suggested that a licence fee would not be a duty of excise this held, at least, where the fee was not imposed in relation to goods sold in the licence period and where the goods were inherently susceptible to regulation, such as tobacco and alcohol (e.g. *Dennis Hotels Pty Ltd v. Victoria* (1960) 104 CLR 529, *Dickensons Arcade Ltd v. Tasmania* (1974) 130 CLR 177). By the late 1980s, licence fees in various states had crept up to around 30% of the value of the goods sold; these were upheld by the High Court as a long-standing exception

[12] State taxes have been successfully challenged on the basis that they impermissibly interfere with interstate trade and commerce under section 92 of the Constitution: e.g., *Fox v. Robbins* (1909) 8 CLR 155 (discriminatory tax on wine); *Hughes and Vale Pty Ltd v. New South Wales* (1955) 53 CLR 247 (one of a series of challenges to State taxes on motor vehicles); *Bath v. Alston Holdings* (1988) 165 CLR 411 (challenge to ad valorem duty on tobacco). A tax will only be struck down if it is a discriminatory burden on interstate trade of a protectionist kind: *Cole v. Whitfield* (1988) 165 CLR 360.

to the excise prohibition.[13] In the 1990s, some states increased tobacco "licence fees" to 100% of the value of the tobacco sold. This prompted yet another Constitutional challenge. In *Ha v. State of New South Wales* (1997) 189 CLR 465, the High Court by majority struck down the fee in question, finding it to be a duty of excise on goods. It was widely recognised that the reasoning extended to similar licence fees in other states and on other goods, notably alcohol and petrol. To protect the States from financial difficulties, the Commonwealth Parliament enacted legislation to tax at 100% any amount recovered from the States in relation to invalidly imposed excise duties: *Franchise Fees Windfall Tax (Imposition) Act 1997* (Cth). This "tax" was returned to the relevant States and was constitutionally permitted. As a result of *Ha's case*, such taxes were, in effect, denied to the States (see Dick 1998; Williams 1999).

In 1965, the economist Mathews had proposed a "general tax on production ... in the form of a 'value-added tax'" to be levied by the States businesses (Mathews 1965). There has been debate about whether a tax imposed at the point of consumption of goods would be an excise and the matter has never been legally tested, as no State has ever attempted to legislate a broad-based consumption tax.[14] In partial substitution, State governments started to levy gambling taxes, a trend noted by some who see states as becoming addicted to gambling revenues (e.g. Williams 1999).

3.3 Local Government

Local government is not recognised in the Constitution. Local governments are generally statutory bodies incorporated by State governments and exercising delegated State legislative power. In 2014, there were 569 local governing bodies eligible to receive federal financial assistance grants (Department of Infrastructure and Regional Development 2017:

[13] *Phillip Morris Ltd. v. Commissioner of Business Franchises (Vict)* (1989) 167 CLR 399; *Mutual Pools And Staff Pty Ltd. v. FCT* (1992) 173 CLR 450. A licence fee for the sale of pornographic videos was struck down: *Capital Duplicators Pty Ltd v. Australian Capital Territory [No 2]* (1993) 178 CLR 561.

[14] The High Court stopped short of finding that a tax on "consumption" of goods is an excise in *Dickensons Arcade Ltd v. Tasmania* (1974) 130 CLR 177. There are suggestions in *Ha v. State of New South Wales* (1997) 189 CLR 465, at 499, that a tax on consumption would not be considered to be an excise; see Hanks and Cass (1999: 649–650; cf. Saunders 1997: 21).

219). The majority of Australia's population lives in urban centres and the earliest local governments were established in the cities of Adelaide, Sydney and Melbourne in the 1840s. However, the size and diversity of the country means that local government areas are extremely diverse, ranging in population from fewer than 100 to close to 1 million people and in size from 2 to 372,571 km^2 (the Shire of East Pilbara, servicing about 20,000 people) (Productivity Commission 2017: 4). Local governments have powers of general competence and deliver services, such as waste management, street safety, parks and libraries, and services to members of the community. Some local governments manage infrastructure including water and sewerage. They can make and enforce local laws and make land-use, development and planning decisions.

Local governments self-fund most expenditures; in 2014–15 on average 90% of expenditures from own-source revenue, about half from property rates, and half from fees, developer charges, fines and investment revenue (Productivity Commission 2017). Local governments exercise delegated legislative power to levy rates (property tax) on immovable property (e.g. Local Government Act (Vic), Part 8). Rates are charged on the value of residential and commercial immovable property in the jurisdiction, with value calculated in various ways.

NSW and Victoria cap the rates that can be levied by local governments in those states, a matter that is the subject of some controversy. The Hawker Report (2003) found some evidence of "cost shifting" to local government by State and Commonwealth governments, putting increased pressure on local budgets while "squeezing" their ability to raise revenues in some cases. The Hawker Report (2003) and the Productivity Commission (2017) recommended the abolition of rate capping and State-mandated exemptions (nonrateable land).

The balance of local government funding is grants from State and Commonwealth governments. Self-funding capacity is variable and some rural and remote councils are heavily reliant on grants. Federal grants directly to local government commenced under the Whitlam Labor government during the 1970s on the advice of the Commonwealth Grants Commission (see Sect. 5.1 below).

The Whitlam government established a program by which funds would be paid directly to Regional Councils for Social Development, bypassing the States, after appropriation from consolidated revenue under section 81 of the Constitution. This was soon abolished, although *Victoria v. Cth* (1975) 134 CLR 338 (*Australian Assistance Plan* case), the High Court by a bare majority (4:3) upheld the appropriation to fund regional councils as valid. This decision may have indicated a relatively expansive view of federal power to appropriate money for spending under section 81 of the Constitution (Saunders 2009: 258). *Pape* in 2009 did not explicitly overturn the case, but the power of the Commonwealth government to fund regional or local initiatives outside section 96 of the Constitution must be in doubt since *Pape*. The Liberal-National Fraser government in 1979 provided to local government 1.52% of net personal income tax collections in the previous year, increased to 2% in 1980–81. This revenue sharing arrangement was dropped during the 1980s but direct grants from the federal government continued although they are currently below this level (Hawker Report 2003: 99 et seq). Commonwealth federal grants to local government are delivered under section 96 of the Constitution via State Government Grants Commissions which allocate the funding between local councils in their jurisdiction, on an "untied" basis without conditions.[15] Fiscal equalisation between councils is one of the national principles for distribution to local government.

Local governments are permitted to borrow under State legislation, usually with approval of the State Minister for Local Government and subject to restrictions related to the nature of security for borrowing. Some local governments borrow from the State government, while others cannot do so and must seek finance on the open market. Local governments are usually restricted to for capital investment and not for recurrent expenditure. In general, Australian local governments have extremely low levels of debt and are debt-averse, although this stance has been criticised, see, e.g., Comrie (2014). There have been various proposals to leverage local government assets or establish a national financing facility for local governments, especially to improve financing for infrastructure (e.g. Ernst & Young 2013).

Regional and local government financing is missing from the Intergovernmental Agreement on Federal Financial Relations. There has long been concern in regional and rural Australia that State governments do not adequately respond to the needs of their communities and that local governments are facing high and increasing infrastructure liabilities (see, e.g., Dollery 2009; Twomey 2008; Brown and Bellamy 2006). The Hawker Report acknowledged the desire for legal recognition of

[15] See, e.g., the Victorian Grants Commission, available at www.dpcd.vic.gov.au/localgovernment/victoria-grants-commission.

local government at the federal level and recommended a tripartite financial agreement and national Summit on Intergovernmental Relations, neither of which has been carried out. The President of the Australian Local Government Association was a member of the former Council of Australian Governments (COAG) and on the National Federation Reform Council which replaced it in 2020.. is only one minor voice in this forum. In 2006, the Commonwealth Parliament unanimously passed a resolution acknowledging that local government is an integral part of Australia's federal system, but this has only symbolic value. Referendums to change the Constitution to provide recognition of local government have been held twice, and have twice failed to pass, since 1973. It seems unlikely that Constitutional recognition of local government will be achieved in the future.

4 Federal Economic and Fiscal Coordination

4.1 National Economic and Debt Management

The Commonwealth Government controls most of the levers for economic management in Australia: monetary, fiscal, and trade and investment policy. The independent Reserve Bank sets the interest rate and controls monetary policy using an inflation target as the main goal (during the COVID-19 pandemic, the Bank has been mainly focused on liquidity and economic recovery). As indicated in Sects. 2 and 3, the Commonwealth government raises 80% of tax revenues and manages the social security (transfer) system, and grants to States, thereby controlling most fiscal policy. Commonwealth Australia had (before the COVID-19 pandemic) relatively low debt across all levels of government, with gross debt of 73% of GDP in 2019 , increased to 84% of GDP in 2021; in contrast, household debt in Australia is among the highest in the OECD.[16]

The first major institution of fiscal cooperation in the federation concerned government borrowing. One of Australia's founders noted that Canadian provinces and US states were "practically free of debt"; in contrast, the Australian States had liabilities "the annual interest on which absorbs more revenue than they have been accustomed to raise, or

[16] OECD, Data: https://data.oecd.org/gga/general-government-debt.htm#indicator-chart (2018, 2021), https://data.oecd.org/hha/household-debt.htm (2018).

are likely to raise, by direct taxes" (Deakin 1902, 1952: 242). On one estimate, the colonies had nearly 15 times the debt of Canada (Saunders 1989). The Commonwealth and the States entered into the first federal financial agreement in 1909. After the Commonwealth government also began borrowing seriously, to fund WWI, it was clear that a coordinated approach was needed and this had not been properly planned in the Constitution. A successful referendum amended the Constitution inserting section 105A to allow the Commonwealth Government to take over State debts. The Australian Loan Council was established in 1926 and it became a forum for coordinated borrowing and enforced strict limits on State borrowing, as well as managing federal loans to the States (Saunders 1989).

The Loan Council was a model for the use of cooperative institutions, whether legislated or informal, to manage the fiscal federation. Some described the Loan Council as involving a surrender of sovereign powers of the States (e.g. Cowper 1932); however, it has been eclipsed in this role by the vertical fiscal imbalance and federal grants power discussed in Sects. 2 and 3 above. The Loan Council operates to the present day as a borrowing and deficit control mechanism, together with binding financial agreements. In response to the Global Financial Crisis of 2008, the Council expanded "fiscal space" for the States and Commonwealth by allowing deficits to creep up (with timelines for reduction). The Loan Council was also the vehicle by which the Commonwealth government provided a timelimited guarantee for State debt to ensure they maintained good credit ratings. In response to the economic impact of the COVID-19 pandemic, this role may be refreshed as governments at all levels take on more debt.

4.2 *From The Council of Australian Governments to the National Federation Reform Council*

The grants power in section 96 of the Constitution has substantial political weight, in particular in forcing states *not* to do certain things (such as levy an income tax). However, it is more difficult for the Commonwealth government to leverage the grants power to regulate and deliver services in large and complex areas of government activity, such as education or health, in respect which it does not have direct legislative power. To facilitate joint federal-state funding and regulation, a series of "soft law" federal-state agreements and institutional arrangements have been established. Intergovernmental agreements are in effect political compacts, which may have aspects legislated at Commonwealth and State level, and engage funds legislatively appropriated.

From 1992 until 2020, intergovernmental agreements were negotiated and managed by the Council of Australian Governments (COAG), a series of councils of ministers, supported by bureaucratic representatives and a secretariat, from Commonwealth, State and territory governments. In some councils, New Zealand was also represented. The COAG councils comprised:

- Federal Financial Relations Council
- Disability Reform Council
- Transport and Infrastructure Council
- Energy Council
- Skills Council
- Council of Attorneys-General
- Education Council
- Health Council
- Joint Council on Closing the Gap
- Indigenous Affairs Council
- Australian Data and Digital Council
- Women's Safety Council.

In 2019, in response to the COVID-19 pandemic, the Liberal/National Morrison government established a so-called National Cabinet of the prime minister and premiers or chief ministers of the States and Territories. On 29 May 2020, the National Cabinet agreed to replace COAG with a National Federation Reform Council. This includes the Prime Minister, Commonwealth Treasurer, premiers, chief ministers and treasurers of States and Territories, and the President of the Australian Local Government Association. To date, the newly elected Labor Albanese government has continued the Council and convened the first meeting under his leadership in June 2022.[17]

[17] See www.federation.gov.au.

The dependence of the States on the Commonwealth (going "cap in hand") in bargaining about future funding has been widely criticised (e.g. Senate Select Committee on the Reform of the Australian Federation 2011).[18] Intergovernmental partnership agreements may be lauded as processes of cooperation and partnership, or criticised as vehicles for Commonwealth interference in areas of State primary responsibility and for being short-term, contingent, uncertain and non-transparent.

An example education funding, which is complicated because of a mix of public and private provision, as well as the division of financial and organisational obligations and responsibilities between State and Commonwealth governments, all subject to overarching standards and equalisation processes. The result was described by Hinz (2017: 35) as a system that, while reasonably well performing when compared with other countries, is "characterised by fragmentation, complexity, suboptimal resource allocation, blurred accountability, and an incoherent policy mix". Education funding in Australia has been subject to ongoing shifts in policy direction and funding arrangements in the last decade. School funding was subject to a major review ("Gonski 1.0" after the Chair, David Gonski) initiated by a Labor Government in 2011 which proposed significant changes in the allocation of school funding to public and private schools. This fed into federal-State 5 year funding agreements at that time, but the findings were controversial and debated. A second review in 2017 by the Liberal-National Government (Commonwealth of Australia 2018a). This, together with other reviews, informed the development of the next 5 year National Schools Reform Agreement between the Commonwealth, State and Territory governments which commenced on 1 January 2019 (Department of Education, Skills and Employment 2018). In 2019–20, the Commonwealth rovided funding of $21.5 billion to support school and early childhood education under the agreed framework and other national partnership agreements (Commonwealth of Australia 2019: 30).

[18] Select Committee on the Reform of the Australian Federation (Australian Senate), *Australia's Federation: An Agenda for Reform*, Report (June 2011), for example, in education funding.

4.3 *The Intergovernmental Financial Agreement*

The Intergovernmental Agreement on the Reform of Commonwealth-State Financial Relations of 1999,[19] requires all of the GST revenue collected by the Commonwealth government to be paid to the States and Territories, applying principles of horizontal fiscal equalisation. The equalisation analysis is carried out by the Commonwealth Grants Commission. The difficult financial situation in which the States found themselves in the late 1990s, after license fees on tobacco, alcohol and fuel were struck down as "excises" (Sect. 3.2.2 above), was an important contributing factor to this successful fiscal reform under the Liberal-National government led by Prime Minister Howard. The GST is administered federally by the ATO and is, legally speaking, a Commonwealth tax.

The Intergovernmental Agreement was legislated in a Schedule to *A New Tax System (Commonwealth-State Financial Arrangements) Act 1999* (Cth) with *A New Tax System (Managing the GST Rate and Base) Act 1999*. The latter Act states in section 10 that it is the "intention" of the federal government to abide by the Agreement. The State and Territory governments have a right of unanimous decision-making and veto, by means of the Council because of the requirement that "the rate of the GST, and the GST base, are not to be changed unless each state agrees to the change" (section 11). Changes to the GST law are also required to be consistent with: (a) maintaining the integrity of the GST base; (b) administrative simplicity; and (c) minimising compliance costs for taxpayers. The Act cannot bind future federal (or state) Parliaments – it can be amended by an ordinary Act of the federal Parliament and the agreement is unenforceable as a matter of constitutional law (Saunders 2000: 99). The Agreement is administered by the Council for Federal Financial Relations comprising the treasurers of the Commonwealth, States and Territories, an arrangement which will presumably continue under the new Federation Reform Council. Agreement objectives include collaboration in achieving fair and sustainable financial arrangements; enhanced public accountability; reduced administration and compliance overheads; stronger incentives to implement economic and social reforms; the ongoing provision of GST payments to the States and Territories; and

[19] Available http://www.federalfinancialrelations.gov.au/content/intergovernmental_agreements.aspx.

the equalisation of fiscal capacities between States and Territories. The Agreement was amended and updated in 2009.

Payment arrangements under the Intergovernmental Agreement are established under Schedule D, which explains that financial transfers comprise four categories of payment: (a) National Specific Purpose Payments (SPPs) in respect of key service delivery sectors; (b) three types of National Partnership payments: (i) project payments; (ii) facilitation payments; (iii) reward payments; (c) general revenue assistance, consisting of: (i) GST payments; and (ii) other general revenue assistance; and (d) National Health Reform funding. Payments are legislated under the *Federal Financial Relations Act 2009 (Cth).*

5 Horizontal Fiscal Equalisation

5.1 *History of Equalisation and the Commonwealth Grants Commission*

The need for horizontal fiscal equalisation (HFE) across States and Territories, because of their differing tax capacities and spending needs, was identified early in the life of the Australian federation. In general, the States with smaller populations (and often extremely large land masses) were less able to raise adequate revenue for their infrastructure and services needs. Initially, grants from the Commonwealth to States were made on a per capita basis, but there were needs in the smaller (population-wise) states and extra grants were provided to needy claimant states in many early years (Brown 1952).

The second major federal fiscal innovation after the Loans Council was the establishment of the Commonwealth Grants Commission (CGC) as an independent agency in 1933, under Commonwealth legislation and not by Constitutional amendment. The CGC originated out of dissatisfaction of the States about previous grant processes who called for an independent expert body to prevent "log-rolling" and abuse of Commonwealth grants to States. The CGC was introduced at the same time as a failed attempt to secede by the Government of Western Australia in 1933 (a referendum vote on secession was passed by a significant majority of the Western Australian people, but the majority of votes in a majority of States was not achieved, so the referendum failed) (CGC 1995: 16). The CGC had the role of assessing claims by States for grants of financial assistance to support functioning at a level not significantly below that of other states.[20] After uniform income taxation was established in 1942, the capacity of all states including previously self-sufficient states of Victoria and NSW fell far short of increasing expenditure demands, while the Commonwealth had surplus budgets. Large grants have been paid from the Commonwealth to the states in every year since 1942, with a portion always calculated on an equalisation basis.

In 1973, the CGC was re-established as an independent statutory authority with the role of assessing the relative financial capacity of all the States so as to recommend to the Commonwealth the allocation of financial assistance grants "at standards not appreciably different from the standards of government services provides by the other States".[21] The CGC provides advice to the Treasurer on the allocation among the States and Territories of the GST revenue based on its assessment of HFE relativities. This forms the basis for the annual Determination of GST relativities issued by the Treasurer. From 1981 to 2018, the mission of the CGC was full and comprehensive equalisation, in which a given pool of funds were to be distributed among the States and Territories. From 1999, the pool of revenue to be equalised was capped at the GST revenue, so that horizontal equalisation was a "zero-sum game". The standard of full equalisation commenced as "not appreciably different" capacities to deliver services, but evolved to the "same" capacity by the year 2000 (Productivity Commission 2018: 67). The Commission defined "equalisation" in 2010 as follows (2010: 34):

> State governments should receive funding from the pool of goods and services tax revenue such that, after allowing for material factors affecting revenues and expenditures, each would have the fiscal capacity to provide services and the associated infrastructure at the same standard, if each made the same effort to raise revenue from its own sources and operated at the same level of efficiency.

The GST equalisation analysis is carried out each year by the Commission based on the average level of revenue collection and service delivery across states and calculated over the previous three years. For example, an

[20] Commonwealth Grants Commission (CGC), About us, https://www.cgc.gov.au/about-us.

[21] *CGC*, About us, https://www.cgc.gov.au/about-us; *Commonwealth Grants Commission Act 1973 (Cth)* as amended; CGC (1995).

assessment in 2018–19 would average the result over the *previous* three years (2017–18, 2016–17 and 2015–16) and the relativity factor would then be applied for the *next* year (2019–20). Actual expenditures or policies are not relevant, except in so far as they may affect the average against which all states are judged. Applying the average, the GST relativity is calculated.This is then applied to modify the per capita allocation, in the formula:

$$\frac{\text{Adjusted State population} \times \text{GST revenue}}{\text{Adjusted State population}}$$

(where Adjusted State population is the estimated State population on 31 December in the payment year, multiplied by the GST relativity).

The pool for equalisation is capped by total GST revenue. The result is that all States and Territories receive a grant of GST revenue but some States are "donors" while others are "recipients" of equalisation. The full equalisation approach of the CGC has two components. First, it aimed to bring all states and territories up to the strongest fiscal capacity in the federation. Historically, this has meant equalising all states to the fiscal capacity of NSW or Victoria, but in more recent years, it has meant equalising to the fiscal capacity of Western Australia, because of the mining boom. The second element of equalisation was to ensure that government services could be delivered to the same standard in all States, "if each state made the same effort to raise revenue from its own sources and operated at the same level of efficiency" (Australian Government 2018b: 7).

The factors that have the biggest impact on HFE relativities are mining royalties; land and property sales and taxable land values; remoteness of the population; the share of Indigenous people in the population (both discussed in Sect. 7 below); payrolls of large companies; the existence of big cities; and the existence of Commonwealth Payments for Specific Purposes (Table 2). The HFE determination applies directly only to the GST, but the effect of specific Payments is "equalised" away over time, because most State taxes and other grants are taken into account in applying the formula.

The distribution of GST revenues, and relativities, are shown in Table 3, for 2017–18, 2018-19 and the average relativity since 2000. Table 3 shows that in 2017–18, the NSW received 87.67% of its per capita GST revenue and the Victoria received 93.24%. Western Australia received a very low proportion of 34.43% of its per capita GST allocation. On the

Table 2 Revenue and expenditure categories for equalisation assessment

Expenses	*Revenue*	*Capital*	*Other payments*
Schools education	Payroll tax	Net investment	Commonwealth Payments for Specific Purposes
Post-secondary education	Land tax	Net lending	
Health	Stamp (transfer) duty		
Housing	Insurance tax		
Welfare	Motor taxes		
Services to communities	Mining revenue		
Justice	Other revenue		
Roads			
Transport			
Services to industry			
Depreciation			
Other expenses			

Source CGC, The GST Distribution Model available at www.cgc.gov.au

other hand, South Australia received 144% of its per capita allocaiton and the Northern Territory received an enormous 466% of its per capita allocation (three categories of mining royalties, remoteness and Indigeneity are significant in this result).

5.2 *The "Reasonable Equalisation" Approach and Top-Up for Western Australia*

The arrangements for payment of the GST on general revenue assistance basis, subject to HFE under the Intergovernmental Agreement were reasonably stable for two decades. However, the Agreement began to show cracks as a result of the resources boom. The massive increase in the price and export of iron ore located in Western Australia meant that it became the fiscally strongest state under the HFE analysis because of its capacity to raise revenues through mineral royalties and other taxes, in the period from 2002 to 2014. The consequence, subject to a lag because of the HFE averaging approach, led to Western Australia being a large donor of GST to other States and Territories. The impact on the Western Australian budget was severe because the rolling averaging approach meant that it remained a large donor even after the resources

Table 3 GST distribution relativities and outcomes

	NSW	*VIC*	*QLD*	*WA*	*SA*	*TAS*	*ACT*	*NT*
2017–18 GST relativity	0.87672	0.93239	1.18769	0.34434	1.43997	1.80477	1.19496	4.66024
Population[a]	7,915,069	6,385,849	4,965,033	2,584,768	1,728,053	524,677	415,916	246,726
GST entitlement $m	17,791	15,268	15,110	2,285	6,374	2,417	1,266	2,928
2018–19 GST relativity	0.85517	0.98670	1.09584	0.47287	1.47727	1.76706	1.18070	4.25816
Population[c]	8,052,909	6,532,744	5,041,416	2,617,739	1,740,939	525,707	420,123	245,946
GST entitlement $m[b]	18,442	17,261	14,794	3,315	6,887	2,488	1,328	2,805
Average relativity since 2000[d]	0.90126	0.89103	1.03502	0.72395	1.28004	1.68175	1.20221	5.09715

[a]As at 31 December 2017. *Source* Australian Demographic Statistics, December 2017 (ABS Cat. No. 3101.0)
[b]Estimate. Based on GST pool forecasts as presented in the Commonwealth's 2018–19 Budget
[c]Estimate based on State population forecasts as presented in the Commonwealth's 2018–19 Budget
[d]Average from 2000–01 to 2018–19. Relativities prior to 2009-10 reflect the CGC's calculation of a pool comprising of GST only (relativities previously recommended by the CGC were based on a pool comprising of both GST and health care grants)
Source Commonwealth of Australia (2018b, Table 1, p. 3)

boom had ended. As in 1933, but this time because of its good fortune, significant political unhappiness in Western Australia about fiscal equalisation was the trigger for negotiation of a new political compromise phased in from 2020.

Tshe Commonwealth government established an inquiry into HFE and made interim top-up grants to Western Australia. Following a Productivity Commission report (2018), the Commonwealth Parliament passed a bill for a new equalisation formula to commence in 2021–22, by amendment to the *Federal Financial Relations Act* and *Commonwealth Grants Commission Act*.[22] It is notable that the new approach was not achieved by an amendment to the Intergovernmental Agreement on Federal Financial Relations (which would have required unanimous agreement of all the States and Territories); nor does it implement many of the recommendations in the Productivity Commission report. The Explanatory Memorandum for the bill explained that the GST distribution system had worked reasonably well but "the mining boom revealed that it does not function well when faced with economic shocks".[23]

Information about Commonwealth Government funding to the States and Territories is provided in the annual federal budget.[24] The revenue sharing relativity for the 2020–21 year is set out in Table 4; this will be topped up by additional payments of $1.4 billion over three years to Western Australia to ensure a floor on the relativity factor of 0.7 (which is much more than the factor of 0.449 indicated in Table 4). Additional short-term transition payments are paid to the Northern Territory if needed.

The new "reasonable equalisation" regime for general revenue assistance does the following (in summary):

1. The HFE regime will transition to a "reasonable equalisation" approach over the years to 2026–27 which will benchmark the fiscal capacity of each State and Territory to the stronger of either NSW

[22] *Treasury Laws Amendment (Making Sure Every State and Territory Gets Their Fair Share of GST) Act 2018* (Cth).

[23] Explanatory memorandum to *Treasury Laws Amendment (Making Sure Every State and Territory Gets Their Fair Share of GST) Act 2018* (Cth), p. 7 [1.11].

[24] See www.budget.gov.au for all budget documentation especially Budget Paper No. 3: Federal Financial Relations.

Table 4 GST revenue sharing relativity 2020–21

Item	*For this state*	*The GST revenue sharing relativity for the 2020–21 payment year is*
1	New South Wales	0.91808
2	Victoria	0.95992
3	Queensland	1.04907
4	Western Australia	0.44970
5	South Australia	1.35765
6	Tasmania	1.89742
7	Australian Capital Territory	1.15112
8	Northern Territory	4.76893

Source *Federal Financial Relations (GST Revenue Sharing Relativities for 2020–21) Determination 2020*, Clause 5 (Commonwealth Treasurer Josh Frydenburg, 1 April 2020)

or Victoria, the most populous (and, for most of the last century, the most prosperous) of the States;

2. A minimum GST revenue sharing relativity (or "floor") will be introduced, at the discretion of the Commonwealth Treasurer for any individual State or Territory;
3. The GST revenue pool will be permanently boosted with additional Commonwealth funds.

5.3 *Lack of State Tax Reform*

It was the intention of the 1999 Intergovernmental Agreement on Federal Financial Relations that the distribution of GST revenue on a general assistance basis, subject to HFE, would provide a growing revenue base for the States. This was in exchange for the State and Territory governments reforming and harmonising some of their State taxes. Some reform was achieved at the time, but the State governments still levy a large number of taxes with diverse structures, bases and rates, generating complexity and compliance costs for businesses operating nationally. States also tend to compete down their tax bases. Australian experience of State tax reform suggests that federal fiscal competition is not always a good thing. Tax competition led to the demise in Australia of what has been called the most efficient tax base of all (inheritance or estate duty) and contributed to the failure of the States, even the richest and most populous, to agree on how to enact income taxes when this became possible after WWII. The States have a poor record at developing uniform laws and regulatory regimes in any field and it is difficult to rely on them retaining a single tax base unless forced upon them.

The challenge of State tax reform was addressed in the NSW Review of Federal Financial Relations (NSW Government 2020). Many State tax reforms that support equity and efficiency, such as transitioning from stamp duties to land taxes, may in the short term *increase* rather than decrease vertical fiscal imbalance. State tax reform requires federal cooperationincluding additional Commonwealth funding, as well as leadership by the wealthiest states, as was done in 1999 when the GST was enacted.

Resource taxation has also been a thorny issue in the Australian federation. The State governments are sovereign owners of mineral resources and they have the primary right to levy royalties on extraction. The Henry Tax Review took special note of state royalties, identifying over 60 different and complex royalty arrangements (Australian Treasury 2009: Table 2.19). A key finding was that States tended to under-price mineral resources in their royalty systems (given the level of profit derived, in particular, from iron ore and coal in the last decade). This un-used State fiscal capacity caused the HFE issues for Western Australia, described above. In 2012, the Gillard Labor government enacted a mineral resource rent tax (MRRT) to apply to iron ore and coal; however, this reform failed, and on a change of government, the MRRT was repealed. There is no scope here to discuss the complicated tax and federal issues arising from the MRRT, or why it failed (see, e.g., Eccleston and Hortle 2016; Murray 2015). However, one consequence of the enactment of the MRRT—and perhaps a contribution to its failure because of the treatment of State royalties in that regime – was the reform of royalties in a number of States, leading to them raising more revenue from mining in their jurisdiction (e.g. de Souza et al. 2017, Murray 2015). Royalties remain important revenue sources for some State governments, as indicated in Sect. 3 above. This will continue to be taken into account in the HFE process but, in effect, to a more limited extent in future.

6 Vertical Fiscal Imbalance

6.1 *Australia's High Vertical Fiscal Imbalance*

Vertical fiscal imbalance (VFI) arises when subnational governments have inadequate revenues to fund their expenditure responsibilities. Australia's

VFI is one of the largest of any federation (Bird and Smart 2009; Koutsogeorgopoulou 2007; Webb 2003). The Commonwealth raises more than 80% of taxes in the federation, and controls the most important tax bases of income and consumption as explained in Sect. 3 above. Figure 2 shows the share of State own-source and grant revenues, divided into general revenue assistance (GST revenues) and specific purpose payments (conditional grants). Overall, State and Territory governments raise just over half of the revenue required to finance their expenditure responsibilities and the balance must be provided by grants from the Commonwealth Government.

The high level of VFI in Australia was one of the issues addressed by the 2015 White Paper for reform of the federation, which was quickly abandoned (DPMC 2015). However, the problem existed from the beginning of federation. It was left by the founders in 1901, to be

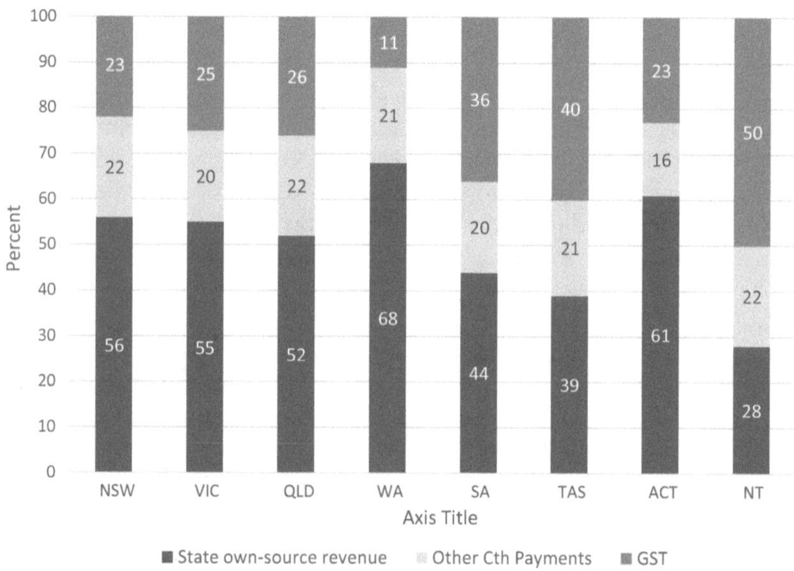

Fig. 2 State own-source and grant revenue, 2017–18 (*Source* Commonwealth of Australia 2018b, Figure 1). Total state revenue figures are sourced from the States' 2018–19 Budgets, with the exception of SA, which is sourced from its 2017–18 Mid-Year Budget Review. Payments from the Commonwealth figures are sourced from the Commonwealth's 2018–19 Budget)

resolved in the arena of federal-state political negotiation rather than by legal allocation of taxing powers. However, VFI has been exacerbated in ways that could not have been foreseen in 1901, through the judicial interpretation of the meaning of "excise" and the takeover of the income tax base by the Commonwealth Government as explained in Sect. 3.

Bird and Smart observe that vertical fiscal "imbalance" has long been seen to require "balance" as a solution, such that "every tub should stand on its own bottom in the sense that the revenues from sources under control of each level of government should be sufficient to finance expenditures" (Bird and Smart 2009: 73). But it is easy to make a fetish out of "balance". The main argument that fiscal capacity should be "balanced in a federation is that subnational governments need a "hard budget constraint" to ensure financial responsibility (Australian Treasury 2009: 671; Bird and Smart 2009: 119). If a government thinks it is going to be bailed out, or that it can come back and request more money next year, it will become inefficient and wasteful in its spending. However, achieving a hard budget constraint does not necessarily require that state and local governments must fund all or even most of their spending from their own taxes. As explained by the Australian Treasury (2009: 672):

> In a developed federation, it can be expected that there is some base level of goods and services that all sub-national governments will provide and that requires a commensurate amount of revenue. This revenue can be provided by the national government. ... So that they can meet the preferences of their citizens, sub-national governments should have the capacity to raise tax revenue to fund significant marginal expenditure beyond the base level. ... the question becomes how much of their own tax revenue State governments need in order to fund significant marginal expenditures.

It has been said that this is outcome of Australian fiscal federal system—thus, "the normal accountability that economists talk about is present" (Boadway 1997: 166). The States raise *marginal* revenues from State taxes which they do occasionally increase or decrease in response to local political demands, and in competition with other states, but a significant proportion of their core functions are funded from federal grants.

The principle of a hard budget constraint does not indicate *how much* revenue should be raised by taxation at the subnational level to fund "significant marginal expenditure". Tax sharing arrangements involve guesswork about how much revenue should be allocated to the subnational level and may be too rigid for governmental needs. For example, the tax-sharing arrangement briefly in place in 1976, under which State and local governments received a fixed proportion of Commomwealth income tax revenues, created a hard budget constraint that was both inflexible and unpredictable. States were dependent on a fixed share of federal revenues that they could not modify and took direct cuts to their budget if the federal government cut its tax rates.

Bird and Smart further argue that greater transparency is needed through the allocation of taxation and expenditure responsibilities, so that "citizens [are] less confused as to what exactly they are paying for in taxes and who should be held accountable for both taxes and expenditures" (2009, 73; 83). In Australia's federation, State and local governments may be more "accountable" to the Commonwealth government, because of their dependence on grants, than to their local population. Saunders suggests that both the responsibility of the executive to parliaments, and the accountability of elected representatives to citizens, may be "distorted" if revenues come from "formula-based" grants from another tier of government rather than from direct taxation (2000: 100).

However, in a federal system in which all levels of government are democratically elected, it may be better to think of accountability as layered (Rubin 2006). The Australian system ensures accountability of governments to the citizens as a whole, via the Commonwealth Parliament (which legitimately taxes and appropriates grant revenues). If there is a mismatch between the political party elected at Commonwealth level which raises the revenue, and that elected at State level which spends it, does this make the governments less accountable? This situation is not uncommon in Australia. On one view, a Commonwealth government is likely to be stricter with its grants to States of a different political persuasion than otherwise, potentially enhancing the budget constraint. On the other hand, State dependence on federal grants may hinder sensible planning about major expenditures, while detailed federal direction in specific purpose payment agreements may not be appropriately designed, monitored or implemented. A consequence may be that neither States nor the Commonwealth is properly accountable for the use of the funds or outcomes from grants.

6.2 *Reforming the GST*

The federal financial arrangements explained in Sect. 5 mean that half the revenues distributed to states and territories are "sourced" from the GST as "general revenue assistance" subject to HFE (as shown in Fig. 2). Since 2000, with numerous albeit relatively minor amendments to the GST law have been unanimously agreed, in line with the Agreement principles of maintaining the integrity of the tax base, simplicity of administration and minimising compliance costs. For example, recently, the Commonwealth, States and Territories agreed to extend the GST base to cover digital service downloads (the "Netflix tax") and imports of low-value goods (the "Amazon" tax).[25]

However, the chief limitation of the GST is the originally enacted base and rate. To date, no government has been prepared to address the challenging equity and political issues associated with GST reform that would raise the rate or broaden the base of the GST so as to raise more revenue. Australia's GST raises a lower share of total revenue than do similar consumption taxes in many other countries. It is levied at a rate of 10% with significant exemptions in the base (about half of the household consumption base is exempt). The decline in share of household spending and low GST coverage is illustrated in Fig. 3.

The NSW Review concluded that the GST does not raise enough revenue to fund core services and it is no longer a "growth" tax base for the states (NSW Government 2020; confirming earlier findings, e.g. GST Distribution Review 2012). The new "reasonable equalisation" approach to HFE and distribution of GST revenues, explained in Sect. 5.2 above, commits the Commonwealth government to ost the pool of revenue to be distributed as general revenue assistance beyond the revenues raised by the GST itself. The increase will reach $9 billion by 2028–29. This is an acknowledgement of the need of State and Territory governments for more revenues to deliver on their core expenditure responsibilities of education and health.

[25] Australian Taxation Office, GST on imported services and digital products, https://www.ato.gov.au/Business/International-tax-for-business/GST-on-imported-goods-and-services/GST-on-imported-services-and-digital-products/.

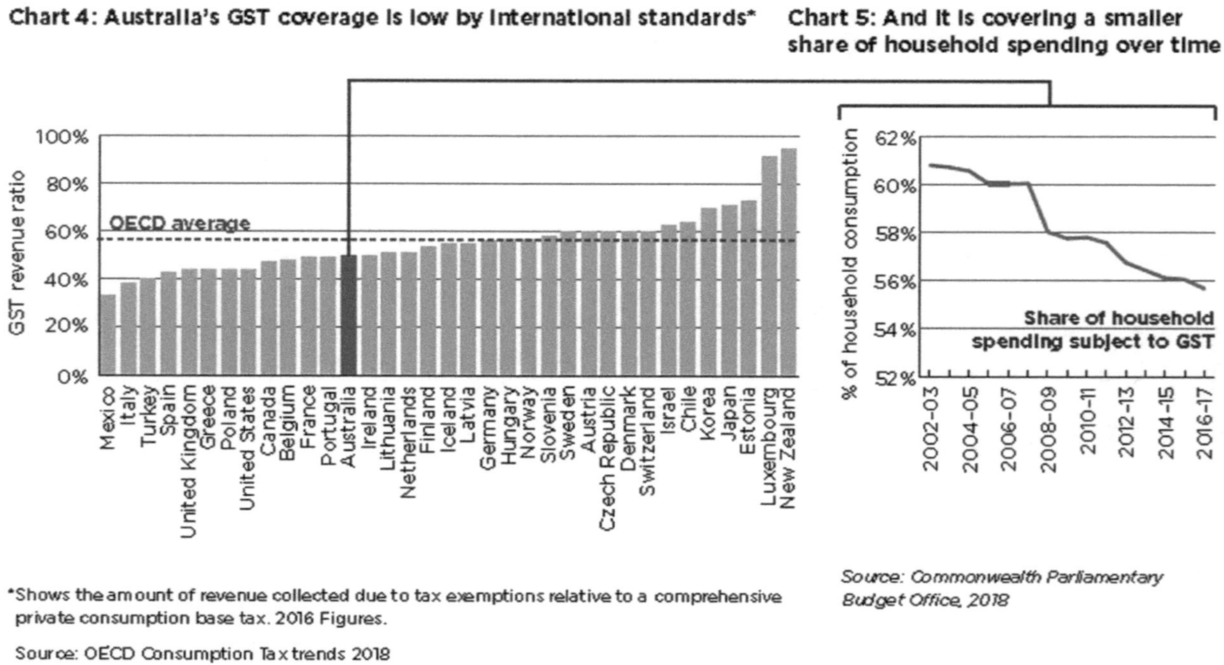

Fig. 3 GST coverage (consumption) (*Source* NSW Review of Federal Financial Relations, Charts 4 and 5, Discussion Paper, 2019, p. 15)

6.3 A New Approach to Revenue Sharing Between the Commonwealth and the States

Attempts to reform Australia's model of fiscal federalism in the last two decades have almost all "non-starters" (Bruerton and Hollander 2018). The *Henry Tax Review* (Australian Treasury 2009) initiated by the Rudd Labor Government raised many issues to do with fiscal federalism and state tax reform. The Abbot Liberal/National Government White Paper (DPMC 2014), with substantial research and consultation, was abandoned in 2015 by Prime Minister Turnbull of the same party. The Re:Think tax reform process (Australian Treasury 2014) launched by the same government was abandoned. The NSW government has proposed State tax reform following its Review (NSW Government 2020) but it is unclear if this will proceed. A key issue in all of these reform processes is whether some part of the tax base should be "returned" to the States, or whether a better revenue sharing approach should be adopted.

The national income tax law and administration has generated significant economic and fiscal gains for Australia and has avoided issues of tax competition, base erosion and complexity. In this author's view, it would be a backward step to "return" income tax law-making or collection to state governments. History suggests that the Australian population would oppose the enactment of State income taxes. Allocating some (necessarily limited) income tax base to the States would be unlikely to address fiscal sustainability challenges and may lead to tax competition. It could also lead to distributional issues across rich and poor states (see, e.g., Eccleston and Warren 2015). Shifting the taxing authority to subnational governments has significant disadvantages.

In this author's view, sharing income tax revenue is a different matter and has much to recommend it. The income tax (as the largest federal tax besides the GST) implicitly funds other grants to the States but, unlike the GST, State and Territory governments do not bear any responsibility for maintaining the integrity of the income tax base. They are not incentivised to carry out economic reforms that would generate a fiscal benefit for the Commonwealth government through greater income tax revenues, rather than a direct benefit to States. The federal government has a political incentive to reduce income tax rates or revenues which is unchecked by state governments that must maintain core public expenditures. The HFE reforms outlined in Sect. 5.2 expand the size of the pool to be distributed to the States, implicitly recognising the need for sharing of more revenue.

However, the "top-up" of the GST pool for general revenue assistance delivers additional amounts out of Commonwealth consolidated revenue without any commitment from States to reform their own tax systems, or to take any responsibility for the management of the federal tax base.

A reform to federal financial arrangements that retains the law and administration of the income tax and GST at the Commonwealth level but shares the revenue of both income tax and GST on a more equal basis with the States and Territories could provide more, and more secure, revenue for their core expenditure responsibilities. This could be implemented as part of a new federal financial agreement in exchange for a State tax reform package. The new Federal Financial Agreement can be implemented in legislation and reformed institutions; an amendment of the Constitution would not be necessary. An alternative could be to amend the Constitution to embed the financial arrangements, and establish a Financial Council, similar to the Loan Council, that would from time to time govern the federal financial agreement. However, the referendum process for Constitutional amendment makes this difficult to achieve.

6.3.1 Inspiration from the German Revenue Sharing System

The reform proposal suggested here takes inspiration from the German system approach. While superficially different, the German fiscal approach is similar in many respects to Australia. In Germany, as in Australia, the personal income tax, corporate income tax and Value Added Tax (VAT) are legislated at the federal level and contribute about 80% of tax revenues.[26] In both countries, taxes under subnational control are comparatively negligible in scope and revenue. However, in Germany, unlike Australia, the Basic Law establishes rules for sharing of revenues from each tax between the federal, State (*Länder*) and local governments. Most importantly, the personal income tax, corporate income tax and VAT in Germany are established as "joint taxes" (*Gemeinschaftssteuern*) under FRG Basic Law, Art 106 and are thereby subject to approximately equal division between the central government and the Länder, with a component distributed to local governments. The division of revenues from these core taxes is made on an entitlement basis, without conditions.

[26] The German VAT is levied at a higher rate and raises more revenue than the Australian GST, contributing about one third of all tax revenues. Overall, the tax level and expenditure level as a proportion of GDP in Germany is significantly higher than Australia.

Most comparative analyses of fiscal federalism obscure the centralised nature of German taxation, implying that Germany has low VFI (e.g. DPMC 2015, Figure 3.1; see also Kim 2015). In fact, the centralisation of taxation in Germany is strikingly similar to Australia. The key difference is that the Basic Law provides that where any revenues from a tax flow to the *Länder*, the tax law must receive the assent of the *Bundesrat* which is the legislative organ that represents the *Länder* at the federal level, comprising delegations appointed by their governments. Nonetheless, as Fuest and Thone write (2008: 16):

> The design of the shared taxes is controlled by the central government. The Länder governments admittedly have joint influence on tax legislation through the Bundesrat. But the Bundesrat is a federal legislative organ. The collective voice of the Länder governments [in that chamber] has little to do with subnational tax autonomy, seeing as the legislators of individual Länder - the state parliaments - have no influence on tax legislation.

The conceptual starting point for the German revenue sharing system is that there is an *entitlement* to the "joint tax" revenues in the *Länder* which are then *accountable to their own population for expenditures*. The "joint tax" revenues to which they are entitled are not subject to federal conditions, as is the case for the Australian general revenue assistance grants of the GST (topped up), but in contrast to Commonwealth Specific Purpose Payments. There are some circumstances in which conditions are required in the German system, for example for "joint tasks" for the improvement of living conditions; to fund large investments in particular states needed to ensure economic stability; or to equalise economic power across the federation, promote economic growth or deal with disasters or emergencies (Arts 91a and 91b, 104b of the FRG Basic Law). No doubt, the range of joint taxes, and federal control, is a matter for constant political debate, as in any federation (see, e.g., Jochimsen 2013).

6.3.2 *Establishing the Income Tax and GST as "Joint Taxes" in Australia*

There seems never to have been any serious consideration of the German revenue-sharing approach as a model for Australia. The German model was briefly discussed in the Federation White Paper *Issues Paper 5* (DPMC 2015) and was studied four decades ago (Rydon and Wolfsohn 1980; Mathews 1980). One reasons why the approach has been ignored is a preoccupation with the *Bundesrat* as the legislative forum for a state voice on centralised tax laws in Germany. The inadequacies of the Australian Senate for achieving this goal may have been perceived as an obstacle. Thus, Mathews observed in 1980 that the German system is "more successful than the Australian system seems to be in reconciling political power and fiscal responsibility" (Mathews 1980: 341).

However, the Australian institutional fiscal landscape has changed significantly since 1980. The Agreement on Federal Financial Relations could be renegotiated to establish the personal income tax and the GST as "joint taxes", the revenue from which is shared on an entitlement basis among Commonwealth, State and Territory governments. It is important to share both income tax and GST revenues because the GST is too small to fund core state expenditures, while the income tax is too large "Joint taxes" would be subject to HFE. Other taxes such as excises and tariffs serve policy goals that are better dealt with at the Commonwealth level, including public health, environmental policy and trade policy. It would be appropriate for all levels of government to have a direct stake and responsibility for the sustainability of Australia's most important taxes in the longer term. Scope for conditional and special grants from the Commonwealth would remain, under s 96 of the Constitution. Different sharing proportions could be applied to each kind of tax and local governments could be included with a specific, smaller share, as is done in the German Federation. The company income tax and superannuation fund taxes are legally part of the general income tax law in Australia; however, it is possible to track company and superannuation tax revenues, rate and base separately and so they may be either included or excluded from the revenue sharing agreement.

In Germany, although tax law is centralised, the administration of taxes is handled by *Länder* authorities that act on behalf of the federation where the revenues go to the central government (Art 108 of the FRG Basic Law). The opposite occurs in Australia, where the income tax and GST are administered nationally by the ATO. However, this should not be an impediment to extending revenue sharing to personal income tax. The cost of administration of the GST is shared between the States and Territories. The GST Administration Performance Agreement (2020–23) which requires them to pay the Commonwealth for the agreed costs of administering the GST.[27] This approach could be extended to the future management of the personal income tax as a "joint tax".

When the total funds currently granted from the Commonwealth are considered, the proposal to *share equally* on an entitlement basis the revenues from the personal income tax and GST would not be a dramatic change. The estimate for personal income tax revenues in 2021–22 was about $240 billion, and for GST revenues about $72 billion, or $312 billion in total.[28] For the 2021–22 year, total payments to the States were estimated to be $167 billion.[29] An agreement to share equally the "joint tax" revenues from personal income tax and GST with the State and Territories would transfer a total of $56 billion. This could be expanded by including some corporate income tax revenue as a "carrot" to encourage states to participate in a package that could include reforming state taxes.

This "joint tax" proposal would not necessarily increase funding to the States, but it would change the *conditionality* of intergovernmental transfers. The equal sharing of personal income tax and GST revenues on an entitlement basis would remove much of the scope for conditionality for Commonwealth payments to the states, currently delivered in Specific Purpose Payments associated with agreements. However, the new approach does not have to eliminate conditionality from federal-State grants. The overall allocation to States and Territories could be determined through the "joint tax" approach and then a second stage could allocate a proportion of this total to partnership and specific purposes agreements establishing national indicators and standards. It should be noted that a proportion could also potentially be shared with local governments.

[27] GST Administration Performance Agreement (1 July 2020–30 June 2023), available https://www.ato.gov.au/About-ATO/Commitments-and-reporting/In-detail/GST-administration/GST-Administration-Performance-Agreement-(1-July-2020---30-June-2023).

[28] Commonwealth of Australia, Budget 2022–23, Paper 1, Statement 4, Table 4.5: Reconciliation of Australian Government general government (cash) receipts, 2021–22, available https://budget.gov.au/2022-23/content/bp1/index.htm.

[29] Commonwealth of Australia, Budget 2022 23, Budget Paper 3, Federal Financial Relations, Table 1.1, available https://budget.gov.au/2022-23/content/bp3/index.htm.

A modified approach could be to share a lesser proportion of the income tax and GST with the states on an entitlement basis, with the remainder to be subject to partnership and specific purpose agreements as is done currently. For example, the Intergovernmental Agreement could transfer one third of personal income tax and GST revenues unconditionally to state and territory governments. This would be a 50% increase on the general revenue assistance of $75 billion in 2021–22 and it would leave room for negotiation of partnership or specific purpose grants above that threshold. Such a change may be a more incremental and acceptable move from our current system to a more sophisticated revenue sharing system in future.

A further challenge concerns the relationship between the sharing of personal income tax revenue, GST revenue and HFE. There may be a good argument that only a portion of the distributed "joint taxes" should be equalised horizontally across states. This requires insulation of that proportion from the HFE relativities calculation, which could be achieved by a sequential distribution. This is likely to be a matter of significant political debate.

6.3.3 *Towards Limited Sharing of the Income Tax Base?*

The NSW Review proposed a limited, experimental, sharing of federal income tax revenues with the states. The proposal differs from the "joint tax" proposal above, as the sharing would be "based on the state in which the income is earned to ensure states are accountable for revenue raising and expenditure" (NSW Government 2020: 59). The income tax revenue is proposed to be quarantined from the CGC's calculation of GST relativities. The stated goal is to deliver greater revenue to a state which undertook reforms to support economic recovery, and to ensure that benefits are not redistributed to other states. This would require a calculation of the "entitlement" of a state to personal income tax. It is not clear how this would be achieved other than on a per capita basis. The Review proposed a pilot to be designed by the NSW government with the Commonwealth government, for example substituting a set of "smaller" agreements (not including the large education and health grants); there is not, yet a response from the Commonwealth on its view of this proposal.

7 Federal Fiscal Policy for Indigenous Self-Government

7.1 *Australia's Failure to Recognise Indigenous Fiscal Self-Government*

An increasingly important challenge in the Australian federation is recognition of Indigenous sovereignty through treaty and other governance recognition processes. Other challenges include fiscal compensation for land taking, and revenue sharing from exploitation such as mining. The movement for the Recognition of Indigenous first peoples in the Australian Constitution (Davis and Langton 2016) produced the Uluru Statement which calls for a First Nations voice in the Commonwealth Parliament and for agreement process with all Australian governments.[30] The Albanese Labor Government was elected in May 2022 on a platform that included a commitment to implement the Uluru Statement. Before these developments, Indigenous peoples such as the Dja Dja Wurrong and Yorta Yorta in Victoria and the Noongar through the South West Land and Sea Council in Western Australia, had taken significant steps towards self-determination in substantial agreements with State governments that cover land, income, assets and services (Langton and Longbottom 2012).

However, there remain many limits on the exercise of Indigenous self-governance and recognition of land title (see Langton et al. 2003, 2006). Indigenous organisations around the country, especially in remote areas, often struggle to develop effective self-governing processes, lack capacity and confront unstable and poorly funded administrative and institutional arrangements for the implementation of agreements and community governance.

State governments, under the Constitution; and, by legislation, Territory and local governments, are exempt from Commonwealth taxation. Similarly, many Indigenous governing entities, such as Native Title and Land Councils are exempt from taxation. Indigenous corporations, associations and trusts are usually not-for-profits that qualify as charitable

[30] A Referendum Council was established to advise and lead debate on recognition of Indigenous peoples in the Constitution: see https://www.dpmc.gov.au/indigenous-affairs/constitutional-recognition. See also http://referen-dumcouncil.org.au/events/uluru-statement-from-the-heart. In the State of Victoria, a Treaty process has been legislated and is underway; see https://www.aboriginalvictoria.vic.gov.au/treaty.

entities which are exempt from federal and state taxation. The exemption from taxation vacates some fiscal space for the raising of revenues by Indigenous organisations from a range of sources. However, there is little formal recognition of their responsibility for Indigenous expenditures. These processes are not recognised as fiscal self-government for the community concerned or in the federation.

Public and policy attention about fiscal matters for Indigenous peoples usually focuses on the apparently "high" level of government expenditures "on" Indigenous people and widespread failure of federal and state governments in delivering policies to enable Indigenous peoples to share in the economic wellbeing of the nation. The Productivity Commission Indigenous Expenditure Report has the purpose to contribute to "closing the gap" to overcome Indigenous disadvantage. The most recent report finds, that in 2015–16, "nationally, Australian Government plus state and territory government direct expenditure on services for Aboriginal and Torres Strait Islander Australians was AUD$33.4 billion" or an estimated $44,886 per capita expenditure, "around twice the ratio for non-Indigenous Australians" (Productivity Commission 2017: xii). The estimate includes a share of mainstream expenditures, and Indigenous-specific expenditures. The main reasons for higher expenditures are greater intensity of service use because of greater need; for example, health needs; a younger population therefore greater per capita use of childcare and schooling; and greater per capita expenditure on incarceration of Indigenous compared to non-Indigenous people. A further reason is the higher cost of providing services to Indigenous people in remote locations or targeted support such as Indigenous liaison officers in hospitals.

The second way in which Aboriginal and Torres Strait Islander people are taken into account in the fiscal federation is through the HFE process for equalising GST revenues across the States and Territories, discussed in Sect. 5. The HFE process takes account of a factor of "Indigeneity" and a factor for "remoteness". Together with mining production (royalties), these two factors are among the most important in the HFE relativities, as illustrated in Fig. 4 (and see Table 2).

The "Indigeneity" factor in the HFE formula reflects increased cost and higher demand for services affecting education, health, justice services, welfare and housing and services to communities. The distribution of the Indigenous population combined with the large "per capita" expenditure allocation is the reason for the importance of this factor. The

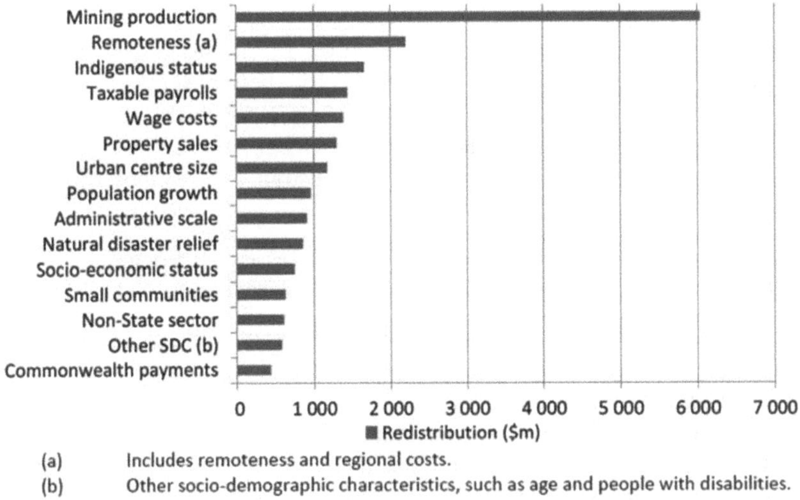

Fig. 4 Main contributors to relativities for horizontal fiscal equalisation (*Source* Commonwealth Grants Commission, trends in horizontal fiscal equalisation [Information Paper CGC 2016-01, April 2016], Figure 5)

State of NSW has the largest population of Aboriginal people by number but they comprise a small fraction of the state's population and hence New South Wales is a net donor on this factor. In contrast, Aboriginal people make up more than 30% of the Northern Territory's population. The "remoteness" factor takes account of community size, distance, cost of delivery of services such as electricity, and road length. This also reflects particular features of service delivery for Indigenous people in remote communities.

The additional funding under HFE is paid to State or Territory governments in the grants process. There is no entitlement to this funding by Indigenous peoples themselves in the State or Territory, and no direct accountability or consultation with Indigenous people about this funding. The last time a significant allocation of funding was explicitly made by the Federal Government to an Indigenous representative organisation was to the Aboriginal and Torres Strait Islander Council (ATSIC), which was established in 1990 and abolished in 2005 (Pratt and Bennett 2005). Since then, Australia has not had a representative Indigenous body with a budget for services.

In sum, Australia's federal fiscal arrangements have not kept up with the significant developments in recognition of Indigenous sovereignty through treaty processes, or the need for better support for self-governance, agreements and native title. A greater recognition of Indigenous self-government requires attention to be paid to fiscal matters, especially grants, revenue sharing and responsibility for expenditures.

7.2 *Inspiration from Canada for Recognising Indigenous Fiscal Self-Government*

In contrast to Australia, developments in Canada during the last two decades show that federal fiscal policy has been recognised as fundamental to the realisation of Aboriginal self-determination. The evolving Canadian approach to federal relations explicitly incorporates recognition of Indigenous first peoples (see, e.g., Prince and Abele 2003). This part presents ideas drawing on developments in fiscal federalism and public finance concerning First Nations' fiscal self-government in Canada, (see further Stewart 2017).

Canadian treaties with First Nations address tax and expenditure policy, revenue sharing and own-source revenue responsibilities. Some agreements address the relationship between First Nations and provincial governments, or allow for a sharing of taxing power and "fiscal space" between provincial and Aboriginal governments (Boucher and Vermaeten 2000: 151). For example, the Nisga'a Treaty contains taxation provisions and represents "the beginning of a greater attempt to weigh Aboriginal interests in tax policy" (Borrows and Rotman 1998: 809). Some tribes have established self-governing territories that are responsible for delivery of all services to the local area and levy taxes on their own populations as well as drawing on other revenues to fund services. The Northern Territories exercise powers delegated by the Canadian Parliament. Land claims settled in the North, for example with the Nunavut, Gwich'in, Sahtu and the Dogrib, include royalty sharing with the Canadian government with respect to mineral, oil and gas.

In 2006, the Canadian Government enacted the First Nations Fiscal Management Act, an optional regime to promote the economic development of participating First Nations by empowering them to collect property tax and to borrow. More than 300 First Nations are scheduled under the Act and many collect property tax or other local revenues under its authority. The Act established institutions with shared governance including a First Nations Tax Commission which regulates the approval of property tax and other local revenue laws and a First Nations Finance Authority, which has since 2014 issued more than CAD $1.3 million in Indigenous finance bonds for participating First Nations governments to finance community projects.[31]

In 2015, the Canadian Government released a policy setting out the fiscal approach for self-government for First Nations that have a comprehensive land and self-government agreement (Government of Canada 2015), presented as "Canada's collaborative self-government fiscal policy".[32] Principles include that all levels of government share responsibility for the financing of Aboriginal self-government, to ensure that communities have access to public programs and services that are reasonably comparable to those available to other Canadians living in communities of similar size and circumstance; and that Aboriginal governments should receive reasonably consistent and equitable allocations of federal funding.

What can we bring to Australia from the Canadian experience? First, a move towards recognition of Indigenous fiscal self-governance in Australia would recognise expenditure responsibilities and independent revenues where possible and agreed by the communities and other levels of government. Importantly, suggesting that Indigenous organisations can take a level of responsibility for fiscal self-government, and may have access to resources such as native title payments and benefits, does not absolve the federal, state, territory and local governments in Australia of their responsibilities to Indigenous and other local citizens. The principle of equalisation of services, which is set out in the Canadian First Nations fiscal governance approach, would also be critical in Australia.

A pathway towards fiscal self-government could be negotiated based on the Indigenous land and community agreements and organisations which now exist around the country or linked to ongoing treaty processes. Accompanying the recognition of Indigenous fiscal self-government, a collaborative fiscal policy should be established that explicitly recognises an entitlement to a share of revenues by Indigenous self-governing organisations. State, Territory and Commonwealth governments must continue

[31] First Nations Financial Management Board, https://fnfmb.com/en.

[32] Government of Canada, https://www.rcaanc-cirnac.gc.ca/eng/1566482924303/1566482963919 (viewed 10 September 2020).

to deliver services. However, as Indigenous fiscal self-government is established, some funding should be redirected through self-government structures of Indigenous communities which would be supported to develop capacity to provide such services.

8 Future Directions

In 2020, the relatively stable process of intergovernmental agreement-making and grant distribution was disrupted by the COVID-19 pandemic. State and Territory governments have been highly visible during the pandemic, as most governmental interventions, both prohibitive and enabling, have been carried out by State governments, applying legislative powers of emergency and disaster. Initially, a reasonably cohesive national response was initiated under the National Cabinet formed to respond to the crisis. Since COAG ceased operations and the new National Federation Reform Council was formed, with it is unclear what shape federal governance will take in future under the Albanese government.[33]

No details have been provided about future collaborative governing arrangements since the abolition of COAG. A failure to develop alternative arrangements would leave a significant vacuum in detailed inter governmental negotiation and cooperation across a range of fields. In the midst of the pandemic, the NSW Review of Federal Financial Relations sought to restart the debate about taxation and allocation of responsibilities between State and federal governments. Albanese government is unlikely to make any dramatic changes before its budget scheduled for October 2022.

The Australian federation under the Constitution of 1901 has delivered, over the last 120 years, a generally stable and fair democracy and economic prosperity shared among most Australians. Nevertheless, today, reform is needed to address fiscal challenges. It is clear that current arrangements do not serve Australians well. The need for reform has been exacerbated by the COVID-19 pandemic, but the significant fiscal challenge of the pandemic and need to restart the economy is likely to be

[33] Prime Minister Albanese has expressed support for federation reform but there is no indication of what shape this might take: see, e.g. https://www.abc.net.au/news/2022-06-18/energy-health-national-cabinet-albanese-premiers/101160606.

the first priority of the Commonwealth government. The fiscal sustainability of state and territory governments, which have core responsibility for delivering core government services of education, health, policing and infrastructure, is the first significant challenge discussed in this chapter. The second challenge is how to achieve a fiscal bargain that will support needed State tax reform to release resources to the economy and improve efficiency and equity overall. Chapter takes inspiration from Germany and argues that a "joint taxation" approach for income tax and GST is suitable for Australia. The second challenge to reform HFE in response to significant disputes between States and Territories; this has been partly addressed by recent reforms including a top-up of revenues. The third challenge to address the lack of any policy or legal framework for Indigenous fiscal self-government in Australia. This chapter recommends the model adopted in Canada for Indigenous fiscal self-government and support.

References

ABS (Australian Bureau of Statistics). 2019a. *Estimates and Projections, Aboriginal and Torres Strait Islander Australians, 2006–2031*, ABS 3238.0 (latest issue released 11/7/2019), https://www.abs.gov.au/ausstats/abs@.nsf/Latestproducts/3238.0Main%20Features402006%20to%202031?opendocument&tabname=Summary&prodno=3238.0&issue=2006%20to%202031&num=&view=.

ABS. 2019b. *Australian Demographic Statistics*, ABS 3101.0, June 2019 (latest issue released 19/12/19), https://www.abs.gov.au/AUSSTATS/abs@.nsf/Lookup/3101.0Main+Features1Jun%202019?OpenDocument.

ANAO (Australian National Audit Office). 2020. *Award of Funding Under the Community Sport Infrastructure Program*, Report No 23 of 2019–20 (15 January), https://www.anao.gov.au/work/performance-audit/award-funding-under-the-community-sport-infrastructure-program.

Appleby, G. 2009. "There Must Be Limits: The Commonwealth Spending Power", 37(1) *Federal Law Review*, 93.

Appleby, G. and McDonald, S. 2011. "The Ramifications of *Pape v Federal Commissioner of Taxation* for the Spending Power and Legislative Powers of the Commonwealth", 37(2) *Monash University Law Review*, 162–143.

Binns, K.J. and Bellis, L.V. 1956. "Uniform Taxation with States Taxing Incomes", *The Economic Record*, 50 63, in Prest and Mathews *, 374.

Bird, R. and Smart, M. 2009. "Assigning State Taxes in a Federal Country: The Case of Australia", in *Melbourne Institute—Australia's Future Tax and Transfer System Policy Conference*, Melbourne, 73, available www.taxreview.treasury.gov.au.

Boadway, R. 1997. 'Tax Assignment in the Canadian Federal System' in Warren, N. (ed.), *Reshaping Fiscal Federalism in Australia* (Australian Tax Research Foundation) 166.

Borrows, J. and Rotman, L.I. 1998. *Aboriginal Legal Issues: Cases, Materials and Commentary* (Butterworths: Toronto).

Boucher, E. and Vermaeten, A. 2000. "Changes to Federal Transfers to Provinces and Territories in 1999", in H. Lazar (ed.), *Toward a New Mission Statement for Canadian Fiscal Federalism* (McGill-Queen's University Press: Montreal, Ottwa), 131.

Brown, H.P. 1952. "Some Aspects of Federal-State Financial Relations", in G. Sawer (ed.), *Federalism* (Cheshire), 49–70.

Brown, A.J. and Bellamy, J. (eds.). 2006. *Federalism and Regionalism in Australia: New Approaches, New Institutions?* (ANU Press: Canberra), available https://press.anu.edu.au/publications/series/anzsog/federalism-and-regionalism-australia.

Bruerton, M. and Hollander, R. 2018. "Introduction", in M.Bruerton, T. Arklay, R. Hollander, and R. Levy (eds.) *A People's Federation* (Sydney: The Federation Press), 1–34.

Butlin, S.J. 1954. "The Problem of Federal Finance", *The Economic Record* 7–18 (May 1954), in W. Prest and R.L. Mathews, *The Development of Australian Fiscal Federalism: Selected Readings* (1980), 461.

Carling, R. 2007. "A State Income Tax for Australia?" Paper 9 for *Atax UNSW Personal Income Tax Reform Symposium*, Sydney.

Cominos, D. and Dwyer, T. 1999. "Constitutional Problems in the Goods and Services Tax", 28 *Australian Tax Review* 69.

Committee for Economic Development of Australia(CEDA). 1975. *Fiscal Federalism.*

(CGC) Commonwealth Grants Commission. 1995. *Equality in Diversity: History of the Commonwealth Grants Commission*, 2nd edition, available at www.cgc.gov.au.

CGC. 2009. *The Last 25 Years*, available at www.cgc.gov.au.

CGC. 2010. *Report on GST Revenue Sharing Relativities: Review Volume 1—Main Report*. Canberra.

Commonwealth of Australia. 2012. *GST Distribution Review Final Report.* http://gstdistributionreview.gov.au/content/Content.aspx?doc=reports.htm.

Commonwealth of Australia. 2018a. *Through Growth to Achievement: Report of the Review to Achieve Educational Excellence in Australian Schools* (March 2018) (Gonski Review), available https://www.dese.gov.au/quality-schools-package/resources/through-growth-achievement-report-review-achieve-educational-excellence-australian-schools.

Commonwealth of Australia. 2018b. *Productivity Commission Inquiry into Horizontal Fiscal Equalisation: Government Interim Response* (July), available https://treasury.gov.au/publication/p2018b-308096.

Commonwealth of Australia. 2019. *Budget 2019–20, Budget Paper No. 3, Federal Financial Relations*, available https://archive.budget.gov.au/.

Commonwealth of Australia. 2020. *Economic and Fiscal Update, Statement by the Treasurer Mr Josh Frydenburg and Assistant Treasurer Mr Mathias Cormann* (July).

Commonwealth of Australia. 2022. *Budget 2022–23*, available at www.budget.gov.au.

Comrie, J. 2014. *Debt Is Not a Dirty Word: Role and Use of Debt in Local Government*, Australian Centre of Excellence for Local Government and Institute of Public Works Engineering Australasia, available https://www.uts.edu.au/sites/default/files/ACELG_Role-Use-of-Debt.pdf.

Copland, D.B. 1924. "Some Problems of Taxation in Australia", *The Economic Journal* (September), 387–397 in W. Prest and R.L. Mathews, *The Development of Australian Fiscal Federalism: Selected Readings* (1980).

Cowper, N. 1932. "The First Financial Agreement: Its Effect Upon the Relations Between the Commonwealth and the States", *The Economic Record*, 173–190.

Davis, M. and Langton, M. (eds.). 2016. *It's Our Country: Indigenous Arguments for Meaningful Constitutional Recognition and Reform* (Melbourne University Press: Melbourne).

Deakin, A. 1902. "The Chariot Wheels of the Central Government", published by La Nauze, J.A. 1952. "The Chariot Wheels of the Central Government", *The Economic Record* (November), 239–244.

Department of Education, Skills and Employment, Commonwealth of Australia. 2018. *What Is the National School Reform Agreement? Fact Sheet*, available https://docs.education.gov.au/system/files/doc/other/what_is_the_national_school_reform_agreement_5.pdf.

(DFAT) Department of Foreign Affairs and Trade, Commonwealth of Australia. 2020. *Foreign Investment Statistics*, https://dfat.gov.au/trade/resources/investment-statistics/Pages/statistics-on-who-invests-in-australia.aspx (viewed 7 February 2020).

Department of Infrastructure and Regional Development, Commonwealth of Australia. 2017. *Local Government National Report 2014–15* (Canberra).

Department of Prime Minister and Cabinet (DPMC), Commonwealth of Australia. 2014. *White Paper for Federation Issues Paper 1.*

Department of Prime Minister and Cabinet (DPMC), Commonwealth of Australia. 2015. *White Paper for Federation Issues Paper 5*, COAG and Federal Financial Relations.

Department of the Treasury, Commonwealth of Australia. 2009. *Review of Australia's Future Tax System: Final Report*, www.taxreview.treasury.gov.au.

Department of the Treasury, Commonwealth of Australia. 2014. *Re:Think Tax Reform Discussion Paper*.

De Souza, S.V., Dollery, B. and Kort, M. 2017. "A Critical Evaluation of Australia's Mineral Resources Rent Tax", 40 *International Journqal of Public Administration* 6, 472–480.

Dick, R.A. 1998. "A Loss of State Autonomy: Implications of the *Ha* and *Hammond* Decisions" 27 *Australian Tax Review* 30.

Dollery, B. 2009. "Themes in Contemporary Australian Local Government" 68 *Australian Journal of Public Administration* 2, 137–138.

Eccleston, R. and Hortle, R. 2016. "The Australian Mining Tax Debate: Political Legacies and Comparative Perspectives", 51 *Australian Journal of Political Science* 1, 102–109.

Ernst & Young. 2013. *National Financing Authority for Local Government: Options Assessment*, Report for Department of Regional Australia, Local Government, Arts & Sport. Available, https://www.regional.gov.au/local/lgifr/files/national-financing-authority-for-local-government-options-assessment-20130416.pdf.

Eccleston, R. 2005. *The 30 Year Problem* (Australian Tax Research Foundation: Sydney).

Eccelston, R. and Krever, R. 2017. "The Future of the Australian Federation: Intergovernmental Financial Relations Amid Growing Fiscal Pressures", in R. Eccelston and R. Krever (eds.) *The Future of Federalism: Intergovernmental Financial Relations in an Age of Austerity* (Edward Elgar: Cheltenham).

Eccleston, R. and Warren, N. 2015. "The Devil Is in the Detail: The Distributional Consequences of Personal Income Tax Sharing in the Australian Federation", 30 *Australian Tax Forum* 713.

Fenna, A. 2017. "The Fiscal Predicament of Australian Federalism", in M.Bruerton, T.Arklay, R. Hollander, and R. Levy (eds.) *A People's Federation* (Sydney: The Federation Press) 134.

Freebairn, J., Stewart, M. and Lei, P. 2015. *Reform of State Taxes in Australia: Rationale and Options*, Report: Melbourne School of Government, University of Melbourne.

Fuest, C. and Thöne, M. 2008 *Reform des Finanzföderalismus in Deutschland* (Stiftung Marktwirtschaft).

Galligan, B. 1995. *A Federal Republic: Australia's Constitutional System of Government* (Cambridge University Press: Cambridge).

Government of Canada. 2015. *Canada's Fiscal Approach for Self-Government Arrangements* (Treaties and Aboriginal Government, Aboriginal Affairs and Northern Development, Canada), available https://publications.gc.ca/site/eng/9.839481/publication.html.

Government of New South Wales (NSW). 2019. *NSW Review of Federal Financial Relations: Working Together for a Better Future*, Stakeholder Discussion Paper (October), https://www.treasury.nsw.gov.au/federal-financial-relations-review.

Government of New South Wales. 2020. *NSW Review of Federal Financial Relations: Final Report.* https://www.treasury.nsw.gov.au/federal-financial-relations-review.

Grattan, M. 2020. "Sports Grants Rort and a Cabinet Reshuffle Deliver a Wild Start to Parliamentary Year", ABC News, *The Conversation*, 7 February 2020.

Hanks, P. and Cass, D. 1999. *Australian Constitutional Law: Cases and Materials* (6th edn., Butterworths: Sydney).

Hinz, B. 2017. "Policy Coherence Across the Education Continuum in Australia: Understanding and Improving Service Delivery", in M. Bruerton, T. Arklay, R. Hollander, R. Levy (eds.), *A People's Federation* (The Federation Press: Sydney).

House of Representatives Standing Committee on Economics, Finance and Public Administration. 2003. *Rates and Taxes: A Fair Share for Responsible Local Government* (Hawker Report), Parliament of Australia.

Hunter, J.S.H. 1977. *Federalism and Fiscal Balance: A comparative Study.*

Jochimsen, B. 2013. "Fiscal Federalism in Germany: Problems, Proposals and Chances for Fundamental Reforms", in C. Rowe and W. Jacoby (eds.), *German Federalism in Transition: Reforms in a Consensual State* (Routledge), 84.

Jotzo, F. 2020. "The Bushfire Crisis Has Given the Government a Political 'Out' to Its Climate Change Problem", ABC News (6 January 2020), https://www.abc.net.au/news/2020-01-06/bushfires-climate-change-opportunity-to-change/11839530.

Kim, J. 2015. "The Role of Intergovernmental Fiscal Institutions: The Case of Revenue Sharing", in Junghun Kim and Hansjorg Blochliger (eds.), *Institutions of Intergovernmental Fiscal Relations: Challenges Ahead* (OECD Publishing), 11.

Koutsogeorgopoulou, V. 2007. "Fiscal Relations Across Levels of Government in Australia", OECD, *Economics Department Working Paper 541.*

Laffer, K.M. 1942. "Taxation Reform in Australia", *The Economic Record*, 168–179 in R. Prest and R. Mathews (eds.) 1980. *The Development of Australian Fiscal Federalism: Selected Readings* (ANU Press: Canberra), 297.

Langton, M., Tehan, M., Palmer, L. and Shain, K. (eds.). 2003. *Honour Among Nations? Treaties and Agreements with Indigenous Peoples* (Melbourne University Press: Melbourne).

Langton, M., Mazel, O., Palmer, L., Shain, K. and Tehan, M. (eds.). 2006. *Settling with Indigenous People: Modern Treaty and Agreement Making* (The Federation Press: Sydney).

Langton, M. and Longbottom, J. (eds.). 2012. *Community Futures, Legal Architecture: Foundations for Indigenous Peoples in the Global Mining Boom* (Routledge).

Mathews, R. 1965 "Business Taxes in relation to problems of Australian State Finance", *Economic Papers* No. 20, 1–18 in Prest, R. and Mathews, R. (eds.) 1980. *The development of Australian fiscal federalism: Selected readings* (ANU Press: Canberra) 401.

Mathews, R. (ed.). 1980. *Federalism in Australia and the Federal Republic of Germany* (ANU Press: Canberra).

Menzies, R. 1961 "The Challenge to Federalism", 3 *Melbourne University Law Review* 1.

Mills, R.C. (Chair), Scullin, J.H. and Spooner, E.S. 1942. *Report of the Committee on Uniform Taxation* (Commonwealth Government Printer: Canberra).

Morabito, V. 1997. "Commonwealth Taxes, State Governments and the Doctrine of Intergovernmental Immunity", 26 *Australian Tax Review* 182.

Murray, I. 2015. "The Minerals Rent Resource Tax is Dead, Long Live Resource Rent Taxes", 40 *University of Western Australia Law Review* 111.

Pratt, A. and Bennett, S. 2005. "The End of ATSIC and the Future Administration of Indigenous Affairs" (Current Issues Brief No. 4, Parliamentary Library, 2004–05), www.aph.gov.au/About_Parliament/Parliamentary_Departments/Parliamentary_Library/Publications_Archive/CIB/Current_Issues_Briefs_2004_-_2005/05cib04.

Prest, R. and Mathews, R. (eds.) 1980. *The Development of Australian Fiscal Federalism: Selected Readings* (ANU Press: Canberra).

Prince, M.J. and Abele, F. 2003. "Paying for Self-Determination: Aboriginal Peoples, Self-Government, and Fiscal Relations in Canada" (Paper presented at Reconfiguring Aboriginal-State Relations, Canada: The State of the Federation, School of Policy Studies, Queen's University).

Productivity Commission. 2018. *Horizontal Fiscal Equalisation*. Report No. 88 (Commonwealth of Australia: Canberra).

Productivity Commission. 2017. *Indigenous Expenditure Report* (Commonwealth of Australia: Canberra).

Reinhardt, S. and Steel, L. 2006. *A Brief History of Australia's Tax System*, available https://treasury.gov.au/publication/economic-roundup-winter-2006/a-brief-history-of-australias-tax-system.

Rubin, E. 2006. "The Myth of Non-bureaucratic Accountability and the Anti-administrative Principle", in M. Dowdle (ed.), *Public Accountability: Designs, Dilemmas and Experiences* (Cambridge University Press: Cambridge), 83–114.

Rydon, J. and Wolfsohn, H.A. 1980. "Federalism in West Germany: The Functions and Relations of the Different Levels of Government, Advisory Council for Inter-governmental Relations", Information Paper No 8 (Australian Government Publishing Service: Canberra).

Saunders, C. 2009. "The Sources and Scope of Commonwealth Power to Spend", 20 *Public Law Review* 260.

Saunders, C. 2000. "Federal Fiscal Reform and the GST", 11 *Public Law Review* 99.

Saunders, C. 1997 "The High Court, Section 90 and the Australian Federation", in N. Warren (ed.), *Reshaping Fiscal Federalism in Australia*, 21.

Saunders, C. 1989. "Government Borrowing in Australia", 17 *Melbourne University Law Review* 187.

Select Committee on the Reform of the Australian Federation. 2011. *Australia's Federation: An Agenda for Reform*, Report (Australian Senate).

Smith, J. 2004. *Taxing Popularity* (Australian Tax Research Foundation: Sydney).

Smith, J. 1992. *Fiscal Federalism in Australia: A Twentieth Century Chronology*.

Stewart, M. 2011. "Australia", in G. Bizioli and C. Sacchetto (eds.), *Tax Aspects of Fiscal Federalism: A Comparative Analysis* (Kluwer Law: Netherlands), 137–180.

Stewart, M. 2017. "Two Ideas for Renewal of Australia's Fiscal Federal Democracy", in M.Bruerton, T.Arklay, R. Hollander, and R. Levy (eds.), *A People's Federation* (Sydney: The Federation Press), 164–182.

Stone, P. and Waters, S. 1992. "Immunity from Taxation Under Section 114 of the Constitution", 66 *Australian Law Journal* 601.

Twomey, A. 2008. "Regionalism—A Cure for Federal Ills?", 31 *UNSW Law Journal* 467.

Warren, N. 2006. "Benchmarking Australia's Intergovernmental Fiscal Arrangements: Final Report", NSW Government, www.treasury.nsw.gov.au.

Webb, R. 2003. "Public Finance and Vertical Fiscal Imbalance", Research Note No 13 2002–3, Parliamentary Library of Australia, available http://www.aph.gov.au/library/pubs/rn/2002-03/03rn13.htm.

Williams, J. 1999. "'Come in Spinner': Section 90 of the Constitution and the Future of State Government Finances", 21 *Sydney Law Review* 627.

World Bank. 2019. *Gross Domestic Product 2019*, https://databank.worldbank.org/data/download/GDP.pdf (viewed 18 August 2020).

Brazil

Fernando Rezende, Alexandre Cialdini, and Bernardo Motta

1 Introduction

The Federal Republic of Brazil has eight and a half million square kilometers—about half the total area of South America. Its population of 211 million inhabitants is unequally dispersed among twenty-six states a federal district and five thousand five hundred and seventy municipalities.

Respectively, Economist, Senior Researcher and Advisor on Public Finance, Federalism and Fiscal Policy; Fiscal Auditor Assistant of the Ceará State Finance Secretary; Economist and private consultant.

F. Rezende (✉)
Brazilian School of Public and Private Administration, Getulio Vargas Fondation, Rio de Janeiro, Brazil
e-mail: herrzende@gmail.com

A. Cialdini
Ceará State Finance Secretary, Eusébio, Brazil

B. Motta
Lisbon, Portugal

J.-F. Tremblay (ed.), *The Forum of Federations Handbook of Fiscal Federalism*, https://doi.org/10.1007/978-3-030-97258-5_2

Brazil follows the global trend, with an average population life expectancy of 79 years projected for 2030 (United Nations, 2015). This increase in life expectancy at birth is caused jointly by a reduction in infant mortality and by greater survival at older ages. The year 2018, in Brazil, was considered the year of the end of the demographic bonus, in the sense that the population from 15 to 64 years of age in total started to fall after reaching 69.5% a year before. According to a recent work published by the UN,[1] the group aged 60 or over, which represented only 4.9% of the total population in 1950, increased its participation to 11.9% in 2015. The expected trend is that it continues to grow almost continuously until the end of this century, reaching 34.1% and 39.4%, respectively, in the years 2060 and 2100.

It is worth noting that Brazil has already undergone rapid urbanization during the second half of the last century when the share of the urban population went from 36% in 1950 to 87% today. The UN projects that in 2050, 92.4% of the Brazilian population will live in cities. In comparison with the rest of the continent, urbanization in Brazil was faster than in Latin America, since 1992.[2]

Most of the population is in the seven Southern states, where the demographic density reaches 79 inhabitants per square kilometer. Although the Center-West and the Amazon regions represent more than 60% of the territory, they account for only 16% of the population. Population density is also high in the nine poor coastline Northeast states where nearly 27% of the inhabitants reside in a 1.5 million square meters perimeter.

Concentration is even greater at the local level Over half of the Brazilian population (57.4% or 120.7 million inhabitants) is concentrated in only 5.8% of the municipalities (324 municipalities), which are those with more than 100 thousand inhabitants. The 48 municipalities with more than 500 thousand inhabitants concentrate almost 1/3 of the population (31.7%, or 66.5 million people). On the other hand, in most municipalities (68.2%, or 3,670 municipalities), with up to 20 thousand people, only 15.2% of the country's population live (32.0 million people). Of the 17 municipalities with a population of more than one million inhabitants, 14 are state capitals. These municipalities concentrate 21.9%

[1] See United Nations (2019).

[2] See United Nations (2018).

of the country's population. The municipality of São Paulo remains the most populous in the country, with 12.25 million inhabitants, followed by Rio de Janeiro (6.72 million), Brasília (3.0 million) and Salvador (2.9 million).

Africans brought in during the slavery era and a large inflow of migrants from every corner of the world, especially in the late nineteen and early twenty centuries, contributed to the multiple faces that characterize the Brazilian population nowadays. Despite that, intermarriage and cultural assimilation produced a quite homogeneous society. The Portuguese official language is spoken by everybody everywhere and cultural values do not differ to a significant extent.

The demographic concentration mirrors the concentration of economic activity. The same seven Southern states account jointly for 70% of the Gross Domestic Product,[3] which reached about 1.9 trillion US dollars in 2018 (3.4 trillion in purchase power parity), placing Brazil among the leading group of world countries in terms of economic size. A modern agribusiness and a growing service economy contribute to a well-balanced composition of the domestic output. Recent data (2019) point to an economic structure more akin to those of industrialized countries with the dominance of services (about 63% of the GDP) and a sizable manufacturing sector (about 18% of the GDP). A still important agriculture sector (4% of the GDP) reflects the recent expansion of highly productive farms that emerged out of the incorporation of modern technologies in rural areas.

From a regional standpoint, economic size does not translate directly into political influence on national policies, due to a bias in regional representation in the National Parliament in favor of the less developed North, Northeast and Center-West regions. As these regions have a higher number of sparsely populated states that are entitled to a minimum of eight representatives in the Lower House, while Southern highly populated states are subjected to a maximum of seventy, they exert strong influence on decision-making related to fiscal and intergovernmental relations issues.[4] The political imbalance in the states' representation in the Lower House is reinforced by an equal representation in the Federal Senate (three per state). Even though this is a common federal feature,

[3] The last data available is for 2017. See IBGE (2019a).

[4] On imbalances in political representation see Serra and Afonso (1999).

the extended role of the Senate in the Brazilian federation—every legislation, not only those directly related to federal issues, must pass through both legislative houses before being sanctioned by the President—creates additional difficulties.[5]

Imbalances in political representation are the result of the dominance of the regional issue in the formation and consolidation of the Brazilian federation. The federal regime put into place by the first republican 1891 Constitution empowered the states with a substantial degree of autonomy and sowed the seeds for local government's autonomy. Since then, subnational autonomy and regional balance became intertwined issues and have been emphasized as essential values to keep internal cohesion in a very economic and socially unequal society.[6]

Inequality is, therefore, one of the main features of the country. Part of the South and the Southeast—particularly the state of São Paulo—present indicators of economic development akin to those of the modern industrialized countries: a high level of per capita income, a high degree of urbanization, and diversification in industrial production.

At the same time, large portions of the country—especially in the North and Northeast—still shows the classical signs of underdevelopment: low per capita income, poor sanitary conditions, and widespread poverty. It is worth noting, however, that poverty is not associated only to regional imbalances in economic development, for the developed regions amasses a large number of people that live below the poverty line.

Regional economic disparities are also great among municipalities. According to a hierarchy of municipalities constructed by the National Bureau of Geography and Statistics, in general, the higher the hierarchy, the higher the GDP per capita. Metropolises, in 2017, had GDP per capita 2.15 times higher than local centers and, as well as regional capitals (R$34,190.09), metropolises (R$42,170.42) had a GDP per capita higher than the national (R$31,702.25). The other classes of the urban hierarchy had GDP per capita below the national average (Fig. 1).

Apart from intermittent periods of authoritarian rule, democracy evolved over time and achieved high standards after the middle eighties. A multi-party system allows for a fairly diversified composition with

[5] This particular aspect led Alfred Stepan to consider Brazil an extreme case of a demo constrained federation. See Stepan (1997).

[6] On the importance of the regional issue see Souza (2005).

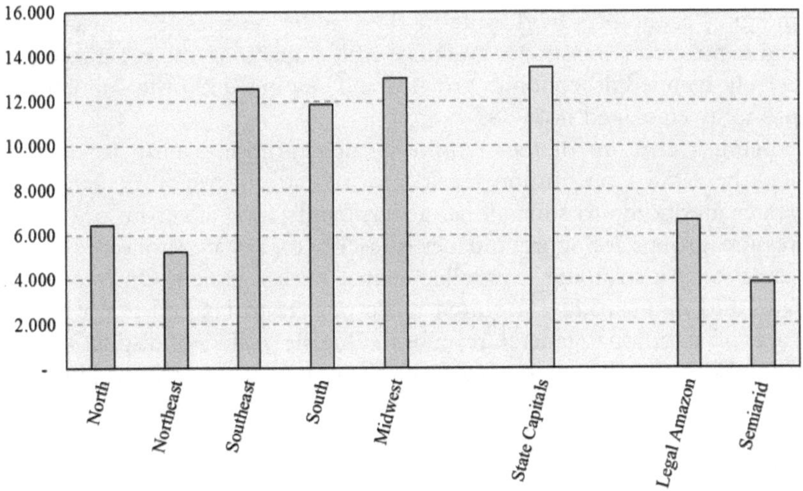

Fig. 1 GDP per capita, by selected regions—US$ (2017) (*Note* 2017 average exchange rate: 1 US$ = R$3,19. *Source* Adapted from IBGE [2019b])

respect to the distribution of political power in the federation. Despite this, governability is achieved by means of coalitions that contribute to increasing the weight of small political parties in national politics, beyond their real size. The practice of forming coalitions contributed to the stability of Brazilian democracy, that passed two important tests: the impeachment of two presidents in the past three decades. One in 1989 and the other in 2016, following the rules established in the Constitution. Over time, however, as this process of partisan fragmentation kept growing it also raised problems for governance, since it demands complex negotiations to reach a national agreement on matters of national interest and takes time to be approved, especially in moments where agility is required, as in times of crisis.[7]

A stable democratic regime and sound institutional arrangements contributed to help the Brazilian economy muddle through the turbulences generated by a sequence of external financial crisis that hit

[7] With 35 parties, registered with the Superior Electoral Court, Brazil is the country with the largest number of parties in the world according to The Quality of Government Institute, University of Gothenburg. https://bit.ly/3e4yyMi.

emerging economies worldwide in the middle nineties. Yet, macroeconomic policies adopted to attenuate the impact of these turbulences severely hampered economic growth, and impinged on the subnational autonomy envisaged in 1988.[8]

Being a creature of the transition from authoritarianism to democracy, the 1988 Constitution reacted to two strong forces: demands for greater autonomy to subnational governments and calls from organized pressure groups for more and better access to a State-sponsored social protection. In so doing it installed a dual fiscal regimen. On one hand, states and municipalities acquired more powers to tax and got a higher share of traditional federal revenues. On the other, a distinct set of compulsory levies—the so-called social contributions—was assigned to the federal government to finance pensions and free access to health and social services to every Brazilian citizen regardless of previous contribution to a social security system. As the extended social rights had to rely on the federal ability to raise enough money to meet a steep rise in social spending, besides generating large surpluses in the public accounts to keep inflation at bay, recourse to social contributions fed a process that reversed the fiscal decentralization intended by the 1988 Constitution, despite pressures faced by states and municipalities to increase social spending, without room to improve their tax revenues.

Over time, equality, autonomy, efficiency and growth objectives collided. Increasing reliance on federal collected social contributions eroded subnational autonomy and aborted the intention to promote efficiency and accountability in public policies through decentralization, as earmarked grants from the federal government, supported by revenues from such contributions, became necessary to finance the provision of social services at the subnational level. At the same time, vertical and horizontal imbalances increased in so far as the basis of equalization funds lost importance over time. In addition, the economic inefficient social contributions created further obstacles to economic growth. Therefore, as we will argue in the concluding section of this chapter, an overhaul of the Brazilian fiscal federalism system is in desperate need.

[8] For details see section on Fiscal Federalism and macroeconomic management.

2 The Structure of Government and the Assignment of Resources and Responsibilities

Brazil is a three-tier federation. According to the 1988 Constitution, states and municipalities are independent units of the Brazilian Federation. Both have explicitly tax powers and share with the federal government responsibilities concerning the role of the State in services provision and development policies. A growing direct relationship between the federal and local governments, mostly on social policies, is a source of intergovernmental conflicts and of increasing complexity in fiscal relation.

Through various legislations that impose unfunded mandates, the federal government added more financial problems that are a source of intergovernmental conflicts. There are many examples of legislation recently passed in the Brazilian Congress with those characteristics, including the national floor for the remuneration of teachers, and the obligations arising from the new legislation for the collection and treatment of waste, as well as obliging states and local governments to include payments to community health workers as personnel expenses to enforce the limit set in the Fiscal Responsibility Law for such expenses..

The formal assignment of expenditure responsibilities follows the subsidiary principle. Thus, the Constitution assigns the provision of basic urban and social services (urban roads, water supply and sewage, public transportation, street lightning, primary education and basic health and social assistance services) primarily to local governments, who shall count on technical and financial assistance from the federal and states governments to carry out these responsibilities on a proper basis. Following the usual pattern, the federal government is solely responsible for the armed forces, foreign relations, international trade and money control.[9]

For public service like education, health, social assistance and public safety, the Constitution envisages concurrent responsibilities. Due to this lack of clarity, in practice it is possible to see a trend toward the decentralization of public expenditures in education, health and public safety, the first two with more protagonism from local government and the latter mostly at the state level. Social assistance, however, is largely carried out

[9] For a detailed account of the division of responsibilities in the Brazilian federation see Piancastelli (2006).

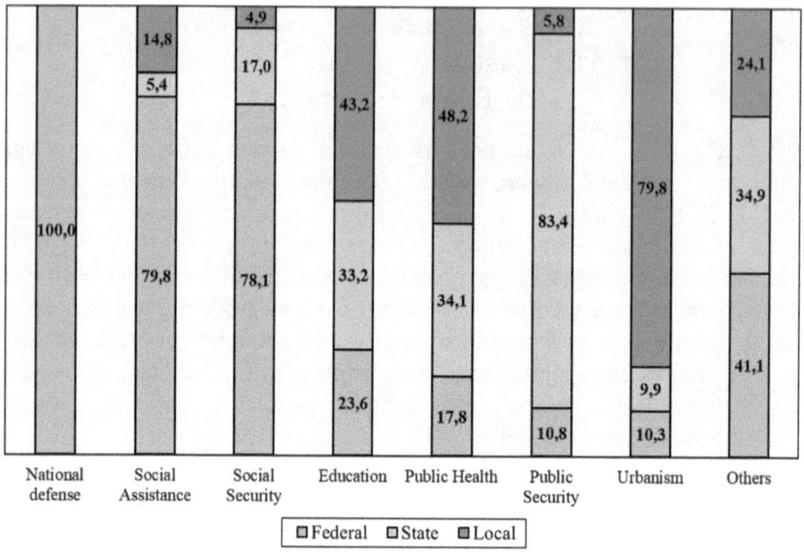

Fig. 2 Non-financial expenses, by function and level of government—% (2017) (*Source* Own elaboration. *Primary source* FINBRA/STN and SIGA BRASIL)

by the federal government through income transfers to poor families the elderly and disabled citizens (Fig. 2).

Sanitation is a case in point, since it has been decentralized to the Municipalities, where most of them do not have the resources to attend to the needs of their inhabitants, especially in poor neighborhoods of the big cities. Data from the National Sanitation Information System (SNIS)[10] show that 35 million of Brazilians do not have access to treated water and about 100 million do not have a sewage collection service.[11]

On the tax side, the federal government is solely responsible for applying taxes on income—corporate and personal—foreign trade, and rural property, as well as on payroll. The federal government can also make use of contributions intended to intervene in the economic domain

[10] https://bit.ly/3hzkAo2.

[11] In the Federal Senate of Brazil, a Bill, which defines the new regulatory framework for basic sanitation (PL 4,162/2019), a project already analyzed by the Chamber, is now going to the virtual Plenary for remote voting by senators. https://bit.ly/2zrkCwO.

and of any other potential tax source not explicitly attributed to the state or local governments by the constitution (residual powers).

But, the most important measure adopted by the federal government to occupy the tax basis originally reserved to states and municipalities was carried out through increases in revenues from contributions earmarked to social expenses (PIS/COFINS) by increasing the rates levied on the import and sale of gasoline, diesel oil, liquefied petroleum gas (LPG), aviation kerosene and alcohol, as well as on the provision of services. One important reason for that was the need to divert part of these revenues to meet the targets set for the primary results of the fiscal accounts.

In fact, there are two reasons why the Union has been making increasing use of contributions: (1) due to its non-submission to the revenue sharing system; and (2) due to the DRU[12] system, which makes it possible to distort the final character of the contribution.

Federal and state governments concur in the field of taxes applied on goods and services through a variety of regimes. The former is entitled to a tax on manufacturing goods and to the social contributions earmarked to finance pensions, health and social assistance. The latter is empowered to a kind of VAT, which, however, does not cover services, transportation and telecommunications excepted. General services are taxed by the local governments, who are also entitled to tax ownership and sales of urban property and apply user charges. An inheritance property tax and a motor vehicle tax are also under the states' jurisdiction (Figs. 3 and 4).

Despite of the constitutional separation of tax powers, subnational governments do not dispose of total autonomy to apply their most important taxes. A complementary law to the Constitution set the basic rules to be followed by states and municipalities with regard to the state value-added tax—the ICMS—and the municipal services tax—the ISS. These laws narrow the scope of state and local governments' legislators with regard to the definition of the tax basis but do not interfere with rates. Rates of the states' VAT are only constrained by a constitutional provision that prohibits internal transactions to be taxed at a rate lower than the smaller one applied to interstate sales.

[12] The Federal Revenue Untying (DRU) comprises a set of provisions that have been implemented by successive constitutional amendments, the objective of which is to increase budgetary flexibility, by canceling the effect of the linkages established by the Federal Government and, later, copied by subnational governments.

	Determination of		Tax collection and administration	Shares in Revenue (%)				
	Base	Rate		F	S	L	R 1/	All orders
Federal								
TAXES								
Income Tax – IR	F	F	F	49.0%	21.5%	24.5%	3.0%	100.0%
Tax on Manufactured Goods – IPI	F	F	F	49.0%	29.0%	25.0%	3.0%	100.0%
Other taxes	F	F	F	100.0%				100.0%
FEES	F	F	F	100.0 percent				100.0 percent
CONTRIBUTIONS								
On sales of goods and services	F	F	F	100.0%				100.0%
On payroll earmarked to primary education	F	F	F	Shared under special legislation 2/				
State or Provincial								
TAXES								
Motor Vehicle Property Tax – IPVA	S	S	S		50.0%	50.0%		100.0%
Tax on Circulation of Goods and Services – ICMS	F, S	F, S	S		75.0%	25.0%		100.0%
FEES	S	S	S		100.0 percent			100.0%
CONTRIBUTIONS	S	S	S		100.0%			100.0%
Local								
TAXES								
Urban Land and Territorial Tax – IPTU	L	L	L			100.0%		100.0%
Tax on Services – ISS	F	F, L	L			100.0%		100.0%
FEES	L	L	L			100.0%		100.0%
CONTRIBUTIONS	L	L	L			100.0%		100.0%

Fig. 3 Tax assignment for various orders of government (F = Federal; S = State; L = Local; R = Regional. *Primary sources* Federal Constitution and Federal Revenue Service. 1/ amount chanelled into a regional development fund. 2/ Two thirds go to the states on a derivation basis. States and municipalities can have access to the other third on a project basis)

	US$ billions – 2019 /1	percent of GDP
FEDERAL		
Direct Collection	**419,9**	**22,9**
TAXES	**143,4**	**7,8**
Income Tax - IR	107,7	5,9
Tax on Manufactured Goods– IPI	14,1	0,8
Others	21,6	1,2
FEES	**2,2**	**0,1**
CONTRIBUTIONS	**267,7**	14,6
Social Security	97,4	5,3
Others	170,3	9,3
Fines and Active Debt	6,5	0,4
AVAILABLE REVENUE (Total minus Constitutional Transfers)	**349,7**	**19,0**
STATE OR PROVINCIAL		
Direct Collection	**177,3**	**9,7**
TAXES	**160,3**	**8,7**
Tax on Circulation of Goods and Services – ICMS	133,8	7,3
Others	26,5	1,4
FEES	**6,9**	**0,4**
CONTRIBUTIONS	**10,0**	**0,5**
Other (fines, interest and debt)	0,0	0,0
Constitutional Transfers from Federal	**34,5**	**1,9**
States and Federal District Participation Fund – FPE	19,7	1,1
Fund for Education - FUNDEB	5,2	0,3
Others	9,6	0,5
AVAILABLE REVENUE (Total minus Constitutional Transfers to Local)	**162,5**	**8,9**
LOCAL		
Direct Collection	**48,7**	**2,7**
TAXES	**39,3**	**2,1**
Tax on Services – ISS	18,1	1,0
Urban Property Tax – IPTU	12,9	0,7
Others	8,3	0,5
FEES	**3,0**	**0,2**
CONTRIBUTIONS	**6,5**	**0,4**
Other (fines, interest and debt)	0,0	0,0
Constitutional Transfers from Federal	**35,7**	**1,9**
Municipalities Participation Fund – FPM	22,9	1,2
Fund for Education - FUNDEB	9,2	0,5
Others	3,6	0,2
Constitutional Transfers from States	**49,3**	**2,7**
Tax on Circulation of Goods and Services – ICMS	26,7	1,5
Fund for Education - FUNDEB	16,1	0,9
Others	6,5	0,4
Total local revenues	**133,7**	**7,3**
TOTAL	**645,9**	**35,2**
GDP	**1.835,8**	**-**

Fig. 4 Government revenues by level—2019 (*Source* Adapted from Afonso e Castro [2019] with update observations by the authors. 1/ 2019 average exchange rate: 1 US$ = R$3,95)

Restrictions imposed on the subnational governments' ability to implement their most important taxes do not mean that the tax system is harmonized. Residual legislative powers of the states' governments allow for great differences with regard to rates applied to each category of goods, ways to reduce the effective tax burden (reduction in the tax base, for instance), special regimes for small businesses, criteria adopted for the utilization of tax credits paid on inputs used to produce exempted exported goods, and preferred tax rates for food and other essential consumption items.

Another source of differences in tax burden imposed on the same goods across the federation arose out of demands from less developed states to apply a reduced rate on goods shipped from the more industrialized South and Southeast states to North, Northeast and Center-West regions to allow consumer states to reap part of the revenues from interstate sales. As a result, a 7% rate applies to shipments from South/SE to North/NE/Center-West regions, whereas a 12% rate applies to interstates sales flowing in the opposite direction. The same 12% rate applies to inter-regional transactions. This mixed origin-destination principle caused distortions in resource allocation and provided a strong incentive to tax evasion. It also led to the main weapon used in the so-called fiscal war in which Brazilian states have been engaged to attract investments and the location of new industries to their jurisdictions.[13]

Brazilian legislation on ICMS taxation has increased the degree of autonomy and heterogeneity of subnational governments. The circulation of goods and interstate and intercity transport and communication services means that the ICMS is levied at a rate set by each state, as shown in Fig. 5.

Although it seems complex, understanding this ICMS table is simpler when we look at it by following only three steps:

Step 1: see the location of the State of Origin in the vertical column.
Step 2: find the destination (destino) state, on the horizontal line.
Step 3: at the intersection of the two lines (State of origin x State of destination) you will obtain the rate applied in the operation. In the transversal line (colored highlight) it is possible to see the rate applied internally within each State. It is important to remember

[13] See Varsano (1999).

	DESTINO																											
ORIGEM	AC	AL	AM	AP	BA	CE	DF	ES	GO	MA	MT	MS	MG	PA	PB	PR	PE	PI	RN	RS	RJ	RO	RR	SC	SP	SE	TO	EX
AC	17	12	12	12	12	12	12	12	12	12	12	12	12	12	12	12	12	12	12	12	12	12	12	12	12	12	12	4
AL	12	18	12	12	12	12	12	12	12	12	12	12	12	12	12	12	12	12	12	12	12	12	12	12	12	12	12	4
AM	12	12	18	12	12	12	12	12	12	12	12	12	12	12	12	12	12	12	12	12	12	12	12	12	12	12	12	4
AP	12	12	12	18	12	12	12	12	12	12	12	12	12	12	12	12	12	12	12	12	12	12	12	12	12	12	12	4
BA	12	12	12	12	18	12	12	12	12	12	12	12	12	12	12	12	12	12	12	12	12	12	12	12	12	12	12	4
CE	12	12	12	12	12	18	12	12	12	12	12	12	12	12	12	12	12	12	12	12	12	12	12	12	12	12	12	4
DF	12	12	12	12	12	12	18	12	12	12	12	12	12	12	12	12	12	12	12	12	12	12	12	12	12	12	12	4
ES	12	12	12	12	12	12	12	17	12	12	12	12	12	12	12	12	12	12	12	12	12	12	12	12	12	12	12	4
GO	12	12	12	12	12	12	12	12	17	12	12	12	12	12	12	12	12	12	12	12	12	12	12	12	12	12	12	4
MA	12	12	12	12	12	12	12	12	12	18	12	12	12	12	12	12	12	12	12	12	12	12	12	12	12	12	12	4
MT	12	12	12	12	12	12	12	12	12	12	17	12	12	12	12	12	12	12	12	12	12	12	12	12	12	12	12	4
MS	12	12	12	12	12	12	12	12	12	12	12	17	12	12	12	12	12	12	12	12	12	12	12	12	12	12	12	4
MG	7	7	7	7	7	7	7	7	7	7	7	7	18	7	7	12	7	7	7	12	12	7	7	12	12	7	7	4
PA	12	12	12	12	12	12	12	12	12	12	12	12	12	17	12	12	12	12	12	12	12	12	12	12	12	12	12	4
PB	12	12	12	12	12	12	12	12	12	12	12	12	12	12	18	12	12	12	12	12	12	12	12	12	12	12	12	4
PR	7	7	7	7	7	7	7	7	7	7	7	7	12	7	7	18	7	7	7	12	12	7	7	12	12	7	7	4
PE	12	12	12	12	12	12	12	12	12	12	12	12	12	12	12	12	18	12	12	12	12	12	12	12	12	12	12	4
PI	12	12	12	12	12	12	12	12	12	12	12	12	12	12	12	12	12	18	12	12	12	12	12	12	12	12	12	4
RN	12	12	12	12	12	12	12	12	12	12	12	12	12	12	12	12	12	12	18	12	12	12	12	12	12	12	12	4
RS	7	7	7	7	7	7	7	7	7	7	7	7	12	7	7	12	7	7	7	18	12	7	7	12	12	7	7	4
RJ	7	7	7	7	7	7	7	7	7	7	7	7	12	7	7	12	7	7	7	12	20	7	7	12	12	7	7	4
RO	12	12	12	12	12	12	12	12	12	12	12	12	12	12	12	12	12	12	12	12	12	17.5	12	12	12	12	12	4
RR	12	12	12	12	12	12	12	12	12	12	12	12	12	12	12	12	12	12	12	12	12	12	17	12	12	12	12	4
SC	7	7	7	7	7	7	7	7	7	7	7	7	12	7	7	12	7	7	7	12	12	7	7	17	12	7	7	4
SP	7	7	7	7	7	7	7	7	7	7	7	7	12	7	7	12	7	7	7	12	12	7	7	12	18	7	7	4
SE	12	12	12	12	12	12	12	12	12	12	12	12	12	12	12	12	12	12	12	12	12	12	12	12	12	18	12	4
TO	12	12	12	12	12	12	12	12	12	12	12	12	12	12	12	12	12	12	12	12	12	12	12	12	12	12	18	4
EX	4	4	4	4	4	4	4	4	4	4	4	4	4	4	4	4	4	4	4	4	4	4	4	4	4	4	4	

Fig. 5 Inter-federative diagram of ICMS rates (*Source* Conselho Nacional de Política Fazendária [CONFAZ] Constitutional Amendment 87/2015 and Federal Senate Resolution No. 13, OF 2012. https://bit.ly/2XVNPJU)

that this is the general rate, but it can be different depending on the product or service. In addition, it should be noted that the application of the interstate ICMS rate for imported products is 4% (according to Federal Resolution N° 13/2012).

With respect to the municipal tax on services, a constitutional amendment[14] exempted exports from this tax and allowed for the imposition of a ceiling and a floor on rates by a complementary law to avoid great variation and curb harmful competition in metropolitan areas. Even though, other less visible means to give fiscal benefits, such as reduction in tax base and better terms for payment may compensate for that.

Fiscal competition among the Brazilian states gained new impetus in the mid-nineties following a wave of foreign direct investments in the

[14] Constitutional amendment 37/2002. A top rate of 5% was imposed afterwards.

Brazilian automotive sector so as to avoid them being located within the old area polarized by the Sao Paulo metropolitan region. Due to the mixed origin-destination principle applied to the state VAT, neighboring states could shift the burden of the fiscal incentives offered to foreign investors to the state of Sao Paulo itself which houses the most important consumer market. In what came to be known as a fiscal war, Southern states (Parana, Rio de Janeiro and Rio Grande do Sul, mainly), succeeded in luring investors to locate new plants in their territories adding additional benefits, such as the provision of infrastructure and training programs for the labor force, to the more usual tax concessions.. Despite studies that pointed out the irrationality of the fiscal war to attract investments, politicians and public administrators alike deem it to be a good response to the absence of a federal policy to avert increases in an already high degree of concentration of manufacturing activities in the country.[15]

One must have in mind, however, that the state VAT, despite still being the tax that most collects tax revenue in the federation, is losing dynamism. Due to structural changes in the dynamic of the Brazilian, and global, economy the ICMS tax base is shrinking. Besides the non-application of this tax to the provision of services, it also faces a decreasing share of industry in the national output, and the erosion of its pillars—telecommunications, energy, and fuels—due to new technologies, foreign competition and the loss competitiveness of important sectors (Rezende, 2019).

Of course, the conflicts that arose out of the fiscal war made it very difficult to implement any proposal for harmonizing the tax system and propelling tax administrators to cooperate. Cooperation is also hampered by conflicts related to the taxation of natural resources—oil in particular. In oil, as well as in electricity generation, the 1988 Constitution adopted a destination principle for the states VAT to avoid producer states to reap all the revenues from these important tax bases. However, as revenues from oil and electricity came to represent a sizable portion of the taxes collected by the states' treasuries, producer states claimed that this exception to the general rule do a lot of harm to their finances, not allowing them to implement adequate environmental protection policies to deal with the side effects of the natural resources exploration. Several attempts

[15] For details on fiscal competition in Brazil see Varsano (1997).

to negotiate a truce among the Brazilian states to put an end to the fiscal war never succeed and still is an important obstacle to be removed.

The absence of clear definitions relating to the functions of government to be performed by each federal order is a major source of renewable conflicts. that come up whenever measures adopted by the federal government reduce revenues from the income and manufacturing taxes that form the basis of the present revenue sharing system. Or when federal sponsored legislation interferes on subnational tax autonomy, as has been the case of the exemption granted to exports from the states value-added tax. In such cases, demand for financial compensation becomes a permanent focus of conflicts, as these compensations have to be negotiated annually during the regular budgetary process. On the expenditure side, changes in rules governing federal financial aid to social programs carried out at the subnational level are also a source of intermittent conflicts.

Conflicts among the states and their municipalities are also noteworthy. The possibility granted to state legislators by the 1988 Constitution to set the criteria for dividing one-fourth of the proceedings of the states' VAT that belongs to their municipalities should be mentioned. Quite often, state legislators change the formula applied to establish the municipal quotas to benefit political allies or to introduce other variables that although justifiable (give a premium to environmental conscious local administrators) affect the distribution of resources and in so doing raise objections from losers.

A council formed by the states' finance ministers created in the seventies is the sole attempt to have an institution in charge of mediating conflicts. Presided by the federal finance minister it worked properly during the authoritarian regimen for obvious reasons. After re-democratization, the federal government could no more impose rules that had to be obeyed by all and this council, albeit in formal existence, was deprived of any power to harmonize states' tax policies and lost credibility, becoming unable to enforce legislation that prohibits special tax concessions by any state without unanimous approval of all the twenty-six states and the federal district.

A long tradition of applying symmetric arrangements to asymmetric situations makes it difficult to avoid conflicts or find proper solutions. In the fairly heterogeneous Brazilian federation, symmetric arrangements cannot lead to a proper equilibrium among subnational government units. Symmetry is reflected in equal powers being granted by the Constitution to every state or municipality whatever its size, region and economic and social realities. Well-developed industrialized states and frontier ones have to abide by the same rules with regard to administrative organization, tax powers and expenditure responsibilities.

What seems to be a contradiction is the result of adopting uniform rates for earmarking states and local government's revenues to health and education expenditures in a situation of huge horizontal fiscal disparities. Cialdini et al. (2014), in a seminal paper presented at the III Iberoamericanas Conference on Local Financing, demonstrated enormous asymmetry between Brazilian Municipalities, with a population above 80 thousand inhabitants.

The study identified municipalities with more than 80 thousand inhabitants with similar socioeconomic vulnerabilities, and concluded that, even being in the vicinity of developed regions or cities (that is, segregated within the same space), the low per capita income was a common feature.

The work raised 100 municipalities in a situation of great socioeconomic vulnerability. These municipalities were selected because their common characteristics were the low purchasing power of the population—88.5% of the population lived with a per capita household income of up to US$300. Associated with low per capita income, the poor indicators in education and health outcomes, the low coverage of sanitation services, endemic violence and, most importantly, the lack of money in the municipal coffers to face this precariousness.

The same goes for big metropolitan cities and small rural municipalities where differences are even greater. Both have similar organizational structures, a directly elected legislative body and direct access to federal funds.

Even though subnational governments enjoy a greater degree of constitutional autonomy, the amplitude of the legislative power of the federal government, both in fiscal and regulatory matters, means that their decision-making power has been curtailed. By means of complementary laws to the Constitution, the federal government defines the framework within which states and local governments can set norms for applying and collecting their own taxes. Federal legislation also establishes detailed provisions concerning the elaboration and execution of subnational budgets. As regards regulation, the detailed rules of the federal laws leave almost no room for the states in areas such as public utilities, environmental protection and the exploration of natural resources.

In fact, local governments have more autonomy than the states insofar as they are entitled to regulate the use of municipal land and the provision of urban services, impose user charges and to define their own norms for collecting the property taxes. In general, they also have a reasonable degree of autonomy over their budgets as, on average, about 40% of their revenues come from general-purpose grants.

It is worth noting that municipal autonomy can also be seen in the political arena, with an increased significance of municipal elections within the national context, at the expanse of state politics. Researches have shown that the Brazilian population not only cares more about municipal elections in comparison with state elections, but also favors mayors over governors when it comes to importance and political power (Arretche and Schlegel, 2014).

Through earmarked grants and control of the subnational debt the federal government increased its influence on subnational policies. It should be noted that the process of controlling the indebtedness of Brazilian states and municipalities has always been a concern reported in several studies. At the end of the 1980s, Rezende and Afonso (1988), carried out an analysis showing the need for broad institutional control, a well-defined public finance regulatory framework and the need to reformulate accounting and statistical procedures.

In the mid-90s the last century, the vast majority of states and large municipalities were insolvent, bowed down by excessive debt and the fact that the end of hyperinflation had exhausted the mechanism of corrosion of the real value of their expenses. This fact started to change with the intense renegotiation of the debt of the States and Municipalities, with the Union and the approval of the Fiscal Responsibility Law, which established fiscal rules for the Union, States and Municipalities, on the control of expenses and debt, among others aspects.

Coupled with hard budgetary constraints that were put into place to sustain macroeconomic stability, the degree of freedom of state governors to allocate budgetary resources had been reduced to very little. This is especially true for policies in the so-called "standardized policy system" part of the National Public Policy Systems, where the access to resources is subject to different types of conditions (Souza e Fontanelli, umplished, 2015). The situation is somewhat better at the local level, the big metropolitan cities aside, since the criteria applied to divide the municipal share on federal taxes is biased toward smaller municipalities and penalizes the states' capital cities, that houses one-third of the GDP and one-fourth of the population but gets only 10% of this pie.

Conversely, subnational governments can interfere with national policies only by means of their representatives' actions in the national Congress. That happens when proposals for federal regulation on the use of natural resources, the provision of public services or the exercise of tax powers at the subnational level affect states and local governments' interests. However, due to the fragmentation of political parties and the nature of the electoral process, representatives from the states in the Lower House and in the Senate do not always act in accordance with states' governors, weakening subnational influence on national politics.

3 Intergovernmental Transfers and Fiscal Disequilibria

Despite of the tax powers assigned to states and local governments by the Constitution, data on tax collections by each layer of the federation shows a remarkable degree of vertical imbalance. The federal government alone responds to a little more than 70% of all the money extracted from businesses and families through various taxes. The states collect about 22% of total tax revenues, the rest coming from the local governments' own taxes (Fig. 6).

	US$ Millions 1/	percentGDP 2/	Amount per capita (in current US$) 2019 3/	percent of total local revenues
Shared taxes	**49.252**	**2,68**	**57.4**	**32,0**
Tax on Circulation of Goods Services – ICMS	26.654	1,45	127,9	17,3
Tax on Motor Vehicle Ownership – IPVA	6.232	0,34	29,9	4,05
Fund for the Compensation of Exports – FPEx	271	0,01	1,3	0,18
Fund for Education - FUNDEB	16.096	0,88	77,2	10,46
Local Revenues 4/	153.931	8,39	738,5	100.0%

Fig. 6 Provincial government constitutional transfers to local governments—2019 (*Primary source* National Treasury Secretariat, Federal, Finance Minister. 1/ 2019 average exchange rate: US$1 = R$3,95. 2/ GDP = [US$ Millions] = 1.835.756. 3/ POP = 208.436.323. 4/ Own Revenue plus current and capital transfers)

Three distinct regimes attempt to address the vertical disequilibria: (a) a conventional revenue sharing system; (b) a separate set of rules concerning the share of states and local governments in revenues from specific taxes; (c) conditional transfers.

The pillar of the revenue sharing system is the participation of states and local governments in the proceedings of the federal income and manufacturing taxes.

According to the 1988 Constitution, 21.5% of federal revenues from these taxes go to the states and 24.5% to the municipalities.[16] Nevertheless, the erosion of the basis of the revenue sharing had a strong impact on horizontal fiscal disparities. When these percentages were adopted these taxes represented 50.8% of total revenues of the federal government, but over time they shrank to less than 33.6% due to the growing importance of social contributions earmarked to pension, health and social assistance in federal tax collections that are not shared in the federation.

Therefore, the revision of the apportionment formula faced strong opposition from states and municipal governments as the erosion of the basis for the equalization funds blocked any attempt to do. Consequently, a provisory arrangement negotiated in 1989 that set up in the quotas of each state and municipality in these funds were frozen since then on the basis of the coefficients prevailing at the time the Constitution was promulgated[17] and the previous practice of making adjustments in light of updated income and population estimates was abandoned.

Another important component of the revenue sharing system, the 25% share of local governments in their states' VAT collections, suffered the same setback. According to rules inserted in the Constitution, sthree-fourths of the municipal share is distributed according to the value-added in each local jurisdiction and the rest follow rules set by the respective states' legislators. Municipalities with a strong economic basis benefit from the first criteria, whereas the formulas adopted by the states tend to favor political allies and are subjected to frequent changes.

Outside the realm of the equalization transfers it is worth noting that local governments also gets 50% of revenues from the rural property

[16] The share of municipalities grew by two percentual points since 1988 by means of two constitutional amendments approved in 2007 and 2014.

[17] The shares of each state were established by CONFAZ. As to municipalities, a percentage was set for all municipalities within each state, so as to prevent the creation of new municipalities from having outside effects.

tax collected by the federal government and from the motor vehicle tax applied by the states.

The Rural Property Tax (ITR) is charged to the owners of rural property and the collection is equally divided between the Union and the municipality where the property is located. However, it is also possible for the tax to be monitored and collected by the municipalities, by means of an agreement with the Union, in which case the total collection will remain with the municipality, which will nevertheless bear the costs of administration and tax collection.[18] The Motor Vehicle Property Tax (IPVA) is incumbent upon and collected by Brazilian states, which transfer 50% of the amount collected to Municipalities, where vehicles are licensed.

Royalties from the exploration of natural resources should also be mentioned. Federal legislation establishes the rules for compensating states and municipalities from the extraction of oil, mining and loss of land due to inundation provoked by hydroelectric dams. Municipal governments are the main beneficiaries of royalties that in some cases enrich the local purse beyond reasonable levels. The current laws regarding the distribution of oil royalties reflect political arrangements made throughout the second half of the last century and are based mostly on geographical criteria (Serra, 2005). The legislation in place, known as Oil Law,[19] provides that the resources of the oil exploration be divided between central, state and local governments by a criterion that largely benefits the states and municipalities where the production takes place, with only a small amount being destinated to other federative units via the Special Petroleum Fund.[20]

The combination of the erosion of the revenue sharing basis with the freezing or the quotas attributed to each federal/entity plus the proliferation of other transfers led to the absence of any criteria guiding the intergovernmental flow of resources in the federation. As a result, the

[18] See, on the subject, the terms of the agreement that can be made by the Federal Revenue of Brazil and the Municipalities. https://bit.ly/3kgzbpD.

[19] Law n° 9.478/1997.

[20] It is worth noting that this distribution criterion was changed by the Law n° 12.734/2012, that increases the amount destinated to the Special Petroleum Fund. However, these changes are not in effect due to a legal appeal made by the State of Rio de Janeiro that questions its constitutionality, and that awaits trial in the Supreme Court up to this date.

share of the federal government in total disposable revenues remained more or less where it was in the late eighties, whereas the municipalities got a bigger slice of the pie at the expense of the states (Fig. 7).

One undesirable consequence of expanding transfers to municipalities without a concomitant revision to the distribution formula was the proliferation of small new units. More than one thousand municipalities were created after 1988, since the distribution formula rewarded districts that decided to "emancipate" themselves, either because they were home to major industries, in which case they would receive a high quota of the state ICMS, or because they had few people, in which case they would benefit from the apportionment under the FPM.

Worse still is the outcome regarding the horizontal distribution of fiscal resources. Of the total amount collected by the states, nearly three-fourths belong to the seven states that comprise the South and Southeast region. Among the municipalities, the twenty-six more important metropolitan cities raise more than 60% of total local governments' own revenues. Moreover, as each specific transfer follows its own logic to distribute the

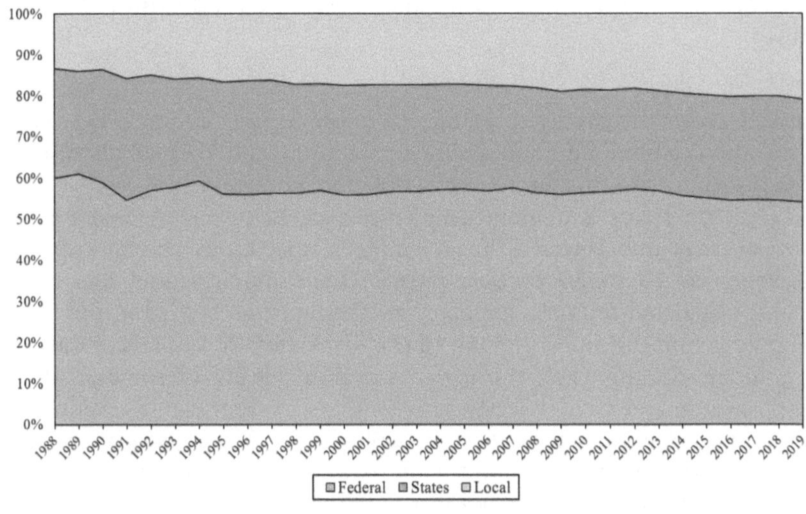

Fig. 7 Federative Division of Available Revenue—% of Total (1988–2018) (*Source* Own elaboration. *Original source* Afonso e Castro [2019] with update observations by the authors)

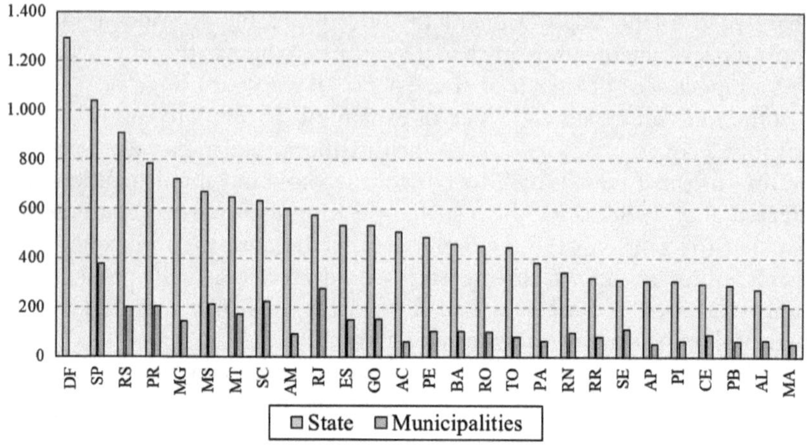

Fig. 8 Tax Revenue Per Capita, by state and municipal governments—US$ (2018) (*Notes* 2018 average exchange rate: 1 US$ = R$3,65. Revenue from taxes, fees and improvement contributions, minus contributions to Fundeb and other deductions, and, in the case of states, constitutional transfers to municipalities. *Source* Authors elaboration. *Primary source* FINBRA/STN and IBGE)

money across the twenty-six states, the federal district and near five thousand and five hundred municipalities, an enormous horizontal disparity in the distribution of fiscal resources across the federation surface.[21]

Data on states and municipalities per capita revenues illustrate the size of these imbalances. Current budgetary per capita revenues can be as much as 20 to 30 times greater in small municipalities located in thinly populated regions, compared to the figures recorded in the more populous municipalities. Among states, disparities are less severe but still significant. In this case, the low population density of some states in the Amazon and Center-West regions means that per capita revenues of these states are more than three times higher than the national average. More densely populated states in the Northeast, with the single exception of little Sergipe, are among those with the lowest per capita revenues (Fig. 8).

[21] The extent of the fiscal gaps can be seen in Prado et al. (2003).

Horizontal inequalities are particularly severe in metropolitan areas and other big urban agglomerations where the outcome is determined by the manner in which economic activity and population are distributed geographically. In general, municipalities with an important manufacturing sector and a small population have *per capita* budgets several times higher than the regional average, due to their share in states' tax collections. At the other extreme, municipalities with a very large population and a fragile economy, usually functioning as a dormitory city in these areas, are severely under-financed, having *per capita* budgets well below the regional average.

Among the conditional transfers, the more important are those that are meant to complement the parcel of states and local government's revenues earmarked for health activities. According to the rules, states must allocate 12% of their budgetary revenues to health and 25% to education, whereas municipalities must spend the same amount on education and 15% to health. But in both cases a uniform rate applied to a very large horizontal fiscal disparities enlarge, instead of reducing, disparities among resources and needs at the state and local levels. To the rules of the same sector enshrined in the Constitution establish that the federal government has to transfer 15% of the net primary revenues to health and 18% to education.[22]

However, the lack of uniformity in the interpretations and transparency in the calculation of the indicators, caused a proliferation of creative accounting practices due to the uneven interpretations of the 34 Courts of Accounts existing in Brazil. Almost all of these practices also generated discomfort with the current fiscal rule—the LRF, causing the loss of the effectiveness of the rules and preventing the accounts of governors and mayors from being rejected.

According to Vieira et al. (2019), in 2018 values, public spending on health in the Union went from R$60.3 billion in 1995 to R$116.7 billion in 2015, corresponding to a 94% growth in the period. Spending by states and the Federal District also increased significantly (257%), from R$19.8 billion to R$70.6 billion. However, the greatest fiscal effort was

[22] With the approval of the Constitutional Amendment nº 95 in December 2016, the health and education spending floor is no longer a percentage of revenue, but equals the amount spent in 2017 adjusted for inflation. This is a temporary rule, since the amendment provides for the possibility of revising the correction index after ten years and has a total validity period of twenty years.

made by the group of municipalities, whose total expenditure totaled R$84.2 billion in 2015, representing an increase of 437% in relation to the R$15.7 billion allocated in 1995.

The lack of a well-designed institutional arrangement that could fulfill the role of introducing rationale in the system and mediate conflicts of interest is a big handicap for a better functioning intergovernmental fiscal relation. Brazil does not actually have a fiscal equalization transfer system, but rather a constitutionally mandated revenue sharing mechanism that delivers automatically a fixed proportion of income and manufacturing federal taxes' revenues, plus other minor taxes, to states and local governments on the basis of predetermined fixed rates.[23] Coupled with the superimposition of specific purpose grants, the absence of an equalization thrust in the general-purpose transfers is responsible for a fairly high degree of horizontal disequilibria in the distribution of fiscal resources in the Brazilian federation and add to the difficulties faced to achieve cooperation in public policies.

4 Fiscal Federalism and Macroeconomic Management

The success of a monetary stabilization plan adopted in 1994 to close an era of high inflation had important consequences for the federal finances. For decades, inflation made it easy to curb budgetary deficits as tax revenues were fully indexed and most of the expenditure items were not. Thus, by postponing payments and adjusting nominal salaries and pensions only once a year, fiscal disequilibria were easily corrected.

A stable currency brought structural imbalances to light. Expenditure on personnel and social security benefits showed the real effect of a paternalistic approach to past policies concerning employment and pensions across the federation. At the same time, a tight monetary policy to protect the Brazilian economy from external shocks raised the amount of money required to serve the public debt.

In the beginning of this new era, price stability was anchored on the overvaluation of the new currency—the real—but the successive external financial crisis that hit emerging economies in the second half of the

[23] The 1967 original formula established that the states quotas would be directly related to population and inversely related to per capita income, whereas the municipal quotas would grow with population size but at a decreasing rate.

nineties—Mexico (1995), Southeast Asia (1997), Russia (1998) forced the Brazilian government to abandon its policy to control the exchange rate in 1999 and let the national currency float. Thus, monetary stability came to depend upon responsible management of the fiscal accounts and fiscal discipline took the place of the exchange rate as the anchor that should avert inflation to drift away.

The new inflation target regime, adopted in 2000, relies on a proper work of monetary and fiscal policies. The National Monetary Council formed by the Finance and Planning Ministers and the President of the Central Bank set targets for the inflation rate for two years in a row, as well as the interval within which the actual result may differ from the desired outcome. The Central Bank is in charge of bringing inflation as close to the mark as possible, making use of the interest rate to adjust expectations and force convergence toward the target. To that end, the Central Bank has enjoyed a fairly large degree of autonomy, even though it does not have formal independence from the national government.

In the fairly decentralized Brazilian federation, the enforcement of fiscal discipline required important institutional changes. A Fiscal Responsibility Law—FRL, inspired by the highly praised New Zealand experience was enacted in 2000. This law intends to enforce fiscal discipline at the federal, state and local governments, as well as, at all three branches of power, the executive, legislative and judiciary. The law works through the imposition of objective and clear rules to be observed in administering revenues and expenditure policies, the public debt and government assets. Among the norms set by the FRL, it is worth noting:

(a) Limits for personnel spending—remuneration of public employees shall not exceed 50% of net current revenues at the federal level and 60% at the subnational level;
(b) Indebtedness limits—outstanding debts cannot exceed two times current revenues for the states and 1.2 times for local governments. With regard to debt service, annual payments cannot surpass 11.5% of current revenues in both cases. In addition, resources from new loans cannot exceed 16% of current revenues in any fiscal year;
(c) Provision for recurrent expenditures—public authorities cannot take actions that create future expenses lasting for more than two years without pointing to a source of financing or a compensating cut in other expenses.

(d) Special provision for electoral years—the law prohibits outgoing governors and mayors (last year in office) to anticipate tax revenues through short-term loans, give wage increases and contract new public servants.

Failure to fulfill obligations imposed by the FRL was subjected to several administrative and more serious misbehaviors, including the loss of the mandate, incapability for having a job in the public service, fines and imprisonment. It is worth emphasizing that all levels of government, the federal one included, had to abide by the conditions established in the FRL.[24]

To make feasible the adherence of states and big municipalities to the new rules concerning the public debt, previous debts with the federal government were refinanced in favorable terms for a period of thirty-five years, but, unlike previous bail-outs, the beneficiaries of such renegotiations became prohibited to issue new bonds and were required to transfer between 11 and 13% of their current revenues to the federal treasury on a monthly basis during the duration of these contracts. To assure enforcement, debt-refinancing contracts entitled the federal government to sequester states and local government's revenues from federal transfers in case of failure to comply with the agreed rules.

In the beginning the hard budgetary constraints put into place by the Fiscal Responsibility Law together with the revenue sequestration mechanisms mentioned above, brought control to the public finances. Since its inception, the public sector as a whole spared a sizable amount of money to revert the ascending trajectory of the total public sector debt to the GDP ratio. Primary surplus, that is, the balance between total revenues and non-financial expenditures rose steadily in the 1999–2005 period, stabilizing up to 2008, with states and local governments contributing with approximately one-fourth of the overall result. In 2009 when it began to fall e returned to a primary deficit starting in 2014, the deterioration in fiscal results was more pronounced in the federal government.[25] Thus, after having reached 81% of the GDP in 2002, the general government gross debt fell up until 2014 when it reached 57%. However,

[24] Despite its isonomic conditions, the debt limits set by the law only impacts state and local governments, given that federal debt limits have never been established.

[25] See IFI (2017).

with the political-economic crisis that took place, the debt-to-GDP rose quickly, closing 2019 at around 88%.[26]

The outbreak of the 2008 financial crisis reached Brazil in an unfavorable fiscal condition. Stimulus to public spending aimed to counteract the impact on the economy brought a new wave of measures hoping that it would insulate the Brazilian economy from the winds that blew from the northern hemisphere. It worked for a time, but as expected did not last long. From 2008 to 2012 the average rate of growth was 3.7%, but since then it showed signals of fatigue. A renewed attempt to follow the same line did not achieve the same effects, leading to a deterioration of the primary balance in the fiscal accounts, as the general government's primary result went from primary surplus of around 3.1% of GDP in 2012 to −0.5% in 2015,[27] thus restoring a scenario similar to the one that preceded the enactment of the Fiscal Responsibility Law. It was time to rein in the march of the carriage, but the federal authorities choose to do the opposite.

Therefore, in light of its poor handling of the 2008 financial crisis, since 2014, Brazil is facing the worst economic crisis of its history. Between 2014 and 2019, the country's GPD has shrunk by 3.1%. As fiscal problems mounted, the commitment to fiscal responsibility lost political support and the disposition to apply the penalties put into place by the FRL for personnel and indebtedness ratios was relaxed, opening some holes in the measures adopted in 2000. Besides, the consequences for the federation were big, especially at the level of the states and bigger municipalities, due to the more room allowed to sustain expenses through an increase in the public debt and non-recurrent revenue, which amounted on average to 1% of the GDP between 2009 and 2013.

In addition, present concerns point to the consequences of a lengthy period of budgetary restrictions on economic growth and income inequality. As public investment plunged, notably at the federal level, road construction and maintenance suffered a severe setback and is now seen as an important handicap for keeping the pace of commodities' exports. In the social area, difficulties to improve quality of education and health

[26] In order to enable a greater time span in the comparison, these percentages refer to the series calculated from the methodology used until 2007. In the new methodology, the values for 2014 and 2019 are 52 and 76%, respectively.

[27] General Government Public Finance Statistics of the National Treasury Secretariat. https://bit.ly/30Wt6aT.

services increased problems low-income people face to access better-paid jobs and escape the poverty trap.

Coupled with high indebtedness ratios, the fall in public savings brought public investment along with it. The average rate of public investment evolved to around 3% of the GDP only in the early 2000 years, down from the already low 4.2% ratio registered in the second half of the nineties and shows no sign of having any condition to improve to a significant degree in the short run. As a matter of fact, since 2016 the net investment in non-financial assets, i.e. excluding capital depreciation, has been negative—minus 0.2% of the GDP in 2018. Contrasting with the situation that prevailed in the seventies, when the public sector accounted for a sizable part of total gross capital formation in the Brazilian economy, the present reality point to a State that now responds for less than 20% of the annual rate of capital accumulation in the country.

Concerns about the problems a low level of public investment generate for economic growth and inequalities in income distribution led to a search for alternative means of investment financing through the recourse to public and private partnerships for gathering resources to finance infrastructure projects, without bringing the expected results so far.

Whatever the possibility of exploring alternatives, the need to restore public investments is compelling. In less developed regions, privatization or partnerships will not attend to the needs of infrastructure modernization. In metropolitan areas, access for low-income families to basic urban services will be denied in the absence of public investments. All the same, health and education infrastructures deserve more attention, especially from state governments.

However, new measures intended to reverse the deterioration of the fiscal accounts did not have time to show significant improvements given the difficulties to restore conditions for recovering economic growth and the approaching of the calendar for a new round of general elections. The most significant fiscal measure was the approval of Constitutional Amendment n° 95 in December 2016, introducing the *New Fiscal Regime*, a fiscal rule that limits for twenty years the growth of federal primary expenditures to the rate of inflation from the previous year. Aside from attempts to alleviate the burden heavily indebted states faced to administer their precarious financial situation, there was no room to pay attention to the need to reform fiscal federalism in a time of increasing conflicts among states and municipalities over who was entitled to tax digital services.

Furthermore, In the midst of economic and political conflicts that dominate the electoral campaign any attempt to put a fiscal federalism reform on the national agenda failed… New proposals for reforming the tax system did not pay attention to it and therefore were doomed to fail, repeating what happened in the last three decades.

But it is not possible anymore to do it again Challenges the Brazilian fiscal federalism face with the impact of the digital revolution on the tax universe, can't be ignored anymore.

5 Challenges to Fiscal Federalism: Institutional Rigidity, Conflicts and Impediments to Reform

A thorough reform of the Brazilian fiscal federalism model is long overdue, but far from being endorsed by public authorities and politicians. In the midst of strong antagonisms, every federal entity fears that a structural reform could run against their particular interests.

The challenges that have to be faced to achieve a broad understanding of proposals for a new fiscal federalism model are big. A new model will have to be able to reconcile tax harmonization, macroeconomic fiscal discipline, subnational autonomy, and governments that are efficient in the use of the fiscal resources and accountable to its citizens.

Even if an agreement can be achieved, a high degree of institutional rigidity makes it hard to find a way to set up a pathway to carry out the reform. Brazil has one of the more extensive constitutional chapters on the tax system and fiscal federalism in the world. Therefore, every minor change demands amendment to the Constitution, and complementary laws to set up new rules for intergovernmental transfers.

During the process of writing the 1988 Constitution several changes were adopted to increase the influence of less developed states in every matter related to their fiscal interests, namely:

(a) States in the more developed regions were assigned maximum of 70 representatives in the lower house, whereas those in poorer regions were allowed to elect 8.[28]

[28] As São Paulo is the most populous state, instead of the more than 110 parliamentarians to which he would be entitled, he has 70 and the excess seats in this account are given to those who have not reached the minimum of eight, such as Acre, Rondônia, Roraima, Amapá and Tocantins.

(b) At the same time, the bicameral regimen that is a common feature of federal countries was tweaked so that every change in the rules that deal with federal issues have to pass through both houses;
(c) New states were created at that time in the North and Center-West regions, leading to a situation in which representatives of the North, Northeast and Center-West regions had a qualified majority in the Senate (more than two-thirds of the votes) and a comfortable position in the lower house, allowing them to block any changes that run against their particular interests.
(d) Previous constitutional rules that prohibit members of local government councils, in municipalities with less than 300 thousand inhabitants to be remunerated were erased, thus leading to a wave of multiplication of the number of municipalities in the country.
(e) Furthermore, provisory rules set up in 1989 to distribute funds that should reduce fiscal disparities were frozen since then, leading as mentioned above to opposite results.

Altogether, these measures reinforced imbalances in the political representation of subnational governments on the national parliament adding to the difficulties to implement major changes. Therefore, intergovernmental transfers that should function as a fiscal equalization regime make the opposite, due to rules adopted in 1989 that resisted any proposal to correct fiscal imbalances since then.

On the other side of the table, the hard budgetary constraints faced by the federal government did not allow him to use a firm hand to conduct a discussion to search for some agreement to overpass resistance to changes. In this context, every attempt to reform the fiscal federalism regimen over the last three decades was doomed to fail.

What could be done to walk out of this trap? My proposal is to install a national dialogue on federalism to explore in detail the problems that accumulate over time, before incurring again the same error of the past thirty years of putting upfront a detailed proposition of a constitutional amendment to the Constitution to be discussed in the national parliament.

That means not to start the discussion by the end. Solutions for every big problem demand to be exposed in a clear way what are the problems that need to be solved and how to search for alternatives that could reconcile distinct perceptions of the problem. Besides, it is almost impossible to solve all problems at once. A more reasonable approach is to set up a path to be followed in steps, choosing carefully the first one that could remove barriers to proceed along the way until the end of the route.

In the Brazilian case, this is very important due to the variety of problems that accumulated over time. First of all, it is important to bring states and municipalities to the same table. Up to now, this did not happen, so it is very important to do it this time. The position of the states is more or less known and reflects the wall erected in 1989, even though this wall does not any more reflect the diversity of situations that we face nowadays,

The same is not true in the case of the local governments. Over time they formed two groups that differ in terms of the number o inhabitants. One congregates those with a population above 80 thousand residents and the other those below this threshold. Each of them belongs to a political organization that does not share a common view regarding any discussions on fiscal reforms.

Why is so? This format was conceived a long time ago and does not anymore reflect the situation we encounter nowadays, but in the midst of the fog that obstructs a clear vision of alternatives, they cling to the old arrangements till something new can be perceived. As in the case of the states, the pattern of regional disparities is very different nowadays, but in doubt about what to do it seems better to wait until things can be clearly exposed.

Why this was not sufficient to change the rules? The main reason is the abovementioned political arrangement that blocks the attempts to do that, To give a good example of the conflicts that surround any tentative to do that it is worth mentioning that in 2012 the supreme court declared that the ongoing criteria to share the national fund created to reduce the effect of the concentration of the state's tax basis in the more industrialized states was unconstitutional and, therefore had to be changed. In 2013 the President of the Senate at the time installed a special commission to present suggestions to do that, to no avail. The deadline arrived and nothing has been done. So, an extension was conceded and the parliament approved in a hurry a new law that in practice changed nothing, but gave an excuse to keep things untouched until now.

It is not possible anymore to avoid the need to reform the Brazilian fiscal federalism nowadays. On the one hand, under the present Constitution states have the power to tax goods and some specific services like telecommunications, energy and transportation, whereas services in general are in the realm of local governments, a situation which is clearly not possible to sustain anymore.

On the other, technological innovations, coupled with the globalization of economic activities are disrupting the old standard of business organization worldwide. With the advancement of the so-called Digital Economy, it becomes impossible to attach the main tax basis to a specific location as digital transactions generate conflicts both at the international level and within a federation. Putting it in simpler terms, the territory is not anymore, a reference to allocate tax powers.

In that case, the usual criteria for operating a regimen of fiscal equalization will also need to adapt. Fiscal equalization was a solution for the fact that revenues from the traditional tax basis were concentrated in richer parts of the federal territory, Therefore it was necessary to transfer resources to less fortunate entities so as to get as close as possible to the ideal of providing all members with enough resources to attend to the basic needs of their population.

In this new world, fiscal equalization will need to adopt a new formula to operate equalization transfers. Perhaps the guide for this should be the principle inscribed in the German Constitution, which says that every citizen should have access to equal opportunities to ascend the social ladder, regardless of the place of birth and residence.

Recourse to socioeconomic data could be a new guide to devise a formula to reach the purpose of equalization transfers, especially in countries like Brazil where economic and social disparities are still great and tend to increase in the wake of the advance of the digital economy, which ask for better qualification of the labor force.

As we mentioned before, this will not be easy, but insofar as technological innovations will also call for a thorough reform of the Brazilian tax system, there might arise an opportunity to move ahead. One of the reasons for the failure of several attempts to reform the tax regimen in the last thirty years was the fact that none of them dealt with this at the same time. Now it is impossible not to do it again for reasons already mentioned.

To that end, we might put in place the proposal we made few paragraphs above to install a federal dialogue aimed at putting in perspective the main points of conflicts and adopt a strategy to move from those that are seen as easier to reach an agreement to those that face more barriers to surpass, in order to go ahead. Some preliminary ideas to put in place this dialogue are presented below.

First there will not be easy to reach an agreement on how to unify the tax basis of subnational governments, since the bigger municipalities will resist the idea of giving away the power to collect revenues for a basis that is growing to share a basis that is shrinking. Second, adopting a uniform basis for taxing goods and services might increase regional disparities that might run against the interests of the less developed states. Third, as mentioned above, that will call for a thorough reform of the intergovernmental transfers of resources to reduce vertical and horizontal disparities among states and local governments Fourth, this will have to come jointly with measures to promote intergovernmental cooperation to improve the quality in the provision of basic services to the population and open up the room to investments aimed at reducing regional inequalities.

As we pointed out, instead of putting out a proposal for reforming fiscal federalism at once, we have to move cautiously. The first step should deal with rewriting the rules for apportioning the resources from the federal funds that should equalize state and local governments revenues, to reduce distortions that accumulated over time,.alongside alternatives to move toward a unified basis for taxing goods and services, A joint approach could start the federative dialogue and make it easier to reach an agreement to move on since gains and losses from one side could be compensated by the other. Could the impact of the Covid-19 pandemic be a turning point in the history of the Brazilian fiscal federalism? The health, social and economic crisis stemming from the Covid-19 pandemics represents one of the greatest challenges faced by governments around the world in the last century. At the time of writing this article, the virus has infected hundreds of millions of people, leading to millions of deaths. Brazil, in particular, has become a hotspot for the disease, registering some of the highest infection and death rates in the world, among the most populous countries in the world.

Due to the unique territorial dimension of this crisis, subnational governments have a key role to play in the containment measures and the provision of health care (OECD, 2020). Therefore, it is not surprising that some aspects of federalism have become central in the midst of the crisis, especially in Brazil, which, as explained in this article, already faced several challenges in this arena. Although it still may be too early to fully assess the federal response in Brazil, it is possible to draw some early conclusions and even postulate possible consequences and paths for the Brazilian federation.

With regard to the immediate response to the health crisis, it is worth highlighting two central aspects. First, a Supreme Court ruling that reaffirmed the constitutional guarantee of subnational governments autonomy in matters of health and epidemiological surveillance, allowing states and municipalities to implement the international guidelines for medical and health measures to contain the virus, despite the resistance of the central government.[29] The second aspect concerns the relevance of the Unified Health System (SUS), one the largest public and universal healthcare systems in the world, that operates in a fairly decentralized way. As a matter of fact, subnational governments account for about 60% of the financing of consolidated government expenditure on the health function, executing 86% of the expenses (Graziane et al., 2020).

The economic fallout has affected central and subnational finances, both by the falling tax revenue and by the increase in spending. Since subnational governments in Brazil are not able to issue public debt and have limited access to loans (that typically are subjected to a financial guarantee from the central government) it was up to the central government to provide some temporary fiscal relief. This was done via the compensation of the loss of revenue from the participation funds, by an emergency aid to subnational entities, and by increased transfer of resources from the Ministry of Health to the state and municipalities, amounting up to BRL 80 billion.

There is, however, some indication that this crisis may become an inflexion point in the Brazilian federative relations. The central government chose to relinquish its privileged position to coordinate a national response strategy. One silver lining, however, has been the unprecedented cohesion and cooperation of states and municipalities, in light of the central government's abstention. Governors and mayors, together with the National Congress, assumed the leadership in the battle against the virus, and used political and popular pressure to force the central government to take some action.

One can only suppose if this newfound alliance will go on in the next years, during the structural reforms at play, ultimately leading to a strengthening of subnational entities and a decentralization process, or the old ways will return and deepen, following the progressive deterioration of subnational public finance. Those who managed to survive, will see.

Only by recognizing the need to establish a federal dialogue it could be possible to find ways to succeed in conducting the huge task that lay

[29] ADI 6.341.

ahead. It is not easy but it can be done. And the opportunity to learn from the experiences of other countries that will be provided by the initiative of the Forum of Federations offers a good opportunity to Brazil.

References

Afonso, J. R. R. and Castro, K. P. 2019. "Carga Tributaria Brasileña en perspectiva histórica: Estadísticas revisadas". *Tax Administration Review*, v. 45, p. 139–154. https://bit.ly/3hw6JPp

Afonso, J. R. R. and Cialdini, A. S. 2016. "Os Municípios e a Lei de Responsabilidade Fiscal: de conceitos a indicadores. Gestão Pública e Direito Municipal: tendências e desafios". *Série IDP-Saraiva.*

Arretche, M. and Schlegel, R. 2014. "Os estados nas federações: tendências gerais e o caso brasileiro". *Inter-American Development Bank - IADB.* Discussion Paper IDB-DP-334. https://bit.ly/3hlpipc.

Cialdini, A. S. 2020. "A Lei de Responsabilidade Fiscal: O processo de formulação e seus efeitos nos Estados brasileiros" (*Tese de doutorado*). ISCSP/ ULisboa.

Cialdini, A. S., Perre, G. and Ribeiro, S. 2014. "Vulnerabilidades Socioeconômicas dos Municípios Brasileiros: Uma Análise dos Municípios Populosos, com Baixa Receita per capita - o g100". *3rd edition of the Ibero-American Days of Local Financing*. 13–14 august 2014. São Paulo-Brazil.

Graziane, E. Afonso, J. R. R. and Ribeiro, L. 2020. "Política pública da saúde e dever de enfrentamento da calamidade: financiamento e responsabilização". In *Governance 4.0 para Covid-19 no brasil*, org. G. Mendes, H. Santana, and J. R. R. Afonso. Coleção IDP. Almedina. São Paulo (in press).

IBGE. 2019a. *Produto interno bruto dos municípios 2017.* Coordenação de Contas Nacionais. Rio de Janeiro. https://bit.ly/3cV7GND.

IBGE. 2019b. *Sistema de Contas Regionais: Brasil 2017.* Coordenação de Contas Nacionais. Rio de Janeiro. https://bit.ly/2B1pzgv.

IFI. 2017. *Relatório de Acompanhamento Fiscal Nº4.* Senado Federal. https://bit.ly/37vbsfk.

Ministry of Health. 2006. "Diretrizes operacionais dos Pactos pela Vida, em Defesa do SUS e de Gestão". Brasil. Secretaria Executiva Brasília (Série A. normas e Manuais técnicos).

OECD. 2020. "The Territorial Impact of COVID-19: Managing the Crisis Across Levels of Government". *OECD Policy Responses to Coronavirus (COVID-19).* https://bit.ly/3NUvaVN.

Piancastelli, M. 2006. "The Federal Republic of Brazil". In *A Global Dialogue on Federalism, Vol 2: Distribution of Powers and Responsibility in Federal Countries*, eds Akhtar Majeed, Ronald L. Watts and Dougls M. Brown.

Mc Gill-Queens University Press for the Forum of Federations. Montreal and Kingston.

Prado, S. Quadros, W. and Cavalcanti, C. 2003. "Partilha de Recursos na Federação Brasileira". FUNDAP, São Paulo.

Rezende, F. 2019. "Expectations And Frustrations: The Recentralization Of Power And The Expansion Of Federative Conflicts And Imbalances". *30 Years of the Brazilian Federal Constitution perspectives for Brazilian Federalism*, 59.

Rezende, F. and Afonso, J. R. R. 1988. "O (Des)controle do Endividamento de Estados e Municípios- Análise Crítica das Normas Vigentes e Propostas de Reforma". IPEA, *Texto para Discussão Interna, N.132*. Rio de Janeiro.

Ricardo Varsano. 1997. "A Guerra Fiscal do ICMS: Quem Ganha e quem perde". IPEA, *Texto para Discussão*. Brasília.

Serra, R. V. 2005. "Contribuições para o debate acerca da repartição dos royalties petroliferos no Brasil". *Tese (doutorado)* - Universidade Estadual de Campinas, Instituto de Economia, Campinas, SP, 289 p.

Serra, J. and Afonso, J. R. R. 1999. "Federalismo Fiscal à Brasileira: Algumas Reflexões". *Revista do BNDES*, Rio de Janeiro, v.6, n. 12, p. 3–30.

Souza, C. 2005. "Constitutional Aspects of Federalism in Brazil". In *A Global Dialogue on Federalism, Vol 1: Constitutional Origins, Structure and Change in Federal Democracies*, eds. John Kincaid and G. Alan Tarr. Mc Gill-Queens University Press for the Forum of Federations. Montreal and Kingston.

Souza, C. and Fontanelli, F. 20015. Sistemas Nacionais de Políticas Públicas (mimeo).

Stepan, A. 1997. "Toward a New Comparative Analysis of Democracy and Federalism: Demos Constraining and Demos Enabling Federations". Coréia do Sul (mimeo).

United Nations, Department of Economic and Social Affairs, Population Division. 2015. "Population 2030: Demographic challenges and opportunities for sustainable development planning". (ST/ESA/SER.A/389).

United Nations, Department of Economic and Social Affairs, Population Division. 2018. *World Urbanization Prospects: The 2018 Revision*. https://bit.ly/3e3BIA0.

United Nations. 2019. *World Population Prospects 2019*. https://bit.ly/3e16lpH.

Varsano, R. 1997. "A Guerra Fiscal do ICMS: Quem Ganha e quem perde". IPEA, *Texto para Discussão*. Brasília.

Varsano, R. 1999. "Subnational Taxation and Treatment of Interstate Trade in Brazil: Problems and a Proposed Solution". *ABCD-LAC Conference*, Valdivia, Chile.

Vieira, F. S., Piola, S. F. and Benevides, R. P. D. S. 2019. "Vinculação orçamentária do gasto em saúde no Brasil: resultados e argumentos a seu favor". IPEA. *Texto para Discussão*. nº 2516. Brasília. https://bit.ly/2UNoTlN.

Canada

Jean-François Tremblay

The fundamental structure of the Canadian federation was established by the Constitution Act of 1867 which specifies the allocation of taxation powers and spending responsibilities among the federal and provincial governments. The federal government was initially intended to play a relatively dominant role in a fiscally centralized federation. Some of the areas that were exclusively assigned to the federal government included the regulation of trade and commerce, money and banking, public debt and property, criminal law, national defence, foreign affairs, postal service and navigation and shipping. Provincial governments were given exclusive responsibilities over the management and sale of public lands, hospitals, education, administration of justice and other matters of local nature including control of municipalities. At the time, the role of the government in the social policy sphere, including in the areas of health care and education, was very limited while regulating commerce, trade and banking were central to economic policy. Provinces were also given more limited taxation powers than the federal government. Over time however,

J.-F. Tremblay (✉)
Department of Economics, University of Ottawa, Ottawa, ON, Canada
e-mail: jtrembl2@uottawa.ca

J.-F. Tremblay (ed.), *The Forum of Federations Handbook of Fiscal Federalism*, https://doi.org/10.1007/978-3-030-97258-5_3

and particularly with the development of the welfare state in the post-World-War II period, the role of provincial governments has expanded considerably. The growth of public spending in health care, education and social services has resulted in a federal structure which is much more decentralized today than what was initially envisioned. Provinces have also progressively occupied a greater share of the tax room resulting in a tax system today which is among the most decentralized in the world.

Provincial governments are now responsible for over half of direct public expenditures (Finance Canada, 2020a). They enjoy extensive autonomy in designing programs and regulations in key areas of social and economic policy, and fund a substantial share of their expenditures through their own taxes. At the same time, there are various mechanisms in place to promote policy harmonization and cooperation in matters that are important to the economic and social union. These include mechanisms to induce harmonization of tax policies and public services, as well as intergovernmental agreements in the areas of labour market, environmental and immigration policies, among others. There are also measures to maintain horizontal equity across provinces including an extensive equalization system designed to ensure that all provincial governments have the capacity to provide public services of comparable quality.

This chapter outlines key features of Canadian fiscal federalism as it operates today, it discusses some of the successes of the federal model as well as various tensions that exists and explores upcoming challenges.

1 General Features of the Country

The Canadian federation is composed of ten provinces and three territories. The latter are located in the northern part of the country and are sparsely populated, largely by First Nations. Territorial governments do not have powers specified by the Constitution. Their powers are delegated by the federal government. Despite that, the territories increasingly operate as provinces and are heavily involved in the development of relationships with First Nations. Local governments do not have constitutional status either. They are creatures of provincial governments. All powers of local governments are therefore mandated by the provinces.

The total population of the country was over 35 million in 2016. Approximately 60% of the population lives in the two largest provinces of Ontario and Quebec. There are two official languages, English and French. Quebec is the only province where French speakers constitute the majority, but there are significant francophone minorities in other provinces. The indigenous population represents close to five percent of the total population of the country. There are some indigenous self-governments that have been established through agreements with the federal and provincial governments. The powers and responsibilities of these self-governments are diverse, but they generally involve some control over land, resources and the provision of various public services.

Canada has a parliamentary system within a constitutional monarchy in which the British monarch is the official head of state and is represented in Canada by the governor general. There is a bicameral national parliament that includes an elected House of Commons and an appointed Senate. Executive powers are vested with the cabinet headed by the prime minister. The cabinet is responsible to Parliament. Democracy is exercised within a multi-party system although it has historically been dominated by two major political parties. Provincial legislatures have a single elected chamber. Elections at federal, provincial and municipal levels are held periodically, usually every four years. In recent years, the federal government and almost all provincial governments have adopted fixed election dates.

Various institutions promote accountability in Canadian governance including regular democratic elections at all levels of government. Moreover, federal and provincial governments are fully autonomous in their respective areas of jurisdiction and they have access to all broad-based taxes. Provincial governments are responsible for raising a high share of their revenues through their own taxes, they have essentially complete autonomy in setting their tax policy and are responsible for managing their budget balance and incurring public debt when necessary. These various dimensions of autonomy and responsibility lead to high accountability at both orders of government. There is also a high level of transparency in public accounts and in budgetary processes safeguarded by independent auditing mechanisms and an independent press. Basic rights, such as freedom of speech and religion, are guaranteed by the Charter of Rights and Freedom, which is written in the Constitution. The treaty rights of indigenous people are also protected by the Constitution.

Canada is among the world highest-income countries. Gross domestic product (GDP) per capita was equal to US$49,031 in 2019.[1] Although

[1] Per capita GDP based on purchasing power parity, retrieved from the World Bank database.

the economy is dominated by service industries, there are sizeable natural resource and manufacturing sectors. Natural resources, especially oil and gas, are mainly located in western provinces while the manufacturing sector is concentrated in the central provinces of Quebec and Ontario. This has important implications for fiscal federalism and different aspects of economic efficiency. The Canadian economy is highly open to international trade. Approximately 32% of domestic production was exported in 2019, although roughly three-quarters of exports are heading to the United States and a considerable share of total exports consists of primary commodities.

2 The Allocation of Expenditure Responsibilities

The Constitution sets the powers and responsibilities of the federal and provincial governments. While most areas of jurisdiction are assigned exclusively to one order of government, there are a few joint responsibilities. Both levels of government enjoy high autonomy in their areas of exclusive jurisdiction, although there are sometimes disagreements about jurisdiction in various areas. The allocation of functions is outlined in Table 1. In addition to functions that are clearly national in scope, such as defence, foreign affairs, regulation of trade, banking and monetary policy, the federal government is also responsible for unemployment insurance, criminal law and various other components of economic policy.

Provincial governments have exclusive legislative authority over the main pillars of social policy such as health care, education and social welfare. In the cases of education and social welfare, some responsibilities are delegated to local governments who are usually involved, to various degrees, in the delivery of services. The federal government is indirectly involved in the financing of health care, post-secondary education and social welfare through the provision of transfers to provincial governments, as outlined later, and in the case of education, through the provision of scholarships, student loans and funding to post-secondary institutions. The federal government is also responsible for population health, for providing health care services to First Nations, for regulating pharmaceuticals, medical devices and food and contributes to research and innovation in the health sector.

Importantly, provincial governments have jurisdiction over natural resources. That comprises exclusive authority over exploration, development, conservation and management of non-renewable resources, forestry

Table 1 Legislative responsibilities and effective allocation of functions

Function	*Legislative responsibility*	*Effective allocation of function*
Defence	Federal	Federal
Foreign affairs	Federal	Federal
Regulation of trade and commerce	Federal	Federal
Banking, currency and bankruptcy	Federal	Federal
Criminal law	Federal	Federal
Unemployment insurance	Federal	Federal
Navigation and shipping	Federal	Federal
Patents and copyrights	Federal	Federal
Postal services	Federal	Federal
Sea coast and fisheries	Federal	Federal
Indigenous people	Federal	Federal and provincial
Immigration	Federal and provincial	Federal and provincial
Agriculture	Federal and provincial	Federal and provincial
Pensions	Federal and provincial	Federal and provincial
Health care	Provincial	Provincial
Administration of justice	Provincial	Provincial
Civil and property rights	Provincial	Provincial
Natural resources	Provincial	Provincial
Municipal institutions	Provincial	Provincial
Education	Provincial	Provincial and local
Social welfare	Provincial	Provincial and local
Local services	Provincial	Local

Source Canadian Constitution, Sections 91 to 95, and Boadway (2007)

and electrical energy. It also includes regulation and management of resource exports to the rest of the country, as well as the exclusive right to tax renewable and non-renewable resources. This has profound implications for various dimensions of fiscal relations among governments, including horizontal fiscal balance and equalization, as well as for economic policy in the federation.[2] In recent years, it also led to conflicts between provinces over the construction of interprovincial oil and gas pipelines.

Provinces are responsible for cultural issues, which is particularly important in the French-speaking province of Quebec, although there are important federal agencies in the cultural sector including the Canadian Broadcasting Corporation, the Canadian Radio-television and Telecommunications Commission and the National Film Board of Canada, among others. Provincial governments have the power to regulate financial markets and labour markets. The Constitution also provides provinces with the authority to legislate on all matters of local nature. This has been interpreted to include various aspects of environmental policy and of transportation policy that are more local in scope, among others.

There are shared responsibilities in the areas of pensions, immigration and agriculture which, in practice, are exercised in a variety of ways. For example, the Canada Pension Plan is legislated by the federal government but any change to policies governing the plan requires the approval of at least seven provincial governments representing at least two-thirds of the Canadian population. Nine provinces participate in the plan. The Quebec government operates its own public pension plan.

In the case of immigration, the federal government has agreements with several provinces according to which provincial governments can select a given proportion of immigrants based on the particular labour market needs of the province, and can manage labour market integration programs. This applies essentially to economic immigrants, that is, those that are admitted through the merit-based system that takes into account various characteristics of immigration applicants including education and proficiency in one or both official languages. Even though all provinces can participate in such agreements with the federal government, the province of Quebec has been most heavily involved in immigration policy. Recently, the surge in the number of individuals claiming

[2] See Boadway et al. (2013) for a detailed discussion of the various challenges that decentralized natural resource management raises in the Canadian federation.

refugee status after crossing the border between Canada and the United States has exposed the need for additional federal-provincial cooperation in this area. This sudden rise in the number of refugee applicants has raised tensions between the federal government, which is responsible for managing refugee claims, and provincial and municipal governments which are providing various social services and housing to claimants. The provinces that are particularly affected have called for financial support from the federal government to help cover the additional costs.

Municipal governments are under the jurisdiction of provincial governments. In principle, each province has full discretion in determining which responsibilities to devolve to municipalities. In practice, however, the set of responsibilities transferred to the local level is relatively uniform across provinces. There are single-tier and two-tier local governments. Single-tier municipalities are responsible for providing all public services delegated by the provincial government, although some services are often provided jointly by neighboring municipalities, generally to take advantage of economies of scale. In two-tier local governments, the upper tier (e.g. region or county) is responsible for services that are more adequately provided over a broader geographical area, while the lower tier (e.g. town or village) are tasked with services that are more local in nature or for which potential economies of scale are more limited.

The extent of expenditure decentralization is highlighted in Table 2. Provincial and territorial governments carry out over three-quarters of total expenditures in health and over 90% of education spending. All

Table 2 Share of expenditures (%) by functions and level of government, 2019

	Federal	*Provincial/territorial*	*Municipal*
Defence	100.0	0.0	0.0
Public order and safety	32.4	31.8	35.8
Economic affairs	27.6	53.3	19.1
Environmental protection	28.8	24.0	47.2
Housing and community amenities	22.0	26.9	51.1
Health	21.4	77.4	1.1
Recreation, culture and religion	29.5	25.3	45.2
Education	8.3	91.7	0.0
Social protection	58.3	36.1	5.6

Source Statistics Canada, Table: 10-10-0024-01. Expenditure functions are grouped according to the Canadian Classification of Functions of Government sub-national governments combined account for well over two-thirds of expenditures in public order and safety, economic affairs, environmental protection, housing and community amenities, and recreation and culture.

Aside from the allocation of powers and responsibilities, the Constitution imposes on the federal and provincial governments joint obligations to provide basic public services to everyone and to pursue equality of opportunity and regional economic development. These constitutional obligations have been argued to justify some federal contribution to a wide range of public services and programs that have an important equity dimension, including in areas of provincial jurisdiction (Boadway and Hobson, 1993). This has been particularly important in the establishment of several provincial programs in the areas of education and health care. For example, in the 1950s and 1960s, the federal government provided cost-sharing grants to provincial governments to encourage the creation of public health care insurance programs and to guarantee the attainment of national standards, even though health care in an exclusive provincial jurisdiction.

The federal and provincial governments have the constitutional right to borrow. The borrowing ability of local governments, however, is limited by provincial governments in various ways. Typically, municipalities can only borrow to finance capital expenditures, they often face debt limits and are sometimes subject to strict conditions with respect to budget balance.

3 Taxation Powers

The federal and provincial governments have unrestricted access to the main broad-based taxes, namely personal and corporate income taxes as well as consumption taxes, as outlined in Table 3. Taxes on natural resources are restricted to provincial governments while the federal government has sole access to taxes on international trade. Local governments rely heavily on the property tax which is their main source of revenues. All levels of government impose various user fees, although the relative importance of user fees as a revenue source is much greater at the local level.

As indicated in Table 4, the federal government dominates the income tax field, which includes personal income and corporate income taxes, while provincial governments occupy two-thirds of the consumption tax

Table 3 Allocation of main taxation powers

	Tax base	*Tax rate*	*Collection and administration*
Personal income tax	Federal	Federal and provincial	Federal and provincial
Corporate income tax	Federal	Federal and provincial	Federal and provincial
Consumption taxes	Federal and provincial	Federal and provincial	Federal and provincial
Property tax	Provincial	Provincial and local	Provincial and local
Resource taxes	Provincial	Provincial	Provincial
User fees	Federal, provincial and local	Federal, provincial and local	Federal, provincial and local

Table 4 Share of revenues (%) by source and level of government, 2019

	Federal	*Provincial/Territorial*	*Municipal*
Incomes taxes	61.7	38.3	0.0
Consumption taxes	33.0	65.7	1.3
Property tax	0.0	15.0	85.0
Taxes on international trade	100.0	0.0	0.0
Social contributions	64.3	35.7	0.0

Source Finance Canada (2020a), *Fiscal Reference Tables*

base and local governments collect 85% of property taxes. The federal government also raises over 60% of social contributions, which at the federal level consist mainly of contributions to the Canada Pension Plan and to the unemployment insurance system.

The federal and provincial governments have their own distinct income taxes. However, there are intergovernmental agreements that facilitate tax collection and management and that promote tax policy harmonization. In the case of the personal income tax, the federal government is responsible for collection and management in all provinces except Quebec. The tax base is determined by the federal government but provinces retain high flexibility in setting tax policy. They can set their own structure of tax rates, and therefore determine the degree of progressivity, as well as province-specific tax credits and special provisions. In contrast, in Quebec, the provincial personal income tax is fully managed and collected by the provincial government. Nonetheless, it remains fairly well harmonized with the personal income tax systems of the federal government and of the other provinces.

The federal government also collects corporate income taxes in all provinces except Quebec and Alberta. As for the personal tax, the federal government sets the tax base, but provinces can choose their tax rates and credits. The tax collection agreement precludes provincial governments from using tax credits and special provisions that discriminate against corporate taxpayers from other provinces. As part of the tax collection agreement, there is also a formula-apportionment system used to allocate the taxable income of firms that have activities in more than one province. This greatly limits firms' opportunities for tax-avoidance through profit-shifting. The formula is based on the allocation of sales and payroll of firms across provinces.

There are also tax collection agreements for the value-added tax in some provinces. In five of them—Newfoundland, Nova Scotia, Prince Edward Island, New Brunswick and Ontario—there is a single value-added tax, the harmonized sales tax (HST), which is managed and collected by the federal government. The tax base is set by the federal government and is therefore fully harmonized across the participating provinces. Each provincial government can set its own tax rate which is imposed on top of the federal rate—currently set at 5%. The federal government transfers to each province the provincial share of revenues on a derivation basis. There is also a tax collection agreement between the federal government and the province of Quebec, although in that case, both governments impose their own distinct taxes, and both are collected by the provincial government. Three provinces—Manitoba, Saskatchewan and British Columbia—collect their own sales taxes and one province—Alberta—does not have any provincial sales tax. In these four provinces, the federal government independently collects its own value-added tax.

The lack of sales tax harmonization across all provinces remains an important concern. It potentially imposes various types of efficiency costs on the Canadian economy. For example, the fact that the tax bases of the HST and of provincial sales taxes in provinces that do not participate in the tax collection agreement are defined differently likely distorts the efficient allocation of firms and economic activity across provinces as well as patterns of interprovincial trade. Moreover, the lack of harmonization tends to increase the compliance costs of firms that have activities in more than one province and the costs of tax administration and collection for governments (Boadway and Shah, 2009; Anderson, 2010).

4 Intergovernmental Fiscal Transfers

The system of intergovernmental transfers is composed of federal transfers to provincial governments, including equalization transfers and specific-purpose transfers, to municipal governments and to territorial governments, as well as transfers from provincial governments to municipalities.

4.1 Equalization

The equalization transfer system constitutes the main general-purpose transfer program. As stated in the Canadian Constitution, the federal government is committed to providing monetary transfers to ensure that all provincial governments have the capacity to provide reasonably comparable levels of public services at reasonably comparable levels of taxation. In practice, this commitment is achieved by providing transfers to provincial governments with fiscal capacities below the national average.

Five tax bases are included in the calculation of provincial fiscal capacities: personal income taxes, corporate income taxes, consumption taxes, property taxes and natural resource revenues. For all of these except natural resource revenues, the capacities of provincial governments to raise revenues are computed by applying the national average tax rate on the estimated size of provincial tax bases. Equalization entitlements are determined by the gap between the fiscal capacities of each provinces and the national average. Since equalization entitlements are based on fiscal capacities, payments to each province are related to their potential tax revenues, not their actual tax revenues. This ensures that provincial governments' incentives to raise own-source revenues are preserved. It is also consistent with the broad objective of ensuring that provincial governments have capacities to provide comparable public services but without requiring them to undertake the same levels of public expenditures.

In the case of natural resource revenues, the calculation of provincial fiscal capacities is different. Half of actual resource revenues, not potential revenues, are included in fiscal capacities. Moreover, to guarantee that the equalization entitlement of any given province is not affected negatively by the inclusion of natural resource revenues, the actual entitlement of each province is equal to the maximum amount obtained by either including half of resource revenues in entitlement calculations or fully excluding natural resource revenues.

Equalization transfers are entirely financed out of the federal government's general revenues. Provincial governments with fiscal capacities above the national average do not contribute to financing the system. Moreover, as discussed below, other federal transfers to provinces are largely unrelated to provincial fiscal capacities. This implies that there is no explicit equalization of fiscal capacities for provinces with above-average capacities. As a result, substantial fiscal disparities remain between provinces that receive equalization payments and provinces that do not. To guarantee that the system remains affordable for the federal government, a ceiling is imposed on the growth of total equalization payments. This ceiling is determined by the three-year moving average of the GDP growth rate.

In 2019–2020, five of the ten provinces received equalization. The non-recipient provinces were Newfoundland, Ontario, Saskatchewan, Alberta and British Columbia. For several years, and up until 2018–2019, the two largest provinces in terms of population, Ontario and Quebec, were recipient of equalization although in the case of Ontario the per capita amount was relatively small.

The equalization system is based only on the capacities of provincial governments to raise revenues. It does not take into account differences across provinces in expenditure needs or in the costs of providing public services. This is potentially important to the extent that the average costs of providing public services will vary with the demographic structure of the population and between urban and rural areas, for example. Even though the federal government supports provincial government expenditures in particular areas through specific-purpose transfers, it is sometimes argued that omitting expenditure needs and costs in the calculation of equalization entitlements limits the ability of the system to fulfill the equalization mandate set by the Constitution.

The equalization system is reviewed every five years following consultations with the provinces, although it is not clear that these consultations always had a large impact on the outcome. In effect, the federal parliament has full authority to change the parameters of the system. Therefore, changes are effectively determined as part of the budgetary process of the federal government, and without any formal requirement to obtain the agreement of provinces. This also applies to the specific-purpose transfers described below. In contrast to other federations, such as Australia India and South Africa, there is no fiscal commission in Canada with the mandate of providing recommendations on the intergovernmental transfer system. However, the Council of the Federation, which includes as members all provincial and territorial Premiers, sometimes serves to promote consultation and negotiations with the federal government on a wide range of issues including intergovernmental transfers. Finance ministers of the federal, provincial and territorial governments also meet regularly, as do deputy ministers, and fiscal transfers would often be discussed at such meetings. Intergovernmental relations also take place through sectoral meetings involving federal and provincial ministers and deputy ministers responsible for specific areas, some of which are highly relevant for the transfer system, such as health care.

4.2 Specific-Purpose Federal Transfers to Provinces

The main specific-purpose transfers are the Canada Health Transfer (CHT) and the Canada Social Transfer (CST). These contribute to the financing of provincial programs in health care, post-secondary education, social assistance and social services, early childhood development and child care. These transfers are allocated among provinces on an equal per capita basis. Therefore, they are unrelated to the actual level of spending by provincial governments in the programs that the transfers are intended to support. Given that the federal government collects more taxes, in per capita terms, in provinces with higher fiscal capacities, these transfers indirectly contribute to horizontal balance among provinces.

As for equalization, the CHT and CST are determined as part of the budgetary process of the federal government. The annual growth rate of the CHT is currently set equal to the three-year moving average of the GDP growth rate. A minimum growth rate of three percent applies if the three-year moving average of GDP growth falls below three percent. The annual growth rate of CST is currently set at three percent. The commitment of the federal government to the future growth of these transfers provides some stability and predictability to provincial governments in their own budgetary process. However, it has been argued that the growth rate of the CHT will fall short of the growth rate of provincial governments' expenditures in health care in the next several years leading to a gradual retreat of federal support for health care.

There are some broad conditions associated with these transfers although in practice provincial governments retain high autonomy and flexibility in designing and delivering public services. For example, CHT requires that provincial health insurance systems satisfy five broad principles which are specified by the Canada Health Act: insurance coverage must be universal and accessible to all independently of personal income, it must apply to a list of insured health care services, it must be portable across provinces and the system must be administered publicly. In principle, financial penalties can be imposed on provinces that do not comply with the Canada Health Act, although in practice non-compliance issues are usually addressed through federal-provincial discussions.

When first introduced, federal transfers for health care and social assistance were structured as cost-sharing grants. Under the Hospital Insurance and Diagnostic Services Act of 1957 and the Medical Care Act of 1966, the federal government covered roughly half of provincial governments' health care costs.[3] These costs sharing arrangements provided provinces with a strong incentive to establish public health care systems and all provinces had done so within a few years. Similarly, under the Canada Assistance Plan, established in 1966, the federal government covered half of the cost of provincial social assistance programs. These cost-sharing arrangements were eventually replaced by block transfers subject to general conditions, but unrelated to the level of spending by provincial governments. Part of these block transfers were cash transfers and part took the form of income tax points transfers.

There are also several federal transfer programs for infrastructure financing. These often take the form of matching grants or cost-sharing arrangements with subnational governments. Some of them are specifically intended for local governments. The Gas Tax Fund is one important example. It is a permanent federal transfer that represents an important share of the total federal contribution to municipal infrastructure.

[3] The Hospital Insurance and Diagnostic Services Act covered half of costs of hospitals and diagnostic services while the Medical Care Act included the costs of the services of doctors provided outside hospitals.

The amount of this transfer was originally determined as a share of the federal gas tax, although it is effectively financed from federal general revenues. The transfers serve to finance a wide range of municipal projects that includes infrastructure for transportation, water and waste management, recreation, culture, tourism, etc. The funds flow through provincial governments and are allocated across provinces and territories on an equal-per-capita basis.

There are several other programs such as the Building Canada Fund, the Canada Strategic Infrastructure Fund, the Green Infrastructure Fund, the Public Transit Infrastructure Fund, and the Clean Water and Wastewater Fund. These are all essentially structured as cost-sharing arrangements with provincial and local governments intended for projects of national, regional or local scope. Various types of infrastructure projects are eligible under these different programs including infrastructures for transportation, public transit, water supply, wastewater treatment, sport, recreation, culture, waste management, green energy, disaster mitigation, etc.

4.3 Territorial Formula Financing

The three northern territories do not receive equalization transfers, the Canada Health Transfer or the Canada Social Transfer. A different federal transfer program, called Territorial Formula Financing, is in place to guarantee that territorial governments have the capacity to provide public services of comparable quality as those provided by provincial governments. This transfer program is designed to reflect the higher costs of providing public services in northern territories where communities are often isolated and sparsely populated. The transfers received by each territorial government are determined by taking into account the capacities to raise revenues as well as measures of expenditure needs. These transfers are unconditional.

4.4 Provincial Transfers to Municipalities

Local governments rely heavily on transfers from provincial governments. Most are specific-purpose grants, usually intended to support municipal spending in transportation, recreation, culture and the environment. There are also provincial transfers to local school boards for the financing of primary and secondary education. School board expenditures are also partly financed with local property taxes although provincial transfers generally represent a much greater share of total expenditures. General-purpose grants usually account for a small share of municipal revenues. Importantly however, some of the general-purpose grants have an equalizing component, often meant to compensate for disparities in capacities to raise property tax revenues. The way that these equalization components are structured varies across provinces. Some take into account only disparities in fiscal capacities while other also consider expenditure needs. In all cases, however, given that general-purpose grants represent a small portion of municipal revenues, their equalizing effects are limited.

4.5 *Vertical Fiscal Gaps*

The extent of fiscal decentralization and vertical fiscal gaps are shown in Table 5. The federal government collected 40% of total own-source revenues of all government levels in 2019 while the shares of provinces/territories and local governments were approximately 47% and 13%, respectively. Decentralization is even more pronounced on the expenditure side. The direct expenditures (i.e. expenditures excluding transfers to other governments) of all subnational governments represented 73% of the total. The vertical fiscal gaps, measured by the share of transfers in total revenues, was equal to approximately 20% at the provincial/territorial level and 44% at the local level. Thus, local governments rely much more heavily on transfers from other governments than do provincial governments. In fact, compared to other federations, the share of federal transfers in subnational government revenues is relatively low.

Table 5 Fiscal decentralization and vertical fiscal gaps, 2019

	Federal	*Provincial/territorial*	*Local*
Own-source revenues	343,302	402,644	111,557
Transfers from other governments	1,131	98,549	87,775
Total revenues	344,433	501,193	199,332
Direct expenditures	234,592	436,364	193,347
Share of transfers in total revenues (%)		19.7	44.0

Note Numbers in first four rows are expressed in millions of current Canadian dollars
Source Finance Canada (2020a), *Fiscal Reference Tables*

Table 6 shows the share of major federal transfers in provincial government revenues for each province. There is high variation in the extent to which provinces rely on federal transfers, although much of that variation essentially reflects the distribution of equalization payments. Major federal transfers represented between 8 and 14% of provincial revenues in the five provinces that did not receive equalization payments in 2019–2020. In contrast, major transfers accounted for over 30% of revenues in Prince Edward Island, Nova Scotia and New Brunswick where equalization payments weigh most heavily in provincial revenues.

The Canada Health Transfer and the Canada Social Transfers accounted for about 74% of major federal transfers to provinces. Thus, specific-purpose transfers were approximately three times larger than general-purpose transfers. However, as mentioned earlier, the conditions associated with the CHT and the CST are broad and have very limited impact on the effective autonomy of provincial governments.

Table 6 Major federal transfers as percentages of provincial governments' revenues, 2019–2020

	Canada Health Transfer	*Canada Social Transfer*	*Equalization*	*All major federal transfers*
Newfoundland and Labrador	5.9	2.1	0.0	8.0
Prince Edward Island	7.8	2.8	19.5	30.1
Nova Scotia	9.5	3.4	18.3	31.2
New Brunswick	8.4	3.1	20.5	31.9
Quebec	7.8	2.8	11.2	21.7
Ontario	10.0	3.6	0.0	13.6
Manitoba	8.3	3.0	12.8	24.1
Saskatchewan	8.5	3.1	0.0	11.5
Alberta	10.1	3.7	0.0	13.8
British Columbia	9.3	3.4	0.0	12.7
All provinces	9.1	3.3	4.5	16.8

Source Finance Canada (2020a), *Fiscal Reference Tables*, and Finance Canada (2020b), *Federal Support to Provinces and Territories*

5 Macroeconomic Management

Both senior orders of government are involved, in different ways, in macroeconomic management. Business cycle stabilization is most actively conducted by the federal government. However, given the extent of fiscal decentralization, both in terms of taxation and expenditures, the fiscal decisions of provincial governments can potentially have significant effects on aggregate demand and on the business cycle. Despite this, there is no formal mechanism or fiscal rules in place to coordinate fiscal policies among governments. Following the 2008–2009 financial crisis, the federal government led the charge to stimulate the economy although most provincial governments also adopted expansionary fiscal policies albeit without formal coordination. The federal government adopted a fiscal stimulus package in 2009 in which additional infrastructure spending was a key element. Much of the added federal funds required matching expenses by the provinces and municipalities, so the federal measures indirectly induced, to some degree, increased stimulus expenditures by subnational governments. However, this was not the result of a concerted effort by the federal and provincial governments, and the matching requirements imposed on subnational governments have been the source of some tensions. Much of the fiscal policy measures in the early stages of the Covid-19 pandemic were also conducted by the federal government.

Fiscal policy, for the purpose of economic stabilization, is sometimes conducted more actively by provincial governments, especially when there are negative economic shocks that affect specific parts of the country. In such cases, economic stabilization is best achieved with province-specific fiscal policies that are more difficult to implement by the federal government.

Monetary policy is conducted by the Bank of Canada which is a federal crown corporation although it is, in practice, largely independent from the federal government. It generally operates in a framework of inflation targeting even though its official mandate gives it broad responsibilities to regulate credit and the national currency in order to promote national economic well-being, to mitigate business cycle fluctuations and to protect the external value of the Canadian dollar. The Bank of Canada responded fairly aggressively to the financial crisis of 2008–2009, complementing the expansionary fiscal policies that were put in place at the federal and provincial levels. The Bank's key interest rate was kept very low for an extended period and quantitative easing measures were used to further stimulate the economy. As in the United States, housing prices had increased significantly in the pre-crisis period, and continued to do so to some extent during the economic recovery, although price increases and market over-heating were very uneven across different provinces and metropolitan areas. Regional asymmetries in the evolution of the housing market during the recovery and in the period that followed complicated somewhat the conduct of monetary policy which inevitably establishes credit market conditions that apply in the country as a whole. The Bank of Canada also react swiftly and very aggressively when the Covid-19 pandemic started in Canada, initially by lowering its key interest rate near the effective lower bound.

The federal and provincial governments manage their public debts independently and with complete autonomy. There are no rules or restrictions governing debt accumulation at either government level. Of course, all governments are subject to credit ratings which affect their borrowing costs and influence decisions over debt management. There is no contemporary tradition of bail-out by the federal government for provincial governments facing budgetary difficulties so the latter have strong incentives to manage debt accumulation prudently.

In the 1990s, the federal government debt-to-GDP ratio was considerably higher than the average provincial debt-to-GDP ratio. However, as a result of a dramatic fiscal turnaround, the federal debt was lowered from close to 70% of GDP in the mid-1990s to below 30% of GDP just before the start of the 2008–2009 financial crisis. The expansionary federal fiscal policy that was implemented in response to the financial crisis and the recession that followed had a relatively limited impact on the federal debt. The federal debt-to-GDP ratio increased to approximately 34% by 2012–2013 before starting to decline again. In contrast, the provincial governments' debt-to-GDP ratios have increased since the mid-1990s in most of the non-oil producing provinces, including in the three most populous provinces, namely Ontario, Quebec and British Columbia. The immediate fiscal implications of the Covid-19 pandemic are much more important than those of the 2008–2009 financial crisis and will have a sizeable impact on debt-to-GDP ratios at both the federal and provincial levels.

Given the high degree of tax decentralization in the Canadian federation, tax policy harmonization is central for the efficiency of the internal economic union. The tax collection agreements between the federal and provincial governments greatly facilitate harmonization. For instance, the fact that provinces are precluded from discriminating against firms from other provinces in setting corporate tax policy is important for the efficiency of the common market. Moreover, the formula-apportionment system used to allocate corporate taxable income across provinces is important for mitigating incentives for tax competition among provincial governments and for tax-motivated profit-shifting by firms. This is critical for preserving the ability of governments to raise significant revenues from the corporate tax in the Canadian economic union in which there is high mobility of goods, investment and firms.

There are intergovernmental agreements intended to foster the good functioning of the internal common market. Of particular importance is the Canadian Free Trade Agreement (CFTA) that took effect in 2017 in replacement of the Agreement on Internal Trade adopted in the mid-1990s. The CFTA establishes rules that govern internal trade and investment and that are intended to prevent, or mitigate, frictions to the mobility of goods, services, labour and investment within the internal common market. For instance, it includes measures to promote regulatory harmonization across provinces and eliminate regulatory barriers to interprovincial trade. It promotes labour mobility and the establishment of a common labour market by encouraging the harmonization of occupational standards and credential recognition practices across provinces. It also establishes common practices in public procurement meant to level the playing field across provinces and promote broader competition for government contracts.

6 Response to the Covid-19 Pandemic

All three levels of government have been heavily involved in implementing response measures to the Covid-19 pandemic. While provincial governments are responsible for health care, all levels of governments have responsibilities with respect to public health. The Public Health Agency of Canada, which is a federal government agency, is responsible for preparing and responding to health emergencies, preventing and controlling infectious diseases and coordinating communications and responses during health crisis situations. The federal government is responsible for air transportation and border control and in the weeks that followed the start of the pandemic has implemented control measures in airports, closed the land border with the United States to non-essential travel and enacted the Quarantine Act requiring international travellers to self-isolate for 14 days after returning from abroad. Provinces have their chief medical officers and have all established their own public health response measures such as restrictions on gatherings, imposition of lockdowns, non-essential business and school closures, testing and tracing strategies, self-isolation rules, etc. This relatively decentralized approach has led to extensive variations across provinces in response measures and strategies. Arguably, this has been quite effective given that the spread of the virus and outbreaks have been uneven across provinces and have required province-specific reactions and response measures.

Both orders of government have also contributed to economic response measures although the federal government shouldered much of the effort. The federal government quickly implemented the Canada Emergency Response Benefit program to provide income support to workers, as well as loan, rent support and wage subsidy programs for businesses. It also provided income support through tax payment deferrals as well as income support for students, among other measures.

As a result of the pandemic, provinces have intensified pressure on the federal government to increase transfers for health care, both in the short run to help cover the immediate health care costs of the pandemic and on a more permanent basis. Before the pandemic, provinces had been demanding that the federal government increase the Canada Health Transfer to help them cope with the rapidly rising health costs associated with population aging. The pandemic has certainly made requests for higher CHT transfers more urgent, at least from the perspectives of provinces.

7 Challenges to Canadian Fiscal Federalism

Apart from immediate challenges raised by the Covid-19 pandemic, there are a number of other longer term challenges to fiscal federalism in Canada that call for reforms of fiscal arrangements, or for the adoption of new elements in the federal fiscal architecture, as well as additional cooperation among governments. Some of these issues are briefly outlined below.

Like many other countries, Canada is facing a demographic challenge. Population aging will continue to exert substantial pressure on public finances through both revenue and expenditure effects. A lower proportion of working-age individuals will lead to downward pressure on total employment and on government revenues. At the same time, the increase in the old-age dependency ratio will induce increased spending on health care, public drug programs, other social services and income-support programs including publicly funded pensions. In fact, according to Robson and Laurin (2015), age-sensitive expenditures are projected to increase from 13.0% of GDP to 15.6% of GDP between 2014 and 2035. Given the allocation of responsibilities between orders of government in Canada, these projected revenue and spending pressures could potentially be quite disruptive to fiscal balance across the federal and provincial governments.

Pressures from demographic changes on the finances of the federal government will be relatively limited, at least on the expenditure side. The Canada Pension Plan is the main federal program sensitive to population aging. However, given that the program is now largely funded, the impact of aging on the cost of pension benefits to the government will be relatively limited. On the other hand, most of the programs in which expenditures are highly sensitive to the old-age dependency rate are under provincial responsibility, including health care which represented 37% of total program spending by provincial/territorial governments in 2016 (Canadian Institute for Health Information, 2018).

Demographic trends will therefore require additional expenditure and revenue decentralization in the Canadian federation. Further revenue decentralization could be implemented by increasing federal transfers to provinces, by transferring tax room to provincial governments, or in other words, by decentralizing taxation, or by adopting revenue-sharing arrangements that could serve to increase provincial government revenues without further decentralizing taxation. The additional revenue decentralization required could be reduced by pre-funding some of the provincial public services that are highly sensitive to the old-age dependency rate, or by lowering provincial debt levels so as to create future fiscal room, although any efforts on those fronts will not eliminate altogether the need to decentralize revenues. Adapting to this pressure will be one of the key challenges to fiscal relations and the particular approach that will be used to achieve federal-provincial fiscal balance will potentially have profound effects on the efficiency and distributional properties of the Canadian tax system (Tremblay, 2012).

In the area of health care, there have been long-standing discussions to adopt a national public insurance program for prescription drugs, either as complement or as replacement to existing provincial programs.

Currently, the costs of drugs are supported by public insurances provided by provincial governments, employer-provided insurances, and out-of-pocket expenses incurred by individuals. However, provincial programs generally cover a limited range of prescription drugs and a considerable proportion of the population is not covered by employer-provided insurances. One recent proposal, supported by an advisory council established by the federal government, is to introduce a new national drug insurance program that would provide universal and harmonized coverage across provinces. This would be a publicly funded program that would cover the costs of a wide range of prescription drugs deemed medically necessary. According to that particular proposal, the program would be administered by a federal agency that would be responsible for setting the list of covered drugs and negotiating drug prices with pharmaceutical companies. The introduction of a single-payer system would potentially reduce the costs of prescription drugs, and the adoption of a nationally-set list of covered drugs would ensure some uniformity of coverage across provinces. Although the program could include some co-payments by individuals, it would increase the share of total costs supported by the public sector.

Given that health care is a provincial jurisdiction, provincial governments would need to agree to participate in this new program, and the establishment of the program would require a high level of cooperation among governments. One option that has been put forward would be to implement it through a new dedicated federal transfer to provinces that would cover at least the additional costs to provinces relative to their current programs. As with the establishment of public health care insurance in the 1950s and 1960s, the federal government would likely have to play a leadership role by offering a conditional, and financially attractive, transfer to induce provinces to participate. Nonetheless, as in other areas, provinces could also be given the option to opt-out of the program. Opting-out provisions, leading to asymmetric arrangements across provinces, have worked relatively well in the past, with respect to labour market programs for example, and have sometimes facilitated the establishment of new programs.

The contentious issue of carbon pricing has been at the forefront of federal-provincial relations in the last few years. To achieve the emission reduction target of the Paris Agreement on climate change, the federal government has committed, in 2016, to implementing a carbon-pricing system across the country, and has later adopted a plan under which a carbon tax is imposed in all provinces that do not have a carbon-pricing system. The federal carbon tax includes a consumer levy on fuel and a tax on large industrial emitters. It has now been imposed in four provinces, while the other six have implemented a carbon price, either through a carbon tax or a cap-and-trade system.[4] In order to be exempted from the federal carbon-pricing backstop, provincial systems must meet benchmarks specified by the federal government with respect to the level of emission coverage and the pricing level (Environment and Climate Change Canada, 2017).

While the system is so far succeeding at imposing a carbon price across the country, despite court challenges launched by some provincial governments, there will remain considerable dis-harmonization along various dimensions. Among the provinces that have their own carbon-pricing system, there are substantial variations in coverage of carbon sources as well as in pricing (Dobson et al., 2019). Moreover, while federal carbon tax revenues will be returned to households as tax rebates, that is not the case in some of the provinces that adopted their own carbon-pricing system. While the fact that revenues from the federally imposed carbon-pricing backstop are returned to citizens is arguably consistent with accountability principles (Snoddon, 2018), it does raise distributional issues given that revenues are not returned to citizens under some of the provincial carbon-pricing system. In any case, it is not clear that all the efficiency and equity benefits of a fully national system are obtained under the current approach.

Maintaining horizontal balance in the Canadian federation is always a challenge, although with the relatively low prices of oil and gas in the last few years, the issue has not been as salient as in the past. Nonetheless, any substantial increase in oil and gas prices in the future will surely bring back the question of horizontal balance at the forefront of federal-provincial fiscal relations and generate pressure to reform the equalization system. Many features of the system remain controversial. First, the treatment of natural resource revenues is a source of tension, partly because of the fundamental conflict between the provincial ownership of resources, as stipulated by the Constitution, and the constitutional mandate of equalization imposed on the federal government (Dahlby, 2014;

[4] The Alberta government has recently announced that it will abolish the provincial carbon tax which will presumably lead the federal government to eventually impose the federal backstop in that province.

Boadway et al., 2015). Second, some provinces, notably Ontario, have argued that the equalization obligation of the federal government cannot be properly met with an equalization system that does not take into account differences across provinces in expenditure needs or in the costs of providing public services. To address this issue, there have been proposals to include in the calculation of equalization entitlements measures of costs based on indicators of public sector wages, construction costs and percentage of the population living outside metropolitan areas, as well as measures of needs based on demographic and expenditure indicators (Gusen, 2012; Courchene, 2013).[5]

There are intense fiscal pressures on municipal governments arising from several different sources including increased urbanization, growing demand for locally provided services to citizens and businesses, as well as infrastructure needs. At the same time, local governments do not have access to a diversified set of tax bases. They rely largely on property taxes, user fees and transfers from other governments, mainly provincial governments. Moreover, many of the services that they provide must meet standards set by the provincial government, or are defined by provincially set mandates. Limited flexibility on both the revenue and expenditure sides of their budget makes it difficult for municipal governments to respond to changing circumstances and to address some of the challenges they face. Given the increasingly important role of municipal governments in promoting growth and competitiveness, especially through the provision of infrastructure, there is growing interest in providing more revenue autonomy to municipal governments, whether that is achieved by diversifying their tax bases or through revenue-sharing arrangements with other government levels.

References

Anderson, G. (2010), *Fiscal Federalism: A Comparative Introduction*, Oxford University Press.

Boadway, R. (2007), 'Canada', in *The Practice of Fiscal Federalism: Comparative Perspectives*, Anwar Shah (ed), Forum of Federations/McGill-Queen's University Press, Montreal.

[5] See Dahlby (2014) for a detailed analysis of proposals to include costs and needs indicators in the calculation of equalization payments.

Boadway, R. and P. Hobson (1993), *Intergovernmental Fiscal Relations in Canada*, Canadian Tax Paper no. 96, Canadian Tax Foundation, Toronto.

Boadway, R. and A. Shah (2009), *Fiscal Federalism: Principles and Practice of Multiorder Governance*, Cambridge University Press.

Boadway, R., S. Coulombe and J.F. Tremblay (2013), 'Canadian Policy Prescriptions for Dutch Disease', *IRPP Insight no. 3*, Institute for Research on Public Policy, Montréal.

Boadway, R., S. Coulombe and J.F. Tremblay (2015), 'The Dutch Disease and the Canadian Economy: Challenges for Policy-Makers', in *Thinking Outside the Box*, K. Banting, R. Chaykowski and S. Lehrer (eds), McGill-Queen's University Press, p. 31–65.

Canadian Institute for Health Information (2018), *National Health Expenditure Trends, 1975 to 2018*, Ottawa.

Courchene, T. (2013), *Surplus Recycling and the Canadian Federation*, Mowat Centre for Policy Innovation, School of Public Policy and Governance, University of Toronto.

Dahlby, B. (2014), 'Reforming Equalization: Balancing Efficiency, Entitlement and Ownership', *SPP Research Papers* 7:22, The School of Public Policy, University of Calgary.

Dobson, S., J. Winter and B. Boyd (2019), 'The Greenhouse Gas Emissions Coverage of Carbon Pricing Instruments for Canadian Provinces', *SPP Research Papers* 12:6, The School of Public Policy, University of Calgary.

Environment and Climate Change Canada (2017), *Technical Paper on the Federal Carbon Pricing Backstop*, Ottawa.

Finance Canada (2020a), *Fiscal Reference Tables*, Ottawa

Finance Canada (2020b), *Federal Support to Provinces and Territories*, Ottawa.

Gusen, P. (2012), *Expenditure Needs: Equalization's Other Half*, Mowat Centre for Policy Innovation, School of Public Policy and Governance, University of Toronto.

Robson, W. and A. Laurin (2015), 'Adaptability, Accountability and Sustainability: Intergovernmental Fiscal Arrangements in Canada', *Commentary no. 431*, C.D. Howe Institute, Toronto.

Snoddon, T. (2018), 'The Rocky Road to Canada-wide Carbon Pricing', *C.D. Howe Institute E-brief*, Toronto.

Tremblay, J. F. (2012), *Fiscal Problems, Taxation Solutions: Options for Reforming Canada's Tax and Transfer System*, Mowat Centre for Policy Innovation, School of Public Policy and Governance, University of Toronto.

Ethiopia

Sisay Regassa Senbeta and Yakob Bekele Hundie

1 Introduction

Ethiopia is one of the oldest countries and, unlike other African countries, was not colonized albeit the brief occupation by Italy from 1936 to 1941. The country is home to ancient civilization which is witnessed by obelisks and rock-hewn buildings, ruins of temples and other archeological findings that are well-known for their fascinating monuments, architectural artifacts, unique scripts and metal tools. Ethiopia is also the only country in Africa with its own indigenous written alphabet, the *Ge'ez*. It has its own calendar which is based on the old Alexandrian or Coptic calendar.

The country is endowed with plenty of historical, social, cultural, linguistic and religious diversities. It consists of more than 76 ethnocultural communities, which are constitutionally referred to as the "Nations, Nationalities and Peoples." According to *Ethnologue*, 88 languages exist

S. R. Senbeta (✉)
Addis Ababa University, Addis Ababa, Ethiopia
e-mail: sisayregassa@gmail.com

Y. B. Hundie
Forum of Federations, Addis Ababa, Addis Ababa, Ethiopia
e-mail: Yakob@forumfed.org

J.-F. Tremblay (ed.), *The Forum of Federations Handbook of Fiscal Federalism*, https://doi.org/10.1007/978-3-030-97258-5_4

in Ethiopia, of which 86 are living and 2 are extinct. The other dimension of diversity is the coexistence of different religions of significant population: Orthodox Christianity being the most numerous (43.5%) followed by Islam (33.9%) and Protestant Christianity (18.6%). Although the number of their followers are small, Catholicism (0.7%) and other traditional faiths (2.6%) are also practiced.

With an estimated population of 105 million as of 2018, Ethiopia is the second most populace country in Africa next to Nigeria (World Bank, 2019). Of these, the Oromo ethnic group accounts for 34.4%, the Amhara 27%, the Somali 6.2%, the Tigray 6.1%, the Sidama 4%, the Gurage 2.5%, the Welaita 2.3%, the Hadiya 1.7%, the Afar 1.7%, the Gamo 1.5%, the Gedeo 1.3%, the Silte 1.3%, the Kefficho 1.2% and others 8.8% (World Bank, 2019). Encompassing an area of 1.1 million Square Kilometers, it is geographically located in the north-eastern part of Africa, more exactly at 4 and 14 degrees north, 33 and 48 degrees east. It is a landlocked country bordering Sudan and South Sudan on the west, Eritrea on the north, Djibouti and Somalia on the east, and Kenya on the south.

2 Federalism in Ethiopia

Before the introduction of federal form of government in 1991, Ethiopia had been ruled by a tradition of an extremely centralized unitary system. The creation of the modern Ethiopian State was started by Emperor Tewodros II (1855–1868) in the 1850s and completed by Emperor Menelik II (1889–1913) through the conquest and incorporation of a large extent of territories and a wide range of ethnocultural groups of the southern, eastern and western parts of today's Ethiopia (Zewde, 2002; Markakis, 2018). This culminated in the creation of a strong centralized and oppressive new empire anchored on the assimilation and/or subordination of all Ethiopian cultural communities to one language (Amharic) and one religion (Orthodox Christianity) (Esheté, 2010; Gudina, 2007). Emperor Haile Sellassie (1930–1974) continued this process by pushing further the cultural hegemonizing and the centralization of the State to finally create a unitary Ethiopian state and establish monarchial absolutism. The *Dergue* regime (1974–1991), which came to power after a popular uprising that removed the monarchy in 1974, further sustained a centralized tyrannical Ethiopian state with entrenched centralization of administrative, political and economic powers.

Since the overthrow of the socialist government [*Dergue* regime] by the Ethiopian People's Revolutionary Democratic Front (EPRDF) in 1991, the country introduced a federal system of government. The main factor that brought about this change was the dissatisfaction of the various ethnic groups in the then existing system of government, some of whom were engaged in armed struggle for secession. Hence, the introduction of the federal form of government in 1991 was to avoid the disintegration of the country which implies that the federation in Ethiopia is the "holding together" federation. As per the 1995 constitution, the federation comprises of the Federal Government and the nine-member States[1] both of which have legislative, executive and judicial powers. Addis Ababa, the capital city of the Federal government, has been given a constitutional status of self-government. Dire Dawa, another self-governing Federal city which does not have a constitutional recognition, was also established under federal proclamation.[2]

The defining feature of the Ethiopian federal system is the right of ethnocultural communities (nations, nationalities and peoples) to self-determination. To begin with, the foundation of the federal constitutional dispensation, as clearly stated in its preamble, is the outcome of the consent of each ethnocultural community to form a shared economic and political community capable of ensuring a lasting peace, a dependable democratic order and rapid and equitable socio-economic development. This is nowhere reaffirmed other than in Article 8 of the constitution which pronounces nations, nationalities and peoples as the ultimate bearers of sovereignty. Article 39 further guarantees the unconditional right of "Nations, Nationalities and Peoples" to all aspect of self-determination. The constitution in article 39(5) defines a Nation, Nationality or People similarly to mean "a group of people who have or share a large measure of a common culture or similar custom, mutual intelligibility of language, belief in a common or related identities, a common psychological make-up, and who inhabit an identifiable, predominantly contiguous territory." But there are no clearly defined attributes that

[1] Article 47(1) of the Ethiopian Federal Constitution, Member States of the federation are Tigray, Afar, Amhara, Oromia, Somali, Benishangul Gumuz, Southern Nations, Nationalities and Peoples, Gambela and Harari.

[2] Initially, Dire Dawa was created under federal proclamation as a temporary solution to the claims made by the Oromia and Somale regional states over the city.

differentiate nations from nationalities and peoples or nationalities from the other two.

Accordingly, each nation or nationality has the right to use and develop its own language, to express and promote its culture and to preserve its history. It also has the right to establish its own self-administration within its territory, be it at local or regional level, and to be fairly and proportionately represented in state and federal governments. The scope of this right ranges from a mere preservation and exercise of cultural distinctiveness to a full measure of self-government and even unilateral secession to form an independent sovereign state. This suggests that not only the foundation but also the continuity of the Ethiopian state is at the mercy of each ethno-cultural community.

The country has experienced demand for statehood and even secession by different ethnic groups. For example, the people of Sidama have long since demanded statehood. It is, however, recently that they succeeded to create their own regional state through referendum. Following this, more than a dozen nationalities in the SNNP region have started demanding for statehood. Though there were ethno-national opposition political parties such as the Oromo Liberation Front (OLF) and the Ogaden National Liberation Front (ONLF) which pursued secession even prior to the establishment of the federation, there has hardly been any serious attempt to secede. In fact, the EPRDF has been against the exercise of the right of secession, and it has discouraged any demand of this sort both through persuasion and by the use of force.

3 The Structure of Government

There are two Houses at the Federal level: The House of Peoples Representatives (HoPR) and the House of Federation (HoF). The HoPR, which is composed of members representing the Ethiopian people as a whole elected for five-year terms in single-seat constituencies according to a first-past-the-post principle, is the highest authority of the federal government. It has powers to legislate in all matters that fall under federal jurisdiction. Currently, the HoPR has 547 members of which 22 seats are reserved for minorities. The maximum number of seats for elected representatives in the House of Peoples' Representatives is 550, of which at least 20 seats are reserved for representatives of minority Nationalities and Peoples. The FDRE Constitution does not define what "minority Nationalities and Peoples" mean. It was left to the HoF to define them.

In 1995, the House, with the recommendation from the National Electoral Board, defined minority nationalities as those nationalities or peoples that are too small in number to make up a constituency so as to have their own representatives in the House of Peoples Representatives (HoPR).

The HoF, a more or less non-legislative house represents the diverse ethnocultural communities,[3] is bestowed with important powers and functions pertaining to, among other things, self-determination of ethnic communities, inter-state disputes, the sharing of federal grants and proceeds from joint revenues among regional states and constitutional interpretation. The powers of the HoF in legislation are limited only to its participation in the constitutional amendment, determination of undesignated powers of taxation and initiation of laws on civil matters necessary to establish and sustain one economic community.

As per Article 73(2) of the constitution, government power is assumed by the political party or coalition of political parties that has the largest number of seats in the house of peoples' representatives. The executive is made up of the prime minister as the head of government and the council of ministers. Both are appointed by and accountable to the HoPRs, and they have collective responsibility for any decision they make together.[4] The President, who is elected in a joint session of both houses for a term of six years, only has ceremonial and symbolic powers.

Under the current Ethiopian federal system, subnational governments have four levels, i.e., State, Zonal, Woreda and Kebele governments. With the exception of the state of the Southern Nations, Nationalities and Peoples (SNNP) and a few States with more than one nationality, where they have elected cabinets, Zones do not have a legislative organ. In States with a strong majority nationality, Zones are decentralized arms of the regional government, being responsible for coordinating and monitoring the activities of Woredas.

The constitution makes only a passing reference to local governments, in that it does not specify their structures, status and powers. States, are empowered to establish their own administration "that best

[3] As per Article 61(2) of the Ethiopian Federal Constitution, each ethnocultural group is represented by at least one member, and one additional representative is guaranteed for each one million of its population.

[4] See Article 72 of the Federal constitution.

advances self-government".[5] In doing so, however, they are constitutionally required to devolve adequate powers to local governments so as to enable participatory governance. Article 39(3) of the constitution, in addition, provides each ethnocultural community the right to establish its own self-government.

In practice, states have established at most three levels of local government: Zones, Woredas and Kebeles. Woredas, arguably the most influential local government, are established under States' constitutions. The others are created through ordinary regional laws. In urban areas, city administrations are equivalent to Woredas.

Constitutionally, Ethiopia is the Federal Democratic Republic with a parliamentary form of government[6] in which the executive is accountable to the legislature. The system of government relies almost exclusively on representative democracy. There are only few elements of direct democracy whereby people make decisions through referendum. Only demands for self-government, statehood and secession by a "nation," "nationality" or "people" and settlement of border disputes between States need a referendum to come into effect. In practice, referendums were held few times. The one which is held in 2000 is to solve the question of identity of the *Silte* community. The settlement of Oromia–Somali and Oromia–SNNP border disputes also required a popular vote (Fiseha, 2012). The most recent one is the referendum that was held in 2019 to determine the statehood question by the People of Sidama that was a Zone in SNNP.

Electoral politics has remained contentious in Ethiopia. Although a series of elections have been held since 1995, none has been competitive except for the 2005 national and local elections. On the one hand, the ruling party has used the power of incumbency and its strong organizational capacity to repress the oppositions and control the results of elections (Lyons, 2010; Abbink, 2017). On the other hand, the opposition parties have not been viable enough to mobilize the people beyond the capital city and certain urban areas because of their limited resources and the intimidation of the ruling front. As a result, the EPRDF and its affiliates monopolized the politics of Ethiopia throughout the period closer to three decades of post-*Dergue* (Lyons, 2010).

[5] Articles 50(4) and 52(1) of the Ethiopian Federal Constitution.

[6] Articles 1 and 45 of the Ethiopian Federal Constitution.

Accountability of government is one of the fundamental principles of the Ethiopian constitution. Since government power can only be seized through periodic elections conducted every five years, the election is one of the mechanisms that ensure accountability. Public officials or elected representatives are held accountable if they fail in their public duties. Elected representatives can also be recalled if they lose the confidence of their electorates.[7] However, given the relative lack of electoral competition and the domination of electoral politics by a single party at all levels of government, election has not, in practice, played much role in promoting the accountability of governments.

The constitution also provides for an extensive list of fundamental rights and freedoms of citizens and groups, which impose limits on the power of the government. A Human Rights Commission and an ombudsman that are responsible for the HoPRs were established as per the constitution to ensure the protection of human rights and freedoms. Auditors-general have also been established to ensure the financial accountability of government at federal and state levels. These institutions have, however, been blamed by many to be weak and partisan, and they have fallen short of fulfilling their responsibilities.[8] The judiciary lacks independence and impartiality to protect human rights. Until recently, there has been no independent free press vibrant enough to reflect the voice of the people, and the operations of the civic society have been impaired with highly restrictive government laws and actions. Therefore, ensuring accountability has been a major challenge in Ethiopia (Makundu, 2018).

4 Social and Economic Development

Ethiopia has made significant progress to become one of the world's fastest growing economies in recent years. According to the World Bank (2019), the country has been growing at an average growth rate of 10.4% from 2004 to 2018. This led to significant reductions in the proportion of people living in extreme poverty from 71.7 to 27.3% in 2015. Income inequality, as measured by Gini coefficient of 39.1 in 2015, is among the

[7] Article 12 (1, 2 and 3) of the Federal Constitution.

[8] Goshu, Wondemagegn T. (2015) The Ethiopian [National] Human Rights Commission and Its Contribution to Constitutionalism. Ethiopian Constitutional Law Series 5 (2015).

lowest in the world. Despite robust economic progress, the country still remains one of the poorest nations in the world with a per capita GDP of $702 and a HDI of 0.463 in 2017, which is well below the average value of the Sub-Saharan Africa (0.537). Agriculture is the mainstay of the economy absorbing 66.02% of the total employment while contributing 31.1% of GDP. The service sector dominates the economy as its share in GDP stood at 36.5% while the contribution of industry to the GDP is slowly increasing to reach 27.3%.

Though Ethiopia has been one of the fastest growing economies for the last 10–15 years, there has been a low or lack of structural transformation of the economy. This slow or lack of structural transformation is compounded by a very slow demographic transition that impeded the nation from reaping the benefit of demographic dividend. As a result of lack of economic structural transformation and slow demographic transition, the number of jobs created every year has not been catching up with the new entrants into the labor force. Moreover, jobs created were not "quality jobs." This led to the national crisis of youth unemployment that has been threatening the socio-political stability of the country.

The government of Ethiopia has been pursuing what it refers to as Democratic Developmental State development ideology where the state plays crucial role in the economy. As a result, the state heavily intervenes in different sectors of the economy, particularly infrastructure and heavy industries. According to the Constitution, the ownership of all lands and natural resources is in the hands of the state. Despite the recent signals of privatization, postal service, telecommunication, electricity and aviation are monopolies of the state. The financial sector of the economy is dominated by government-owned financial institutions (banks and insurance). This has contributed to increased government spending, budget deficits and public debt from both domestic and foreign sources. Foreign investors are not allowed to involve in banking, insurance, microcredit and saving and broadcasting and mass media services.

The state-led policies have indeed contributed for the abovementioned socio-economic progress registered over the last few years. The progress, nevertheless, seems to reach its limit mirrored in the declining growth rate and the corresponding challenges of high unemployment, soaring inflation, foreign exchange shortage and increasing foreign debt burden. The distortions and inefficiencies resulting from excessive government interventions hampered the development of the private sector and hence the economy. Ethiopia is one of the low-income countries that have a relatively high public investment rate with the lowest estimated marginal returns. In contrary, its rate of private investment is relatively too low (World Bank, 2016).

5 Allocation of Expenditure Responsibilities

Ethiopia adopted a dual federal system in which most of the executive powers of each level of government coincide with its legislative powers. The Constitution assigns expenditure and regulatory responsibilities to the federal government and the regional states, leaving the residual powers with the latter. The division of powers set out in the constitution[9] favors the Federal government in legislation and policy-making. Consistent with the traditional theory of public finance, the Constitution of the FDRE puts the stabilization functions, authority concerning monetary and fiscal policies, under the federal government's sphere of influence. The federal government is also mandated with the formulation and implementation of policies for national social and economic development, strategies and plans. The responsibility to establish national standards and basic policy criteria for health, education and science and technology are also among the mandates of the federal government. States can also develop and implement policies, strategies and plans within their respective geographic jurisdictions given that they do not contradict with the general policy directions and standards set by the federal government.

Nevertheless, no regional policies or strategies have yet been devised and implemented. Rather, States have been implementing the policies and plans developed by the federal government. These policy documents and development plans cover areas of competence that are constitutionally assigned to the regional governments (Fiseha, 2005). The replication of federal policies at the regional levels is mainly due to the dominance of a single party, the EPRDF, which was a coalition of four ethnic/regional parties, i.e., the Oromo Democratic Party (ODP), the Amhara Democratic Party (ADP), the Southern Ethiopia Peoples Democratic Movement (SEPDM) and Tigray Peoples Liberation Front (TPLF). Since the adoption of the federal system in 1995, this coalition has controlled power at all levels. On the surface, the EPRDF looked like a

[9] See Articles 51, 52 and 55 of the Ethiopian Federal Constitution.

decentralized party. But practically, it functioned in a centralized manner with its *democratic centralism* as a principle of internal organization. As a result, central government hegemony in policy-making over the States has prevailed since the introduction of the federal system.

On a legislative sphere, States have constitutional power in areas of labor, commercial and penal codes, as well as civil laws except on matters that the HoF believes require uniform provisions.[10] While the power to legislate on land and natural resources is reserved for the federal government, the administration as per federal law is States' power.

The assignment of allocative functions basically follows the *subsidiarity* principle. Given the fact that residual powers reside in them, States are responsible for the provision of basic social services. The provision of primary education, health care and drinking water is administered by local governments. Local governments in urban areas have wider responsibilities, including such municipal functions as local roads, slaughter houses, recreational centers, fire protection, public libraries, street lighting, waste management, sewerage and urban land administration (Garcia and Rajkumar, 2008).

The federal government is entrusted only with those public services with a significant degree of non-excludability like national defense and foreign affairs. It provides services with significant economies of scale and that promote the consolidation of one economic community such as air, rail and water transport and major roads linking two or more States and postal and telecommunication services. Furthermore, the federal government also has a regulatory power over inter-state commerce, foreign exchange and money supply, which is crucial for the preservation of internal common market (Table 1).

The division of expenditure assignment lacks clarity as to the specific limits of the framework powers assigned to both levels. Moreover, there is significant overlaps, concurrency and sharing are observed in the division of powers. However, the mechanism of intergovernmental relations (IGRs) in Ethiopia does not have adequate constitutional foundation and is practically weak and poorly institutionalized. As a result, there is no effective mechanism to deal with these overlapping and concurrency issues. The relations tend to be dominated by the federal government and

[10] Article 55 sub 3, 4, 5 and 6 the Ethiopian Federal Constitution.

Table 1 Legislative and executive responsibilities of different levels of government

Powers/Responsibilities	*Legislation*	*Execution*
Foreign relations	Federal	Federal
Economic, social and development policy	Federal and State	Federal and State
Inter-state and foreign trade	Federal	Federal
Defense	Federal	Federal
Police and public security	Federal and State	Federal and State
Monetary and financial policy	Federal	Federal
Education and health	Federal	State
Land and natural resources	Federal	State
Water-bodies and rivers linking more than one state	Federal	Federal
Citizenship, immigration, refuge and asylum	Federal	Federal
Political parties and election	Federal	Federal
Air, rail, water and sea transport	Federal	Federal
National roads	Federal	Federal
Labor, commercial and penal laws	Federal	Federal and State
Civil law	Federal and State	Federal and State
Civil service	Federal and State	Federal and State
Patents and copyrights	Federal	Federal
Possession and bearing of arms	Federal	Federal
Residual powers	State	State

Source The Constitution of the FDRE

violate some of the most important principles of intergovernmental relations of equality, partnership and mutual consent. The hitherto endeavors made to strengthen intergovernmental relations are by far gloomy. The fact that most intergovernmental concerns and issues are dealt with through the party channel has undermined the need to institutionalize IGRs. The recent initiative on the development of IGRs law seems, however, to be a positive step in consolidating the system.

The Ethiopian constitution gives much emphasis to equity, equality and pluralism. These principles are reflected both in the political and economic realms, and they are embodied in the institutions of the federal system. Equality among individuals, groups including gender and cultural communities are guaranteed.[11] In addition to having equal rights with

[11] See the preamble and Articles 41(3 and 5) and 89(1, 2, 4 and 7) of the Federal Constitution.

men, women are constitutionally entitled to affirmative measures with the aim to rectify the inequality and discrimination they have suffered from. Two key examples of areas where such affirmative measures have been applied are education and public employment. In addition to getting special support when they join universities, women are required lower scores in nationally administered high school and university entrance exams. Though there is no imposed obligation on the private sector, the Federal Civil Service Proclamation No. 1064/2017 provides a preferential treatment for women candidates over male candidates in recruitment, promotion, transfer, redeployment, education and training (See article 48/2). The constitution also imposes an obligation on the government to provide special assistance to the disabled, elderly, children and those ethnocultural communities least advantaged in socio-economic development. The government at all levels is also constitutionally obliged to ensure that all Ethiopians have equal opportunity to and equitable benefit from the country's development.[12]

The constitution gives wider space for the government to play an active role in the socio-economic life of the people. In addition to the provision of basic public services such as education and health, governments at different levels are required to create employment opportunities, eliminate poverty in its different forms and promote economic growth.[13] Anchored on its socialist background, the policies of the ruling government also affirmed this constitutional provision of government involvement to the extent of determining the pace and direction of the country's development. Guided by the above values and principles, state policies and plans are geared towards agricultural development, poverty reduction and promotion of equitable basic services, all of which have objectives of ensuring equity. This has, indeed, hampered the development of the private sector. Recently, the government took a bold decision towards broadening the participation of the private sector. Apart from planning to privatize key state-owned enterprises, a Public–Private Partnership (PPP) Framework was provided to promote semi or purely private

[12] Article 89 of the Federal Constitution.

[13] See Articles 89(8) and 90(1) of the Federal Constitution.

solutions to the development of public infrastructures as an alternative to public provision.[14]

The excessive emphasis on equity at times brought tradeoffs with efficiency. For example, the unconditional nature of most of the federal transfers has promoted equity but only at the expense of efficiency in utilizing the funds. Since no strings have been attached to the transfers, there has not been accountability on the part of the receiving States in reducing infrastructural deficit and improving service delivery (Shah and Fesehatsion, 2015). Crucial services such as telecommunication and electricity have been provided by the federal government based on the principle of equal access sacrificing the effectiveness and competitiveness of the sectors.

There are a number of channels through which the federal government influences subnational expenditure decisions. Being the major and most powerful one, the party channel has been used to guarantee uniform policies and development plans across the levels of government. Complementary but equally important are the federal policy documents which cover areas which are purely the jurisdiction of subnational governments. Although they have not been as influential as the abovementioned two channels, certain specific-purpose federal transfers such as Millennium Development Goals/Sustainable Development Goal (MDG/SDG) grants have also been used to influence subnational policies and actions. The other channel is the now Ministry of Peace which was formerly known as the Ministry of Federal Affairs. This Ministry which grew out of the office for Regional Affairs within the Prime Minister's office, though mandated to bring the four emerging States on par with the others, had served to control these States until 2001. This might prove the existence of some degree of *de jure* asymmetry among subnational jurisdictions during the early years of the federal experiment though the constitution, as per Article 47(4), provides them with equal powers and rights.

The Ethiopian Constitution does provide a mechanism for addressing intergovernmental disputes. It is the House of the Federation, as the final interpreter of the constitution, which has the power to resolve interstate or Federal-State government disputes and misunderstandings. The legal

[14] A Proclamation to provide for the Public Private Partnership, Proclamation no 1076/2018, *Negatit Gazeta* 24th year, No. 28. Addis Ababa, February 22, 2018.

framework[15] provides a room for the conflicting parties to resolve their conflicts by themselves through peaceful means and discussion before the case is presented to the House for a final decision. Until now, intergovernmental dispute over constitutional division of powers is rare. The only case in this regard is the dispute between the federal government and the State of Oromia over the power to levy and collect tax on proceeds from the sale of property and proceeds from renting properties such as house, which was then solved through discussion with the help of the House.

6 Taxation Powers

The tax assignment in Ethiopia is largely in accordance with the economic principles of fiscal federalism and common practices of other federations. There are, however, marked differences in some respect. In comparison to other federations, the constitution gives much more detailed provisions regarding the division of power of taxation. It clearly specifies which layer of government has what tax powers. This helps a great deal in reducing potential intergovernmental disputes over tax powers.

The division of taxation powers is mainly structured according to the categories of taxpayers or particular things as sources of revenue; in that, the two levels divide tax sources rather than the tax bases. The only exceptions are custom duties over which the federal government has exclusive control and land-use fees, which is the sole domain of States. Generally, the constitution provides three categories of taxation powers: exclusive federal, exclusive state and concurrent taxation powers (Article 96, 97 and 98). Each level of government has legislative as well as administrative powers over sources exclusively allocated to it. Revenues derived from concurrent sources of taxation powers were to be levied and collected jointly by the two levels of government until the power to levy and administer the taxes was given to the Federal government through a constitutional amendment.

States levy and collect taxes from farmers, cooperatives, enterprises they own, employees of State and private companies, small-scale mining operators and State services. On the other hand, the Federal government has taxation powers over importers and exporters, employees of Federal

[15] Consolidation of the House of the Federation and the Definition of its Powers and Responsibilities Proclamation, Proclamation no. 251/2001, Article 24, *Negarit Gazeta*, 7th Year, No. 41, Addis Ababa, July 6, 2001.

and International Organizations, properties and enterprises owned by the Federal government, lotteries and other games of chance, air, rail and sea transport, federal services and monopolies. Corporations, enterprises owned jointly by the federal and State governments, and any gas, petroleum and large-scale mining operators are made to be concurrent revenue sources.

The lucrative sources of revenue are assigned to be either exclusive federal powers or concurrent. For instance, the revenue of the federal government from customs, taxes and charges on imports and exports, constitute about 34.3% of total federal revenue in 2016/17. The other major sources of federal revenue are profit, VAT and excise taxes on enterprises owned by federal government. The residual powers of taxation are not given to either of the two levels of government. Rather, taxes that are not designated should be determined by the two-thirds majority vote in a joint session of the House of the Federation and the House of Peoples' Representatives (Article 99) (Table 2).

The designation of levying power over Value Added Tax (VAT) to the Federal government reveals serious practical problems in the assignment of undesignated taxation powers. The name VAT does not appear in the constitutional division of powers of taxation. In substance, it is similar to sales tax which is designated to the federal government and States according to the categories of the taxpayers. This is also confirmed in the federal VAT proclamation, which considers VAT as a replacement of sales tax. Though the decision of the joint houses mentions nothing regarding administration and sharing revenues, the Federal government, by treating just like one other source of concurrent power, administers and shares the revenues to the States based on the formula determined by the HoF. It delegated the States to collect and utilize the proceeds of VAT collected from individual traders. Furthermore, the states quitted collecting sales tax from eligible individual traders since the introduction of VAT. These all suggest that, contrary to the understanding of the two houses at the time of their decision, the VAT and sales are practically taken as similar taxes (Lencho, 2012).

Though both the Federal government and States enjoy legislative as well as executive powers over revenue sources reserved to them, the legislative sphere has been held sway by the former. Not only the exclusive federal sources but also the concurrent ones fall under the federal legislative jurisdiction. At times, the legislative power of the federal government

Table 2 Tax assignment in Ethiopia

Tax types/Sources	*Legislation*	*Collection*	*Revenue sharing*
Custom	Federal	Federal	Federal
Payroll tax			
Employees of State and private enterprises	State	State and Local	State and Local
Employees of Federal Government and International Organizations	Federal	Federal	Federal
Income tax (corporate and personal)			
Private companies and Company Patent Rights	Federal	Federal	Federal and States
Bank Deposit Interest Earnings and Federal Companies	Federal	Federal	Federal
Small-scale Mining Operators, Individual Traders, State Companies, Private Properties and Individual Patent Rights	State	State	State
Royalties			
Large Scale Mining, Gas and Petroleum Operators	Federal	Federal	Federal, State and Local
Small scale Mining Operators	State	State and Local	State and Local
VAT and turnover			
Exports and Imports, Federal Enterprises	Federal	Federal	Federal
Companies	Federal	Federal	Federal and State
State Enterprises and Individual Traders	State	State and Local	State and Local
Excise			
Exports and Imports, Federal Enterprises	Federal	Federal	Federal
Companies	Federal	Federal	Federal and State
State Enterprises and Individual Traders	State	State and Local	State and Local
Fees and charges			
Federal Services	Federal	Federal	Federal
State Services and Land Use	State	State and Local	State and Local

Source The FDRE Constitution and Minutes of the Decisions of the Joint Sessions of the Two Houses even extends to the exclusive taxation powers of States. VAT and income tax proclamations are good examples in this regard.

In a similar fashion to the assignment of expenditure responsibilities, the division of taxation powers is limited only to the federal government and the regional states. The Federal constitution does not assign any taxing power to the local governments for their fiscal powers are left to be determined by the States. However, local governments are assigned almost no taxation powers in the constitutions of the States. The only power they have is to collect payroll tax, land-use fees and agricultural-income taxes on behalf of the States. However, they are not allowed to use the revenues they collected to finance their expenditure responsibilities until they get them back in the form of transfer from States. The case of urban local governments is to some extent different since these entities have several revenue sources, which include rents from and sales of municipal property, urban land-lease fees, charges and fees from municipal services and penalties (Aytenew and Tesfaye, 2012). In some big cities, these revenue sources cover up to 66% of the total expenditures of the local governments (Werner and Nguyen-Thanh, 2007).

From the discussion on the allocation of expenditure and tax powers to the local level, it can be evidently concluded that local governments have hardly had the authority and resources to effectively engage in democratic self-rule. They were to a large extent administrative organs over which regional authorities had a strong controlling power. The expenditure responsibilities of the local governments are limited mainly to the administration of States' social services. Despite the constitutional commitment to empower local governments, one can, therefore, argue that the practice of decentralization has failed to bring about genuine self-rule at a local level.

7 Intergovernmental Fiscal Transfer and Revenue Sharing

Ethiopia's fiscal federalism is characterized by a high degree of vertical as well as horizontal fiscal imbalances. This is in fact an inherent challenge faced in every federation. But the problem is much more severe in Ethiopia and is vividly seen in the intergovernmental fiscal relations between the federal government and the States. During the period 2012/13–2016/17, the share of the revenues collected by the States in the total national government revenue collection was 21% while their share in total national public expenditures was 44.04%. The ratio of the revenue collected by the States from their own revenue sources to total actual expenditure on average was only 23.81% over the same period. This shows that, on average, more than 76% of the expenditures of the States were covered by transfers from the federal government (Table 3).

There is a high level of heterogeneity among the States in Ethiopia in terms of population, geographical size, level of development, natural resource endowment etc. For example, the largest state both in terms of population and area is Oromia with a population of 36.5 million and 359.6 thousand square kilometers while the smallest one is Harari which has a population of 251 thousand and an area of 0.34 thousand square kilometers. In terms of the level of development, the four states of Afar, Benishangul Gumuz, Gambella and Somali are, relatively, less developed. As a result, the fiscal capacity of the States differs considerably. The per capita own revenue collected by the strongest state is more than 6 times that of the weakest. The States with the highest per capital own revenue are Dire Dawa City Administration and Harari, owing mainly to their urban nature. Tigray State, with a relatively small population size and better revenue collection effort, has been collecting relatively high per capita revenue. Those States that have large population size such as Oromia, Amhara and SNNP have low per capital revenue collection (Table 4).

Table 3 Intergovernmental budgetary relations (2012/13–2016/17)

Year	*National government revenue*		*National government expenditure*		*States own revenue as percentage of their expenditure*	
	States share	*Federal share*	*States share*	*Federal share*	*Excluding Addis Ababa*	*Including Addis Ababa*
2012/13	18.14	81.86	42.70	57.3	20.70	36.90
2013/14	20.34	79.66	44.66	55.34	21.68	39.78
2014/15	22.47	77.53	43.73	56.27	22.57	39.77
2015/16	22.1	77.9	43.12	56.88	24.48	42.85
2016/17	21.95	78.05	45.99	54.01	29.64	52.21
Average	**21.00**	**79.00**	**44.04**	**55.96**	**23.81**	**42.30**

Source MoFEC, Fiscal Policy Directorate

Table 4 Per capita revenue collection by states in Ethiopian Birr, 2016/17

Regions	*Tigray*	*Afar*	*Amhara*	*Oromia*	*Somali*	*BG*	*SNNP*	*Gambella*	*Dire Dawa*	*Harari*
PC revenue	895.3	372.3	423.3	320.8	394.4	556.3	356.3	850.7	1,943.4	2,005.6

Source MoFEC and CSA

Recognizing the inevitability of fiscal imbalances, the Constitution lays down legal basis for intergovernmental fiscal transfers. There are two fundamental provisions that are directly related to intergovernmental fiscal transfers. Article 94 states that the federal government may provide states with grants in the form of assistance or loan, so long as it does not deter the balanced development of States. The other provision is related to the concurrent powers of taxation. As stipulated in Article 98, there are certain revenue sources that are owned jointly by the two levels of government. The mechanism used to distribute both joint revenues and federal grants among the levels of government is determined by the House of Federation.

The constitution does not specify any principle, specific criteria or guiding procedure for the design of the grant. The HoF, therefore, seems to have complete freedom and flexibility in designing the grant scheme. For the last 25 years, the dominant transfer mechanism used to address both the vertical and horizontal imbalances has been the Federal General-Purpose Grant (FGPG). The FGPG is a formula-based equalization grant which aims at equalizing the fiscal capacities of States so that they are enabled to provide comparable level of public services to their electorates. The transfer system is strongly influenced by the experience of the Australian federation as it considers both expenditure needs and fiscal capacity of States.

The grant pool is solely determined by the federal government. Upon the recommendation of the Ministry of Finance, the Council of Ministers every year decides upon the total pool and presents it as part of the federal government budget to the House of the People's Representatives for approval. Over the period 1996/97–2018/19, the total pool for the FGPG nominally shows an increasing trend. The only exception is the year 1999/00 where, because of the Ethio-Eritrean war, the federal grant decreased significantly. As can be seen from Table 5, the total pool of

Table 5 FGPG as percentage of total federal government budget

Fiscal year	*2014/15*	*2015/16*	*2016/17*	*2017/18*	*2018/19*	*2019/2020*
FGPG (in '000,000 Et. Birr)	51,520.40	76,808.64	87,871.71	115,624.59	135,604.73	138,140.86
Total Federal Budget (in '000,000 Eth Birr)	178,565.91	223,397.82	274,373.20	320,803.60	354,481.67	386,954.97
% of Grant	**28.85**	**34.38**	**32.03**	**36.04**	**38.25**	**35.70**

Source MoFEC Data Base

FGPG has shown an increasing trend in nominal terms over the period 2014/15–2019/20, though the trend has been unstable when measured as a share of federal budget.

The FGPG formula is designed by the Secretariat of the HoF with technical support from external consultants, and it is approved by the HoF periodically. Once approved, the formula serves for three to five years. The existing grant formula was adopted by the HoF in 2017 to serve for three consecutive years (2017/18—2019/20). The formula uses a relative fiscal gap-filling approach to distribute the federal grant where the total pool is distributed based on the relative fiscal gap of States. The relative fiscal gap is measured as a ratio of fiscal gap of each state relative to the sum total of fiscal gap of all states. The formula is developed based on the estimation of relative fiscal gaps, which involves the estimation of the relative revenue capacities and expenditure needs of States. The representative tax system (RTS) and representative expenditure system (RES) were used to assess States' revenue capacities and expenditure needs. Fiscal gap calculations are used to determine relative fiscal gaps of the States to distribute the available pool of resources. The FGPG Formula places greater emphasis on equity as the primary concern in the system is to provide all Ethiopian nationals equal access to publicly funded social services as clearly stated in Article 41(3) of the constitution.

In addition to the general-purpose unconditional grant, the country has experiences of specific-purpose conditional transfers. One of such grants is the Millennium Development Goals (MDGs) specific-purpose grant (Legesse et al., 2016). Similar to the FGPG, this grant is allocated to all the nine regions and Dire Dawa City Administration since 2011. The transfer is made using the FGPG formula. The grant was earmarked for capital expenditures in six selected sectors, i.e., rural roads, water (drinking water and irrigation), health, education, agriculture and small and medium enterprise development. And it aimed at contributing to the achievement of Millennium Development Goals. The MDGs grant design exhibits six key features: its amount is discretionary; its spatial allocation is formula-driven; its usage is partially earmarked; it is monitored by the Federal government on a project by project basis; it is accompanied by a rigorous reporting and the key role is played by regions, not Woredas (Legesse et al., 2016). The evaluation by the World Bank confirms that it was a very successful program.

Starting from 2014/15, the MDGS grant was changed into Sustainable Development Goals (SDGs) grant and its amount is decreasing over time. Previously, the SDG grant was to finance projects in water, education, health, agricultural development and rural road sectors. Eventually, however, the States, more specifically the four relatively developed ones, are instructed to use the grant for the development of integrated agro-industry parks. During the past eight years (2012–2020), the FGPG and MDG/SDG grants have been the two most dominant transfers. The relative size of the latter on average was about 18.6% of the total transfer, excluding other specific-purpose transfers, while the remaining 81.4% of the total transfer came from the former.

In addition to the MDGs/SDGs grant, Ethiopia has been using other specific-purpose transfers. The major ones include the Road Fund, Productive Safety Net Program (PSNP), Urban Safety Net Program (USNP), General Education Quality Improvement Program (GEQIP) and Urban Local Government Development Program (ULGDP) (Desisa, 2014). Most of these programs allocate the grant using the FGPG formula. But few developed their own formula for the allocation. All the specific-purpose grants have been implemented without the knowledge and involvement of the House of Federation. Since the FGPG does not take the MDG and other specific-purpose transfers into consideration, there is a lack of integration among the different grant programs.

Shared revenue from joint tax sources is the other source of subnational finance. Sharing revenues from joint revenue sources is one of the salient characteristics of intergovernmental fiscal relations in Ethiopia. The House of Federation approved the first and only revenue sharing formula in 1997 and the decision to implement it was made in March 2003. All the revenues derived from such joint sources are allocated among the levels of government on a derivation basis (origin principle). Since the constitution (Art. 98) gives the power of concurrent taxation to the federal government and regional states, there is no reference to local governments as the formula considers the Federal government and States as the only sharing parties.

Recently, a revision is made both on the formula and the administrative mechanisms of joint revenues. In the revised system, an equalization element is introduced in the sharing of revenues from indirect taxes such as VAT and excise while the revenues from direct taxes are still to be allocated on a derivative basis. The share of States from such tax bases is now distributed among themselves using the FGPG formula. The share of States from such taxes is made to be increased from 30 to 50% of the total proceed. There is also an increase in the share of revenues from royalties from 40 to 50%. Local governments are also to share from the royalties derived from oil, petroleum and large-scale mining operations to compensate for any negative externalities. The main change brought about by this revision is, however, in making the system of concurrent revenue sharing more transparent, principles-based and simple (HoF, 2019) (Table 6).

Despite the revision, there are still serious concerns on the sharing of revenues derived from oil, petroleum and large-scale mining operations. In fact, currently, Ethiopia does not earn noticeable revenue from extraction of high-value natural resources relative to the size of the economy. The available data show that the share of this subsector is less than 1% of the GDP and is dominated by the export earnings from gold (which covers more than 60%) (Moore Stephens, 2018). However, the future of the nation in terms of natural resource revenues seems bright given the country's potential in this regard and the advances in exploration and extraction technologies.

The current and revised share of States from such revenues (50%), therefore, is so big to expose the country to different challenges. Since the tax bases for such revenues are unevenly distributed, favoring States in the allocation will definitely lead to fiscal inequities, and hence unbalanced development, among States. Due to the volatile nature of the revenues

Table 6 The existing joint revenue distribution formula

	Tax sources	*Types of tax*	*Share of federal government*	*Share of regional government*
1	Enterprises jointly owned by the federal and regional governments	a. Profit taxes	Share in capital	Share in capital
		b. Personal income tax from employees	50%	50%
		c. Sales tax (VAT), service and excise taxes	70%	30%
2	Private share companies (corporations)	a. Profit tax	50%	50%
		b. Sales tax (VAT), service and excise taxes	70%	30%
		c. Taxes from dividends due to shareholders	50%	50%
3	Large-scale mining and petroleum and gas operations	a. Profit tax	50%	50%
		b. Royalties	60%	40%

Source House of Federation (2019)

derived from these resources, high dependence on resource revenue will expose States to macroeconomic instability. What is more, the lack of absorption capacity of States will also cause substantial efficiency losses as a result of misspending.

Since woredas, with the exception of few urban areas, do not have any taxing powers, the major source of their budget has been State-local transfers, which cover about three-fourth of woredas' expenditures. States have been allocating about half of their budget to the local governments to ensure sustainable delivery of local public services. For example, for the period between 2011/12 and 2016/17, States on average transferred 44.5% of their budget to local governments. Most States use similar approaches to local fiscal transfers. The transfer is a general-purpose equalization transfer which aims at the financial capacities of local governments to provide comparable level of local public services.

The equalization formulae were developed largely on the basis of local expenditure needs. Only three states tried to assess the fiscal capacity of local governments. The expenditure needs of local government were assessed using average unit cost approach based upon historical expenditures. Though the States exerted much effort in designing the formulae using quantitative data and rigorous analysis, a number of drawbacks that are related to efficiency, equity and accountability were observed. The approach they used treats urban and rural woredas as well as large and small municipalities in the same way. The expenditure needs assessment did not comprehensively cover important local services. No transfer is available for capital expenditures while covering almost all recurrent expenditures. Since they did not provide any incentives for efficient and effective budget utilization, they failed to ensure results-based accountability.

8 Macroeconomic Management

The stabilization functions are mostly under federal control. This follows from the fact that the expenditure levels of regional states are dependent heavily on the grants from federal government and monetary policy is the mandate of the federal government. The federal government has complete authority over monetary policy. The National Bank of Ethiopia is entrusted with the power to develop and implement the country's monetary policy in a way that ensures price and exchange rate stability and healthy financial system. It is, therefore, in charge of printing money, setting the official interest rate, controlling the nation's entire money supply, managing the country's foreign exchange, gold reserves and government bonds and licensing and supervising banks, insurances and other financial institutions.

The National Bank of Ethiopia, being accountable to the Prime Minister, is not an independent institution. The independence of the central bank is also compromised due to the fact that appointments of its management and board of directors are made by the prime minister, without the approval of the parliament. As a result, the bank has been operating under the direct rule of the federal executive. The federal government's misguided monetary policies are, in part, blamed for the high and increasing rates of inflation that eroded the gains on poverty reduction.

In the monetary policy framework of the National Bank of Ethiopia and national economic plans, it is emphasized that the primary goal of monetary policy has been maintaining price and exchange rate stability in a way that creates a conducive macroeconomic environment for rapid and sustainable growth. The target is indicated to be maintaining inflation within a single digit and ensuring a stable exchange rate that encourages export growth. The direction has been to maintain the growth of broad money on a par with the growth of nominal GDP, to keep the interest rate paid on deposits at the minimum at equal or slightly higher than the annual rate of inflation (positive or zero real interest rate on deposits) and to hold an adequate level of foreign reserves (NPC, 2016: 14). However, the nominal rate paid on deposits is about half the inflation rate making the real interest rate on deposits negative for many years. This, in part, explains the poor saving mobilization in the country (PSI, 2019).

Since the largest proportion of the budgets of the States is dependent on the grant from the federal government, the role of the States in influencing the macroeconomic conditions of the country is practically negligible. This, as indicated earlier, is the consequence of centralizing trend of Ethiopia's fiscal federalism. Not only do the most important sources of revenue belong to the Federal government, but States' spending is also largely dependent on non-compulsory Federal transfers. The transfer pool is simply determined by the federal government, and there is no any legislative or regulatory rule guiding the determination of the total pool. Furthermore, the States' borrowing rights are limited to internal sources and are subject to preconditions set by the federal government. The federal government has provided, by law, the terms and conditions under which States can borrow. It is the Ministry of Finance that determines the amounts to be borrowed by individual States taking into account the national fiscal policy and macroeconomic stability. States are required to provide the Ministry with all the necessary information required.

In practice, there has not yet been significant divergence between federal and State tax laws. This may be due to the tax harmonization provision in the Federal Financial Administration Law which requires the Federal government and State to harmonize their tax policies and systems. The Ministry of Finance is responsible to lead, coordinate and ensure the tax harmonization. In fact, this does not have a constitutional basis so that it may not be binding upon regions if they adopt divergent tax policies which, in effect, adversely affect the macroeconomic stability. The other reason, which is more appealing, is the smooth relationship between the two levels which is primarily facilitated by the party channel.

The Federal government, at least at plan level, pursues a prudent fiscal policy primarily aimed at ensuring macroeconomic stability for sustainable economic growth through financing expenditures mainly from tax revenues and maintaining budget deficit below 3% of GDP to be financed without compromising macroeconomic stability. The objective of the fiscal policy extends beyond achieving macroeconomic targets of price stability and sustained growth to shaping the political economy of the country by supporting inclusive development and productive investments.

The framework for debt management is established through the fiscal policy and financial administration laws of the federal government. No bond can be issued without the authorization of the House of Peoples' Representatives and all loan agreements are required to be approved by the House of Peoples' Representatives. Each loan is issued in the country's *Negarit Gazeta,* the official federal government Gazette, to ensure transparency and accountability in debt management.

One area that can show macroeconomic instability is the overall fiscal operation of the government. During the last five years (2013/14–2017/18), the average annual gross domestic investment and saving have been 38.62% and 22.46% of GDP, respectively. This has led to a huge annual saving gap. The federal government has been using external and domestic borrowing to fill the resource gap. As a result, the country's debt has risen significantly. Ethiopia is now at high risk of debt distress. Government debt to GDP ratio, which had been 47.2% on average between 2007 and 2017, reached an all-time high of 61.8% in 2018 (IMF, 2019). As debt servicing obligations are posing very high risks, the government has decided to refrain from financing new projects with non-concessional debt in 2018/19. The growth of broad money has also remained strong registering 26.12 for the last decade (National Bank of Ethiopia, 2018). This has been one of the major reasons for soaring inflation which stood above a single-digit target at about 13% in 2018.

The level of public expenditure has also been significantly higher than domestic resource mobilization. For example, in 2016/17 government expenditure and revenue to GDP ratios were 18.2 and 14.9, respectively. This gave rise to an overall budget deficit of 3.3% of GDP which is against the fiscal rule of the government which set the fiscal deficit not to exceed 3% (IMF, 2019). The external trade is also characterized by large trade deficit owing to both poor performance of exports and continued high levels of imports. In 2018, Ethiopia exported $7.1 billion and imported

$19.2 billion, resulting in a negative trade balance of $12.2 billion (World Bank, 2019).

9 The Ethiopian Federal System and Response to Pandemics: Lessons from Coronavirus

Powers related to health and health-care matters are shared between the federal government and regions. The constitution in its article 51(2) clearly empowers the federal government to develop and implement national healthcare policy, strategy and plans. The Federal government is also entrusted with the power to set and implement national standards and basic policy criteria for public health (see Article 51 sub 3). Apart from following up and coordinating the implementation of health programs across the nation, the Federal government provides technical, material and financial support to States. Despite the constitutionality, the powers and functions of the federal government as specified by federal laws include establishment and administration of federal hospitals, control and supervision of the proper execution of food, medicine and health-care administration and regulatory functions, promotion and coordination of research activities and prevention and controlling of epidemic and communicable diseases and coordination of measures tackling the problem.[16]

On the other hand, States are mandated with the powers of formulating and executing their own health policies and strategies (Article 52[2c]). All health-related powers which are not given to the Federal Government are also reserved to the states as per Article 52(1). States are therefore mainly responsible for the provision of both preventive and curative health services. They have practically been very active in these areas.

Similarly, both levels of government are responsible for the public health emergency response (See Article 89(3) of the constitution). They have the duty to manage any kind of disaster and to provide appropriate support to those affected by the disaster. In times of epidemic or other

[16] See Proclamation No. 1097/2018, Definition of Powers and Duties of the Executive Organs of the Federal Democratic Republic of Ethiopia Proclamation, *Federal Negarit Gazeta*, 25th Year No. 8 (November 2018); and Regulation No. No. 301/2013 Ethiopian Public Health Institute Establishment Council of Ministers Regulation, *Federal Negarit Gazeta*, 20th Year No. 10 (January 2014).

kind of emergency such as the current Covid-19, the power of the federal government goes beyond what is mentioned above. The Federal Government, as per Article 94(2) of the constitution, has a spending power in the sense that it can provide States with emergency assistance and loans. It also has a constitutional power to declare State of Emergency (SoE) either nationally or in some parts of the country (See Articles 51(16), 77(10) and 93). In this regard, the federal government can take all necessary measures "to protect the country's peace and sovereignty, and to maintain public security, law and order." It can also suspend or limit basic human and democratic rights enshrined in the Constitution with the exception of changing the nomenclature of the State and restricting right of nationalities to cultural liberty, right to equality and freedom from inhuman treatment. According to the constitution, states are also allowed to declare SoE within their respective geographical jurisdiction.

What one can learn from the above division of powers is that powers on matters of health services fall under framework powers where the federal government are entrusted to formulate a nationwide framework policies and legislations, broad enough to leave adequate rooms for the States to develop and implement their own specific policies that fit their local circumstances. There is also a lack of clarity and specifics in the division of powers. There are a wide range of gray areas where it is impossible to make demarcations on the specific boundaries of each level's jurisdiction. The proper implementation of these powers, therefore, requires effective intergovernmental interactions, coordination and collaboration.

To the contrary, however, there have never been well-established processes and institutions to facilitate intergovernmental relations (IGRs) in the health sector. Coordination and collaboration among the levels of government using proper channels of IGRs have been rare and weak. This is what has been witnessed in the government's response against the Covid-19 pandemic. Since the outbreak, the government of Ethiopia at different levels took measures to prevent and contain its spread. At the federal level, a National Ministerial Committee (NMC) was established to mobilize coordinated response to Covid-19 and agreed on certain cautionary and preventive measures even before the confirmation of the first case in Ethiopia. Following the occurrence of cases in the country, the federal government resorted to more powerful actions such as closing schools and nightclubs, shutting all land borders, suspending flights to highly affected countries, instructing civil servants to work from home and university students to take their courses virtually and banning large gatherings including religious events. To prevent importation, all travelers entering Ethiopia are now required to spend 14 days in quarantine.

On the contrary, States' response, and of local governments, came very late. Initially, their effort was limited to creating awareness. They have later on started to take serious measures to the extent of banning inter- and intra-state movement of people, though the legal basis for the former action is questionable as inter-state travel seems to be the jurisdiction of the federal government. Tigray regional state went even further to declare state-wide SoE. Coffee houses, bars, nightclubs, large markets and billiard halls have been closed. Selected social activities such as a wedding have also been banned.

Though the hitherto response made by the federal government has been relatively robust there is a lack of effective coordination and cooperation among the levels of government. This can be evidenced by differences in the measures taken by the federal and state governments and the absence of States in the national committee. No IGR platform has been formed yet to coordinate the response against coronavirus. One single effort that can ever be mentioned in this regard is the discussion among federal and state communication heads and officers that was held at the office of the prime minister on how to effectively create public awareness about the pandemic.

Allocating about $150 million to finance activities aimed at tackling the pandemic, the federal government has been strengthening its surveillance, diagnostics and medical care capacity. In an effort to combat the outbreak at subnational level, it has provided States with medical supplies and equipment including testing kits. It has also been mobilizing additional funds from both internal and external sources. However, there has not yet been any special fiscal transfer planned or effected to the regions as part of the effort to fight the spread of the virus.

10 Concluding Remarks

By any standard, Ethiopia is a highly centralized federation. It is so both in design and practice. The division of powers greatly favors the federal government. It is, however, in practice that the federal government has grown so forcefully even to the extent of undermining the roles and status of the States and local governments. Ethiopia's experiment with ethnic federalism has not yet faced a more practical challenge. The major reason for this is the hitherto one-party political dominance across the nation.

The fact that the ruling coalition, the EPRDF, together with its satellite allies in some of the regions has seized power both at the federal and State level ever since the introduction of the federal system makes it difficult to fully put the federal dispensation into practice thereby judge its workability thereof. The party, with its organizing principle of democratic centralism, has ruled the country in an extremely centralized manner.

Currently, the ruling coalition is in deep crisis. The crisis started with friction over the distribution of power within the party and hence the state, after losing its center of gravity following the death of the late Prime Minister Meles Zewawi. The popular protest and uprising that had prevailed in States of Oromia and Amhara during the pre-reform period also exacerbated the internal fissures. The root cause of the protest was the long-standing grievances related with land, administrative boundaries, governance and the perceived inequity in opportunities and distribution of infrastructure.

The recent change in the leadership of EPRDF brought with it a massive wave of reforms with some relevance to fiscal federalism. Pertinent in this regard is the change in the inter-party power relations within the ruling coalition and the widening of the political space. The loosening of democratic centralism means member parties of the coalition and the States they ruled will become more assertive of their interests and autonomy. The weakening of the coalition as a result of the continuity of power struggle within the ruling party is already undermining the power of the center. The widening political space has also encouraged people to express their demands more freely than ever. Demands for statehood have already flourished in the ethnically diverse State of the Southern Nations, Nationalities and Peoples. Many pan-Ethiopian nationalist opposition parties are also pushing for constitutional amendments.

The increasing demand for statehood according to the provision in the constitution will have significant implications on the fiscal relationship among the different tiers of governments. Currently, regional states cover, on average, only about 20% of their expenditure from their own revenues. That is, on average about 80% of the expenditures of the regional states is covered by the grants from the federal government. More importantly, the largest proportion of the expenditure of the regional states is recurrent. The smaller regions barely cover their recurrent budgets and sometimes borrow from through the federal government to cover basic recurrent expenditures towards the end of the budget year. With the proliferation of statehood in different parts of the country, particularly in SNNP, will lead to many small states that cannot cover their expenditure on basic services. This, in turn, leads to the increasing development gap between the larger and smaller regions which fuels internal frictions.

These all indeed have direct implications on the intergovernmental power relations between the federal and State governments. The move towards a more open democratic space will most probably bring a more devolved federal arrangement against the previously centralized practice. It may end the dominance of the federal government. However, no one can be certain about the nature and extent of the change in the federal system. Only time will tell as to what will happen to the Ethiopian centralized fiscal federalism.

References

Abbink, J. 2017. "Paradoxes of electoral authoritarianism: the 2015 Ethiopian elections as hegemonic performance." *Journal of Contemporary African Studies*, Vol. 35, No. 3: 303–323.

Abehodie, W. and R. Krever. 2018. *Subnational Value Added Tax in Ethiopia and Implications for States' Fiscal Capacity*. Institute of Development Studies, Working Paper 75, Brighton.

Ayitenew, Z. and Y. Tesfaye. 2012. "The Constitutional Status of Local Government in Federal Systems: The Case of Ethiopia." *Africa Today*, Vol. 58, No. 4: 88–109.

Berhanu, B., Y. Seleshi and A. Melesse. 2014. "Surface Water and Groundwater Resources of Ethiopia: Potentials and Challenges of Water Resources Development." in Melesse, A. W., Abtew and S. Setegn (eds.), *Nile River Basin: Ecohydrological Challenges, Climate Change and Hydropolitics*, 97–119. Cham: Springer.

Desisa, D. F. 2014. *Conditional Grant Allocation and its Implementation in the Ethiopia Federal System: A Comparative Study of Afar, Amhara, Oromia and Somali Regional National States*. MA Thesis. Addis Ababa University, Ethiopia.

Eshete, A. 2010. "Keynote Addresses—Abuses and Uses of Cultural Diversity: African Past, Ethiopian Present" in A. Habtu (ed.), *Equality and Unity in Diversity for Development: 5th International Conference on Federalism Opening Plenary*, 35–47, Addis Ababa: Forum of Federations.

FDRE. 2010. Financial Administration Council of Ministers Regulation. "Regulation No. 190/2010." *Negarit Gazeta*, Year 16, No. 55 Addis Ababa, October 4, 2010.

FDRE. 2009b. Proclamation to Provide for the Financial Administration of the Federal Government of Ethiopia. "Proclamation No. 648/2009." *Negarit Gazeta*, Year 15, No 56, Addis Ababa, August 6.

FDRE. 2009a. Proclamation to Provide for the Registration and Regulation of Charities and Societies. "Proclamation no. 621/2009." *Negarit Gazeta*, Year 15, No. 25, Addis Ababa, February 14.

FDRE. 1995. The constitution of the Federal Democratic Republic of Ethiopia. "Proclamation No. 1/1995." *Negarit Gazeta*, Year 1, No 1, Addis Ababa, August 21.

FDRE. 2002. Value Added Tax Proclamation, "Proclamation No. 285." *Negarit Gazeta*, Year 8, No. 33, Addis Ababa, July 4.

Federal Democratic Republic of Ethiopia. 2016. *Growth and Transformation Plan II (GTP II) (2015/16–2019/20)*. Addis Ababa: National Planning Commission.

Fiseha, A. 2006. "Theory versus Practice in the Implementation of Ethiopia's Ethnic Federalism." in D. Turton (ed.), *Ethnic Federalism: The Ethiopian Experience in Comparative Perspective*, 131–164. Oxford: James Currey.

Fiseha, A. 2012. "Ethiopia's Experiment in Accommodating Diversity: 20 Years' Balance Sheet." *Regional and Federal Studies*, Vol. 22, No. 4: 435–473.

Fiseha, A. 2019. "Federalism, Development and the Changing Political Dynamics in Ethiopia." *International Journal of Constitutional law*, Vol. 17, No. 1: 151–176.

Fiseha, A. 2005. *Federalism and Accommodation of Diversity in Ethiopia: A Comparative Study*. Nijmegen: Wolf Legal.

Fritsch, E. 1999. "The Liturgical Year and the Lectionary of the Ethiopian Church." *Warszawskie Studia Teologiczne*, Vol. XII, No. 2: 71–116.

Fulea, D. 2014. *Conditional Grant Allocation and Its Implementation in the Ethiopia Federal System: A Comparative Study of Afar, Amhara, Oromia and Somali Regional National States*. MA Thesis, Addis Ababa University, Addis Ababa, Ethiopia.

Garcia, M. and A. Rajkumar. 2008. *Achieving Better Service Delivery through Decentralization in Ethiopia*. Washington DC: World Bank.

Goshu, W. 2015. "The Ethiopian [National] Human Rights Commission and its Contribution to Constitutionalism." *Ethiopian Constitutional Law Series*, Vol. VI.

Gudina, M. 2007 "Ethnicity, Democratisation and Decentralization in Ethiopia: The Case of Oromia." *Eastern Africa Social Science Research Review*, Vol. 23, No. 1: 81–106.

House of Federation. 2019. *Revision of the Concurrent Revenue Sharing Formula of Federal Democratic Republic of Ethiopia* . Unpublished, 2019.

House of Federation. 2017. *The Federal General-Purpose Grant Distribution Formula (2017/18–2019/20)*. Addis Ababa.

International Monetary Fund. 2018. "The Federal Democratic Republic of Ethiopia: Staff Report for the 2018 Article IV Consultation." *IMF Staff*

Country Reports, Vol. 18, No. 354, IMF, December 4, 2018. Accessed September 18, 2019.
International Monetary Fund. 2019. *General Government Gross Debt (as %age of GDP)*, [Time Series Data Set] Generated September 16.
Legesse, B. et al. 2016. *Ethiopia—Evaluation of MDGs Specific Purpose Grant to Regions*. Washington DC: World Bank.
Lencho, T. 2012. "The Ethiopian Tax System: Excesses and Gaps." *Michigan State International Law Review*, Vol. 20, No 2: 327–380.
Lyons, T. 2010. "Ethiopian Elections: Past and Future." *International Journal of Ethiopian Studies*, Vol. 5, No. 1: 107–121.
Makundu, R. and F. Rasmussen. 2018. *IMS Assessment Report–Ethiopia in Transition: Hope amid Challenges*. Copenhagen: International Media Support (IMS).
Markakis, J. 2018. *Ethiopia; Anatomy of a Traditional Polity*. 2nd Ed. Addis Ababa: Shama Books.
Ministry of Finance and Economic Development (MoFEC). 2018. *Fiscal Policy and Recent Development, No. 3*. Addis Ababa: MoFEC Publishing.
Ministry of Foreign Affairs of the Netherlands. 2019. "Climate Change Profile: Ethiopia." *Reliefweb*. April 2018, (accessed August 15, 2019.)
Munro-Hay, S. 1991. *Aksum: An African Civilization of Late Antiquity*. Edinburgh: Edinburgh University Press.
National Bank of Ethiopia (NBE). 2018. *Annual Report 2017/18*. Addis Ababa: NBE Publishing.
National Plan Commission (NPC) of the FDRE. 2016. *Growth and Transformation Plan II (GTP II) (2015/16–2019/20): Volume I: Main Text*, Addis Ababa: NPC Publishing.
Phillipson, D. 2012. *Foundations of an African Civilization. Aksum and the Northern Horn, 1000 BC–AD 1300*. Woodbridge: James Currey.
Policy Research Institute. 2019. *Saving Promotion and Mobilization in Ethiopia: Implications for Economic Growth (Amharic)*. FDRE, Addis Ababa.
Population Census Commission of the FDRE. 2008. *Summary and Statistical Report of the 2007 Population and Housing Census*. Addis Ababa: CSA Publishing.
Shah, A. and B. Fesehatsion. 2015. *Financing Subnational Governments in Ethiopia: Options to Enhance Fairness, Objectivity, Transparency and Simplicity of Federal and Regional Fiscal Transfers.*. Unpublished.
Stephens, M. 2018. *Third Report EEITI Report for the Year Ended 7th July, 2016*. Addis Ababa: Ethiopian Extractive Industries Transparency Initiative (EEITI).
The FDRE House of Peoples' Representatives. 1996. *Minutes of the 1st Joint Session of the House of Federation and the House of Peoples Representatives (Meskerem 26, 1996 E.C. in Amharic)*. Addis Ababa: Secretariat of the House of Peoples' Representatives' Archive.

Vaughan, S. 2006. "Response to Ethnic Federalism in Ethiopia's Southern Region." in D. Turton (ed.), *Ethnic Federalism: the Ethiopian Experience in Comparative Perspective*, 181–207. Oxford: James Currey.

Werner, J. and D. Nguyen-Thanh. 2007. *Municipal Infrastructure Delivery in Ethiopia: A Bottomless Pit or an Option to Reach the Millennium Development Goals?* Institute of Local Public Finance, Working Papers 01–2007. Langen.

World Bank, 2016. *Ethiopia's Great Run–The Growth Acceleration and How to Pace It*. Washington DC: World Bank.

World Bank, 2019. World Development Indicators. *Ethiopia, 1984–2018*. [Time Series Data File] Generated August July 29, 2019.

Zewde, B. 2002. *A History of Modern Ethiopia, 1855–1991*, 2nd ed. Addis Ababa: Addis Ababa University Press.

Fiscal Federalism in Germany

Yannick Bury and Lars P. Feld

From the year 2020 onwards, major constitutional changes have inverted former principles of German fiscal federalism and have led to further vertical fiscal imbalances. The latest reform of Germany's fiscal federalism strengthens the federal level in general and the executive branches

This article is an updated and supplemented version of Feld, L.P., and J. von Hagen. 2007. "Federal Republic of Germany." In A. Shah (ed.), *The Practice of Fiscal Federalism: Comparative Perspectives*. Montreal & Kingston/London/Ithaca: McGill-Queen's University Press. We thank Lars Other and Mustafa Yeter, both from the staff of the German Council of Economic Experts, for very valuable research assistance and comments.

Y. Bury · L. P. Feld (✉)
Walter Eucken Institute, Freiburg, Germany
e-mail: feld@eucken.de

Y. Bury
e-mail: yannick.bury@bunderstag.de

L. P. Feld
University of Freiburg, Freiburg, Germany

J.-F. Tremblay (ed.), *The Forum of Federations Handbook of Fiscal Federalism*, https://doi.org/10.1007/978-3-030-97258-5_5

at the federal and state (Laender) tiers of government in particular at the expense of the Laender and their parliaments, respectively. The autonomy of German Laender continues to decline, while their executives will keep an already substantial influence on federal policies.

From the early years of the German constitution (*Grundgesetz*), Germany has been characterized as a unitary federal state.[1] Even though there have been attempts by some Laender to obtain higher tax autonomy since, the majority of the Laender has favored comprehensive fiscal equalization to provide every Land with the financial resources to meet its legal obligations and related spending needs. As a result, the Laender have not returned to the tax autonomy they had in the pre-war Weimar constitution.[2] The Laender executives, however, have kept the influence on tax laws via the second chamber of parliament, the *Bundesrat*, an influence that had been ensured by the intervention of the allies. Under constitutional law, this legislative power on tax policy resulted from administrative responsibilities of the Laender rather than from actual tax setting competencies.[3]

On this constitutional basis, an increasing degree of cooperation and centralization in fiscal powers has evolved after 1949. After the federal level exerted a major influence in the fields of public housing and culture, which the Grundgesetz assigns exclusively to the Laender, the Laender demanded a fundamental reorganization of fiscal competencies.[4] This was followed by the Fiscal Reform Act of 1969, aiming at relocating powers between the Laender and the federal level. In addition to this reorganization of competencies, the Fiscal Reform Act also established a new fiscal equalization scheme between the Laender and thus effectively raised fiscal cooperation to an even higher level. These core characteristics of this fiscal equalization system remained unchanged until 2019.

After the reform act of 1969, several attempts to reform this system took place, some of them triggered by decisions of the Constitutional

[1] See Hesse, K. 1962. *Der unitarische Bundesstaat*. Karlsruhe: C.F. Müller.

[2] See Oeter, S. 1998. *Integration und Subsidiarität im deutschen Bundesstaatsrecht*. Tübingen: Mohr Siebeck.

[3] See Feld, L.P. and J. von Hagen. 2007. "Federal Republic of Germany." In A. Shah (eds.), *The Practice of Fiscal Federalism: Comparative Perspectives*. Montreal & Kingston/London/Ithaca: McGill-Queen's University Press.

[4] See Blankart, C.B. 2017. *Öffentliche Finanzen in der Demokratie*. Munich: Franz Vahlen.

Court. Two decisions in 1986 and 1992, e.g., resulted in bailouts of the Laender Bremen and Saarland.[5] After unification in 1990, the five East German states were integrated into the system in 1995. After another ruling by the Constitutional Court in 1999 and in the light of growing concerns about resulting disincentives of the system, a Commission for the Modernization of the Federal Order was created in 2003. It was supposed to be the starting point of a major revision of German federalism.

After the grand coalition, elected in 2005, re-entered the reform process of the federal system, a first reform step of Germany's fiscal federalism succeeded in 2006. The major achievement of the Reform Act of 2006 was a disentanglement of federal and Land responsibilities. As the assignment of constitutional tasks to the different levels of government is prerogative for the fiscal constitution, this disentanglement of tasks was key to reform Germany's *fiscal* federalism. Subsequently, the reform of federalism continued in a second step with a strengthening of subnational fiscal responsibility in 2009, as a debt brake for the Laender was introduced to limit their ability to compensate for the lack of tax autonomy through indebting themselves in order to finance political projects. While the expenditure side of fiscal federalism was thus reformed, there was almost no progress on the revenue side.

Instead of introducing more tax autonomy, the federal level and the Laender agreed on a major reform of Germany's fiscal federalism in 2017, which has the dimension of the Fiscal Reform Act of 1969 and has been criticized for fundamentally undermining Germany's (fiscal) federalism.[6] The reform act, which came into force in 2020, did not only largely rescind the disentanglements of the 2006 reform but also revokes essential parts of the 1969 Fiscal Reform Act and the basic principle that the Laender themselves are the signors of the equalization scheme and Germany's cooperative fiscal federalism.

In view of this development of fiscal federalism in Germany, this chapter provides an overview of the components of fiscal federalism in Germany. After providing a brief characterization of the country, we

[5] See Ruling of the Constitutional Court, "BVerfGE 86, 148—Finanzausgleich II ", 27.05.1992.

[6] See German Council of Economic Experts. 2017. *Towards a Forward-Looking Economic Policy: Annual Report 2017/2018*. Wiesbaden: Federal Statistical Office, https://www.sachverstaendigenrat-wirtschaft.de/jahresgutachten-2017-2018.html?&L=1.

discuss the division of fiscal powers, the possibilities for different levels of government to generate revenues, and the system of intergovernmental transfers. Besides describing the current situation, we discuss how the latest reform act will change these dimensions of fiscal federalism from 2020 onwards.

1 Overview of the Country

The Federal Republic of Germany is a representative parliamentary democracy with a population of 83.0 million in 2019 and an area of 375,050 square kilometers. In 2019, 10.9 million people, which corresponds to 12% of the population, were foreigners. With 1.48 million people, immigrants from Turkey make up the largest group of foreigners living in Germany, followed by 869,145 immigrants from Poland. In 2019, 1.68 million refugees were registered in Germany, which corresponds to 2% of the total population. Of these refugees, 53% were firstly registered in the years 2015 and 2016. With 698,950 persons, immigrants from Syria represent the largest part of the refugees and the third largest part of all immigrant groups.

The majority of the German population has a Christian religious background; however, most of them are not practicing; 23.6 million people are Roman Catholics and 21.9 million people are Protestants. There are 1.2 million people of Orthodox faith and 300,000 free church followers. About 4.7 million Muslims and 99,000 Jews live in Germany (Table 1).

The German constitution stipulates two layers of government that possess sovereignty. One is the state level, the *Laender*. The Laender in their entirety form the federal level, the *Bund*, which is the second tier of government. As the Laender constitute the federal level, their existence is guaranteed by the Grundgesetz.[7] The Grundgesetz allows for territorial changes of the Laender and of Germany with three important cases in German post-war history.[8] The first case was the creation of Baden-Wuerttemberg through a merger of the former Laender Baden, Württemberg-Baden, and Wuerttemberg-Hohenzollern. The second case

[7] See Grundgesetz, art. 20, abs. 1.

[8] There has also been the interesting case of Schaumburg-Lippe. Despite a majority in a referendum on January 19, 1975 aiming at a re-establishment of the Land of Schamburg-Lippe according to art. 29 of the Grundgesetz, the federal government rejected this territorial change.

Table 1 Basic political and geographic indicator

Official name:	*Bundesrepublik Deutschland (Federal Republic of Germany)*
Population (31 December 2019)	82,885,000
Area (square kilometres)	357,400
GDP per capita in US (2018)	45,578.57[a]
Constitution	1949, written
Orders of government	Representative democracy
Constitutional status of local government	Strong
Official language	German
Number and types of constituent units	Three levels of government: federal (*bund*), states (*länder*), and local (*gemeinden*)
Number of Laender	Before Reunification: 8 Laender and 2 City-States After Reunification: 16 Laender (5 new Laender) and 3 City-States (1 new City-State)
Population, area, and per capita GDP in US of the *largest* constituent unit	Northrhine-Westphalia—population (2018): 17,932,651, area: 34,112.31 sq. km., per captia GDP (2018) US $45,721.70[a]
Population, area, and per capita GDP in US of the *smallest* constituent unit	Bremen - population (2018): 682,986, area: 419.36 sq. km., per capita GDP (2017) US $56,720.6[a]

[a]Exchange rate: 1 EUR = 1.18 USD (ECB reference rate 2018)
Source: Federal Statistical Office (2020)

was Saarland's accession to the Federal Republic and the third case, of course, was unification.

The constitutional barriers for such changes in the territorial boundaries of the Laender are high, as only there the Grundgesetz stipulates mandatory and binding referenda in those Laender, which are involved in possible territorial changes, so that a merger requires the majority of the citizens in every Land involved.[9] In 1996, the planned merger of the Laender Berlin and Brandenburg failed, because only the majority of the citizens of Berlin, but not of the citizens of Brandenburg, voted for

[9] See Grundgesetz, art. 29.

the merger. The Grundgesetz confers severity on the sovereignty of the citizens of the Laender and thus of the Laender themselves.[10]

Before 1990, the Federal Republic of Germany consisted of eight Laender and the cities of Hamburg and Bremen, which hold the legal status of a Land. Unification in 1990 increased the number of Laender to 16, when five East German Laender and the city-state of Berlin entered the Federal Republic. The largest Land is North Rhine-Westphalia with a population of 17.9 million and an area of 34,083 square kilometers. The smallest Land is the city-state of Bremen with 568,006 inhabitants living on 325 square kilometers. Economically, the Laender show considerable differences. While Germany as a whole recorded an annual GDP per capita of 47,535 USD in 2018, Hamburg recorded a significantly higher figure of 76,208 USD, followed by 53,829 USD in Hesse, and 55,646 USD in Bavaria. The three Laender with the lowest GDP per capita are the East German Laender Mecklenburg-West Pomerania with 32,753 USD, Brandenburg with 33,776 USD, and Saxony-Anhalt with 33,001 USD.[11]

Local government does not enjoy the constitutional status of sovereignty. Instead, the municipalities are part of the Laender with their exact legal status determined by each Land's constitution. This leads to varying rights and obligations at the local level across the Laender. Nevertheless, the Grundgesetz protects local government. In particular, the Grundgesetz obliges the Laender to guarantee the principle of municipal self-administration, which means that local governments must be enabled to offer voluntary services in addition to mandatory services they have to provide as delegates of the Laender.[12] This constitutional guarantee obliges the Laender to endow their municipalities with sufficient funds to fulfill their mandatory tasks and to give them financial leeway to offer additional voluntary services.

The number of municipalities has declined considerably since the 1970s. The first wave of municipal mergers took place in the 1970s, during which the number of independent municipalities was reduced by

[10] See Feld, L.P. and J. von Hagen. 2007. "Federal Republic of Germany." In A. Shah (eds.), *The Practice of Fiscal Federalism: Comparative Perspectives*. Montreal & Kingston/London/Ithaca: McGill-Queen's University Press.

[11] GDP and population numbers taken from Federal Statistics Office. 2020.

[12] See Grundgesetz, art. 28 abs. 2.

64%.[13] The second wave coincided with unification, with the number of municipalities in East Germany falling by around 38%, mainly because of municipal mergers there. Since 1991, the number of municipalities has been further reduced by another 33%, resulting in 10.848 politically independent municipalities in 2019.

There are two major differences between German federalism and other, particularly older, federations.[14] First, most of the Laender were newly created and comprised after the Second World War, following the boundaries of the allied occupation zones instead of the historical German states and principalities. The only exceptions are Bavaria, Saxony, and the city-states Bremen and Hamburg. The second peculiarity of German federalism is that it mainly focuses on separating executive tasks rather than legislative competencies across different layers of government.[15] This special understanding of federalism assigns a particularly important role to the executive branches of government. The historical reason for this distinctive kind of federalism can be found in the way Germany was created in the nineteenth century.[16] As Germany emerged from numerous formerly sovereign principalities under Prussian hegemony, federalism was regarded as a mechanism to ensure the influence of the local princes on the newly created federal level. The aim was to decide jointly on a number of policy fields at the federal level and to leave implementation at the level of the principalities. To date, the Grundgesetz still lays down the principle that the Laender must execute (commonly set) federal law within their own responsibility, which leaves them with considerable executive leeway.

Additionally, the focus of German federalism on executive functions can be seen in the composition of the Bundesrat as the second chamber of parliament. Instead of consisting of elected state representatives, it is an

[13] See Fritz, B. and L.P. Feld. 2020. "Common Pool Effects and Local Public Debt in Amalgamated Municipalities." *Public Choice*, 183: 69–99 for more details and for an analysis of the effects of these mergers in the state of Baden-Wuerttemberg.

[14] See Feld, L.P. and J. von Hagen. 2007. "Federal Republic of Germany." In A. Shah (eds.), *The Practice of Fiscal Federalism: Comparative Perspectives*. Montreal & Kingston / London / Ithaca: McGill-Queen's University Press.

[15] See Renzsch, W. 2015. "Bundesstaatlicher Finanzausgleich: Fiskalischer Föderalismus oder funktionale Aufgabenteilung des Grundgesetzes? "In M. Junkernheinrich, S. Korioth, T. Lenk, H. Scheller and M. Woisin (eds.), *Jahrbuch für öffentliche Finanzen*. Berlin: Berliner Wissenschafts-Verlag.

[16] See Oeter, S. 1998. *Integration und Subsidiarität im deutschen Bundesstaatsrecht*. Tübingen: Mohr Siebeck.

assembly of the Laender's executives. Only cabinet members of the state government can be appointed as members of the Bundesrat.[17] Thus, the members of the Bundesrat are the Prime Ministers and senior ministers of the Laender. Note that it is the state cabinets that decide which cabinet members represent the Land in the Bundesrat, while the state parliaments play no role in the formal appointment process. Each member of the Bundesrat carries one vote. The number of members a Land is entitled to appoint is constitutionally set and should (non-proportionally) reflect the differences in the Laender's population. The members of the Bundesrat have to follow an imperative mandate of the state government they represent. Only if all delegates of one Land vote unanimously a Land's votes are counted. If no consensus can be reached within a state government, the respective Land has to abstain entirely from the conflicted vote. Besides the orderly members of the Bundesrat each line-minister of a Land represents their Land in the committees of the Bundesrat, no matter whether they are a member of the Bundesrat itself or not.

German politics is organized as a parliamentary democracy with proportional representation both on the federal and state levels. Federal and Laender executives are elected by their respective parliaments. Between elections, executives need the ongoing trust of the majority of their parliaments to govern. This offers a strong role to political parties. The role of the parliaments manifests itself also in the fact that there are no elements of direct democracy on the federal level and only very narrowly limited elements of direct democracy on the level of the Laender. The only exception to the parliamentary system is the local level as mayors are directly elected, such that they play a strong role on the local level against the local (militia) assemblies. Moreover, there are possibilities to hold referenda on local policy issues on the local level. However, on both, the state and the municipal level, decisions affecting public revenues are strictly excluded from direct democratic decision-making. Elections are held in a four-year term on the federal and in five-year terms on the Laender level. As electoral terms overlap, a year without any municipal, state, or federal election is the exception, which holds governments accountable to voters on an ongoing basis.

Given the strong role of political parties, representatives are heavily dependent on their party to pursue political careers. Candidates depend

[17] See Grundgesetz, art. 51 abs 1.

on their party to put them in a secure position on the party list or to nominate them in a constituency the party is likely to win. Thus, parties can discipline their representatives in parliament. The parties themselves are deeply rooted in German federalism.[18] Their structures follow the federal layers and it is usually the local and Laender party branches that decide on the composition of the party lists as well as the candidates in the constituencies. Talented politicians can make it from the local level directly to the federal level or via the state level to the federal level, but usually the Laender level plays a key role in interlinking all levels within the parties. Conversely, federal policymakers changing to state governments or becoming mayors of large cities is also common. This applies to both the legislative as well as the executive branches of government. A side effect of these recruitment mechanisms and the permeability across federal levels within parties is that politicians pursue a more cooperative than a competitively oriented path of federalism. However, this cooperative prevalence of federalism within parties usually collapses when conflicts of interest arise between the Laender and the federal level. In such cases, the political lines of conflict do usually not follow party lines, but rather the lines of the tiers of government across all parties. The most recent examples for this are the Federal Reform Acts of 2017 and 2019, in which representatives of the Laender across all parties opposed representatives of the federal level across all parties on the issue of state funding.

Since the Second World War, these lines of the German political system have led to stable governments across all levels of government, usually with two-party coalitions in parliament, led by one of the two main parties, CDU/CSU and SPD. Although parties are very influential, their strong role is challenged in recent times due to two factors. First, the fragmentation of the German party system has increased recently. While the vote shares of the two main parties have declined considerably, left- and right-wing parties have been able to establish themselves, making grand-coalitions or coalitions with more than two parties the rule, and turning formerly secure party lists as well as constituencies into more open races. Second, a strong civil society with an influential NGO landscape increasingly engages in political debate and questions the parties' role as dominant political actors.

[18] See Feld, L.P. and J. von Hagen. 2007. "Federal Republic of Germany." In A. Shah (eds.), *The Practice of Fiscal Federalism: Comparative Perspectives*. Montreal & Kingston/London/Ithaca: McGill-Queen's University Press.

While the separation of powers between the legislative and the executive is not very strong due to the parliamentary system, a strong and independent judiciary restricts representatives in parliaments and government. This is, on the one hand, due to the strong role of the constitutional court, which enjoys a high reputation among the population. On the other hand, Germany's civil law system, especially its distinct constitutional and administrative law, effectively restricts policymakers. A second restriction is provided by the federal system and the formation of the Bundesrat as a representation of the Laender governments. Since the Bundesrat has to approve most of the federal lawmaking and majority conflicts often arise in the Bundestag and the Bundesrat with the parties in opposition in the Bundestag holding the majority in the Bundesrat, i.e., a form of divided government, pronounced checks and balances are provided via the Laender governments.

2 The Division of Fiscal Powers

In light of the functional nature of German federalism, spending responsibilities for each level of government follow the assignment of tasks at these levels.[19] Basically, the Laender are responsible for all fields of politics as long as the Grundgesetz does not explicitly assign a specific responsibility to the federal level.[20] Conversely, this means that the Grundgesetz conclusively defines the fields for which the federal level is exclusively responsible, while everything else lies in the responsibility of the Laender.[21] By these means, the constitution explicitly assigns competencies to the various layers of government.

Besides this explicit assignment, there is an implicit assignment of competencies[22] occurring through concurrent legislation of the federal level and the Laender. The Grundgesetz defines policy areas in which legislative power is assigned to the Laender and to the federal level.[23]

[19] See Grundgesetz art. 104a abs. 1.

[20] See Grundgesetz art. 70 abs. 1.

[21] See Grundgesetz art. 73.

[22] See Feld, L.P. and J. von Hagen. 2007. "Federal Republic of Germany." In A. Shah (eds.), *The Practice of Fiscal Federalism: Comparative Perspectives*. Montreal & Kingston/London/Ithaca: McGill-Queen's University Press.

[23] See Grundgesetz art. 74.

If both layers use their legislative powers in these policy areas, federal legislation is superior to legislation by the Laender. The degree to which the federal level uses its legislative powers then implicitly determines the remaining powers of the Laender.

Throughout the Reform Act of 2006 and the associated disentanglement of competencies, the fields of concurrent legislation were reduced. The most important, formerly concurrent, fields in which the Federal Level attained exclusive legislative powers were a defense against terrorism, legislation on citizens' registration as well as legislation on the usage and security of nuclear energy. The Laender attained exclusive legislative competencies in the fields of salaries and pensions of local civil servants, shop-closing times, and assembly rights. Moreover, the Reform Act of 2006 made legislation by the Laender superior to federal legislation in specific areas of concurrent legislation.[24] The most important areas in which legislation of the Laender now outweighs that of the Federal Level are environmental protection, legislation on hunting and fishing, as well as on university admissions. Table 2 provides a list of the disentanglement of formerly concurrent legislation throughout the Reform Act of 2006. Although the reform generally strengthened the legislative role of the Laender against the Federal Level, the general superiority of federal legislation against Laender legislation has remained.[25]

Generally, the political fields explicitly and exclusively assigned to the federal level are foreign affairs and defense policy, immigration and border control, citizenship, aviation, railways, highways and large parts of traffic regulation, postal services, and communication. In addition, the federal level is solely responsible for payments and pensions of public servants employed at the federal level. In all of these fields, the Laender are not involved in federal decision-making via the Bundesrat. Other competencies at the federal level are the unity of law, labor market regulations, social security including healthcare, research policy, and parts of environmental policy, in particular nuclear safety. In these fields, the Laender executives are involved in decision-making through the Bundesrat.

In principle, the Laender are responsible for all remaining fields of policy. However, due to a strong emphasis on equivalent living conditions in connection with skepticism towards competition among states, the only

[24] See Grundgesetz art. 72 abs. 3; art. 84 abs. 1.

[25] See Grundgesetz art. 72 abs. 1.

Table 2 Rearrangement of (former concurring) legislative competencies 2006

Area of Government	*Competency before 2006*	*Competency after 2006*
Legislation on citizen's registration and ID	Concurring	Federal Level
Defense against terrorism	Concurring	Federal Level
Legislation on arms and explosives	Concurring	Federal Level
Legislation on the usage and security of nuclear energy	Concurring	Federal Level
Protection of cultural goods against outflux to foreign countries	Concurring	Federal Level
Support for veterans	Concurring	Federal Level
Legislation on tenure, salaries, and pensions of local civil servants and judges	Concurring	Land
Correction and correction facilities	Concurring	Land
Social housing	Concurring	Land
Shop-closing times	Concurring	Land
Right of assembly	Concurring	Land
Legislation on restaurants and pubs	Concurring	Land
Legislation on general provisions for universities	Concurring	Land
Legislation on general provisions for the press	Concurring	Land
Legislation on gambling	Concurring	Land
Legislation on retirement-homes	Concurring	Land
Legislation on land consolidations	Concurring	Land
Noise abatement (except of noise from traffic)	Concurring	Land
Legislation on hunting and fishing	Concurring	Concurring (Land legislation superior)
Environmental protection	Concurring	Concurring (Land legislation superior
General legislation on regional development	Concurring	Concurring (Land legislation superior
General legislation ond water supply	Concurring	Concurring (Land legislation superior
University admission	Concurring	Concurring (Land legislation superior

Source Report of the Scientific Service of the German Bundestag. 2009. Auswirkungen der Föderalismusreform I relevant fields of policy that remain at the Laender level are education, police services, and, to a lesser extent, regional planning and hospital supply. Moreover, since the Reform Act of 2006, salaries and pensions of state public servants fall into the exclusive responsibility of the Laender. This is of particular importance as 76% of all public servants are employed by the Laender (and 11% by the municipalities).[26] This number is an indicator of another important role of the Laender. The Laender provide public administration, which does not necessarily give them legislative but ample administrative powers. Only the federal employment agency and defense are provided by the federal level. With the Reform Act of 2017, however, the federal level assumes additional administrative competencies on the legislative design of online-administrative services for all levels of government.[27]

Although the Reform Act of 2006 strengthened the regulatory powers of the Laender, the Laender deliberately coordinate themselves in almost all fields in which they possess autonomy. At regular meetings of the state ministers, the Laender mostly agree to adhere to common standards. These standards exert similar effects as legislation at the federal level. Therefore, even in those fields in which the Laender could act autonomously, they mostly decide to act uniformly.[28] The most prominent examples are the regular conferences of the state ministers for education and the interior, the two main areas of state autonomy.

Deviating from the principle that funding responsibilities follow the assignment of tasks, the Grundgesetz defines regional economic promotion, agricultural development, and coastal protection as shared tasks of the federal level and the Laender.[29] Both layers of government are generally obliged to provide fifty percent of economic promotion funding. For agricultural development and coastal protection, the federal level has to provide *at least* fifty percent.[30] Until the Reform Act of 2006, the construction of university buildings, research promotion, educational

[26] See Federal Statistical Office. "Personal des öffentlichen Dienstes " Series 14/6.

[27] See Federal Ministry of Finance. 2017. "Die Neuordnung der Bund-Länder-Finanzbeziehungen" *Monthly Report of the Federal Ministry of Finance*, 8. Berlin.

[28] See Zimmermann, H. 2018. "Deutschland—auf dem Weg zum unitarischen Bundesstaat?" In M. Junkernheinrich, S. Korioth, T. Lenk, H. Scheller and M. Woisin (eds.), *Jahrbuch für öffentliche Finanzen*, 2018–1. Berlin: Berliner WissenschaftsVerlag.

[29] See Grundgesetz art. 91a abs.1.

[30] See Grundgesetz art. 91a abs. 3.

planning, local public transport, and public housing have been shared tasks, too. With the Reform Act of 2006, these fields have been assigned exclusively to the Laender. In order to compensate for the increased financial obligations of the Laender following the assumption of exclusive responsibility for these areas, the federal level granted so-called disentanglement aid for the period from 2009 to 2019. These transfers are de jure earmarked. However, there is no monitoring as to whether the Laender have actually used these funds for the newly assigned competencies.

Besides the constitutionally set shared tasks and financial interlinkages that result from former shared tasks, there are three other areas in which fiscal powers are interwoven across federal levels. First, the federal level provides grants for large investment projects that are carried out by the state or municipal level.[31] In cases where municipalities are the beneficiaries, grants are allocated and administratively executed by the state administrations. During the last years, these grants have been widely extended. With the Federal Reform Act of 2017, federal grants for the subsidization of school infrastructure expenditure of financially weak municipalities were established.[32] In 2019, the federal level and the Laender agreed on additional constitutional changes that establish federal grants to the Laender to support Laender and municipalities in funding digital school equipment and to financially assist the Laender in providing public housing.[33] These latest reforms not only invert some of the disentanglements of the Reform Act of 2006. For the first time, the federal level assumes funding responsibility for educational spending, thus creating a new interweaving in a policy area that used to be the exclusive responsibility of the Laender.

Second, federal legislation often influences sub-federal spending. A recent example is federal legislation that established legal entitlements for childcare. While legislation is passed on to the federal level, the Laender and municipalities must provide childcare capacities locally. Third, the Laender often administers federal tasks without receiving financial compensation from the federal level. This was the case with highway construction, which fell into the responsibility of the federal level but was carried out administratively by the Laender. The latter changed in 2020,

[31] See Grundgesetz art. 104b.

[32] See Grundgesetz art. 104c.

[33] See Grundgesetz art. 104d.

when a newly established federal highway agency became responsible not only for construction but also for the administration of highways.

All of this indicates a strong influence of the federal level on state and local policies and thus on state and local fiscal decisions. The flipside is a high degree of participation by the Laender in federal decision-making processes. Every time a federal law affects the administrative competencies of the Laender or concerns the Laender or municipalities financially, the approval of the Bundesrat is required. This provides the Laender with a strong position to counterbalance the federal level, especially when the Laender act jointly. This leads to a situation where on the one hand the Laender are strongly bound by federal legislation, but on the other hand, the federal level cannot decide much without the consent of the majority of the Laender executives.[34]

As local governments are part of the Laender, their concrete responsibilities differ across states and depend on specific regulations in the states' own constitutions. In all states, municipalities are responsible for services of general interest such as sewerage, waste disposal, school buildings, urban construction, childcare services, or sports and recreation. Moreover, municipalities are free to provide additional public services on their own as long as they do not violate state or federal legislation. Besides these competencies, municipalities take on administrative tasks on behalf of the states or the federal government. The most important is the registration of citizens and permits for buildings and social services. Thus, there is a high level of administrative vertical integration across all layers of government, which is why Germany is referred to as a typical example of executive federalism.[35]

Table 3 shows the differences in legislative and executive responsibilities of the German federal system. We include the EU to indicate the responsibilities that the national level has delegated to the EU. It becomes

[34] See Feld, L.P. and J. von Hagen. 2007. "Federal Republic of Germany." In A. Shah (eds.), *The Practice of Fiscal Federalism: Comparative Perspectives*. Montreal & Kingston / London / Ithaca: McGill-Queen's University Press.

[35] See Zimmermann, H. 2018. "Deutschland—auf dem Weg zum unitarischen Bundesstaat?" In M. Junkernheinrich, S. Korioth, T. Lenk, H. Scheller and M. Woisin (eds.), *Jahrbuch fur offentliche Finanzen*, 2018–1. Berlin: Berliner Wissenschafts-Verlag.; Renzsch, W. 2015. "Bundesstaatlicher Finanzausgleich: Fiskalischer Föderalismus oder funktionale Aufgabenteilung des Grundgesetzes?" In M. Junkernheinrich, S. Korioth, T. Lenk, H. Scheller and M. Woisin (eds.), *Jahrbuch für öffentliche Finanzen*. Berlin: Berliner Wissenschafts-Verlag.

Table 3 Legislative responsibility and actual provision of services by different spheres of government

Legislative responsibility (de jure)	*Public service*	*Executive responsibility*
Federal/land/local		Federal/land/local
EU	Monetary policy	EU
EU	Customs	EU
Federal	Defense	Federal
Federal	Foreign affairs	Federal
Federal	Citizenship	Federal
Federal	Customs	Federal
Federal	Rail and air transport	Federal
Federal	Post and telecommunication	Federal
Federal	Social security	Federal/Land
Federal	Health including health insurance and local health facilities	Federal/Land/Local
Federal	Social assistance (supplementary welfare)	Federal/Land/Local
Federal	Waste disposal	Local
Federal/land joint task	Regional economic policy	Land
Federal/land joint task	Coastline preservation	Land
Federal/land joint task	Agricultural promotion	Land
Federal/land	Digital school equipment	Federal/Land/Local
Federal/land	Environmental protection	Land
Federal/land	Water supply	Local
Federal/land	Sewerage	Local
Land	Law and order	Land
Land	Culture	Land
Land	Schools and education	Land
Land	Universities	Land
Local	Local roads	Local
Local	Sports and recreation	Local
Local	School construction	Local
Local	Public housing	Local

Source Authors' collection on the basis of legal documents

obvious how responsibilities are shared, especially in the execution of public services. This task sharing across layers creates a high opacity for citizens as to which of the three layers of government is de facto responsible for which part of a particular public service. While the Reform Act of 2006 disentangled some of these legislative and executive competencies, the Reform Acts of 2017 and 2019 have rolled back some of these increases in responsibility and transparency, creating a new interweaving especially in the areas of school construction, school equipment, and public housing.

Since the allocation of tasks is prerogative for the spending responsibilities, the spending shares of the different governmental tasks are correspondingly interwoven. This is depicted in Table 4. Defense is the only government function that falls into the exclusive fiscal responsibility of a single (the federal) tier of government, while Local Public Services I is the only category in which the federal level has no spending obligations. On the contrary, apart from defense spending, universities are the

Table 4 Direct expenditures by function and sphere of government

Function	*Federal*	*Land*	*Local*	*All*
Defence	100%	0%	0%	100%
Debt servicing[c]	58%	35%	7%	100%
General administration	14%	27%	59%	100%
Law and order	13%	57%	30%	100%
Schools	0%	81%	19%	100%
Universities	13%	87%	0%	100%
Promotion of pupils, students	37%	35%	28%	100%
Other education	30%	47%	23%	100%
Science and research	74%	23%	3%	96%
Social security	65%	12%	23%	99%
Health, environment, sports, and recreation	9%	40%	51%	100%
Housing, urban development, regional planning	17%	32%	51%	100%
Local public services I[a]	0%	3%	97%	100%
Subsidies	33%	53%	14%	100%
Traffic and communication	45%	20%	35%	100%
Public enterprises	63%	11%	26%	100%
Total	**47%**	**36%**	**17%**	**100%**
Local public services II[b]	5%	60%	35%	100%

Source: Federal Statistics Office, Fachserie 14/Reihe 3.1, Finanzen und Steuern, 2020

[a] According to Federal Statistical Office definition, including street lights, sewerage, waste collection, and street cleaning.

[b] According to the Forum of Federations definition, approximated as mean of law and order, schools, other education, health environment, sports and recreation, housing, urban development and regional planning, and local public services I.

[c] "Zinsausgaben am Kreditmarkt"

only governmental function where the local level has no (at least administrative) spending responsibilities. With the exception of defense, the Laender have spending responsibilities for all other governmental functions, which can be explained by their role as the general provider of public administration services.

Overall, the federal level plays the predominant role in financing public services, accounting for 47% of overall public expenditures, while the Laender account for 36%, and the local level for 17%. The most important driver for this role of the federal level is its main responsibility for social security spending. However, as discussed above, the actual fiscal influence of the federal level is much higher, as its legislation often has a decisive impact on state and local spending. With these allocations and interweaving of governmental tasks and, as a result, fiscal obligations and competencies across the three layers of government, Germany can be characterized as a *unitary* federal state.[36] The federal level has the possibility to protrude into competencies of Laender and municipalities, while the Laender are compensated for this with increased influence on the federal level for their executives. Even though they are not formally involved in decision-making processes on the federal level or on the level of the Laender, municipalities, through their umbrella organizations, which are important, albeit informal, actors in the political arena on the Laender and federal levels, have a strong voice on all issues that affect them. While the tendencies to further intervene in tasks and decisions across government tiers have been ceased somewhat through the Reform Act of 2006 and the associated disentanglements of legislative and executive competencies, they accelerated again with the Reform Acts of 2017 and 2019. As a result, the decision-making system, with its tendencies to shift decisions to higher levels, often contradicts the subsidiarity principle. This applies especially to the interplay between the federal and the state level. Due to the strong role of the executives against the legislatures on all governmental layers, which has increased as a result of the latest Reform Acts, Germany's federal system can not only be described as a unitary but also as *executive* federalism, that often lacks parliamentary oversight over federal fiscal relations, especially on the level of the Laender.

[36] See Hesse, K. 1962. *Der unitarische Bundesstaat*. Karlsruhe: C.F. Müller.

While the expenditure side of the public budget is highly intertwined and rigid, this is all the more true for public revenues. The three main revenue sources of the public budget are the income, corporate, and value added taxes. These three taxes are the so-called shared taxes. The federal level and (via the Bundesrat) the executives of the Laender jointly decide on the bases and rates of these taxes. Tax revenues are divided between the federal level, the Laender, and, to a lesser extent, the municipalities.[37]

Large, but still limited, exclusive tax autonomy is assigned to the federal level, which has the exclusive right to determine tariffs and some indirect taxes.[38] However, the authority to set tariffs was conveyed to the European Union, which reduces the de facto exclusive tax autonomy of the federal level to indirect taxes. The Laender possess even less exclusive tax autonomy. They only have full rate autonomy on the real estate purchase tax and, since 2020, the right to determine the tax base of the local property tax autonomously. For the remaining state taxes, tax bases and tax rates are set uniformly and jointly on the federal level by the Bundestag and the executives of the Laender in the Bundesrat as a result of concurrent legislation.[39] Although the Laender have almost no revenue-raising autonomy, they are responsible for collecting federal, state, and joint taxes due to their role as general providers of public administration services.[40] This offers them de facto a slightly stronger role in revenue collection than the de jure tax competencies would suggest.[41] However, the Reform Act of 2017 reduced the autonomy of the Laender to collect taxes from 2020 onwards. While each Land had exclusive autonomy over legislation concerning its tax administration until 2019, new legislative possibilities allow the federal level, with the consent of the Bundesrat, to establish administrative standards for the collection of taxes which are applicable to all Laender.

The largest exclusive tax-setting power is assigned to the municipal level. Municipalities are allowed to set the tax rates of local business and

[37] See Grundgesetz art. 106 abs. 3.

[38] See Grundgesetz art. 106 abs. 1.

[39] See Grundgesetz art. 105 abs. 2.

[40] See Grundgesetz art. 108 abs. 2.

[41] See Bönke, T., B. Jochimsen and C. Schröder. 2017. "Fiscal Equalization and Tax Enforcement." *German Economic Review*, 18: 377–409.

property taxes, which are both major revenue sources for the local authorities.[42] Until 2020, the tax bases have been jointly determined by the Bundestag and the Laender executives in the Bundesrat at the federal level. Since 2020, the Laender also have the right to set the tax base of the local property tax autonomously.

These tax-raising competencies lead to a situation where the own-source revenues of the state and municipal levels fall short of their constitutionally assigned tasks and thus their actual spending needs. Therefore, there are distinct, complex, and quantitatively important systems of revenue redistribution between the federal level and the Laender and between the Laender and the municipalities, which assign revenues to all layers according to their respective tasks. Moreover, the distribution of revenues across layers of government is, most notably for the Laender, also used to compensate for differences in local revenues among the jurisdictions of the same layer. After the allocation of the respective tax shares of the joint taxes, which follows tax occurrence and redistribution aims, a redistribution scheme among the Laender sets in to increase revenues of all states to approximately 90% of per capita average state revenues. After that, further vertical transfers from the federal level ensure that every Land receives at least 97.5% of average per capita state revenues. All these transfers are de facto unconditional and impose a highly egalitarian revenue situation on all Laender. Even though municipalities enjoy more tax autonomy than the Laender, their own-source revenues also fall short of their spending responsibilities. As municipalities are part of the Laender, it falls into the responsibility of the Laender to endow them with sufficient resources to execute their tasks. Therefore, all states established municipal equalization schemes. In addition to the equalization scheme among the Laender until 2020, the local equalization schemes are primarily vertical systems with horizontal redistribution effects. Only a few Laender have amended their municipal equalization scheme with horizontal components. All of this can be attributed to the general emphasis of German politics and the electorate on an egalitarian rather than efficient distribution of revenues. This is even rooted in the Grundgesetz, where the establishment of equivalent living conditions is defined as a constitutional obligation.[43]

[42] See Grundgesetz art. 106 abs. 6.

[43] See Grundgesetz art. 72 abs. 2.

Throughout the Reform Act of 2006 and as a result of the increases in public debt and the insufficiency of the formerly "golden rule" debt constraint, which stated that the federal and the state governments are entitled to issue debt for themselves in the amount of their annual net investment expenditures, a close-to-balanced-budget rule has been introduced for the federal level since 2016. Since 2020 the Laender face a strict balanced-budget rule. Although the precise formulation of the budget rules of the Laender fall within the competencies of the Laender legislatures, the strict borrowing banning obligations of the Grundgesetz are prerogative to possibly shortcoming rules of the Laender.[44] Local governments were already confronted with budget rules before the Reform Act of 2006. As the Laender are constitutionally obliged to guarantee the financial capacity of their municipalities, and since it remains at least unclear whether the Laender would have to bailout municipalities in the case of a municipal default, they restrict municipal budgetary activities, especially with respect to local borrowing and deficits, and control the fiscal activities of their municipalities. Apart from the Laender that are exposed to credible fiscal rules since 2020 only, German municipalities have never been allowed to run structural deficits. However, the intensity and credibility of restrictions for municipal debt and their surveillance differ considerably across Laender. While the budgets of municipalities in, e.g., Baden-Wuerttemberg are tightly regulated by state legislation, municipalities in North Rhine-Westphalia enjoy much greater discretion.[45] Overall, the Reform Act of 2006 introduced credible restrictions on federal borrowing and borrowing of the Laender, while municipalities face debt restrictions ever since. Moreover, Germany as a whole remains restricted not only by its own fiscal rules but also by the EU Stability and Growth Pact and the Fiscal Compact.

[44] See Burret, H.T. and L.P. Feld. 2013. "Fiscal Institutions in Germany." *Swiss Journal of Economics and Statistics*, 149: 249–290.

[45] See Bury, Y. and L.P. Feld. 2018. "Die Heterogenität der kommunalen Haushalts- und Aufsichtsregeln als Herausforderung im vertikalisierten Fiskalföderalismus." In M. Junkernheinrich, S. Korioth, T. Lenk, H. Scheller and M. Woisin (eds.), *Jahrbuch für öffentliche Finanzen*, 2018–2. Berlin: Berliner Wissenschafts-Verlag.

3 Fiscal Federalism and Macroeconomic Management

Since the foundation of the European Monetary Union (EMU), monetary policy is exclusively assigned to the European Central Bank (ECB) and thus to the European level. According to the European treaties, the ECB was created based on the model of the Deutsche Bundesbank. The ECB enjoys strong independence, but in a hierarchical mandate, it has the primary task to ensure price stability. While the ECB is bound by its mandate, the central bank enjoys instrumental independence, with the exception that state funding and monetization of public debt are strictly prohibited. While monetary policy is delegated to the European level, fiscal policy remains in the national sphere. The only European institutions that affect national fiscal policy are the Stability and Growth Pact (SGP) and the Fiscal Compact, the first one limiting the overall annual deficit of all layers of government to 3% of its GDP and the overall debt burden to 60% of GDP, the latter limiting structural deficits to 0.5% of GDP. However, the credibility of the SGP and its enforcement has been put into question several times since its establishment because of many special permissions and loopholes.[46]

On the national level, the Grundgesetz establishes general economic equilibrium as constitutional obligation for the federal level and the Laender.[47] This became instrumental with the Stability and Growth Law of 1967, which obliges the federal government and the Laender to conduct macroeconomic policies such that price stability, high employment, external balance, and adequate economic growth are achieved.[48] Thus, all governmental layers are responsible for macroeconomic stabilization.

The lack of tax autonomy of the Laender, combined with rigid spending obligations, led the Laender to increasingly rely on transfers and borrowing to meet their spending needs and to finance the state governments' individual political purposes. The consequence is high indebtedness in some Laender. This development culminated in a ruling

[46] See Christofzik, D.I., L.P. Feld, W.H. Reuter, and M. Yeter. 2018. "Uniting European Fiscal Rules: How to Strengthen the Fiscal Framework." Working Paper 04/2018, German Council of Economic Experts, Wiesbaden.

[47] See Grundgesetz, art. 109 abs. 2.

[48] See Stability and Growth Law, paragraph 1.

of the Constitutional Court in 1992, according to which the federal level and the other Laender had to bailout the most highly indebted Laender Bremen and Saarland.[49] However, the Constitutional Court defined strict requirements for such federal bailouts. The most important of these requirements is that there must be a federal state of emergency. This would only be the case if the continued existence of the Land, which seeks bailout, and thus of the federal territory as it stands, is at risk. The Constitutional Court appeared to be strict in the application of this requirement, as it rejected a bailout lawsuit of the highly indebted city-state of Berlin in 2006.[50]

Nevertheless, there are reasons to suspect that a soft budget constraint for the Laender resulted from the Bremen/Saarland ruling.[51] In case of a soft budget constraint, the marginal benefits of additional spending exceed their marginal costs, as the possibility for state policy arises to externalize some of the taxation needed to fund additional spending to taxpayers outside their own Land.[52] This may incentivize state policy to conduct excessive spending and to increase deficits.[53] These tendencies are intensified as all Laender benefit from the favorable credit conditions of the German federal government. Empirical analyses indicate unsustainable debt levels in most Laender.[54] Moreover, the numbers of state debt

[49] See Ruling of the Constitutional Court, "BVerfGE 86, 148—Finanzausgleich II," 27.05.1992.

[50] See Ruling of the Constitutional Court, "2 BVF 3/03," 19.10.2006.

[51] See Feld, L.P. and J. von Hagen. 2007. "Federal Republic of Germany." In A. Shah (eds.), *The Practice of Fiscal Federalism: Comparative Perspectives*. Montreal & Kingston/London/Ithaca: McGill-Queen's University Press; Seitz, H. 1999. "Subnational Bailouts in Germany." ZEI Working Paper B20. Bonn; Rodden, J. 2005. "And the Last Shall be First: Federalism and Fiscal Outcomes in Germany." Department of Political Science, MIT. Cambridge. Mimeo.

[52] See Feld, L.P. and J. von Hagen. 2007. "Federal Republic of Germany." In A. Shah (eds.), *The Practice of Fiscal Federalism: Comparative Perspectives*. Montreal & Kingston / London / Ithaca: McGill-Queen's University Press.

[53] See Hagen, J. von and M. Dahlberg. 2004. "Swedish Local Government: Is There a Bailout Problem?" In P. Molander (ed.), *Fiscal Federalism in Unitary States*. New York: Kluwer/Springer.

[54] See Burret, H.T., L.P. Feld, and E.A. Koehler. 2016. "(Un-)Sustainability of Public Finances in German Laender: A Panel Time Series Approach." *Economic Modelling*, 53: 254–265; Burret, H.T., L.P. Feld and E.A. Koehler. 2017. "Fiscal Sustainability of the German Laender: Time Series Evidence." *Finanzarchiv / Public Finance Analysis*, 73: 103–132; Feld, L.P., E.A. Koehler and J. Wolfinger. 2020. "Modeling Fiscal Sustainability

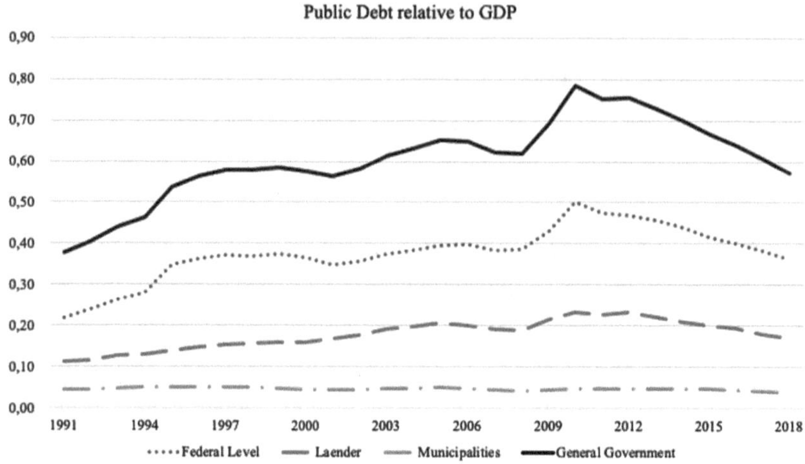

Fig. 1 Public Debt relative to GDP (1991–2018) (*Source* Federal Statistical Office, own calculations)

are likely to increase sharply once demographics will affect pension liabilities of the Laender.[55] The overall debt to GDP ratio was 59.8% in 2019.[56] At about 60% of overall public debt, the federal level bears the largest share, followed by the Laender with 30% of public debt in 2019. While the overall public debt burden quadrupled since 1990, subnational debt tripled.

The development of the public debt stock since reunification is depicted in Fig. 1. Although fiscal sustainability of individual Laender can be put into question,[57] the credible bailout claim of the federation against the Laender prevented individual Laender from falling into sovereign debt crises. This credible bailout claim also prevented the Laender from falling

in Dynamic Macro-Panels with Heterogeneous Effects: Evidence from German Federal States." *International Tax and Public Finance*, 27: 215–239.

[55] See Feld, L.P. and J. von Hagen. 2007. "Federal Republic of Germany." In A. Shah (eds.), *The Practice of Fiscal Federalism: Comparative Perspectives*. Montreal & Kingston/London/Ithaca: McGill-Queen's University Press.

[56] Data according to Eurostat.

[57] See Burret, H.T., L.P. Feld and E.A. Koehler. 2016. "(Un-)Sustainability of Public Finances in German Laender: A Panel Time Series Approach." *Economic Modelling*, 53: 254–265.

into debt crises in situations of particular fiscal stress as, e.g., in the financial crisis of 2008/2009. However, the increase in general government debt during the financial crisis triggered the debate on sustainability of public finances in Germany.

As a reaction to this debate and to counteract the imbalances of increasing spending needs and almost no revenue-raising possibilities on the state level and the associated unfavorable incentives, the federal level and the Laender agreed to implement a fiscal rule into the Grundgesetz in 2009.[58] This fiscal rule states that, since 2016, the federal government is not allowed to run a structural deficit that exceeds 0.35% of GDP. The respective cyclical adjustments have to be symmetric. They enable broader deficit limits in times of economic downturns but require surpluses in booms.[59] In addition to automatic cyclical adjustments, an escape clause is provided. The Bundestag may approve additional credit lines in case of natural disasters, severe economic downturns or other events that are beyond the control of the government. In such cases, an amortization plan of the additionally approved deficits must be provided.[60]

While Article 109 of the Grundgesetz allows the federal level to run a close-to-balanced budget, the Laender are subject to a strict balanced-budget rule since 2020. As on the federal level, deviations from a balanced budget through cyclical adjustments and escape clauses are allowed for. The detailed design and implementation of the fiscal rule for each Land are submitted to the Laender. However, the provisions that apply to the fiscal rule on the federal level have to hold for the fiscal rules of the Laender simultaneously. In particular, even on the state level, only *symmetric* cyclical components are legitimate. Moreover, amortization plans are also required at the Laender level if a state parliament approves higher credit lines in the event of natural disasters or other exceptional events. If the fiscal rule of a Land did not meet the requirements of the Grundgesetz, the Land's own fiscal rule would be overruled by the Grundgesetz. In this case, the Land would not be allowed net borrowing in any case without exception.

58 See Burret, H.T. 2013. "Die deutsche Schuldenbremse als Allheilmittel - eine Analyse im historischen Kontext." *Journal für Generationengerechtigkeit*, 13: 48–65.

59 See Burret, H.T. and L.P. Feld. 2013. "Fiscal Institutions in Germany." *Swiss Journal of Economics and Statistics*, 149: 249–290.

60 See Federal Ministry of Finance. 2012. *Compendium on the Federation's Budget Rule as set out in Article 115 of the Basic Law*. Berlin.

While giving considerable scope for fiscal policy to react to macroeconomic shocks, the design of the German debt brake should limit excessive public borrowing on both federal and Laender levels. Due to cyclically high revenues and low-interest payments, the federal government faced no difficulties in meeting the requirements of the fiscal rule since 2016. To enable the highly indebted Laender Berlin, Bremen, Saarland, Saxony-Anhalt, and Schleswig–Holstein to meet the requirements of the fiscal rule from 2020 onwards, the federal government and the other Laender provided consolidation assistance of 800 million euros (862 million USD) annually to these Laender between 2011 and 2019. Within the framework of the Federal Reform Act of 2017, the federal level and the Laender agreed that the payment of consolidation assistances will continue beyond 2019. Since 2020, however, the federal level bears the consolidation assistances alone, while the other Laender will no longer have to contribute any funds.[61]

By the Reform Act of 2009, a Stability Council was established consisting of the federal ministers of finance and economic affairs, and the state ministers of finance.[62] This council has to monitor the compliance of all tiers of government with the fiscal provisions of the Grundgesetz and the federal law of public budgeting. Since 2020, the Council is mandated to monitor compliance of the Laender with the fiscal rules and is allowed to set uniform standards for the cyclical adjustment of budgetary data.[63] Moreover, the Stability Council has to ensure that all layers of government comply with European fiscal provisions. The Stability Council must provide recommendations if the federal government or a Land fails to comply with the legal provisions. In case of fiscal stress of a particular Land, the Stability Council has to detect and declare a fiscal state of emergency and agree on adjustment measures for the respective Land. It may impose sanctions if a Land does not comply with its adjustment plan. However, these sanctions are limited to a cut in consolidation assistances that are part of the adjustment plan itself. The council is complemented by an independent advisory board.

[61] See Federal Ministry of Finance. 2017. "Die Neuordnung der Bund-Länder-Finanzbeziehungen" *Monthly Report of the Federal Ministry of Finance*, 8. Berlin.

[62] See Grundgesetz, art. 111.

[63] See Federal Ministry of Finance. 2017. "Die Neuordnung der Bund-Länder-Finanzbeziehungen" *Monthly Report of the Federal Ministry of Finance*, 8. Berlin.

While strict fiscal rules for the federal level and the Laender were established by the Reform Act of 2009, German municipalities have never been allowed to run structural deficits. Instead, municipal borrowing is restricted to the amount of public investment expenditures. However, as the Laender are responsible for monitoring municipal finances, compliance with this rule varies considerably across states. Especially, Saarland, Rhineland-Palatinate, Hesse, and North Rhine-Westphalia allowed their municipalities to use short-term liquidity loans to fund current expenditures and to accumulate deficits over a period of years.[64] Hesse launched a debt relief program with which the state and local governments could redeem debt burdens caused by liquidity loans and thus reflecting deficits resulting from current expenditures. Since late 2019 there are ongoing debates whether the federal government should redeem municipal debt burdens in other states without leading to conclusive results.

4 (Fiscal) Federalism During the COVID-19 Pandemic

The COVID-19 pandemic of 2020 is a litmus test for macroeconomic management in Germany's system of fiscal federalism in the situation of an extraordinary economic and societal shock. In addition, it has put the effectiveness of Germany's executive and cooperatively entangled federalism in times of crises to the test.

Despite the strong role of the Laender executives in German federalism, situations are rare in which a wider public takes notice of the crucial role the Grundgesetz assigns to the Laender. The outbreak of the COVID-19 pandemic in 2020 marked such an, also in this regard, exceptional event. There are two reasons that are important to understand the central role the Laender have played during the COVID-19 pandemic. First, times of crises are usually times in which the executive branches of government are central. As discussed above, in German federalism the core executers of public services are the Laender executives. Second,

[64] See Bury, Y. and L.P. Feld. 2018. "Die Heterogenität der kommunalen Haushalts- und Aufsichtsregeln als Herausforderung im vertikalisierten Fiskalföderalismus." In M. Junkernheinrich, S. Korioth, T. Lenk, H. Scheller and M. Woisin (eds.), *Jahrbuch für öffentliche Finanzen*, 2018–2. Berlin: Berliner Wissenschafts-Verlag; Heinemann, F., L.P. Feld, B. Geys, C. Gröpl, S. Hauptmeier and A. Kalb. 2009. *Der kommunale Kassenkredit zwischen Liquiditätssicherung und Missbrauchsgefahr*. Baden-Baden: Nomos.

the Laender constitute the federation and delegate (large) parts of their sovereignty to the federal level. However, policies that may interfere with fundamental personal rights have largely been kept within the sphere of the Laender. Therefore, the federal state of defense constitutes the only case in which the federal level is allowed to universally restrict the right of assembly or free movement of people. By this means, the Grundgesetz uses the assignment of competencies to establish pronounced checks and balances to secure fundamental rights. Establishing the state of emergency[65] or inducing measures that restrict the freedom of assembly or free movement in the case of natural disasters falls into the exclusive competency of the Laender, which are responsible for all policies of civil protection and disaster management.

According to this separation of competencies, it has been the Laender that were responsible for all emergency measures during the COVID-19 pandemic. In the course of the pandemic, all Laender imposed the closures of schools, shops, and restaurants and enacted directives to prohibit all assemblies and meetings of more than three persons. A formal quarantine was, however, not prescribed by any Land. The sequence of inducing these measures differentiated distinctly between the Laender. Bavaria and Saarland, followed by Baden-Wuerttemberg and Hesse, were the first to implement far-reaching measures to reduce personal contacts between people. Bavaria and Saarland have also been the two only Laender that formally established a state of emergency. This aimed at giving the state governments additional policy tools at hand, i.e., using health-care equipment of the armed forces. Thus, instead of sticking to the usually practiced cooperative approach, Germany's federalism showed competitive elements between the Laender during the COVID-19 pandemic.

Besides the Laender, municipal governments played the most important role in implementing emergency measures. In accordance with their state constitutions municipal governments are entitled to implement measures that restrict personal freedom in case of natural disasters that particularly affect respective municipalities. As emergency measures of the state governments evolved gradually, municipalities that were exposed to particular epidemiological risks often imposed emergency measures such

[65] Most of the Laender did not formally establish a state of emergency during the COVID-19 pandemic, but imposed directives to restrict the freedom of movement and assembly.

as curfews and restrictions to the right of assembly before the respective state governments took up containment measures. For these municipalities, the directives of the state governments did then outweigh the measures already imposed by the municipality. However, each municipality was still entitled to implement measures that went beyond the scope of the state directives if there was a local epidemiological necessity to do so.

In addition to civil protection measures, the Laender had two other important functions during the pandemic. These functions came along with their constitutionally assigned tasks of public health protection in general as well as their roles as providers of general public administration services and of hospital supply in particular. Within the Laender's role as provider of the general public administration, public health offices, as well as police and emergency forces are part of the state administrations. Thus, not only the emergency measures by themselves but also the enforcement of these (de jure often identical across states) measures, differed between the states. Within the Laender's role to administer hospital care, the state level was responsible to organize the allocation of patients to hospitals, the safety regulations of hospitals as well as for the supply of hospitals with medical equipment. Also in these regards, the concrete policies of the Laender differed from each other.

Coordinating the emergency measures of the Laender fell into the competency of the federal level. The most important field of coordination was the supply of medical equipment. The federal ministry of health newly organized centralized procurement mechanisms for medical equipment and its distribution to the state governments.[66] While this technical coordination was well perceived by all Laender, an attempt to transform the individual emergency measures of the Laender into a coherent acting of all Laender caused conflicts. The attempt to transform state-individual policies into one coherent policy of all states was initiated by the federal government and triggered by some state prime ministers but encountered sharp resistance by most of the Laender that faced higher epidemiological risks and subsequently already took up stricter containment measures than the rest of the Laender. Thus, the differing reactions of the state governments to the COVID-19 pandemic was one of the rare examples in which the otherwise usual urge of German Laender to cooperate and

[66] The distribution to individual hospitals was then organized by the state governments.

agree to pursue coherent policies failed. The Laender also declined an attempt of the federal level to change the Federal Infection Protection Act. This attempt aimed at shifting far-reaching additional competencies in the case of pandemics from the state to the federal level.[67]

While the implementation of emergency and health-care measures fell into the responsibility of the Laender, the federal level had two explicit competencies to execute. First, the federal government was within its tasks of foreign affairs and border protection responsible for international coordination of emergency measures as well as border protection and closures.[68] The most important role the federal level assumed during the pandemic, however, has been economic emergency measures. The central economic emergency measure has been the provisions for short-time work, which is wage assistance from the federal employment agency for workers, that enables companies to keep them on the job during a crisis without bearing the costs of employment. Via tax moratoriums, liquidity assistance,[69] and liquidity loans the federal level provided an additional 415.8 billion euros (447.2 bn. USD) of public funds. This economic emergency response aimed at counteracting liquidity shortages of businesses during the economic shutdown period. Within few days after the first shutdown measures were imposed by state governments, these funds became effective. Moreover, the federal government provided guarantees over 819.7 billion euros (884 bn. USD) for liquidity loans for companies. To finance these measures, Bundestag and Bundesrat used the escape clause that the fiscal rule of the Grundgesetz foresees and were authorized to take up 217.8 billion euros (238.7 bn. USD) of new debt. According to the provisions of the fiscal rule an amortization table was passed together with the activation of the escape clause. The amortization table states that the newly issued debt will be redeemed within 20 years with an annual debt service of 5 billion euros, starting in the year 2024.

[67] The Infection Protection Act was changed during the COVID-19 pandemic, however, in a distinctly smaller extent than it was intended by the federal government.

[68] The latter caused discussions between some state governments and the federal government, as, e.g., Saarland, Bayern and Baden-Wuerttemberg closed parts of their borders to France and Austria before the federal government officially announced the general closure of borders.

[69] These assistances were designed as direct and non-refundable payments for small and medium sized businesses.

The payout of the liquidity assistance was implemented via the state governments that individually designed the applications and approving procedures for companies to receive funds. Besides the economic emergency measures of the federal level, most Laender set up their own state funds to provide liquidity assistance and liquidity loans to businesses within their state. Some states implemented their own funds proactively before the economic stabilization measures of the federal level were implemented.

Table 5 provides an overview of the federal and state-individual economic emergency measures during the COVID-19 pandemic. In addition to the economic emergency funds, some of the Laender established funds to support the municipalities within their states with additional transfers. These transfers aimed at covering the increased costs of local public services during the pandemic. As of July 31, 2020, all Laender except Thuringia and the city-state of Bremen passed supplementary budgets. In line with the federal level, the Laender parliaments had to activate the escape clauses of their state level fiscal rules to take up new debt to fund their economic emergency measures.

Additional borrowing of the Laender is also depicted in Table 5. Although the federal level and most of the Laender indebted themselves to mobilize substantial funds, sustainability of public finances of the federal government and the Laender is not expected to change. The reason for this are the amortization schedules for newly issued debt, which the Laender had to resolve in the course of enacting the escape clauses of their fiscal rules (see Table 5). According to these schedules, the Laender will have to use substantial amounts out of their budgets in the subsequent years to service the debt they took up during the COVID-19 pandemic. As the Laender have almost no possibilities to raise additional revenues (see next section), servicing the debt of the COVID-19 emergency measures out of their running budgets will substantially reduce fiscal space of the German Laender in the years after the pandemic.

Eventually, Germany's (fiscal) federalism, with the strong role it assigns to the state executives, proved to provide resilient structures to react to an outstanding exogenous shock such as the COVID-19 pandemic. The decentralized decision-making on the municipal and state levels mostly provided healthcare and fiscal policy responses that have been effective and locally suited for the specific regional needs. Moreover, the Laender resisted to use the pandemic as an occasion to shift competencies to

Table 5 Economic emergency measures of the Laender during the COVID-19 pandemic (as of 2020)

Land	*Economic Emergency Measures*	*Borrowing necessary to fund measures*	*Amortization Table*
Federal Level	• Direct payments for SME, self-employed and liberal professions • Liquidity loans • Economic stimulus package	217.8 bn. Euro (255.84 bn USD)[70]	Amortization over 20 years, beginning in 2023
Baden-Wuerttemberg	• Direct payments for SME, non-profit organizations, self-employed, liberal professions, and artists • Liquidity loans • Direct payments to municipalities to compensate for a shortfall in receipts and additional expenditures	5 bn. Euro (5.87 bn UDS)	Amortization over 10 years, beginning in 2024 with annual redemptions of 500 million euros
Bavaria	• Direct payments for SME and self-employed members of the liberal professions and artists • Liquidity loans and guarantees	10 bn Euro (10.96 bn USD)	Amortization beginning in 2024 with annual redemptions of 1/20 of the liabilities

[70] ECB euro reference exchange rate: US dollar (USD): EUR 1 = USD 1.1760 (27th July 2020).

Land	*Economic Emergency Measures*	*Borrowing necessary to fund measures*	*Amortization Table*
Berlin	• Liquidity loans and guarantees • Direct payments for SME, self-employed, liberal professions, and artists	6 bn. Euro (7.05 bn USD)	Amortization beginning in 2023 with annual redemptions of 1/27 of the liabilities
Brandenburg	• Direct payments for SME, self-employed and liberal professions • Liquidity loans and guarantees • Direct payments to municipalities to compensate for a shortfall in receipts and additional expenditures	2 bn Euro (2.35 bn USD)	Amortization beginning in 2022 with annual redemptions of at least 3.3%
Bremen	• Direct payments for SME and artists • Liquidity loans	0.89 bn Euro (1.06 bn USD)	Amortization beginning in 2024 with annual redemptions of 29.6 Mio Euro for 29 years
Hamburg	• Direct payments for SME, self-employed, liberal professions and artists • Liquidity loans	1.5 bn Euro (1.76 bn USD)	Amortization beginning in 2025, equally within 20 years
Hesse	• Direct payments for SME, non-profit organizations, self-employed, liberal professions, and artists • Liquidity loans • Direct payments to municipalities to compensate for a shortfall in receipts • Economic growth package	1.7 bn Euro (2 bn USD)	Amortization over 7 years, according to the difference between the net borrowing allowed and the actual net borrowing during the financial year 2020 required net borrowing

(continued)

Table 5 (continued)

Land	*Economic Emergency Measures*	*Borrowing necessary to fund measures*	*Amortization Table*
Mecklenburg-Western Pommerania	• Direct payments for SME, non-profit organizations, self-employed, liberal professions, and artists • Liquidity loans	0.7 bn Euro (0.82 bn USD)	Amortization over 10 years, beginning in 2024 with annual redemptions of 10%
Lower Saxony	• Direct payments for SME, self-employed and liberal professions • Liquidity loans	8.78 bn Euro (10.3 bn USD)	Amortization beginning in 2024 within 25 years
North Rhine-Westphalia	• Direct payments for SME, non-profit organizations, self-employed, liberal professions, and artists • Liquidity Loans	25 bn Euro (29.4 bn USD)	Amortization over 50 years, in line with the economic situation
Rhineland-Palatinate	• Liquidity loans	0.57 bn Euro (0.67 bn USD)	Amortization beginning in 2024, with a positive business cycle component 15%, with a negative business cycle component 5%
Saarland	• Liquidity loans • Direct payments for SME, self-employed, liberal professions, and artists • Support for municipalities	1.2 bn Euro (1.41 bn USD)	Amortization over 30 years

Land	*Economic Emergency Measures*	*Borrowing necessary to fund measures*	*Amortization Table*
Saxony	• Liquidity loans	6 bn Euro (7.01 bn USD)	Amortization within 8 years specified in the constitution, Actual amortization over 6 years (beginning 2025) with annual redemptions of 1/6 of the liabilities
Saxony-Anhalt	• Direct payments for SME, self-employed, liberal professions, and artists • Liquidity loans	0.259 bn Euro (0.305 bn USD)	Amortization in financial years 2022 and 2023 100 million euros each and approximately 59 million euro remaining in 2024
Schleswig-Holstein	• Liquidity loans	1 bn Euro (1.17 bn USD)	Amortization beginning from 2021, within 20 years
Thuringia	• Direct payments for SME, self-employed and liberal professions	Decision on borrowing not yet taken on the 28th July 2020	Decision on borrowing not yet taken on the 28th July 2020

Source Authors collection. The Table depicts the policy measures resolved until the 28th July 2020 the federal level thereby protecting the federal structure in a situation in which it was exposed to intense stress.

5 Revenue-Raising Responsibilities

The German fiscal constitution provides almost no competencies to generate revenues for subnational units. Tax bases, and rates, with minor exceptions for the latter, are set at the federal level. While the Laender have almost no autonomy to set taxes exclusively, their executives play an important role in tax setting decisions on the federal level via the Bundesrat. Table 6 summarizes the tax setting powers and the allocation of revenues from the various taxes. In the fiscal year of 2018, 46% of all shared, federal, and state tax revenues were assigned to the federal level.

The most important revenue sources in quantitative terms are the shared taxes (*Gemeinschaftssteuern*), i.e., income tax, corporate tax, value added tax, and flat-rate withholding tax. Revenues from these taxes are shared between the federal level, Laender, and municipalities.[71] Tax bases and rates are determined at the federal level, whereby a majority of the Bundesrat and thus the approval of the executives of the Laender is required. The shared taxes are the quantitatively most important revenue sources for the federal level. Revenues from these taxes accounted for 80% of federal tax revenues and 66% of total federal revenues in 2018. The VAT alone accounts for 35% of tax revenues at the federal level. For the Laender, the shared taxes are an even more important source of tax revenue. In 2018, shared taxes made up 86% of state tax revenues and 63% of total state revenues.

While the shared taxes are quantitatively the most important, there are taxes that are exclusively assigned to the federal, state, or local levels. Taxes on insurance, tobacco, coffee, spirits, sparkling wine, intermediate goods, energy, electricity, car, and air-traffic fall under the sole responsibility of the federal government (*Bundessteuern*).[72] Within the Reform Act of 2006, the previously state vehicle tax became a federal tax. The Bundestag has the authority to autonomously determine the bases and rates of these taxes. The revenues from these taxes fall exclusively on the

[71] See Grundgesetz art. 106 abs. 3.

[72] See Grundgesetz art. 106 abs. 1.

Table 6 Tax assignment for various orders of government

	Determination of		*Tax collection and administration*	*Shares in Revenue (%)*			
	Base	Rate		Federal	Land	Local	All orders
Federal							
Mineral oil tax	Federal	Federal	Federal	100%	0%	0%	100%
Tobacco tax	Federal	Federal	Federal	100%	0%	0%	100%
Spirits tax	Federal	Federal	Federal	100%	0%	0%	100%
Sparkling wine tax	Federal	Federal	Federal	100%	0%	0%	100%
Intermediate goods tax	Federal	Federal	Federal	100%	0%	0%	100%
Coffee tax	Federal	Federal	Federal	100%	0%	0%	100%
Insurance tax	Federal	Federal	Federal	100%	0%	0%	100%
Electricity tax	Federal	Federal	Federal	100%	0%	0%	100%
Solidarity levy	Federal	Federal	Land	100%	0%	0%	100%
Motor vehicle tax (since 2009 federal)	Federal	Federal	Federal	100%	0%	0%	100%
Air traffic tax	Federal	Federal	Federal	100%	0%	0%	100%
State or provincial							
Property (wealth) tax	Joint Federal/land	Joint Federal/land	Land	0%	100%	0%	100%
Inheritance tax	Joint Federal/land	Joint Federal/land	Land	0%	100%	0%	100%
Real estate purchase tax	Joint Federal/land	Land	Land	0%	100%	0%	100%
Betting and lottery tax	Joint Federal/land	Joint Federal/land	Land	0%	100%	0%	100%
Fire protection tax	Joint Federal/land	Joint Federal/land	Land	0%	100%	0%	100%

(continued)

Table 6 (continued)

	Determination of		*Tax collection and administration*	*Shares in Revenue (%)*			
Beer tax	Joint Federal/land	Joint Federal/land	Federal	0%	100%	0%	100%
Local							
Business tax	Joint Federal/land	Local	Land/Local	3,7% (2017)	13,9% (2017)	82,4% (2017)	100%
Real estate taxes	Joint Federal/land (from 2020 land may deviate)	Local	Land/Local	0%	0%	100%	100%
Dog tax	Local	Local	Land/Local	0%	0%	100%	100%
Hunting and fishing tax	Land	Land	Local	0%	0%	100%	100%
Secondary residence tax	Land/Local	Land/Local	Local	0%	0%	100%	100%
Beverage tax	Local	Local	Local	0%	0%	100%	100%
Shared taxes							
Personal income tax	Joint Federal/land	Joint Federal/land	Land	42.50%	42.50%	15%	100%
Flat rate withholding tax	Joint Federal/land	Joint Federal/land	Land	44%	44%	12%	100%
Corporate income tax	Joint Federal/land	Joint Federal/land	Land	50%	50%	0%	100%
VAT	Joint Federal/land	Joint Federal/land	Land	50,2% (2018)	46,6% (2018)	3,2% (2018)	100%

Source Federal Ministry of Finance, Steuern von A bis Z

federal level. However, of these taxes, only the energy, tobacco, and, to a lesser extent, the insurance and car tax generate notable revenue.

The taxes whose revenues exclusively flow to the Laender (*Laenderssteuern*) are the real estate purchase tax, the beer tax, lottery, amusement, inheritance, and gift taxes. Even though these are state taxes, the bases and rates of these taxes are jointly set on the federal level by the Bundestag and the Laender executives in the Bundesrat. Since 2006, the only tax for which the Laender have the power to set the tax rate autonomously is the real estate purchase tax. Its tax base is determined jointly on the federal level. Thus, the tax policy of the federal and Laender levels is almost completely harmonized. Actual state taxes accounted for only 8% of the states' tax revenues. The remaining 6% of the states' tax revenues are federal tax payments to compensate the Laender for the conversion of the car tax into a federal tax and for taking on further responsibilities of local public transport services. Notably, the real estate purchase tax, which is the only tax where the Laender have the competence to set the tax rate autonomously, accounts for only 4% of the states' tax revenues.

Other than the Laender, the municipalities have the power to set surcharges on the local business and property tax rates (*Gemeindesteuern*), both of which are important revenue sources for the local jurisdictions. However, there are ceilings for minimum and maximum surcharges. For the local business tax, the tax base is jointly determined on the federal level by the Bundestag and the executives of the Laender in the Bundesrat. Therefore, although municipalities can set surcharges, the tax system is also strongly harmonized on the local level.

Since the year 2020, this changed for the property tax. Following a ruling of the Constitutional Court, the determination of the local property tax base had to be reformed. In June 2019, the federal level and the Laender agreed to a new definition of the property tax base, which is set on the federal level. First and foremost, the reform will confer legislative power over the property tax on the federal level. At the insistence of Bavaria and Baden-Wuerttemberg, however, an opening clause was introduced in accordance with Article 72.3 of the Grundgesetz. This opening clause gives the Laender the right to voluntarily deviate from the federal definition of the property tax base and to set the property tax base autonomously according to their own definition. Both, Bavaria and Baden-Wuerttemberg made use of this new competency. Thus, the reform of the property tax increases the tax autonomy of the Laender and enables minor tax competition not only between the municipalities that set the property tax rate but also between the Laender that can autonomously define the property tax base since 2020.

On the municipal level, with 50% of all municipal tax revenues in 2018, the local business tax is the most important tax revenue source. Local property taxes account for 12.5% of local tax revenues and thus also play an important role in municipal funding. The remaining 37.5% of municipal tax revenues come from the municipal shares in joint taxes. However, local tax revenues account for only 41% of total local revenues, while the remaining 59% are transferred from the Laender, fee revenues, and other revenues, such as property sales or dividends from municipal holdings.[73] Even though tax revenues are not the only important revenue source of German municipalities, local governments actively use their autonomy to set surcharges on tax rates. Therefore, in Germany's highly interwoven system of fiscal federalism, the municipal level is the only sphere where tax competition between jurisdictions arises.[74]

6 Intergovernmental Fiscal Transfers

Germany has an elaborated fiscal equalization system, which arranges fiscal relations among the Laender as well as between the federal level and the Laender. The equalization scheme effectively levels out disparities in per capita revenues of the Laender. The effects of the equalization scheme on fiscal disparities between the Laender for the fiscal year 2019 are depicted in Fig. 2. Without the equalization scheme in place, the Laender would have faced distinct fiscal disparities. Before equalization, per capita tax revenues of Bavaria as the financially strongest Land yielded 172% of the per capita tax revenues of the financially weakest Land Thuringia. The equalization scheme considerably closes these disparities and reduces the gaps in per capita revenues at a rate of up to 70%. The equalization system that was in force until 2019 was established in 1969 as part of the Fiscal Reform Act. The fundamental principle of this equalization system was to put the Laender in the position of the signors of fiscal equalization. Therefore, the system was originally designed as a horizontal equalization system, supplemented by vertical transfers. This principle changed in 2020 when fiscal relations among the Laender and between the Laender and the federal level have been transformed into an entirely vertical equalization system managed by the federal level.

The system in place since 1970 and until 2019 consisted of four steps. First, tax revenues were distributed between the federal level and the Laender according to the distribution of shared taxes in Table 6. Second,

[73] See Federal Statistical Office. 2018. *Kassenmäßige Steuereinnahmen vor Steuerverteilung*.

[74] See Buettner, T. 2003. "Tax Base Effects and Fiscal Externalisties of Local Capital Taxation: Evidence from a Panel of German Jurisdictions." *Journal of Urban Economics*, 54:110–128.

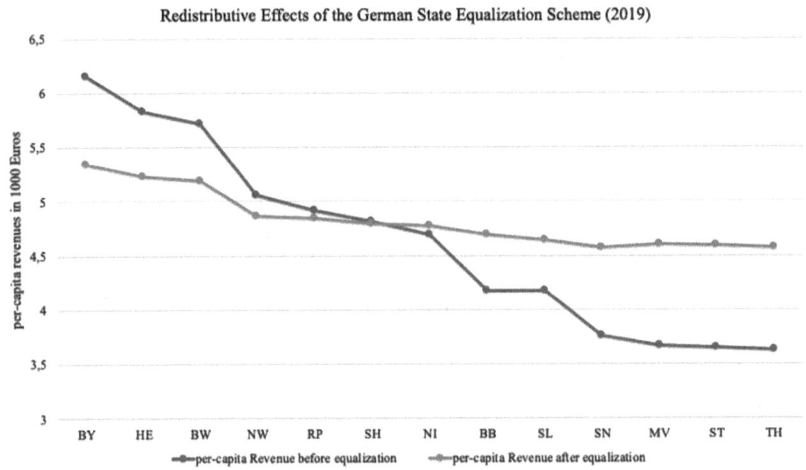

Fig. 2 Redistributive effects of the German state equalization scheme (2019) (*Source* Federal Ministry of Finance, own calculations)

the state shares of the income and corporate taxes and revenues from state taxes were assigned to each Land. This assignment followed population in the case of the income tax, residency in the case of the corporate tax, and occurrence in the case of the state taxes. Moreover, 25% of the VAT revenues were distributed according to the financial strength of the Laender, with the aim to increase the revenue capacity of the poorest Laender. The remaining 75% of VAT revenue was then distributed according to the number of inhabitants. As VAT revenues have been redistributed among the Laender in this way, this step is referred to as primary horizontal equalization.

Third, the secondary horizontal equalization set in. This step was the core of the fiscal equalization system until 2019. Laender with above-average adjusted per capita revenues contributed to the system, while Laender with below-average adjusted per capita revenues received payments from the system. State tax revenues were adjusted in two different ways. On the one hand, 64% of local revenues was included into the revenues of the Land. On the other hand, 12% of the more than proportional increase of state revenues compared to the average of all Laender has been deducted from a Land's revenue. The latter aimed at limiting the absorption of additional tax revenues and thus possible disincentives of the equalization system.

The fiscal gap of Laender receiving payments and the fiscal excess of the Laender contributing to the system was calculated as the difference between a Land's adjusted per capita revenue and the average adjusted per capita revenues of all Laender. Redistribution then took place according to a symmetric progressive formulary schedule that raised the marginal transfers to the receiving Laender to fill up 44–75% of the calculated fiscal gap. The exact rate at which the fiscal gap filled up depended on a Land's relative per capita revenue strength. On the contrary, the fiscal excess of the contributing Laender was skimmed by 44–75%, again depending on a Land's individual relative per capita revenue strength.[75]

The fourth step in revenue distribution was vertical transfers from the federal level to those Laender, which still had an adjusted revenue capacity of less than 99.5% of the adjusted average per capita revenues of all Laender. These vertical transfers filled the gap between a Land's relative revenue and 99.5% of the average per capita revenues of all Laender at a rate of 77.5%. Moreover, the federal level provided transfers to those Laender for which special spending needs were identified politically. On this basis, the Laender in East Germany received additional vertical transfers to deal with high structural unemployment as a consequence of the separation of Germany before 1990. Furthermore, ten small Laender received compensation for the costs of their political administration.

At the end of these four steps, every Land had revenues that amounted to at least 97.5% of the average per capita revenues of all Laender, such that the equalization system among the Laender was highly egalitarian. This highly egalitarian system induced high rates of marginal contribution, which for some recipient states came close to a full absorption of additional tax revenue throughout the equalization scheme.[76] There is

[75] At which concrete rate between 45 and 75% the fiscal gap (excess) was filled up (skimmed) depended on the relative per capita revenue strength of each Land compared to the average per capita revenue strength of all Laender. The lower (higher) the relative per capita revenue strength, the higher was the rate of compensation (skimming). For a detailed description and explanation of the exact tariff formula see Burret. H.T., Y. Bury and L.P Feld. 2018. "Grenzabschöpfungsraten im deutschen Finanzausgleich." *List Forum für Wirtschafts- und Finanzpolitik*, 44: 1–22.

[76] See Burret. H.T., Y. Bury and L.P Feld. 2018. "Grenzabschöpfungsraten im deutschen Finanzausgleich." *List Forum für Wirtschafts- und Finanzpolitik*, 44: 1–22; Baretti, C., B. Huber and K. Lichtblau. 2002. "A Tax on Tax Revenue: The Incentive

Table 7 Vertical fiscal gaps

	Total revenue collected	*Total revenue available, including net transfers for that level of government*	*Expenditures*
	(2018) Mill. USD	(2018) Mill USD	(2018) Mill USD
National	412,298.34	228,927.81	215,045.19
Subnational			
Land	363,035.81	318,334.26	295,769.27
Local	131,194.91	223,514.45	212,605.15
EU	30,710.70	30,710.70	30,710.70
Social security	*319,326.12*	*447,935.96*	*435,492.58*
All levels	1,256,565.88	1,256,565.88	1,189,622.89

Source Federal Statistical Office, Fachserie 14 Reihe 2

also evidence that the system created incentives for excessive borrowing and spending by the Laender.[77] Although some of the vertical transfers had been justified by specific spending needs, all transfers in this system were unconditional. Despite these problems of the system between the federal level and the Laender, Table 7 shows that the system closed fiscal gaps and eased the cost of social security, as these costs are primarily borne by the federal level.

As of 2020, this system, which has shaped fiscal relations among the German Laender for more than 50 years, has been changed fundamentally. The new system breaks the principle of horizontality in fiscal relations among the Laender, as all financial relations are verticalized. Since 2020, the two steps of horizontal redistribution have been eliminated completely, reducing fiscal equalization to a three-step system. After the first step of allocating tax revenues of income, corporate, and state taxes to the federal and the Laender levels and among the Laender according to the same principles as in the old system, the entire redistribution, which took place horizontally, is converted into the vertical VAT

Effects of Equalizing Transfers: Evidence from Germany." *International Tax and Public Finance*, 9: 631–649.

[77] See Feld, L.P. and T. Baskaran. 2010. "Federalism, Budget Deficits and Public Debt: On the Reform of Germany's Fiscal Constitition." *Review of Law and Economics*, 6: 365–393; Feld, L.P. and J. Schnellenbach. 2013. "Verzerrungen im bundesstaatlichen Finanzausgleich." Report for the Laender Bavaria and Hesse. Freiburg.

distribution to the Laender by means of surcharges and deductions. The newly designed vertical VAT redistribution forms the new second step of equalization. It is designed to not only entirely replace the volume of the formerly horizontal funds. The volume of equalization will instead be increased by 4.7 billion USD to meet the increased redistributive goals of the new system. Note, however, that this *increase* in equalization funds comes at the cost of the federal level and not at that of the other Laender.

However, this increased federal funding will not remove horizontal redistributive effects. The reason for this is that, in order to replace the horizontal funds, the redistribution formula of VAT revenues changes: Before 2020, fiscal gaps and fiscal excess were calculated as the difference between adjusted per capita revenues of each land and the average adjusted per capita revenue of all Laender. The adjustment of revenues has changed slightly, as local revenues are now included in the calculation of state revenues with a factor of 75% instead of 64%. The schedule to determine VAT surcharges and deductions that replace the formerly horizontal funds is now linear, filling up (skimming) 63% of the fiscal gap (fiscal excess). Thus, the Laender with above-average per capita VAT revenues are still effectively contributing to the equalization scheme via VAT deductions. In fact, the former explicit horizontal redistribution effects are neither abolished nor substantially reduced, but converted into implicit ones.[78]

Increased additional vertical transfers from the federal level to the Laender form the new third step of the equalization system. The vertical transfers to close remaining fiscal gaps have been expanded, as the upper ceiling of the remaining fiscal gap was increased to 99.75% of the average per capita revenues of all Laender. Also, the rate at which this gap is filled was increased from 77.5 to 80%. Thus, the standard of equalization was not lowered through the removal of the horizontal component. Instead, it has been slightly increased. The politically identified fiscal needs, that constitute further vertical transfers, have also been expanded. The vertical transfers to compensate the Laender for the cost of high unemployment remain, while the vertical transfers intended to compensate small

[78] Only horizontal redistribution effects at the top are slightly reduced. This reduction is, however, not induced through the removal of the horizontal transfer scheme, but through the change of the redistribution tariff from a linear-progressive tariff in the former horizontal scheme to a proportional tariff according to which the VAT deductions are calculated.

Laender for the costs of their political administration have been increased. In addition to these vertical transfers, two new areas of additional fiscal needs have been identified. Laender with financially weak municipalities receive additional vertical transfers from the federal level. Furthermore, Laender with a poor research performance receive additional vertical transfers, which should enable them to build up better research capacities.[79] As before, all transfers paid within the new equalization system remain unconditional.

There is a broad consensus that the reform of the fiscal relations between the federal level and the Laender will not improve the incentives of the German fiscal equalization scheme. Instead, there is reason to expect a worsening of the problems of the old system as well as new problems. In particular, there are three points that cause concerns.[80] Firstly, the reform is not able to reduce the disincentives arising from the high marginal contribution rates.[81] Even though the new linear equalization schedule should be associated with reduced marginal contributions, the increased rate at which local revenues will be included in the calculation of state revenues will counteract this effect. Thus, the reform is not expected to reduce the disincentives of revenue equalization.

Secondly, the transparency of fiscal relations and fiscal accountability declined further through the elimination of the horizontal elements of the redistribution scheme. This loss of accountability and transparency can be seen as a main driver why both, the Laender that formerly contributed horizontal transfers as well as the Laender that received horizontal payments, pushed for the removal of the horizontal component of fiscal equalization. Before the reform, distributional conflicts between contributing and receiving Laender regularly caused tensions between

[79] Poor research performance is defined as the (negative) difference between the per capita research grants a Land receives from the federal level and the average per capita research grants received by all Laender. If the amount of per capita federal research grants received by a Land meets 95% or less of the average per capita research grants of all Laender, the Land is entitled to receive additional transfers out of the equalization scheme. Note that federal research grants are assigned to the Laender based on individual grant applications for specific research projects.

[80] See Feld, L.P., C. Fuest, J. Haucap, H. Schweitzer, V. Wieland and B.U. Wigger. 2016. *Für eine echte Reform der Bund-Länder-Finanzbeziehungen*. Kronberger Kreis Study No. 62. Berlin: Stiftung Marktwirtschaft.

[81] See Burret. H.T., Y. Bury and L.P Feld. 2018. "Grenzabschöpfungsraten im deutschen Finanzausgleich." *List Forum für Wirtschafts- und Finanzpolitik*, 44: 1–22.

both groups. With the removal of the horizontal scheme, these formerly horizontal distributional conflicts between the Laender are converted into vertical conflicts between the entirety of all Laender and the federal level. Now, both groups of Laender can accuse the federal level instead of each other if they face insufficient fiscal resources to pursue their spending projects. Moreover, due to the loss of transparency, the formerly transfer-receiving Laender lose their stigma of conducting bad fiscal policies, while the formerly contributing Laender cannot be accused for lacking solidarity anymore.

Thirdly, as redistribution is fully integrated into the vertical distribution of VAT revenue, parliamentary oversight of fiscal relations is almost completely eliminated. With the horizontal compenent in place, horizontal transfer payments between the Laender were part of the budgets of the Laender and thus part of the parliamentary budgetary processes and votes in all Laender. While the state parliaments had no possibility to reject the payment of (constitutionally determined) equalization transfers, this process established transparency over the redistribution of revenues across the Laender. The distribution of VAT revenues is however determined before the actual state budget processes start. Thus, with horizontal redistribution being integrated into the vertical distribution of VAT revenues, state parliaments will no longer debate nor vote on the redistributive effects of the equalization scheme. Instead, it will be the executives of the Laender and the Federal Ministry of Finance that have full oversight over the redistributional effects of the equalization scheme now.

Besides the transfers resulting from the fiscal equalization system, the federal level may grant financial aid to the Laender if certain conditions are met. These additional vertical transfers have become increasingly important throughout the last years as the federal level and the Laender agreed to expand the fields where the federal government may provide such grants. The most prominent examples are newly established federal transfers to the Laender so that they can endow their municipalities with sufficient funds to improve school equipment in all municipalities and school infrastructure in financially weak municipalities.

The increased and highly rigid fiscal obligations of the federal level against the Laender lower the fiscal space of the federal level itself. However, due to the strong fiscal position of the German federal government, these new obligations as well as possible future financial claims of the Laender against the federal government are not expected to put fiscal sustainability of the federal government at risk.

As compensation for granting additional funds, the federal level received extended control over the use of federal financial aid. As a result of the Reform Act of 2017, the Laender lost their autonomy in designing transfer programs that are partly funded by federal transfers, as they now require the consent of the federal level for the design of these programs. Thus, federal influence and the interweaving of federal and Land policy increased due to the Reform Acts of 2017 and 2019. Furthermore, the control rights of the Federal Court of Audit against the Laender have been extended, as the Court is now allowed to conduct inquiries directly at the level of the Laender and municipalities if they receive federal funds.

Fiscal relations and fiscal transfers between the federal level and the Laender are a regular part of the public debate. However, fiscal transfers between the state and the local levels are quantitatively much more important, as transfer revenues make up for 50% of municipal revenues. Unlike the federal level and the Laender, there are unconditional *and* conditional grants from the Laender to their municipalities. Conditional grants to municipalities usually serve to support municipal investment projects. Only to a lesser extent conditional grants aim to subsidize current expenditures. Conditional grants to municipalities are usually designed as matching grants. Unconditional grants, which aim at closing the fiscal gap between Laender and municipalities, play the most important role in transfer relations between the two subnational layers of government. All Laender are obliged to ensure that their municipalities are adequately endowed so that they can fulfill their compulsory tasks and have fiscal leeway to provide a minimum amount of additional voluntary services on which local councils decide autonomously. The transfer systems between Laender and municipalities differ in design. Basically, there are two types of systems for unconditional transfers to close municipal fiscal gaps. Most Laender use a system that assigns a specific share of aggregated tax revenue of the Land and municipalities to the municipal level. Some Laender, mainly as a result of rulings by their state courts, changed the system to a needs-based system that requires the determination of the specific fiscal needs of every municipality. All transfer systems between Laender and municipalities are predominantly vertical systems with horizontal redistribution effects. Only some Laender amended their transfer systems with actual horizontal redistribution schemes.

There is evidence that municipal equalization can induce adverse incentives on municipalities. For example, Buettner and Wildasin find that grants to municipalities in the state of Baden-Wuerttemberg have a significant effect on spending and borrowing.[82] Similar spending effects are found for municipalities in other states.[83] Beyond flypaper effects, marginal contribution rates are also an issue within municipal transfer systems. This is shown, e.g., by Hauptmeier, who finds that increased contributions rates to the system are associated with lower productive spending of the municipalities in Baden-Wuerttemberg.[84]

7 The Way Forward

Given these institutional arrangements, Germany can be characterized as a cooperative,[85] unitary, and executive federal system. All layers enjoy autonomy on the expenditure side of the public budget. However, fiscal responsibilities follow the constitutionally assigned tasks. As these tasks are often influenced by legislation of higher levels, spending decisions are partly predetermined and rigid for subnational levels. While these legislative influences induce minimum spending levels for certain political areas, there are, however, no restrictions that would impose limits for maximum spending. The only exceptions for the latter arise indirectly through deficit rules for municipalities and, since 2020, for the Laender.

While the spending side is somewhat restricted, this is all the more true for the revenue side. In order to decide on all quantitatively relevant tax bases and rates, the federal level requires the approval of the Laender executives through the Bundesrat. The Laender themselves have almost no autonomy in raising their own revenues or setting taxes. The

[82] See Buettner, T. and D. Wildasin. 2006. "The Dynamics of Municipal Fiscal Adjustment." *Journal of Public Economics*, 90: 1105–1132.

[83] See Baskaran, T. 2016. "Intergovernmental Transfers, Local Fiscal Policy and the Flypaper Effect: Evidence from a German State." *FinanzArchiv / Public Finance Analysis*, 72:1–40.

[84] See Hauptmeier, S. 2007. "The Impact of Fiscal Equalization on Local Expenditure Policies: Theory and Evidence from Germany." ZEW Discussion Paper No. 07–006. Mannheim.

[85] See Scharpf, F.W., B. Reissert, and F. Schnabl. 1976. *Politikverflechtung: Theorie und Empirie des kooperativen Föderalismus in der Bundesrepublik*. Kronberg/Ts: Scriptor.

only minor exception is the real estate purchase tax, which is quantitatively negligible. The local level enjoys the widest autonomy in raising revenues since municipalities decide on surcharges on the local business and property taxes.

This institutional framework not only underlines the *cooperative* nature of German federalism but also its characterization as a *unitary* federal state, that predominately divides the fulfillment of tasks across layers of government instead of assigning areas of policy entirely to single governmental layers. One consequence of this is the historically rooted, particular power that executives have at all layers of government. Cooperation across layers takes place between the executive branches of governments. Especially at the level of the Laender, the parliaments play no considerable role in German federalism. Therefore, the third characterization of Germany's federal system is to be an *executive* federal system.

These federal arrangements entail a number of problems and create adverse incentives for the fiscal performance of subnational entities. The most important one is that the fulfillment of governmental tasks and the fiscal responsibilities associated with it are not transparent. As a consequence, it becomes hard to hold individual tiers of government accountable. This has an impact on the fiscal performance of subnational entities. As it is hard to hold subnational policy fiscally accountable, inhibitions to increase spending are low in some states and municipalities. While at the same time borrowing is the only real autonomous revenue-raising possibility of the Laender, some of them have run excessive deficits. The federal bailouts that were provided for two of them accelerated the soft budget constraint problem.

The 2006 and 2009 Reform Acts aimed at tackling these problems in two ways. First, excessive state borrowing and the soft budget constraint problem are limited through the implementation of fiscal rules for the federal level and, since 2020, for the Laender. Second, transparency and accountability of the different levels of government ought to be strengthened by a disentanglement of tasks and their fulfillment. While these reform steps went into the right direction, they only focused on the spending side of the public budget. The consequent third step towards achieving the goals of the federal reform commissions of 2006 and 2009 of establishing a fiscal constitution that is transparent and that ascribes clear and conceivable accountabilities to all levels of government, would have been to rearrange the revenue side of the budget. Granting more tax autonomy to all layers of government would have been a possibility to bring Germany's fiscal constitution closer to the ideas of Oates' laboratory federalism[86] and to increase the advantages of decentralization in Germany.

Instead, the reforms agreed between the federal level and the Laender in 2017 and 2019 after protracted negotiations rescinded most of the disentanglements of the 2006 reform. It even created new entanglements, with the federal level assuming responsibilities for educational funding, which was the last area of exclusive state autonomy and accountability. While the situation on the expenditure side becomes increasingly intertwined, the same applies to public revenues. Instead of unravelling the revenue side and ascribing revenue-raising and tax-setting autonomy to the Laender, the revenue side has become even more verticalized and thus rigid for the Laender. First, all horizontal elements of the fiscal equalization scheme have been replaced by vertical transfers. Second, the formerly existing vertical transfers from the federal level to the Laender within and outside the equalization scheme have been expanded. Third, the federal level has for the first time assumed funding responsibilities for the local level. Apart from these unfavorable steps, there are also positive aspects of the Reform Act. First, assigning the competencies of highway construction and maintenance solely to the federal level ended the situation in which the Laender had to bear the administrative costs of federal decisions in this area. Second, the strengthening of the Stability Council should lead to a more credible implementation of the fiscal rules for the Laender.

Although there are minor positive aspects to the latest reforms of the federal system, the overall repercussions of the reform remain worrying. Most of the reform steps that took effect in 2020 accelerate unitarianism and a predominant role of the executives in the German federal system. With the recent reforms of German federalism, the Laender degrade themselves and become more and more administrative provinces instead of real federal states. It is noteworthy that it was the Laender that pushed for this design of the latest reform, and not the federal level, although the power of the latter will increase as a result of the reform. Given the complicated negotiation procedures of the German federal system, which are driven by conflicting interests of federal and Laender officials, further reform towards more transparent and accountable arrangements of tasks, revenues, and transfers is unlikely in the near future. What will remain

[86] See Oates, W.E. 1999. "An Essay on Fiscal Federalism". *Journal of Economic Literature*, 37: 1120–1149.

for the time being is an increasingly unitary state within the institutional mantle of federalism.

References

Baretti, C., B. Huber and K. Lichtblau. 2002. "A Tax on Tax Revenue: The Incentive Effects of Equalizing Transfers: Evidence from Germany." *International Tax and Public Finance*, 9: 631–649.

Baskaran, T. 2016. "Intergovernmental Transfers, Local Fiscal Policy and the Flypaper Effect: Evidence from a German State." *FinanzArchiv/Public Finance Analysis*, 72: 1–40.

Blankart, C.B. 2017. *Öffentliche Finanzen in der Demokratie*. Munich: Vahlen.

Bönke, T., B. Jochimsen, and C. Schröder. 2017. "Fiscal Equalization and Tax Enforcement." *German Economic Review*, 18: 377–409.

Buettner, T. 2003. "Tax Base Effects and Fiscal Externalisties of Local Capital Taxation: Evidence from a Panel of German Jurisdictions." *Journal of Urban Economics*, 54: 110–128.

Buettner, T., and D. Wildasin. 2006. "The Dynamics of Municipal Fiscal Adjustment." *Journal of Public Economics*, 90: 1105–1132.

Burret, H.T. 2013. "Die deutsche Schuldenbremse als Allheilmittel – eine Analyse im historischen Kontext." *Journal für Generationengerechtigkeit*, 13: 48–65.

Burret, H.T., and L.P. Feld. 2013. "Fiscal Institutions in Germany." *Swiss Journal of Economics and Statistics*, 149: 249–290.

Burret. H.T., Y. Bury, and L.P Feld. 2018. "Grenzabschöpfungsraten im deutschen Finanzausgleich." *List Forum für Wirtschafts- und Finanzpolitik*, 44: 1–22.

Burret, H.T., L.P. Feld, and E.A. Koehler. 2016. "(Un-)Sustainability of Public Finances in German Laender: A Panel Time Series Approach." *Economic Modelling*, 53: 254–265.

Burret, H.T., L.P. Feld, and E.A. Koehler. 2017. "Fiscal Sustainability of the German Laender: Time Series Evidence." *Finanzarchiv/Public Finance Analysis*, 73: 103–132.

Bury, Y., and L.P. Feld. 2018. "Die Heterogenität der kommunalen Haushalts- und Aufsichtsregeln als Herausforderung im vertikalisierten Fiskalföderalismus." In M. Junkernheinrich, S. Korioth, T. Lenk, H. Scheller and M. Woisin (eds.), *Jahrbuch für öffentliche Finanzen*, 2018-2. Berlin: Berliner Wissenschafts-Verlag.

Christofzik, D.I., L.P. Feld, W.H. Reuter, and M. Yeter. 2018. "Uniting European Fiscal Rules: How to Strengthen the Fiscal Framework. " Working Paper 04/2018, German Council of Economic Experts, Wiesbaden.

Federal Ministry of Finance. 2012. *Compendium on the Federation's Budget Rule as set out in Article 115 of the Basic Law*. Berlin.

Federal Ministry of Finance. 2017. "Die Neuordnung der Bund-Länder-Finanzbeziehungen" *Monthly Report of the Federal Ministry of Finance*, 8. Berlin.

Feld, L.P. and T. Baskaran. 2010. "Federalism, Budget Deficits and Public Debt: On the Reform of Germany's Fiscal Constitition." *Review of Law and Economics*, 6: 365–393.

Feld, L.P., and J. von Hagen. 2007. "Federal Republic of Germany." In A. Shah (ed.), *The Practice of Fiscal Federalism: Comparative Perspectives*. Montreal & Kingston/London/Ithaca: McGill-Queen's University Press.

Feld, L.P., and J. Schnellenbach. 2013. "Verzerrungen im bundesstaatlichen Finanzausgleich." Report for the Laender Bavaria and Hesse. Freiburg.

Feld, L.P., E.A. Koehler and J. Wolfinger. 2020. "Modeling Fiscal Sustainability in Dynamic Macro-Panels with Heterogeneous Effects: Evidence from German Federal States." *International Tax and Public Finance*, 27: 215-239.

Feld, L.P., C. Fuest, J. Haucap, H. Schweitzer, V. Wieland and B.U. Wigger. 2016. *Für eine echte Reform der Bund-Länder-Finanzbeziehungen*. Kronberger Kreis Study No. 62. Berlin: Stiftung Marktwirtschaft.

Fritz, B. and L.P. Feld. 2020. "Common Pool Effects and Local Public Debt in Amalgamated Municipalities." *Public Choice*, 183: 69–99.

German Council of Economic Experts. 2017. *Towards a Forward-Looking Economic Policy: Annual Report 2017/2018*. Wiesbaden: Federal Statistical Office, https://www.sachverstaendigenrat-wirtschaft.de/jahresgutachten-2017-2018.html?&L=1.

Hagen, J. von, and M. Dahlberg. 2004. "Swedish Local Government: Is There a Bailout Problem?" In P. Molander (ed.), *Fiscal Federalism in Unitary States*. New York: Kluwer/Springer.

Hauptmeier, S. 2007. "The Impact of Fiscal Equalization on Local Expenditure Policies: Theory and Evidence from Germany." ZEW Discussion Paper No. 07–006. Mannheim.

Heinemann, F., L.P. Feld, B. Geys, C. Gröpl, S. Hauptmeier, and A. Kalb. 2009. *Der kommunale Kassenkredit zwischen Liquiditätssicherung und Missbrauchsgefahr*. Baden-Baden: Nomos.

Hesse, K. 1962. *Der unitarische Bundesstaat*. Karlsruhe: C.F. Müller.

Oates, W.E. 1999. "An Essay on Fiscal Federalism." *Journal of Economic Literature*, 37: 1120–1149.

Oeter, S. 1998. *Integration und Subsidiarität im deutschen Bundesstaatsrecht*. Tübingen: Mohr Siebeck.

Renzsch, W. 2015. "Bundesstaatlicher Finanzausgleich: Fiskalischer Föderalismus oder funktionale Aufgabenteilung des Grundgesetzes?" In M. Junkernheinrich, S. Korioth, T. Lenk, H. Scheller, and M. Woisin (eds.), *Jahrbuch für öffentliche Finanzen*. Berlin: Berliner Wissenschafts-Verlag.

Rodden, J. 2005. "And the Last Shall be First: Federalism and Fiscal Outcomes in Germany." Department of Political Science, MIT. Cambridge. Mimeo.

Scharpf, F.W., B. Reissert, and F. Schnabl. 1976. *Politikverflechtung: Theorie und Empirie des kooperativen Föderalismus in der Bundesrepublik*. Kronberg/Ts: Scriptor.

Seitz, H. 1999. "Subnational Bailouts in Germany." ZWEI Working Paper B20. Bonn.

Zimmermann, H. 2018. "Deutschland – auf dem Weg zum unitarischen Bundesstaat?" In M. Junkernheinrich, S. Korioth, T. Lenk, H. Scheller and M. Woisin (eds.), *Jahrbuch für öffentliche Finanzen*, 2018–1. Berlin: Berliner Wissenschafts-Verlag.

Republic of India

V. N. Alok

1 Introductory Overview

The Indian constitution is the longest formulated constitution on earth. It was initially espoused by the constituent assembly of India on 26 November 1949 and came into force from 26 January 1950. The Indian constitution is based on federal principles, however, Article one of the constitution affirms that '*India, that is Bharat, shall be a Union*[1] *of States*'. In fact, the constitution has all the features of a federal polity, viz. (a) statutorily mandated two orders of elected government (increased to three in 1993) with clear assignment of responsibilities to federal and state governments as contained in the union list (97 items), state list (66 items) and concurrent list (47 items) of the seventh schedule in the constitution (b) union and states are competent to enact laws and (c) institutions to support a federal polity including techniques for intergovernmental fiscal

[1] Though the term 'union' is used in the constitution, 'Centre' is interchangeably used in this paper.

V. N. Alok (✉)
Indian Institute of Public Administration, New Delhi, India
e-mail: vnalok@gmail.com

J.-F. Tremblay (ed.), *The Forum of Federations Handbook of Fiscal Federalism*, https://doi.org/10.1007/978-3-030-97258-5_6

transfers (IGFT) to correct vertical and horizontal imbalances. The territories of India consist of 28 states and eight union territories including three with the legislature.

India is the largest democracy in the world inhabited by about 1.36 billion people over an area of 3287 thousand square kilometres according to an estimate for 2021 based on Census 2011 (GoI, 2011). Out of total population, more than 0.9 billion were eligible to exercise their adult franchise in 2019 general election for the lower house of parliament. The population represents a large number of ethnic groups and cultures that co-exist in the country which is identified by a diversity of religious beliefs and practices. In fact, India is depicted in the preamble of the constitution as '*sovereign, secular, socialist, democratic republic*' to protect its citizens' social, economic and political rights; liberty of thought, expression, belief, faith and worship; equality of status and of opportunity and to promote fraternity. The Indian subcontinent is the origin of four of the world's major religions; namely Hinduism, Buddhism, Jainism and Sikhism. The largest religious group in India is Hindus which is 79.80% followed by 14.23% of Muslims and 2.34% of Christians.[2] Geographically, India is located in the northern hemisphere and lies in the south of Asia. It is surrounded by the Indian Ocean from the south, the Arabian Sea from the west and Bay of Bengal from the east.

The eighth schedule of the Indian constitution lists 22 official languages, which have been referred to as scheduled languages and given recognition, status, and official encouragement (see Table 1). The largest number of people around 44% speaks Hindi as their primary language, followed by eight percent Bengali, seven percent Marathi seven percent Telugu and so on, according to Census of India Report 2011.[3] The official language of the union is Hindi in the Devanagari script,[4] but the English language is also used by law due to its wide acceptability.

[2] https://www.census2011.co.in/religion.php.

[3] http://censusindia.gov.in/2011Census/C-16_25062018_NEW.pdf, p. 15.

[4] See Article 343 of the constitution (GoI, 2021).

Table 1 Geographical and demographic information

Sr. no.	*Variable*	*Value*
1	Official name	India
2	Area 1000 sq. km	3,287 sq. km
3	Population (2021 estimates) millions	1,361,343
4	Major Religions	Hindu (80%), Muslims (14%), Christians (2%) and Others
5	GDP per capita (US$) (2020—estimates)	2051 US$ [Exchange rate as on 28th February 2021: US$1 = INR74]
6	Constitution: Year and form	1950, Parliamentary democracy, republic
7	Orders of government	Union; States/Union Territories Local: Urban—Municipalities at three levels, i.e. Municipal Corporations (for big cities), Municipal Councils (for small cities) and *Nagar Panchayats (for transitional areas)* Local: Rural—*Panchayats* at three rungs, i.e. district, block and village
8	Constitutional status of local government	Rural and Urban Local Governments recognized in Constitution in 1992 through 73rd and 74th Amendments
9	Official languages	Official languages: 22 Hindi (43%), Bengali (8%), Marathi (7%), Telugu (7%) and Others. Hindi and English are widely used
10	Number and types of constituent units	The union of India consists of 28 States and 8 Union Territories including three (Delhi, Puducherry and Jammu & Kashmir) with the legislature 4516 urban local governments 2,60,485 rural local governments, of which 652 are at the district level, 6,713 at the block level and 2,53,120 at the village level
11	Population, area and per capita GDP in US$ of largest unit	Uttar Pradesh Population (2021 estimates): 230.91 million Area: 240,928 sq. km NSDP (per capita, nominal): INR65704 or $888

(continued)

Table 1 (continued)

Sr. no.	*Variable*	*Value*
12	Population, area and per capita GDP of smallest unit	Sikkim Population (2021 estimates): 0.68 million Area: 7,096 sq. km. NSDP (per capita, nominal): INR425656 or US$5752
13	Per capita NSDP (nominal) (highest)	Goa INR466585 or US$6305
14	Per capita NSDP(nominal)(lowest)	Bihar INR46664 or US$631

Source Government of India (2021a).

1.1 Legal System

The legal system in India is based on common law (Setalvad 1960). Like all other federations, the judiciary interprets the provision of the constitution if any dispute arises. The Supreme Court, an apex body of the legal executive, comprises a chief justice and 33 other judges. A high court exists in every state, while district and session courts are at the district level. The apex court has jurisdiction to give judgements on all disputes between the union and states or between the states. In fact, it is the last court of appeal on civil and criminal proceedings of a high court. The Supreme Court may likewise at its own discretion, grant special leave to appeal any judgement taken by a national court or tribunal. Its verdict is binding on all courts.

India's overall set of laws depends on written law. The judiciary is independent and there exists a separation between the judiciary and the executive. The judicial system in India experiences a shortfall of judges and staff, infrastructural requirements and extraordinary procedural postponements. The lower courts apparently stay feeble and prone to corruption.[5] Foundation of fast-track courts to resolve criminal cases, induction of modern information and communication technology in

[5] A study on corruption in India by Transparency International found in 2005 that, among public services, the lower courts were perceived by the population to be among the most corrupt. India stands at 86th place according to Transparency International's (2020) Corruption Perceptions Index.

courts, national legal literacy mission and additional funding to the judicial system[6] are few measures under judiciary reforms. In general, people have negative perception about the judiciary system as being extremely slow and extraordinarily costly for setting legal disputes (Ram Mohan et al. 2021).

1.2 *Political Parties*

Political parties play a key role in the functioning of democracy. They come together to contest elections and hold power in the government. In India, the concept of multi-party system is at work. The fundamental motivation behind these political groups is to nominate candidates for public office and to get most of them elected as could be expected under the given circumstances. Before each election, each political party announces its election manifesto. When chosen as elected representatives, they try to fulfil the party agenda and the objectives through legislation and programme initiatives. The bureaucracy assists them in these endeavours. The political parties keep opening their gates for new members to join and help the party grow.

Election Commission of India, an autonomous body, is mandated to conduct free and fair elections.[7] The commission gives recognition to political parties and provides symbols to them. There are seven recognized national political parties in India namely, All India *Trinamool* Congress, *Bahujan Samaj* Party (BSP), *Bharatiya Janata* Party (BJP), Communist Party of India (CPI), Communist Party of India-Marxist (CPM), Indian National Congress (INC) and Nationalist Congress Party (NCP).[8] In addition, there are more than 150 regional parties in India.

In the history of Indian politics, there have been three phases which envisage the picture of government stability from past to date. In the first phase, from the very first general election in 1952 till 1977 government at the centre was stable and it was INC which was in power throughout this period. In 1977, many parties including *Janata* Party joined hands and came to power at the centre. They could not survive due to internal

[6] According to Government of India 2006, Rs 2.8 billion has been released by the centre to the state governments since 1993–1994 for developing infrastructure facilities for the judicial system (Department of Justice, Ministry of Home Affairs, online information.

[7] See Article 324 of the constitution

[8] Election Commission of India website accessed at https://eci.gov.in/ on 5 July 2019.

conflicts. INC came to power once again. India, post-1989, witnessed alliance formation and coalition form of governments either by United Progressive Alliance (UPA) led by INC or National Democratic Alliance (NDA) led by BJP. General Election of 2014 was the defining moment when NDA led by BJP won the election with a thumping majority. Within the alliance, BJP alone got the majority by winning 282 seats under the leadership of Narendra Modi. They improved their performance in 2019 election by securing 303 seats. Hence, the government led by BJP is stable due to high number of seats they have secured in the general election.

1.3 Social Norms and Restraints

India is a secular country where state and religion are separated from each other. Being a plural society, harmony and fraternity are maintained between different faiths and religions. Different social norms for different faiths of people pose formidable challenges before governments. Demands for uniform civil codes are raised time and again. The matter remains sensitive even for the judiciary.

1.4 Civil Society

India is bestowed with a vibrant civil society which has played an important role in bringing much-needed changes. Within civil society, there is active participation of non-governmental organizations (NGO's) and other self-help groups who play an important role where and when government fails to perform up to the mark. Some of these NGOs have been recognized and awarded by international organizations, e.g. Kailash Satyarthi, an Indian social activist, won the Nobel Peace Prize in 2014 for waging a peaceful struggle to stop children being exploited as labour instead of attending school. He has also contributed to the development of international conventions on the rights of children (Nobel Prize 2014).[9]

[9] https://www.nobelprize.org/prizes/peace/2014/satyarthi/facts/.

2 Citizens' Charter

The basic goal of the citizen's charter (GoI 2021b)[10] is to empower the citizens in relation to public service delivery. The originally framed six standards of the citizens' charter movement are:

- Quality: improving the quality of services;
- Choice: wherever possible;
- Standards: specify what to expect and how to act if standards are not met;
- Value: for the taxpayers' money;
- Accountability: individuals and organizations and
- Transparency: rules/procedures/schemes/grievances.

In India, the concept of citizens' charter was first adopted at a 'Conference of Chief Ministers of various States and Union Territories' held in May 1997 in the national capital. Department of Administrative Reforms and Public Grievances (DARPG), Government of India, inducted the assignment of synchronizing, framing and making citizens' charter operational. Guidelines for framing the charter and a list of do's and don'ts were conveyed to different government departments/bodies to empower them to bring out focussed and implementable charters. In order to frame the charter, the government organizations at the centre and state levels were advised to formulate a task force with representation from users, senior administration and the cutting-edge staff. The objectives of citizens' charter are mainly fulfilled by the fundamental rights and directive principles of state policy enshrined in the constitution. Fundamental rights like protection of life and personal liberty, freedom of speech and expression helps the citizen in making informed choices and transparency in the system. The directive principles of state policy focusses on promotion of welfare of people, improve the standard of living and public health. The charter, by itself, is not enshrined in the constitution.

[10] https://darpg.gov.in/citizens-charters-historical-background.

2.1 *Basic Economic Indicators*

The economy of India is known as a middle-income emerging market economy. At the time of India's independence the mainstay of the economy was agriculture which contributed more than 50% to the GDP. The economy consistently registered low growth due to extensive centralized state intervention and protectionist economic regulation. Due to alarming economic crises emanated from high fiscal deficit, mounting external trade imbalances, and double-digit inflation, broad economic liberalized policies were adopted in 1991. As a result, India moved from low rate of economic growth to one of the fastest-growing economies in the world. Consequently, the share of agriculture declined significantly due to prominence that service sector acquired with about 55% share in Indian economy.[11]

The BJP government assumed office in early 2014 and during the period 2014–2019, the average GDP[12] (gross domestic product) growth rate in the country was 6.8% against the world's annual average of 3.5%. The per capita GDP in India recorded in 2019 was the US$2169.10 which is equivalent to 17% of the world's average. When the figure is adjusted by purchasing power parity (PPP) the per capita GDP in India is estimated at the US$6754.30 which is equivalent to 38% of the world's average.[13]

India was the fifth largest economy in the world till 2019 and has been pushed back to sixth place in 2020 due to relatively larger impact of the pandemic. Till 2019, India was able to improve its rank on the back of liberalization, globalization, digitization, favourable demographics, and reforms. In the fiscal year[14] 2019–2020, the US$ three trillion Indian

[11] At sub-national level, composition of state GDP and pattern of economic growth differs significantly across states.

[12] GDP is the sum of the gross value added at basic prices, plus all taxes on product, minus all subsidies.

[13] https://tradingeconomics.com/india.

[14] The financial or fiscal year in India commences on 1st April and ends on 31st March of the following year.

economy[15] was at its trough and has gone down further due to the incidence of corona virus pandemic in 2020 and beyond. As a result, the GDP in 2020–2021 has registered a negative growth of 6.6% as compared to positive growth of four percent in the previous year.[16] This contraction in GDP is largely attributed to a very significant contraction in trade, hotels, transport and communication. In fact, all sectors declined except agriculture which continued to grow at three percent. The negative economic growth has limited the fiscal space of the government and made them to revise its fiscal deficit target to 9.3% of GDP in the covid year.[17]

3 The Structure of Government and Division of Fiscal Powers[18]

3.1 System of Governance

A Legislature, a Judiciary and an Executive are three separate and independent branches of governance in India. The arrangement is intended to maintain democracy, avoid autocracy and build accountability framework. While the legislature and the executive branches are interwoven, the judiciary is independent and interprets, among others, the provisions of the constitution. There is a council of ministers[19] with prime minister as the head to aid and advice the president. It is notable that advice tendered by the ministers to the president for any executive action cannot be inquired in any court of law. The president has a tenure of five years and is elected by an electoral college made up of members of parliament of both the upper and lower houses and the state legislatures. Similarly, the vice president has a fixed tenure of five years and is elected by an electoral college comprising members of both houses of parliament. The union cabinet is collectively responsible to the *Lok Sabha* or lower house (house of the

[15] The GDP of India consist of about 20% primary sector (comprising agriculture, fishing, forestry and mining and quarrying), about 25% secondary sector (comprising manufacturing, electricity, gas, water supply and other utility services and construction), and about 55% tertiary sector (services).

[16] Provisional estimate on national annual income released on 31 May 2021 by National Statistical Office, India.

[17] Fiscal deficit in the year 2020–2021 was set at 3.5 of GDP in the beginning.

[18] This section is drawn upon Alok (2011).

[19] See Article 74 of the constitution,

people). The members of the *Lok Sabha* are elected directly on the basis of adult suffrage of a jurisdiction or constituency (comprising on an average 1.5 million voters and 2.5 million people) in a general election held every fifth year or earlier if the *Lok Sabha* is dissolved. The house may have a limit of 550 members, of which 530 are elected from the states and 20 from the union territories.[20]

After every general election, the political party having the majority chooses its leader who stakes his claim to the president to form the government. Under Article 75 of the constitution, the President appoints the prime minister and the remaining ministers in the cabinet. Members of the cabinet must be members of parliament. Other person, who is not a member of either house of parliament, ceases to be a minister after six consecutive months of holding the position.[21]

As discussed earlier, the legislative power rests with the parliament consisting of the president, the *Lok Sabha* (House of the People) or lower house and the *Rajya Sabha* (Council of States) or upper house. The *Rajya Sabha* may have a limit of 250 members, of which 238 are elected by the members of legislative assemblies of states and union territories through open ballot and 12 members are nominated by the president having exceptional expertise or exposure in literature, arts, science and social service.[22] Members sit for alternate terms lasting six years with 33% of the 238 retiring every subsequent year and are qualified for re-appointment through elections.

All bills can be introduced in either houses of the parliament. Only money bills (including the union budget) are presented in the *Lok Sabha*.[23] These bills need to be passed by a simple majority in both houses and consented by the president before it becomes a law. The president has the power to return the bill with a request for amendment, but, the president may not withhold assent if the bill is passed again in its original form. The money bill is deemed to have been passed by both houses in the form in which it was passed by the lower house. If the council of states or upper house does not return the bill to the lower house within

[20] In addition, under article 331 of the constitution, the President may, if he believes that the Anglo-Indian community is not adequately represented in *Lok Sabha*, nominate not more than two members of that community to the house.

[21] See Article 75 of the constitution.

[22] See Article 80 of the constitution.

[23] See Article 109 of the constitution.

14 days, it is considered to be passed by the two houses. In other cases, the suggestions and recommendations of *Rajya Sabha* cannot be overridden unless and until the entire parliament goes for a joint session to break the deadlock.

On the other hand, an ordinance may be promulgated if the president considers it as a requisite to pass legislation during parliament's recess.[24] The ordinance has the similar power as an act of the parliament. However, it ceases to exist in six weeks after the reassembly of parliament except in case it is passed as law by the two houses.

The constitution has an arrangement for a separation of jurisdiction between the parliament and the legislative assemblies of states and union territories to make laws in their respective areas as stipulated in the central and state lists of the constitution. Like parliamentary elections, there is a provision for election, in every fifth year, of assemblies in states and three union territories, i.e. Delhi, Jammu & Kashmir and Puducherry in India to elect members of legislative assemblies (MLAs). Election Commission of India conducts both the elections. MLAs of the political party having a majority choose their leader who stakes his claim before the governor of the state to form the government. On the basis of this exercise, the governor appoints the chief minister and other ministers, as per the former's advice. The governor is appointed by the president of India for five years or earlier. In other five territories, the president appoints an administrator at the advice of the central government. At sub-national level, the state government, headed by the chief minister, has all the powers to (a) legislate matters in the state list of the constitution and (b) administer the state through state civil servants.

Sharp interstate variations can be seen across all 28 states and eight UTs (see Table 2). Population of Uttar Pradesh, the biggest state, is about 340 times more than that of Sikkim, the smallest state. The per capita income of Goa, the richest state is about ten times more than that of Bihar, the poorest state. Their pattern of economic developments is also different. A few states register double-digit economic growth whereas a few others cannot achieve even five percent. This affects the quality of governance across states. As a result, institutions deciding allocation among states have to take all these factors into consideration.

[24] See Article 123 of the constitution.

Table 2 Indian states—some basic facts

No.	*State*	*Area ('000 Sq. km)*	*Population (million) (census 2011)*	Lok Sabha *(lower house) seats*	*SGDP growth rate for 2019–2020 at constant price (2011–2012)*	*Share of states (%) in net proceeds of central taxes (2020–2025)*
1	Andhra Pradesh	162.923	49.58	24	8.16	4.05
2	Arunachal Pradesh	83.743	1.38	2	4.59[a]	1.76
3	Assam	78.438	31.20	14	6.42	3.13
4	Bihar	94.163	104.09	40	10.47	10.06
5	Chhattisgarh	135.192	25.55	11	5.32	3.41
6	Goa	3.702	1.45	2	9.73	0.39
7	Gujarat	196.244	60.44	26	9.19[a]	3.48
8	Haryana	44.212	25.35	10	7.75	1.09
9	Himachal Pradesh	55.673	6.85	3	5.56	0.83
10	Jharkhand	79.716	32.98	14	6.69	3.31
11	Karnataka	191.791	61.09	27	5.95	3.65
12	Kerala	38.852	33.41	19	7.46[a]	1.93
13	Madhya Pradesh	308.252	72.63	28	7.62	7.85
14	Maharashtra	307.713	112.37	48	5.99[a]	6.32
15	Manipur	22.327	2.85	2	7.11	0.72
16	Meghalaya	22.429	2.97	2	8.16	0.77
17	Mizoram	21.081	1.10	1	14.07	0.50
18	Nagaland	16.579	1.97	1	7.05[a]	0.57
19	Odisha	155.707	41.94	21	5.21	4.53
20	Punjab	50.362	27.74	13	5.33	1.81
21	Rajasthan	342.239	68.54	25	5.05	6.03
22	Sikkim	7.096	0.61	1	6.92	0.39
23	Tamil Nadu	130.060	72.14	38	8.03	4.08
24	Telangana	112.122	35.19	17	8.23	2.10
25	Tripura	10.486	3.67	2	9.79	0.71
26	Uttar Pradesh	240.928	199.81	80	3.81	17.94
27	Uttarakhand	53.483	10.09	5	6.87[a]	1.12
28	West Bengal	88.752	91.27	42	7.26	7.52
	All states	3054.265	1178.19	500	4.18	100.00

Note #Union territories are excluded in the table, hence total of all states is not comparable to all India picture

Source Government of India (2020), Ministry of Statistics and Programme Implementation, Government of India and http://loksabhaph.nic.in/

[a]Figures are for the year 2018–2019

At the third tier, elections are also held in every fifth year to elect representatives of *panchayats* (rural local governments) and municipalities (urban local governments). *Panchayat* is constituted, through election, in every state at three rungs, i.e. the district, the intermediate and the village.[25] Intermediate p*anchayat* may not be established in a state having a population not surpassing two million. Similarly for urban areas, municipalities are constituted at three levels, i.e. municipal corporation for a large urban area, municipal council for small urban area and *nagar panchayat* for an area having transition from rural to urban.[26] Though these institutions became legal entities through the 74th constitutional amendment act which is a central act but these institutions are defined in the conformity act (state municipal act) based on population, area and activity.

As the local government is a state subject, the state legislature may make their own rules to conduct elections, in every fifth year, through the state election commission. After the election, the group of elected representatives provides leadership to officials in his/her respective local area for delivery of services and preparation of plans for local economic development and social justice as stipulated in the respective state act. There are separate laws in each state for *panchayats* and municipalities. Similarly, separate schedules, eleventh and twelfth, were inserted, among others, in the constitution in 1993 through the seventy-third and seventy-fourth constitutional amendments for *panchayat* and municipalities respectively. These eleventh and twelfth schedules enumerate twenty-nine and eighteen subjects, respectively. These subjects are only indicative and not exhaustive. Most subjects in these two lists are state concurrent which lead to overlapping. At any case, it is ultimately the authority of state legislature to make laws on these subjects and devolve functions to local governments. In addition, on these matters, the centre and state governments design vertical programmes in which *panchayats* and municipalities are assigned roles.[27] Both the schedules include core municipal functions including waste management, sanitation, primary health, primary education, drinking water, parks, street lights, roads, etc.

[25] See Article 243B of the constitution.

[26] See Article 243Q of the constitution.

[27] See Articles 243G and 243 W of the constitution for assignment of functions to panchayats and municipalities, respectively. These Articles are interpreted differently by many who casually bracket the eleventh and twelfth schedules with union and state lists.

Hence, election is held at three levels, i.e. parliament, state assembly and local governments. In all the cases, there is an in-built feature of accountability of elected representative. Every fifth year, incumbent candidate or party seeks re-election for their people who in turn, approve or disapprove them. Accountability of the governments is also fixed through parliamentary proceedings, media, right to information, autonomous audit, ombudsman, vigilance commissions, etc.

3.2 *Division of Fiscal Powers*

The fiscal powers shared between union and the constituent units, i.e. states in India are mostly stated in the constitution or are specified by the law, like most federations of the world. As mentioned earlier, the powers and jurisdiction of the respective levels of government are set forth in the seventh schedule of the Indian constitution which contains the union list, the state list and the concurrent list (covering areas of joint authority). The residual powers belong to the centre.[28] Therefore, the centre can enter tax fields not classified in the constitution. For example, the central government, under such power, imposed gift tax in the past which was abolished in 1998. Similarly, service tax was also imposed in the beginning of this century under such power. In 2017, the tax has been subsumed under nationwide goods and services tax (GST).

It can be argued that the tax assignment in the Indian constitution is consistent with the theoretical literature on the subject (see Table 3). The special case identified in relation to the power of the states to tax natural resources, like minerals was rectified subsequently by giving dominant power to the Union to levy or regulate the tax on minerals.[29]

However, the Indian constitutional scheme on tax assignment appears to be acceptable on paper, its real working has identified few limitations including the issue of vertical imbalance, despite the fact that considerable number of taxes have been allotted to the states but the buoyant taxes, viz. corporate income tax and personal income tax and custom duties are with

[28] This provision is contradictory to the principle of subsidiarity under which first choice is given to local government.

[29] Mines and Minerals (Development and Regulation) Act, 1957.

Table 3 Indicative legislative responsibility and actual provision of services by different orders of government

Actual allocation of function (de facto)	*Public service*	*Legislative responsibility (de jure)*
Union/state/local level	List each service/function	Federal/state or provincial/local level
Union	Defence	Union
Union	Foreign Policy	Union
Union	Banking, insurance and currency	Union
Union	International trade and commerce	Union
Union	Major minerals	Union
Union	Railways	Union
Union	Postal service	Union
Union	Census	Union
Union	Shipping and offshore exploration	Union
Union	Airways	Union
Union	Patents, copyrights	Union
Union	Citizenship	Union
Union	Interstate trade and commerce	Union
Union	Interstate rivers	Union
Union	Emigration	Union
Union and states	Criminal law and procedures	Union and states
Union and states	Civil procedure	Union and states
Union and states	Marriage and divorce	Union and states
Union and states	Bankruptcy and insolvency	Union and states
Union and states	Education	Union and states
Union and states	Healthcare	Union and states
Union and states	Contracts	Union and states
Union and states	Environment and forests	Union and states
Union and states	Economic and social planning	Union and states
Union and states	Social security and insurance	Union and states
Union and states	Charities and charitable institutions	Union and states
Union and states	Electricity	Union and states
State	Police and public order	State
State	Administration of justice	State
State	Prisons, reformatories etc.,	State
State and local	Public health and sanitation	State
State and local	Agriculture and animal husbandry	State

(continued)

Table 3 (continued)

Actual allocation of function (de facto)	*Public service*	*Legislative responsibility (de jure)*
States and local	Water	State
State and local	Forests	State
State and local	Fisheries	State
State	Minor minerals	State
State	Administration of justice, jails and police	State
State	Civil and property rights	State
State and local	Public lands and natural resources	State
State and local	Local governments (municipalities in urban areas and Panchayats in rural areas)	State
State and local	Water supply and sanitation	State
State	Incorporation of companies	State
Local	Local services	State
State and local	Education	State
State and local	Social welfare	State

the union (see Table 4). Till 2017, even the central excise duty was also assigned to the centre which has been subsumed under GST. As a result, the union government collects around two-thirds of the combined total revenue. The states along with the local governments[30] collect the rest. Since sub-national governments are assigned two-thirds of expenditure responsibilities (see Table 5). This requires enormous amount of fiscal transfers from union to state governments (see Table 6). In any case, vertical imbalance of some degree is viewed as desirable in a federation to guarantee intergovernmental fiscal transfers or redistribution of income to ascertain equity. Such provisions have been designed deliberately by the constitution-makers.

[30] Local governments except municipal corporations collect negligible revenue. For details, see Alok (2009, 2019).

Table 4 Tax assignment to various orders of government

	Determination of		*Collection and administration*	*Share in combined revenue*	
Federal	*Base*	*Rate*		*Federal*	*State*
Personal income tax (non-agricultural)	Union	Union	Union	6.20	4.06
Corporation income tax	Union	Union	Union	10.74	5.85
Union excise duties	Union	Union	Union	8.03	2.48
Customs	Union	Union	Union	4.72	2.97
Taxes on services	Union	Union	Union	4.59	3.15
Total				34.28	18.51
State or provincial					
Tax and land and agricultural incomes	State	State	State	0	0.40
Stamp duties and registration fees	State	State	State	0	3.52
Sales tax	State	State	State	0	20.03
State excise duties	State	State	State	0	3.87
Taxes on transport	State	State	State	0	1.71
Electricity duty					1.14
Entertainment tax	State	State	State	0	0.10
Others	State	State	State	0	1.44
Fees, fines and charges	State	State	State	0	5.56
Total					37.76
Local					
Property tax	Provincial	Local	Provincial	N	N
User fees on water supply	Local	Local	Local		

Note Latest actual data are available only for the fiscal year 2015–16. The same is used. Assignment of taxes has undergone changes since the introduction of nationwide Goods and Services Tax (GST) in 2017

Source Author's computation from Indian Public Finance Statistics, 2017–2018

N—Data not available; * Reliable data on local governmant revenue are not avaible in India. Data from two different sources do not match.

3.3 Sharing of Central Taxes

In spite of the fact that powers have been assigned to both the union and the states, the union cannot appropriate the proceeds of all the taxes collected by them. According to the design of the constitution,

Table 5 Shares of different levels of government in total expenditures

Item of expenditure	*Centre*	*States*	*Total*	*Percent of total expenditure*
A. Interest payment	67.0	33.0	100	16.1
B. Defence	100.0	0.00	100	5.5
C. Administrative service	34.2	65.8	100	4.8
D. Social and community services	19.5	80.5	100	20.1
i. Education	16.9	83.1	100	10.9
ii. Medical and health	10.4	89.6	100	3.9
iii. Family welfare	55.8	44.2	100	0.9
iv. Others	26.4	73.6	100	4.4
E. Economic services	34.5	65.5	100	24.8
i. Agri. and allied services	32.9	67.1	100	8.7
ii. Industry and minerals	66.8	33.2	100	1.8
iii. Power, irri. flood control	4.1	96.0	100	6.5
iv. Tpt. and communication	52.1	47.9	100	5.5
v. General economic services	74.2	25.8	100	1.8
vi. Public works	13.3	86.7	100	0.5
F. Others	52.5	47.5	100	26.4
G. Loans and advances	5.9	94.1	100	2.2
Total	44.5	55.5	100	100.0

Note Latest actual data are available only for the fiscal year 2015–2016. The same is used
Source Indian Public Finance Statistics, 2017–2018

Table 6 Vertical fiscal gaps (in bn INR)

	Total revenue collected	*Total revenue available, after net transfers*[a] *to other level of government*	*Expenditures*
National	27320.93	15846.14	18149.58
State/provincial	18631.94	30106.73	22853.53
Local	NA	NA	
All orders	45952.87	45952.87	41003.11

Note Latest actual data are available only for the fiscal year 2015–2016. The same is used
Source Author's computation from Indian Public Finance Statistics, 2017–2018
[a]Transfer to States is calculated @42% from Total Revenue of National Government as recommended by the 14th Finance Commission for the period 2015–2020 (GoI, 2014).
NA—Reliable data for local governments are not available

revenue from central taxes should be shared with the states to fulfil their necessities.

Since 2000, all union taxes have been brought into a divisible pool and a certain percentage is shared with the states.[31] Historically, only personal income tax and the union excise duties were shared with the states.[32] In addition, the central government used to collect the tax on behalf of the states, under the tax rental arrangements and then allocated the proceeds among the states on the basis of the formula suggested by the successive finance commissions. These were (a) additional excise duties in lieu of sales tax on textiles, tobacco and sugar[33] and (b) grant in lieu of tax on railway passenger fares.

The constitution provides for sharing of all central taxes except (a) stamp duty levied by the centre but collected and retained by the states; (b) integrated goods and services tax (IGST) in course of interstate trade and commerce and (c) surcharge on taxes and duties and any cess levied for specific purposes by the centre. Only net proceeds of tax revenue are shared, after deducting cost of collections.

In 2017, a nationwide goods and services tax (GST) was introduced.[34] The GST replaced a host of indirect taxes being levied by the central and state governments. It subsumed central excise duty, services tax, additional excise duties, central sales tax, additional customs duty commonly known as countervailing duty and special additional duty of customs at the central level; and state value added tax/sales tax, entertainment tax (other than the tax levied by the local governments), octroi or entry tax, purchase tax, luxury tax, and taxes on lottery, betting and gambling at the state level. The primary idea for introducing GST was to reap the benefit of the common market that Indian union of states offers. It was envisioned to bring in efficiency gains in the economy through 'one-nation-one tax' which could ensure better tax buoyancy and compliance,

[31] Following the constitution (eightieth amendment) act, 2000.

[32] Sharing of the income tax was mandatory under Article 270 while that of the union excise duties was discretionary under Article 272 of the constitution. These Articles have been amended.

[33] These commodities were considered to be of national importance and the states did not levy sales tax on these items as per the agreement, in 1956, between the union and the states.

[34] Through constitution (one hundred and one) amendment act.

transparency, ease to production and trade and elimination of cascading effect of taxation. However, the impact of GST in the first three years hints '*an overall disturbing trend and differentiated impact among states*' (GoI 2020, p. 54).

The basic attribute of GST implemented in India is that it is based on the principle of destination-based consumption taxation contrary to the earlier principle of origin-based taxation. It is a dual GST with the union and the states simultaneously levying tax on a common base. Centre levies and collects the central GST (CGST) and states levy and collect state GST (SGST). Rates of both GSTs are equal. In addition, an integrated goods & services tax (IGST) is imposed by the central government on interstate supplies of goods and services and on imports. The GST accounts for 35% of the gross tax revenue of the centre and around 44% of own tax revenue of the states, as per the analysis of the 15th FC.

3.4 Types of Fiscal Transfers in India

Intergovernmental fiscal transfers (IGFT) from the central government to the states in India go as far back as 1919 and have encountered many changes since the Independence of India in 1947. Like most of the nations, globally, there are two purposes of India's fiscal transfer system which includes, first, correcting vertical fiscal imbalances between the union and the states and second, correcting horizontal imbalances in fiscal capacity among the states. These two aims are not always independent of each other and have both been integrated into the actual operation of the system (Kelkar 2019). The IGFT from the centre to states/UTs can be broadly categorized as finance commission (FC) transfers and other transfer or non-FC transfers. The FC transfers comprise (a) devolution to states/UTs from the union tax divisible pool; (b) fiscal transfers to local governments —both *panchayats and municipalities;* (c) revenue deficit grants to states incurring revenue deficit even after the central tax devolution; (d) grants for disaster management and (e) other specific grants. These are made primarily under Article 280 of the constitution, but some of the transfers are mandated under Articles 270 and 275.

Non-FC transfers can be ascribed to article 282 of the constitution which empowers the '*Union or a State to make any grants for any public purpose*'. These transfers include central sector schemes,[35] centrally sponsored schemes[36] (CSS) and compensation to select states/UTs for GST revenue loss (till 2022). Article 282, inter alia, mandated the institution of planning commission to make 'plan transfers' comprising formula-based unconditional transfers and specific purpose transfers some of which were matching grants. The planning commission was abolished in 2015–2016 and distinction of 'plan' and 'non-plan' in budgets was also discontinued. Consequently, as can be seen in Table 7, non-FC transfers have been reduced from 18.57% of gross revenue receipts in 2014–2015 to 13.24% in 2015–2016 after the recommendation of the 14th FC which increased the share of the states in union divisible pool from 32 to 42%. In addition, one can note, a shift in enlarging the total transfers as a share to GDP from 5.76% during the 13th FC period to 6.30 during the 14th FC award period.

3.5 *Union Finance Commission (UFC)*

The constitution stipulates the appointment of an independent finance commission by the president of India every five years to make recommendations on the devolution of central taxes and grants to be given to the states.[37] The commission has a chairman who is appointed based on his experience and eminence in public affairs. His status is at par with the minister in the union cabinet. There are four other members whose qualifications for appointment are based on their experience and special knowledge in economics, public administration, law and government accounting. The terms of reference (ToRs) of the commission, as per constitutional provisions, are

(i) the distribution between the Union and States of the net proceeds of Union taxes and the allocation between the States of the respective shares of such proceeds;

[35] Central sector schemes are hundred per cent funded and executed by the central government on subject in the union list of the constitution.

[36] Centrally sponsored schemes (CSS) are designed and funded by the central ministries to attain national goals largely on subjects in the state list of the constitution. State government implements each scheme with a matching contribution up to maximum fifty percent.

[37] See Article 280 of the constitution.

Table 7 Transfers from the union to states as proportion of gross revenue receipts (in percent)

Commission	*Finance Commission (FC) transfers*			*Other transfer (non-FC)*	*Total transfers*[a] *(4+5)*	*Ratio of FC to non-FC transfers*	*Total transfers as %age of GDP*
	share in central taxes	*grants*	*Total FC transfers*				
1	*2*	*3*	*4*	*5*	*6*	*7*	*8*
FC-XII (2005–2010)	22.03	4.35	26.38	21.01	47.39	55.7:44.3	6.03
FC-XIII (2010–2015)	23.80	3.96	27.75	20.47	48.22	57.6:42.4	5.76
2010–2011	21.68	3.12	24.79	23.87	48.66	50.9:49.1	6.45
2011–2012	25.27	4.35	29.62	23.73	53.35	55.5:44.5	6.17
2012–2013	24.84	3.86	28.70	19.96	48.66	59.0:41.0	5.74
2013–2014	23.79	4.03	27.82	17.93	45.75	60.8:39.2	5.45
2014–2015	23.41	4.28	27.70	18.57	46.27	59.9:40.1	5.35
FC-XIV (2015–2019)	31.37	4.51	35.88	14.74	50.62	70.9:29.1	6.30
2015–2016	29.66	4.96	34.61	13.24	47.86	72.3:27.7	5.93
2016–2017	30.57	4.80	35.38	13.04	48.41	73.1:26.9	6.26
2017–2018	31.87	4.37	36.24	16.77	53.01	68.4:31.6	6.55
2018–2019	32.88	4.05	36.92	15.45	52.38	70.5:29.5	6.39
2019–2020 (RE)	26.15	4.93	31.08	18.61	49.69	62.5:37.5	6.10
FC-XV (2020–2021)—BE	27.93	5.34	33.27	18.22	51.48	64.6:35.4	6.43

Note RE means revised estimate; BE means budget estimates
Source Government of India (2020) Main Report (p. 90)
[a]From 12th FC onwards, transfers include direct transfers to State implementing agencies
FC Transfers include the share in central taxes, general purpose grants and specific purpose grants; and Non-FC transfers include matching grants for vertical programs of union government and other grants

(ii) the principles which should govern the grants-in-aid of the revenues of the States out of the Consolidated Fund of India.

(iii) the measures needed to augment the Consolidated Funds of a State to supplement the resources of the Panchayats and Municipalities in the State on the basis of the recommendations made by the Finance Commissions of the State; and

(iv) any other matter referred to the Commission by the President in the interest of sound finance.

Under the last item, a number of tasks had been relegated to the commission in the past like setting the fiscal rules and goals for the union and states, measures to be taken for sustainable development and the security of ecology and environment, rescheduling and writing-off of states' borrowings, assessment of public expenditure management framework, review disaster management systems, strategic way to deal with public enterprise reform and giving incentives to the states to undertake tax reforms, doing away with the losses of power sector, proposing measurable performance-based incentives for states at appropriate level of government, encouraging ease of doing business, supporting digital economy, etc.

The commission is the agency that suggests the method for allocating the transfers based on revenue sharing. It is not a standing body and is dissolved after it has made the recommendations and submitted the report to the president of India. Till 2021, fifteen UFCs have submitted their reports. The last was the 15th FC which submitted two sets of reports, the first in December 2019 and the second in November 2020 covering the award period 2020–2021 and 2021–2026, respectively.

The recommendations of UFC are traditionally respected and mostly accepted in the parliament and carried out by the executives. The role of the UFC as envisioned in the constitution was waning when the planning commission was appointed through a cabinet resolution in 1950. The planning commission assumed the control to make grants for plan purposes. The extent of the UFC's review was restricted to evaluating the non-plan (generally the expenditure on the establishment) needs of the states and making tax devolution and grants to meet these expenditure responsibilities. However, the mandate of the 14th FC and the 15th FC did not restrict its scope to assessing only the non-plan side of the states' budgets and both the UFCs made suggestions to cover the entire revenue account. Consequently, when the planning commission itself has been annulled in 2015, it did not make any discontinuity (Reddy and Reddy 2019).

3.6 *Constitutional Status of Local Governments and their finances*[38]

Local governments in India, as is the case in many federal countries, are expected to make provisions for essential public services like street lighting, sanitation, roads, drinking water supply, etc. and are authorized to collect some tax and non-tax revenues for the same. However, these resources are inadequate to meet the expenditure responsibilities and are making the local governments to largely depend on their respective state governments for the financial support.

The *panchayats* and municipalities were recognized as an institution of self-government in the statute book with the enactment of the 73rd and the 74th constitutional amendment acts in 1993. Consequently, two sections, *viz.* parts IX and IXA were added to the constitution for *panchayats* and municipalities, respectively. These sections are bigger than American constitution and carbon copies of each other. This accelerated the process of decentralization with greater devolution and delegation of powers to local governments.

With these constitution amendment acts in place, the state legislature is expected to devolve and delegate powers, responsibilities and authorities to the local government so as to empower them to function as institutions of self-government. The state legislature is also expected to devolve some tax and non-tax handles to the *panchayats* and municipalities and also assign to them the revenues of certain state level taxes.

3.7 *Finances of the Local Governments*

In general, the functional responsibilities are closely related to the financial powers given to local government. In reality, there is a significant mismatch between the two, resulting in severe budgetary stress at the local and consequent reliance on intergovernmental fiscal transfers. Even in the progressive states, fiscal transfers, *viz.* revenue sharing and grants are the main sources of finances for the *panchayats* and municipalities. The state finance commission (SFC), which is an autonomous institution to review the financial position of the *panchayats* and the municipalities, respectively, defines these fiscal transfers and makes recommendations to the governor of the state on the principles that should govern[39]:

[38] The section draws upon Alok (2006, 2009).

[39] See Articles 243 I and 243 Y of the constitution.

i. 'The distribution between the state and the *panchayats* and municipalities of the net proceeds of the taxes, duties, tolls and fees leviable by the state, and their allocation between the *panchayats* and municipalities at all levels for such proceeds;
ii. The determination of the taxes, duties, tolls and fees which may be assigned to, or appropriated by, the *panchayats* and municipalities;
iii. The grants-in-aid to *panchayats* and municipalities from the consolidated fund of the state;
iv. The measures needed to improve the financial position of the *panchayats* and municipalities;
v. Any other matter in the interest of sound finance of the *panchayats* and municipalities'.

With few exceptions, the states have verbatim reproduced the constitutional provisions and placed them as the terms of reference for the SFC. However, significant variations are noticed in the approach, methodology and recommendations of the SFCs across states and time. Even though, the following common major heads can be found from these diverse recommendations of about eighty SFC reports attempted at different period of time (Alok 2021). These are: (a) global sharing; (b) assignment of revenue; (c) horizontal distributions; (d) grants-in-aid; (e) devolution of functions and functionaries and (f) other measures. The heads emanate from the constitutional provisions and common pattern found in SFC reports:

Under 'global sharing', revenue receipts of the state are shared from the divisible pool following the recommendations of the respective SFC. However, states differ greatly in how they define the divisible pool, such as total revenue, own revenue, own tax revenue and so on. Under the second head, SFC recommends devolving revenue handles to local governments. Moreover, the SFC makes horizontal distribution among different rungs of *panchayats* and different levels of the municipalities.

In general, the capacity to generate its own revenue is very limited for the local governments. The sources which contribute most to the small kitty of own revenue of local governments are mainly, advertisement tax, professional tax, property tax, taxes on vehicles and animals, theatre tax, developmental charges, fees and fines, rental income from properties, user charges on services, etc.

It may be suggested that the states could enhance the tax base of the *panchayats* and municipalities by assigning a few buoyant sources of revenue to them. However, the states have not been able to use this option as they themselves face limited fiscal space and also because of the perception that the *panchayats* and the municipalities have inadequate organizational and administrative capacity. The reliance on fiscal transfers is eroding their autonomy to use resources as per their own priorities. Moreover, these transfers are often conditional and therefore hardly assist in the requirements of their fiscal capacity building.

It is, therefore, the central government's responsibility to transfer sufficient funds to the local government through (a) UFC mechanism[40] and (b) centrally sponsored schemes (CSSs). UFC mechanism is discussed in the subsequent section. CSSs bring about significant conditional grants to local governments. Developmental ministries of central government design and administer these schemes and assign various responsibilities to the local governments for grass root implementation. The budget provisions to such programmes have registered a significant growth and the institutional mechanisms tend to provide key role to the *panchayats* and municipalities in their planning and implementation.

4 Fiscal Federalism and Macroeconomic Management

The central government, in Indian federation, has a predominant role in macroeconomic management as dependency of a state on centre is high by design. The resource mechanism is small with the states whereas centre has large number of resources. On the other hand, states are responsible for all the basic primary services to the citizens. Hence, the coordination between central and state governments in fiscal arrangements decides the fate of the state and its people. But, the liberalized policies initiated in 1991 provided opportunities for states to control domestic and foreign investment (Singh and Srinivasan 2005; Singh 2007). This has enhanced the autonomy and increased the space of states in designing their own economic policies to compete among themselves and woo corporate investments.

The changing federal fiscal architecture has enhanced the states' public expenditure. It is the fact that '*total state expenditures as a percent GDP are greater than that of the Union*' (GoI 2020, p. 11). With

[40] See Article 280 sub clauses (3) (bb) (c) of the constitution.

such increasing expenditure, decentralization is arguably beneficial for macroeconomic performance (Rodden and Wibbels 2001; Shah 1999). However, the capacity of state governments in spending on infrastructure is constrained due to their inability to take independent decisions to borrow. States have to take the central government's permission for internal borrowing if they are indebted to the latter.[41] As a matter of fact, all states remain in debt to the centre that tends to reschedule the lending. Unlike the centre, the sub-national government can borrow only from internal sources after a prior consent of the parliament. These sources include public sector banks, other state-owned financial institutions and national small savings fund comprising largely household savings deposited in post offices.[42] In addition, State governments resort to idle pension fund created through the mandatory contributions of government employees. Furthermore, many states keep the liquidity by delaying payments to government-owned agencies including the state electricity boards (Singh 2007).

In view of the on-going pandemic and the financial crunch being faced by the state governments, the market borrowing limit of states has been enhanced by the central government from three percent to four percent of state GDP for the year 2021–2022. This temporary measure for a year was decided with a rider that a portion of the additional limit was meant for capital expenditure. In the year 2021–2022, the states are also allowed to borrow 75% of the limit in the initial nine months of the fiscal. In the previous year they were allowed to borrow only up to 50% of the annual limit. However, the states, can also secure short-term debt up to 90 days, at low interest rate from the Reserve Bank of India (RBI)[43] which manages the public debt of the central and the state governments

[41] See Article 293 of the constitution.

[42] The small savings collected through post offices contribute substantially to total household savings.

[43] RBI is the central bank set up on 1 April 1935 and its affairs are governed by a central board of directors appointed by the Government of India in keeping with the RBI Act, 1934. It decides the monetary policy and controls monetary instruments such as bank rate, interest rate, exchange rate, statutory liquidity ratio, cash reserve ratio, etc. to achieve the goals. The primary objective of the monetary policy is to contain inflation while keeping in mind the objective of growth. The RBI Act was amended through the Finance Act, 2016, to provide for an institutionalized framework for a Monetary Policy Committee to maintain price stability, while keeping in mind the objective of growth. The Monetary Policy Committee is entrusted with the task of fixing the repo rate (rate

and acts as a banker to them. An independent statutory body namely public debt management authority is being contemplated to ease RBI out from this role.[44]

The public debt was 73.8% of GDP in the pre-pandemic year. This was a combined total liabilities of centre and states in which the debt of the states was 26.3% of GDP and external liabilities of the centre was 2.9% of GDP.[45] Though combined public debts have been constantly increasing since 2010–2011, the extraordinary situation due to pandemic is turning this constant increase to a giant leap emanated from shrinking GDP and increasing foregone revenue, public spending and liquidity support. However, this increase is at pace with the current global trend.

5 Fiscal Equity and Efficiency Concerns and Intergovernmental Fiscal Transfers

The allocation of resources between the centre and the states and among the states begins with a discussion on vertical fiscal imbalance and horizontal imbalances. The vertical imbalance between the centre and the states was created through the constitutional assignment of expenditure responsibilities and revenue powers. The central government has more resources and state governments carry more responsibilities. In order to correct this vertical imbalance formula-based IGFT from centre to state was envisaged.

In this context, the UFC has been recommending a share from the net proceeds of all central taxes (after deducting cost of collection, cess and surcharges). It started with the recommendation of the 10th FC (award period 1995–2000) which estimated 28% states' share in the divisible pool. Successive UFCs made incremental increase to this share till 32% that the 13th FC recommended for its award period 2010–2015 (GoI 2009). The year 2015, was the turning point for Indian federal finance when the age-old Planning Commission was abolished. The UFC

at which the central bank lends money to banks) to contain inflation. The interest rate on short term (90 days) is equivalent to repo rate which is four per cent in covid times.

[44] https://dea.gov.in/divisionbranch/public-debt-management-cell.

[45] Only central government can borrow from external sources.

acquired the status of the only institution for IGFT between the centre and the States. Consequently, the 14th FC (2015–2020) recommended a quantum jump to this share from 32 to 42%. As explained earlier, a portion of this share was to cover up the discontinuation of various grants that the Planning Commission used to provide. The 15th FC (2020–2026) made it 41% after adjusting the central government share that rose due to the additional responsibility for newly carved out union territories of Jammu & Kashmir and Ladakh.

From the states' aggregate share, the UFC distributes the resources among the states to correct horizontal imbalances. This horizontal devolution by successive UFCs has been based on objective parameters reflecting equity and efficiency considerations. In fact, it has been the endeavour of all UFCs to keep a fine blend of equity and efficiency in their formula for horizontal distribution among states that are heterogeneous in their fiscal capacities. However, no two UFCs adopted identical formula. All of them are of different varieties carrying the flavour of the then UFC. The series of these formulas are divided into two phases and summarized in the box given below:

Box 1: Phases in Horizontal Devolution
Phase 1: From First to Seventh Finance Commission

- Till 7th FC, income tax and union excise duties were shared using different parameters.
- Income tax was broadly shared using population and tax contribution parameters.
- The 3rd FC considered equity parameters like relative backwardness, backward caste/ tribal population, financial weakness, etc. for distribution of union excise duty for the first time.
- In the case of distribution of union excise duty, the 7th FC considerably reduced direct weightage of population and increased weightage of equity parameters, like inverse of per capita income, percentage of poor, etc.

Phase 2: From Eighth to Fourteenth Finance Commission

- 8th FC to 10th FC recommended similar parameters, including equity considerations, for distribution of both income tax and union excise duties.

- After the eightieth amendment to the constitution in 2000, a single sharing formula from the divisible pool of taxes was recommended. Parameters used by earlier finance commissions continued in the formulae.
- Weight for equity parameters increased significantly, with a proportionate decrease in direct weight for population.
- The 10th FC introduced fiscal performance criteria for the first time with 10% weight to tax efforts of states. Later, criteria like fiscal discipline and fiscal capacity were used by finance commissions.

Source: Government of India (2020).

Successive UFCs have been constructing formula comprising parameters and their relative weights. These parameters harmonize the attributes of equity, need and cost disability and performance for horizontal devolution of resources. 'Income distance' with high weights (about 50%) has been used for equity consideration.[46] The criterion is acceptable to all states for redistribution of income among states. It makes the formula more progressive and provides higher IGFT to states with lower per capita income. The UFC uses per capita gross state domestic product (GSDP) as a proxy for state's tax capacity. Generally, low per capita income represents poor state (mostly more populous state) in need of resources to provide comparable public services. As can be seen from Table 8, it was only the 13th FC which used 'fiscal capacity' instead.

'Population' and 'area' of a state represent the 'need' factor. All UFCs used population as a criterion which is simple and transparent. The 15th FC has assigned 15% weight to this indicator. 'Area' of the state is another indicator which reflects need for simple reason—the larger the area, the higher the resource requirement for public services. The 14th FC and the 15th FC assigned 15% weight to this indicator. 'Forest cover' for the first time was used by the 14th FC in the formula. The 15th FC retained it and assigned even higher weight due to the merits of this indicator. It serves two purposes. First, the state needs to be compensated for this 'cost disability', and second, it is considered beneficial for environment purpose in the interest of the nation or even the world.

[46] The 15th FC assigned 45% weight to this criterion.

Table 8 Criteria and weights assigned for horizontal distribution (for states)

Criteria	*11th FC*	*12th FC*	*13th FC*	*14th FC*	*15th FC*
Population	10	25	25	17.5	15.0
Income	62.5	50	–	50	45.0
Area	7.5	10	10	15	15.0
Index of infrastructure	7.5	–	–	–	–
Tax efforts	5	7.5	–	–	2.5
Fiscal discipline	7.5	7.5	17.5	–	–
Fiscal capacity	–	–	47.5	–	–
Demo change	–	–	–	10	12.5
Forest cover	–	–	–	7.5	10.0

Note FC means Finance Commission
Source Reports of various Union Finance Commissions, India

In order to incentivize fiscally prudent states, criteria such as 'tax efforts' and 'fiscal discipline' were used. These criteria reflect performance and efficiency and intend rewarding states for efficient tax collection. This is important as tax evasion and avoidance are high in states. Likewise, 'fiscal discipline' encourages states to adhere to the targets set by the 'fiscal responsibility and budget management act' (GoI 2003), under which revenue deficit, fiscal deficit, public debt, etc. need to be contained. In addition, the 15th FC used 'demographic performance' as a criterion which reflects performance of states in their efforts to move towards the replacement rate of population growth. Such states also get better outcomes in health, the 15th FC believes.

The IGFT arrangements between the states and their local governments stipulate every state to constitute, at regular interval of five years, a state finance commission (SFC), and assign it the task of IGFT to *panchayats* and municipalities from state's kitty. However, state government is not as serious about SFC as the central government is about the UFC. This conclusion can be drawn based on the following general treatments to SFC. First, SFC is not constituted at a regular interval of five years in some states; second, loyal retired civil servants and side-lined politicians are made members of SFC; third, SFC reports sometimes are not placed in the legislative assembly and fourth, if the report is accepted, the money is not released. These practices weaken the institution of SFC (Alok 2021).

A review of the SFCs' reports suggests that IGFT design by SFCs takes into considerations the following fiscal attributes: equity; fiscal needs and

Table 9 Criteria and weights assigned for horizontal distribution (for local)

Criteria	*11th FC*	*12th FC*	*13th FC*	*14th FC*	*15th FC*
Population	40	40	50	90	90
Area	10	10	10	10	10
Distance	20	20	20	–	–
Decent/devolution index	20	–	15	–	–
Revenue efforts	10	20	–	–	–
Deprivation index	-	10	–	–	–
Grant utilization	–	–	5	–	–

Note FC means Finance Commission
Source Reports of various Union Finance Commissions, India

cost disability; fiscal efforts and efficiency. Various indicators reflecting these attributes have been used. These include total population, ratio of backward and tribal population, population below poverty line, population density, population per hospital bed, area, backwardness of the area, remoteness index, distance from state capital, length of road, literacy rate, sex ratio, index of infrastructure, income distance, own income efforts, tax efforts, etc. (Table 9) (Alok 2021).

Local governments receive a large amount of resources from UFC. As mentioned in Table 10, six UFCs, so far, have recommended fiscal transfers to the local governments and attempted to: (a) equalize basic civic services, (b) provide incentives for strengthening accounts and audit and (c) set rules to strengthen SFCs. The recommendations have been subject to considerable criticism mainly on the following grounds:

- The grants provided are too small to make any difference to the functioning of about quarter million local governments.
- The formula used for the allocation among the states were needlessly complicated and proved to be ineffective in promoting the cause of decentralized governments.
- Contours of decentralization across states have never been very clear and each UFC adopted ad hoc approach that too of different variety breaking the continuity. For instance, the fiscal transfers to local government that the 13th FC recommended was not in the form of lump-sum ad hoc grant but a share in the central tax divisible pool so that the local government could share the revenue buoyancy of central taxes. This practice, based on its inherent merits, could have been followed by the successive UFCs, but the 14th FC discontinued it without assigning convincing reasons.
- UFCs attempted, though half-heartedly, to enhance capacity of local governments by making conditional grants. These conditions had been formed based on practices prevalent in a small southern state. It remained difficult for almost all states to fulfil those conditions and claim conditional grants. The next UFC complicated the issue further by recommending different set of conditions to claim performance grants.

Table 10 Union Finance Commission Grants to local governments (in bn INR)

Finance Commission	*Panchayats*	*Municipalities*
10th [1995–2000]	43.81	10.00
11th [2000–2005]	80.00	20.00
12th [2005–2010]	200.00	50.00
13th [2010–2015]	630.51	231.11
14th [2015–2020]	2002.92 (for village *Panchayats* only)	871.44
15th [2020–2021] First report	607.50	292.50
15th [2021–2026]	2368.05	1210.55
Final report	Health sector grants to local[51] governments = 700	

Note bn = billion; INR = Indian Rupee
Source Reports of various Union Finance Commissions, India

6 Covid-19 Pandemic and Fiscal Federalism

Medical emergency arising out of Covid-19 outbreak calls for the intervention of public health which is the constitutional mandate of state and *panchayats* in rural areas and municipalities in urban areas. But, in a disaster-like situation, it becomes the liability of the central and state governments to cooperate and iron-out differences in the prevention of decease outbreaks. Article 47 of the constitution ordains the state to raise the level of nutrition, standard of living and to improve public health. Further, local governments mandate to have a key role in public health, sanitation conservancy, solid waste management, hospitals, primary health centres and dispensaries and family welfare.[47]

In order to prevent the contagion, the central government imposed, in a series, national lockdown of different varieties, after a consultation with all states, by invoking provisions of National Disaster Management Act, 2005 (DM Act)[48]which empowers central and state governments to frame rules and issue executive orders. In fact, the subject 'disaster management' is not specifically mentioned in the constitution. Therefore, parliament exercised its power to enact a law on the subject.

The public expenditure on public health in India, of the centre and states combined, as percentage of GDP has been around one percent. This is considered paltry if compared to other countries, even BRICS nations' with sizable population.[49] Within India, central government shares about thirty percent of total public spending on health. Rest is by states where significant interstate variations can be noted. The per capita expenditure on health in the states of Bihar, Jharkhand and Uttar Pradesh is estimated at about half that of Kerala and Tamil Nadu (NITI Aayog 2019).

The pandemic due to corona virus has exposed the chink and given impetus to health sector. It has highlighted the critical role of local governments and their potential to mobilize the community in arranging quarantine facilities and cooked food for the homecoming migrant

[47] Under eleventh schedule (for panchayats) and twelfth schedule (for municipalities).

[48] The law was enacted by invoking entry 23, namely, 'social security and social insurance, employment and unemployment' in the concurrent list of the constitution of India.

[49] Where USA has the highest spending (around 9–10% of its GDP) on public health, other BRICS nations namely South Africa, Brazil, Russia and China are not too far behind the top.

workers and supporting the frontline health workers at the level of primary health care.

The 15th FC, in its report written in Covid times, took cognizance of the gap and recommended to augment public health expenditure of centre and states in a progressive manner so as to reach 2.5% of GDP by 2025. The commission recommended gigantic support to the health sector through grants-in-aid to all levels of governments including local governments.

Conventionally, the UFC has a separate window to make recommendation for two types of funds, one for disaster response and the other for mitigation. These two funds are envisaged under the DM Act These funds are to be set up at three levels, i.e. national, state and district. Hence, for disaster response, the DM Act stipulates three funds called National Disaster Response Fund (NDRF) at national level, State Disaster Response Fund (SDRF) at state level and District Disaster Response Fund (SDRF) in each district. Similarly, the DM Act provides National Disaster Mitigation Fund (NDMF) at national level, State Disaster Mitigation Fund (SDMF) at state level and District Disaster Mitigation Fund (DDMF) in each district.

The 15th FC has merged these two funds into one and calls it as National Disaster Risk Management Fund (NDRMF) and State Disaster Risk Management Fund (SDRMF). Two windows of DM Act—'mitigation' and 'response' are parts of this fund. The 15th FC was of the view 'that the mitigation fund created should be used for those local level and community based interventions which reduce risks and promote environment friendly settlements and livelihood practices' it further says 'the idea of a mitigation fund addressing risks and vulnerabilities at the local level has become imperative'. Through another window, the 15th FC has allocated INR 700 billion over a period of five years to local governments for health services.

In an early stage of the pandemic, when the Indian economy had lost about 50 days of output due to a series of national lockdowns, the central government announced an economic package that was ten percent of India's national income. The move is to kick-start the economy by (a) wooing investments including foreign through various measures; (b) providing liquidity to small and medium businesses; (c) arranging safety net for an enormous number of poor and migrant workers travelling back to their respective villages; (d) supporting farmers; and (e) holding shadow banking and electricity distributors. However as mentioned earlier, the economy registered a contraction by more than seven percent in 2020–2021.

There was a sign of economic revival but the second wave of more virulent variant of Covid-19, in the second quarter of the year 2021, has affected the momentum of economic recovery. It has also posed an enormous challenge to all levels of governments to vaccinate about 1.36 billion people across states in several locations. This is an extraordinary number by any standard and requires continuous coordination between the centre and states. Under an arrangement, the centre procures the vaccines in bulk at a discount rate and distributes among the states at no cost to the states. One-quarter of the total number is kept for private hospitals to procure at a regulated market price. On the inoculation drive, dialogue between the centre and states takes place at frequent intervals at the political and administrative level. In fact, the coordination between centre and states is at its peak during the current disaster management.

It is observed that the pandemic till date is being controlled through centralized institutional arrangements at centre and states. Public servants and security forces have been enforcing preventive measures. These arrangements need to gradually give way to the decentralized responsibilities of local governments including *Panchayats* and municipalities. These responsibilities include community health care, basic necessities and livelihoods for reverse migrant workers, maintenance of local psycho-socio helpline, and sensitization for physical distancing (Alok 2020a, b).

7 Fiscal Federalism Dimensions of Public Management Framework

7.1 The Way Forward

Allocation of powers and duties is an important aspect of fiscal federalism. In India, there are three orders of governments: central government, state governments and elected local governments which draw their powers from their respective state legislature. The expenditure responsibilities and tax assignments in the Indian constitution are largely consistent with the theoretical framework and are also evolving over the years to address the changing requirements and circumstances. The central government has more resources and state governments carry more responsibilities. In order to correct this vertical imbalance, formula-based IGFT from centre to state is made.

This system of fiscal federalism induced the performance of public sector governance and the economy at the initial stage for about a decade. Thereafter, the public governance was centralized and the economy was on a slow growth trajectory for two decades. The eighties witnessed some recovery but lately surfaced two chronic imbalances, i.e. fiscal and trade. This forced India to go for structural reforms in 1991. These reforms were initiated at the centre to largely correct central policies, institutions and their workings but the shortcomings of fiscal federalism as practiced in the preceding years which had the bearing on low growth, were not attended. Moreover, constitutional amendment was made on a state subject and local governments were brought into the statute books. Fiscal architecture which identified only two orders of governments is unable to absorb these newly created elected bodies. From the fiscal federal perspective following are the factors that inhibited growth and created political tensions in intergovernmental relations among centre, states and local governments.

Firstly, the assignment of functions and powers to centre and state as envisaged in the centre list, state list and concurrent list should be strictly regarded with exceptional deviation needed to correct the shortcomings and '*negative externalities that have surfaced*' (Bagchi 2001, p. 32). Most of the functions are in the state domain. However, there is a tendency at the centre to give advice to states with an intention of micromanagement. In addition, stringent guidelines are prescribed in vertical schemes that central government designs. All these practices erode state autonomy. Concurrent list is too long and provide scope for overlap. On entries mentioned in the list, laws are created with overriding powers to the centre. For example, law on disaster management was created in 2005 by invoking an entry on social security.[50] The law has been used to manage Covid-19 pandemic through a central control due to inherent dominant powers in the law itself. The law hardly empowers the local governments and remains inconsistent to constitutional provision[51] as far as the powers of local governments are concerned.

[50] Entry 23—social security and social insurance; employment and unemployment in the concurrent list of the constitution.

[51] Article 243 ZD of the constitution provides for a district planning committee duly constituted with about four-fifth elected members to consolidate the plans prepared by *panchayats* and municipalities in the district and to prepare a draft development plan for the district as a whole. However, the law on disaster management empowers the

Secondly, tax assignment needs a holistic review. Centre collects revenue through (a) buoyant taxes including taxes on income, foreign transactions, consumption (CGST) and cess and surcharges on taxes (non-sharable with states) and (b) natural resources, e.g. major minerals, spectrum auction, etc. On the other hand, state governments have concurrent power to tax consumption (SGST), state excise on alcohol and agriculture income tax. Local governments except some municipal corporation have limited power and capacity to collect taxes and user charges. Ill administered property tax which is the mainstay covers little for the revenue expenditure requirements of local governments. Both state and local governments have high dependency on devolution and grants from the centre. Sub-national governments particularly *panchayats* and municipalities have limited flexibility to raise resources by levying surcharges on the existing tax handles assigned to them. Similarly, existing mechanism related to sub-national income taxes like profession tax needs to be altered for the resource requirements of state and local governments.

Thirdly, the way IGFT is designed and implemented needs reforms at centre and state. It has been found that vertical imbalance between the centre and states has been rising and many state governments have shown their reliance on devolution and grants from the centre rather than own resource generation to fulfil their expenditure responsibilities.[52] The inefficiency of the machinery involved in IGFT operation has resulted in sub-optimal provision of public services including public health and education at sub-national level. The imbalances both vertical and horizontal get accentuated during the crisis such as Covid-19 pandemic.

In addition to the tax devolution and grants given to the states based on the recommendations of the UFC, the central government gives specific purpose grants for various purposes through the respective ministries. The objective of specific purpose transfers, as mentioned earlier, is to ensure minimum standards of services in respect of those services that are considered meritorious or those services with significant interstate spillovers. However, in Indian context, this has been used as a patronizing instrument to serve political objectives of the ruling parties at the centre to woo the states and the electorate by expanding its reach to

district collector who delegates powers to local authorities including *panachayats* and municipalities.

[52] Government of India (2020).

spend on the state subjects. Further, centrally sponsored schemes which carry specific purpose transfers have been compressed in 2015. They need to be rationalized further. These schemes require matching contribution from states and are full of conditionality. Except a rural employment guarantee scheme which is based on a well-drafted law all other schemes have weak legal base and role ambiguity. There is a scope to consolidate these schemes and reduce the number to just about ten to fifteen. This would ensure a focus by the central government to equalize minimum level of essential services across states.

Fourthly, the institutions designing IGFT have to be technical, autonomous and exogenous. The approach of these institutions has to be based on normative assessment of the fiscal need, revenue capacity and cost disabilities of the state. Such an assessment can create incentives for fiscal indiscipline among the states. One main explanation for the inability of the UFC and the SFC to assess the fiscal needs of the states and local governments is inadequacy of data related to the cost of basic services in different geographical terrains, e.g. hilly, plain, coastal, etc. Second explanation is lack of expertise within the government to quantify fiscal capacity of the states and local governments. Finance commissions both union and state need permanent secretariat that can undertake research and generate adequate data on a continuing basis. While the institution of union finance commission is matured and respected, the similar institution at sub-national level is at its nascent stage as evident from the SFC reports and their treatments by respective state governments. This institution needs to be strengthened through joint efforts of the centre and states as well as the SFC themselves (Alok 2021). Centre can incentivize states by allocating funds for the (a) timely constitution of SFC as per the law; (b) timely acceptance of their recommendations and timely transfer of funds to local governments (Alok 2019).

In addition, the recently implemented GST has maximum implications in Indian federal finance and intergovernmental fiscal transfers. The GST entails uniform tax rates across states reaping the benefit of Indian common market. Tax harmonization of this magnitude has helped the trade and industry to grow. But, the GST is at the initial stage of its implementation and will take some time to evolve and stabilize. The way GST is designed has subsumed buoyant source of state revenues like sales tax/VAT. Further, states are disallowed to take independent decision to levy surcharge on State-GST. Though, such an arrangement is considered appropriate (Mclure 2000). The state of Sikkim, facing a revenue gap, demands the GST Council to give consent to levy a cess on fast-growing pharmaceutical and power sectors (Mint 2021). In the past, Kerala state government has set a precedent in 2019 by introducing a flood cess.

References

Alok V.N. 2006. Local Government Organisation and Finance: Rural India, in Anwar Shah (ed) *Local Governance in Developing Countries*. Washington, DC: The World Bank.

Alok V.N. 2009. Share of Local Governments in the Union Divisible Pool: An Option Before the 13th Finance Commission. *Indian Journal of Public Administration*, LV(1).

Alok V.N. 2011. Tax System and Reform in India: An Analysis from the Perspective of Economic Development and International Trade, in Agencia Brasilleira De Desenvolvimento Industrial-ABDI (2011), Brazil, Russia, India and China (BRIC): Tax System Structure and the Effects on Development and Foreign Trade Performance (eds). Available at https://old.abdi.com.br/Estudo/bric_ingles_final_reduzido.pdf. Retrieved on 7 August 2019.

Alok, V.N. 2019. Financial Matrix for Empowerment: Design of Intergovernmental Fiscal Transfers in India to Rural Local Governments, A Study Report Funded by the 15th Finance Commission, June. https://fincomindia.nic.in/ShowContentOne.aspx?id=27&Section=1. Retrieved on 28 May 2021.

Alok, V.N. 2020a. Emerging Scope of Local Governments in India's Fiscal Architecture in Corona Crisis, 29 June. https://government.economictimes.indiatimes.com/news/governance/emerging-scope-of-local-governments-in-indias-fiscal-architecture-in-corona-crises/76638753. Retrieved on 20 June 2021.

Alok, V.N. 2020b. Covid-19 and Federalism in India, in 50 Shades of Federalism.

Alok, V.N. 2021. *Fiscal Decentralization in India: An Outcome Mapping of State Finance Commissions*. Palgrave Macmillan [Forthcoming].

Bagchi, Amaresh. 2001. Fifty Years of Fiscal Federalism in India: An Appraisal, Kale Memorial Lecture delivered at Gokhale Institute of Politics & Economics, Pune.

Government of India. 2003. Fiscal Responsibility and Budget Management (FRBM) Act, August 26. Available at https://dea.gov.in/sites/default/files/FRBM%20Act%202003%20and%20FRBM%20Rules%202004.pdf. Retrieved on 23 May 2021.

Government of India. 2009. Thirteenth Finance Commission 2010 2015, Vol. 1, Report, December.

Government of India. 2011. Census of India Report, New Delhi.

Government of India. 2014. Report of the Fourteenth Finance Commission, Vol. 1, December.

Government of India. 2020. Finance Commission in Covid Times. Report for 2021–26, by the XV Finance Commission, Vol. 1 to 4, November.

Government of India. 2021a. *India Year Book*. Publication Division, Ministry of Information and Broadcasting.

Government of India. 2021b. Citizen Charter. Available at https://www.india.gov.in/my-government/documents/citizens-charter. Retrieved on 15 June 2021.

Kelkar, V. 2019. Towards India's New Fiscal Federalism, New Delhi, NIPFP, Working Paper No. 252.

Mclure, Charles E. Jr. 2000. Tax Assignment and Sub National Fiscal Autonomy. *Bulletin of International Bureau of Fiscal Documentation*, December.

Mint. 2021. States want to levy cess to end fiscal woes, 17 June.

NITI Aayog. 2019. *Healthy States Progressive India: Report on the Ranks of States and Union Territories*. NITI Aayog, World Bank and Ministry of Health and Family Welfare, New Delhi.

Ram Mohan, M.P et al. 2021. Public Perception of Courts in India: Unmeasured Gap Between the Justice System and Its Beneficiaries. *IIMA Working Paper* 2020, Ahmedabad, IIM. https://papers.ssrn.com/sol3/papers.cfm?abstract_id=3736988. Retrieved on 28 May 2021.

Reddy, Y.V. and G.R. Reddy. 2019. *Indian Fiscal Federalism*. New Delhi: Oxford University Press.

Rodden, Jonathan and Erik Wibbles. 2001. *Federalism and Macroeconomic Management*. MIT. http://web.mit.edu/jrodden/www/oldsite/materials/roddenwibbels_oct26%20(1).pdf. Retrieved on 20 June 2021.

Shah, Anwar. 1999. *Fiscal Federalism and Macroeconomic Governance: For Better or for Worse?* Washington, DC: The World Bank.

Setalvad, M.C. 1960. *The Common Law in India*. London: The Hamlyn Trust.

Singh, Nirvikar. 2007. The Dynamics of Reform of India's Federal System, University of California, Santa Cruz, MPRA Paper No. 2282.

Singh, Nirvikar and T.N. Srinivasan. 2005. Indian Federalism, Globalization and Economic Reform, in T.N. Srinivasan and Jessica Wallack (eds) *Federalism and Economic Reform: International Perspectives*. Cambridge, UK: Cambridge University Press.

The Nobel Prize. 2014. Kailash Satyarthi: Facts. Available at https://www.nobelprize.org/prizes/peace/2014/satyarthi/facts/. Retrieved on 20 June 2021.

Transparency International. 2020. Corruption Perception Index 2020. Available at https://www.transparency.org/research/cpi/overview.

Italy

Elisabeth Alber and Alice Valdesalici

1 Balancing an Inverted Pendulum: Basic Data and Facts

Italy with its population of 60,317,000 (as of 01 January 2020; Istat 2020a) and its territory of 302,068 km^2 is highly diverse, with a persistent North–South divide. The territory is one of the key features that reveals such a diversity with some of the twenty regions being vast and densely populated, others being small and sparsely populated. This comes with stronger or weaker regional economies, and with varying fiscal capacities from one subnational entity to another (i.e. regions, provinces, metropolitan cities, and municipalities). Such a diversity poses manifold

This chapter is the product of a joint effort. However, Elisabeth Alber authored Sects. 1–3 and 8–9, while Alice Valdesalici wrote Sects. 4–7. Whenever used, the term 'State' refers to the central level of government.

E. Alber (✉) · A. Valdesalici
Eurac Research Institute for Comparative Federalism, Bolzano, Italy
e-mail: elisabeth.alber@eurac.edu

A. Valdesalici
e-mail: alice.valdesalici@eurac.edu

J.-F. Tremblay (ed.), *The Forum of Federations Handbook of Fiscal Federalism*, https://doi.org/10.1007/978-3-030-97258-5_7

and differentiated challenges linked to the functioning of mechanisms that must uphold efficient socio-institutional structures and guarantee high-quality public services throughout the entire country.

Italy's envisaged fiscal federalism and its regime of financial relations are also challenged by ongoing reforms in the local government system. In recent years, the territorial administrative structure has undergone numerous changes, not only in terms of the number of municipalities, but also in terms of the organization of second level local entities. Taking reforms at the national and regional level into account, as of 01 January 2020 (Istat 2020b), Italy consists of the following divisions:

- 20 regions (fifteen ordinary and five special ones, with varying degrees of autonomy from one to another),
- 7904 municipalities,
- 14 metropolitan cities (ranked by population size in decreasing order they are: Rome, Milan, Naples, Turin, Palermo, Bari, Catania, Florence, Bologna, Genoa, Venice, Messina, Reggio Calabria, Cagliari),
- 83 provinces,
- 6 free consortia of municipalities,
- 4 non-administrative units (corresponding to the former provinces of the Friuli-Venezia Giulia region).

Several forms of intermunicipal cooperation complete Italy's administrative territorial organization.

In Italy, multiple actors with partially overlapping responsibilities contribute to a varying degree to the system of fiscal federalism and financial relations, with specificities from North to South and from East to West, and with central authorities as the ultimate authority deciding the main rules of the game. By and large, Italy's subnational entities are recognized only with limited taxing powers, and such powers are linked to sources that have little relevance as far as the revenue is concerned. Conversely, they are vested with relevant administrative powers, and this gives rise to a large vertical fiscal gap. Therefore, inter-regional disparities in fiscal capacities are reduced through equalization transfers in order to ensure "the basic level of benefits relating to civil and social entitlements" throughout the entire country [art. 117 par. 2 lit. m Italian Constitution, hereinafter ItConst]. Such a basic level of benefits includes essential levels of public services in the key fields of health, education, social assistance and, to a certain extent, public transport. The functioning of equalization transfers and other purpose-specific grants have always led to conflictual relations between the center and the subnational entities, on the one side, and between one and another subnational unit at the other side (along the North–South divide, and along party ideologies).

Different political narratives have been characterizing not only the formation, but also the development of the Italian regionalism, and its key question of how to best balance the constitutional principles of autonomy and solidarity (Pallaver and Brunazzo 2017). Back in 1948, the Constituent Assembly opted for constitutional asymmetry, and, in more recent times, regional governors (in the North) are calling for ever more political autonomy. It is worth noting that, from the 1990s onwards, it was the Northern League (Lega Nord) that especially called for "devolution". The political party Lega Nord, founded in 1989 by Umberto Bossi from the merger of six northern Italian leagues, aimed at strengthening the North by truly federalizing Italy and envisaging the creation of three macro-areas characterized by regional economies with different fiscal capacities. Today, under the leadership of Matteo Salvini, the Lega Nord has been renamed Lega, and it pursues different objectives. Regionalism is no longer at the top of its political agenda (Albertazzi et al. 2018).

As anticipated, asymmetric arrangements have become the rule rather than the exception in Italy's regionalist and, in part, federal-like form of government, not least because of the country's territorial specificities that characterized the formation of Italy from its very inception. Special regions do enjoy a larger competence catalogue than ordinary regions and they, unlike ordinary regions, also hold separate bilateral relations to the center. Most importantly, they enter into dialogue with the center on an equal footing when it comes to negotiating financial relations.

Against these introductory remarks, at present, Italy's system of fiscal federalism and financial relations can best be defined as an inverted and thus unstable pendulum. The implementation of the fiscal federalism reform package of 2009, which aims at implementing art. 119 of the ItConst and thus at re-shaping financial relations, is far from being concluded. In Italy, with the 2001 constitutional reform, competences have been further decentralized to major policy fields, but necessary implementing legislation in the fields of fiscal powers and financial relations was delayed and, in part, is still lacking. Moreover, the current composition of the second chamber of the national parliament, the senate, does not guarantee the representation of territorial interests. Several attempts have been undertaken to turn the senate into a federal second chamber by changing its composition and overcoming perfect bicameralism in decision-making (the chamber of deputies and the senate have the same powers). Hence, decision-making processes continue to be lengthy and the interests of subnational entities are, if ever, only indirectly reflected.

The structure of this contribution unfolds as follows: Essential data as to Italy's territorial organization, its population, and regional economies are offered in the Sects. 1–2. The reasons for the origins and development of Italy's unequal regional economies and socio-political cultures are discussed in Sect. 2. Section 3 offers a contextual analysis of Italy's regionalist system from 1948 onwards, and a summary of the main principles of the not yet fully implemented system of fiscal federalism and financial relations. Sections 4–7 discuss the relevance and implications of this system in more detail and give examples from the viewpoint of intergovernmental relations as to the allocation of expenditure responsibilities and taxation powers, and as to the mechanisms of equalization, both in relation to the regional and local levels of government. Section 8, instead, assesses recent trends and the role of key actors in the management of Italy's system of fiscal federalism and intergovernmental relations. Finally, Sect. 9 evaluates how the system is affected by the outbreak of Covid-19 (as to early 2020).

2 Framing Regional Economies: A Look Back and Forth

From the viewpoint of economic history, Felice (2018; also 2017) argues that the Italian North–South divide existed before Italy's unification in 1861 and, in some respects, grew even stronger after unification. By referring to data such as the production of specific goods, key infrastructural elements, and components of human capital, Felice shows that the South including Sardinia, at the time of unification, already lacked proper pre-conditions of development (i.e. roads, railways, communications, and level of human capital) compared to those parts of Italy that later on would be named the northern "industrial triangle" (Piedmont, Liguria, Lombardy). Central Italy, instead, occupied an intermediate position.

Back in 1861, the creation of Italy was based on a centralist structure, which aimed at establishing political unity throughout the whole territory by adopting a threefold approach. First, it should protect the unification project against existing centrifugal tendencies. Second, it should compensate the institutional weaknesses of the pre-unification Italian kingdoms. Third, it should unite the very long tradition of local authorities under a common and uniform legislation and administration. In comparison with Northwest Europe, Italy, back then, was generally poor and "making the Italians" (for a clarification of the origins of the expression see Hom 2013) had remained a difficult task also after the conquest of Rome in 1870. In the years to come, the socio-economic North–South divide had been partially reduced, but the central authorities did not manage to properly control and uniform local government within the then three Italian macro-areas (one composed of the Northwest, the Northeast and the Center; and the two other ones being the South and the Islands). Interestingly, unlike today, certain regions in the North were among the poorest (e.g., Trentino-South Tyrol, then part of the Austrian-Hungarian empire). However, it was only in the early 1950s that all regions of the South had fallen behind the regions of the North in economic-industrial terms. This is because of two interlinked factors. First, agriculture came at the forefront in the South. Second, a tariff system and incentives from 1887 onwards had protected industries in the North, while doing so with grain production in the South.

In the aftermath of World War I, Italy moved from a moderate to a strong regional divergence, with the North, unlike the South, profiting from subsidized modernization efforts by local entrepreneurs that managed to prove themselves capable of modernization also in the period during World War I and II. As pointed out by Felice (2018, 15), in terms of per capita GDP, the three "Italies" of 1951 gave way to only two clearly defined "Italies" by 2011, i.e., the North and Center, and the South named Mezzogiorno (see also Dunford 2008). This is because the economic policy favoring the South never really succeeded in empowering southern regional economies. Incentives provided from the central authorities, so Felice, became a source of power for local political elites instead of promoting socio-economic development.

Recent data confirm such an interpretative strand (see Table 1). The GDP per capita (nominal income) in northern regions is significantly higher than the one in southern regions. Some regions/autonomous provinces of Italy are well above the average (such as the autonomous

Table 1 Basic data

	Total area (km², reference year: 2019)	*Population (in millions, as of 01/01/2019)*	*Number of Municipalities (as of 01/01/2019)*	*per capita GDP (reference year: 2018)*
North-West	*57 926*	*16 093 286*	*2 995*	
Piedmont	25 386	4 356 406	1 181	31 490 €
Aosta Valley*	3 260	125 666	74	38 940 €
Liguria	5 416	1 550 640	234	32 250 €
Lombardy	23 863	10 060 574	1 506	38 840 €
North-East	*62 327*	*11 652 827*	*1 388*	
Trentino-South Tyrol*	13 604	1 072 276	282	/**
Autonomous Province of Bolzano/Bozen (South Tyrol)**	7 397	531 178	116	47 040 €
Autonomous Province of Trento (Trentino)**	6 206	541 098	166	38 120 €
Veneto	18 345	4 905 854	563	33 270 €
Friuli-Venezia Giulia*	7 932	1 215 220	215	31 360 €
Emilia-Romagna	22 444	4 459 477	328	36 290 €
Center	*58 084*	*12 016 009*	*921*	
Tuscany	22 987	3 729 641	273	31 540 €
Umbria	8 464	882 015	92	25 290 €
Marches	9 401	1 525 271	228	28 080 €
Latium	17 231	5 879 082	378	33 580 €
South	*73 797*	*13 957 942*	*1 783*	
Abruzzo	10 831	1 311 580	305	25 580 €
Molise	4 460	305 617	136	20 650 €
Campania	13 670	5 801 692	550	18 590 €

	Total area (km^2, reference year: 2019)	*Population (in millions, as of 01/01/2019)*	*Number of Municipalities (as of 01/01/2019)*	*per capita GDP (reference year: 2018)*
Apulia	19 540	4 029 053	257	18 650 €
Basilicata	10 073	562 869	131	21 870 €
Calabria	15 221	1 947 131	404	16 980 €
Islands	*49 931*	*6 639 482*	*767*	
Sicily*	25 832	4 999 891	390	17 680 €
Sardinia*	24 099	1 639 591	377	21 010 €

*Regions having a special/autonomy statute (i.e. basic law) adopted as a national constitutional law. The scope of autonomy and the procedural guarantees as to the scope of autonomy is different in special regions compared to ordinary regions that adopt their statutes with a reinforced regional law

**The two autonomous provinces Trento and Bolzano/Bozen together form the special region Trentino-Alto Adige/Südtirol (South Tyrol) (in short, Trentino-South Tyrol). Unlike in all other regions, in this region most powers are vested with the two autonomous provinces, and not with the regional level. The two autonomous provinces have different political systems, and data as to their subnational governance is collected and represented separately.

Source Own elaboration (based on I.Stat 2020, data extracted on 31 March 2020; Istat, 2020b, 2020c)

province of Bolzano/Bozen), while others are well below the average (such as Calabria). If compared with regional economies at the European level, data regarding the autonomous province of Bolzano/Bozen, an entity also defined as a quasi-federal reality in Italy (Woelk 2013: 126), show how well-off South Tyrol is in economic terms (Eurostat 2019). As an Alpine border territory, South Tyrol is one of Italy's territories that most effectively makes use of its political autonomy and shows how asymmetry in constitutional design can contribute not only to settle a conflict (Alber 2017), but also to enable a territory in the development of socio-institutional capital that suits local needs, and that ultimately leads to prosperity (Valdesalici 2018).

Constitutional design, however, is only one part of the solution. The development of Italy's two-track regionalist State structure from 1948 onwards proves this. The twenty regions, fifteen having an ordinary statute (i.e. basic law) and five having a special statute made different use of their scope of action (with the special region Trentino-South Tyrol being "special among the specials" as it is subdivided into the two autonomous provinces of Trento and Bolzano/Bozen that hold most of the powers). Each special region has developed its own degree of autonomy in terms of the form of government, distribution and use of legislative and administrative competences, and financial arrangements (laid down in the respective special statutes that, unlike the statutes of ordinary regions, have the rank of a national constitutional law). Ordinary regions were established later than special ones and only some of them, most recently, have started negotiations with the central authority over enhancing their competence catalogue (by making use of art. 116 par. 3 ItConst, a constitutionally enshrined procedure providing for the transfer of additional competences from the center to a region; see Arban 2018 and Sect. 9). In sum, from a constitutional viewpoint, Italy essentially includes two categories of regions. The special regions with different degrees of autonomy, and the ordinary ones that are, as a rule, embedded in a multilateral system of intergovernmental relations, but, from the 2001 constitutional reform onwards, have the possibility to bilaterally negotiate the transfer of additional legislative powers with the central government (see Sect. 9 in more detail).

3 Explaining "Federal" Regionalism: Determinants and Their Implications

Most recently, Pallaver and Brunazzo (2017) aptly summed up the creation and the development of Italy's regionalism by defining it as being caught in the pendulum of "federal" regionalism. Especially from the 1970s onwards, with the establishment of the ordinary regions and further reform seasons starting in the late 1990s, Italy has found itself in a sort of pendulum that swings back and forth between phases of centralization and decentralization (Baldini and Baldi 2014: 87). Such phases are typical for federal systems, especially but not exclusively from the viewpoint of fiscal federalism and financial relations. So are the reasons of (reforming) the rules concerning fiscal federalism and financial relations in "mature federations" such as Germany and Switzerland less linked to the growth of power decentralization; they are rather perceived as an opportunity and necessity for enhancing the competitiveness of economic performance, and for bringing coherence to a system by adjusting it to new scenarios (Alber and Valdesalici 2012: 327–328).

In Italy, a not yet fully federal system, the need for a functioning system of fiscal federalism and financial relations does come as a consequence to reform seasons that pursued an ever more decentralized administration (and thus of spending responsibilities). Back in 1948, the Constituent Assembly opted for an asymmetric system of the territorial organization due to the presence of linguistic minorities, secessionist fears, and geographical particularities in the peripherical territories. Supporters of a federation had to come to terms with supporters of a unitary State (Pallaver and Brunazzo 2017: 151–154). The regional two-track design did, however, not properly dismantle Italy's unitary tradition dating back to the unification of Italy in 1861. It took too long to establish ordinary regions. Once they were established in the 1970s and vested with further powers in the late 1990s, they were not endowed with the parallel transfer of civil servants from the central ministries. In addition, the regions themselves did not use the scope of autonomy they were given in order to develop institutional structures that would better suit their needs (by turning available capacity into capability, i.e., the enhanced capacity by collaboratively making use of favorable pre-conditions). Put differently, in 1997–1998, when putting into place a series of measures aiming at creating a more efficient public administration capable of ensuring higher quality (the 'Bassanini Laws'), both the central and regional authorities missed an opportunity to properly implement the reforms (Pallaver and Brunazzo 2017: 155–159). The transfer of powers from the center to the regions by means of ordinary legislation did neither come with the necessary resources from the central ministries to the regions, nor was it supported by the development of proper regional political cultures (Newell 2010). Hence, the greater autonomy given to public administrations in terms of personnel and controls only scarcely succeeded in establishing a relationship of greater trust between the citizen and decentralized administration, not least because the quality of administrative performance and policy output continued to be very different throughout Italy (Vassallo 2013). In addition, the centralistic political party system did not give space to the development of regionally anchored political cultures—with the exception of the systems in place in the special regions Aosta Valley and Trentino-South Tyrol.

The 2001 constitutional reform re-wrote Title V of the ItConst. Regarding the relations between the center and the regions, it revised the distribution of competences and re-shaped their financial relations (art. 117–119 ItConst). Up to 2001, ordinary regions could only legislate in a number of subjects enumerated in the ItConst and only within the framework outlined by a national law. Special regions, instead, were vested with a broader scope of autonomy within the legislative—often exclusive—powers laid down in each autonomy statute. The 2001 constitutional reform eliminated this difference by turning the distribution of legislative powers upside down. Exclusive legislative competences of the center as well as subject matters of concurrent legislation (the center is responsible for the principles and the regions for the details) are now listed in the ItConst (art. 117 par. 2 and par. 3). Regions have residual legislative competences in all remaining areas. While both ordinary and special regions are vested with financial autonomy on the spending and revenue side, the financing systems of special regions greatly differ from that of ordinary regions because of the bilateral negotiations that have been evolving since 1948 (and in the case of Friuli-Venezia Giulia since 1963, with the adoption of its autonomy statute). Each special region enjoys a regime of financial autonomy that is based on a share of State taxes referable to the territory (from 25 to 90 %). Ordinary regions, instead, greatly depend on transfers from the center.

As of early 2020, the envisaged system grounding the regions' finances on "autonomous resources" (i.e. tax-revenue linked to the territorial fiscal capacity, a core principle of the fiscal federalism reform in 2009) has not yet been fully implemented. Put simply, the new system foresees that financial coverage to decentralized responsibilities is to be provided by autonomous resources (including own taxes and tax-revenue sharing on a territorial base) and equalization transfers. In this respect, the central authority will no longer be the paymaster of last resort. The principle of historical expenditure (i.e. transfers calculated on the last year's expenditure) shall be replaced by a model considering standard costs and needs. Such a model shall be calculated against established efficiency benchmarks. All in all, the regime of fiscal federalism and financial relations as laid down in law no. 42/2009 (and its implementing legislation) aims at providing a system resting on five pillars: financial and partially also fiscal autonomy, tax-revenue sharing on a territorial base equalization transfers the criterion of standard costs instead of the principle of historical expenditure, transparent and accountable budgeting performance. Such a system would, at last, implement art. 119 of the ItConst that reads as follows.

"Municipalities, provinces, metropolitan cities and regions shall have revenue and expenditure autonomy. Municipalities, provinces, metropolitan cities, and regions shall have independent financial resources. They set and levy taxes and collect revenues of their own, in compliance with the Constitution and according to the principles of coordination of State finances and the tax system. They share in the tax revenues related to their respective territories. State legislation shall provide for an equalization fund—with no allocation constraints—for the territories having lower per capita taxable capacity. Revenues raised from the abovementioned sources shall enable municipalities, provinces, metropolitan cities, and regions to fully finance the public functions attributed to them. The State shall allocate supplementary resources and adopt special measures in favor of specific municipalities, provinces, metropolitan cities, and regions to promote economic development along with social cohesion and solidarity, to reduce economic and social imbalances, to foster the exercise of the rights of the person or to achieve goals other than those pursued in the ordinary implementation of their functions. Municipalities, provinces, metropolitan cities, and regions have their own properties, which are allocated to them pursuant to general principles laid down in State legislation. They may resort to indebtedness only as a means of funding investments. State guarantees on loans contracted for this purpose are not admissible."

4 Discussing the Rules of the Game: The Allocation-Scheme

As the earlier parts have shown, Italian regionalism is characterized by an asymmetrical design, both as a matter of constitutional law and in terms of effective use of powers transferred to the regions. Five out of twenty regions have a special status: Sicily, Sardinia, Aosta Valley, Friuli-Venezia Giulia, and Trentino-South Tyrol. Trentino-South Tyrol is subdivided in the two autonomous provinces of Trento and Bolzano/Bozen, which, however, regarding their competence catalogue are comparable to a special region. Each special region has not only a different system of powers, but also a different financing system that is, unlike in the case of ordinary regions, bilaterally negotiated with the central authority. Moreover, ordinary regions were granted a large scope of autonomy much later than the special ones. Though at first sight simple, the new criteria of power distribution between the central authority and the regions from 2001 onwards mask extensive ambiguity. It has given rise to tensions and an enormous increase of controversies between the two levels of government. Therefore, the constitutional court ultimately was and is largely re-writing the division of legislative competences, most recently to the detriment of the regions (Palermo and Valdesalici 2019: 298–299).

As anticipated in Sect. 3, implementing legislation as to art. 119 ItConst has been missing for many years, notwithstanding the fact that it was considered a milestone of the 2001 constitutional reform. Only in 2009, law no. 42 laid down the main features and trajectories of the new system. It took another two years until all relevant enactment decrees and bylaws to this framework law were adopted (Valdesalici 2014: 77–81). Considering the complexity resulting from the implementing legislation, several unexpected political drawbacks, and the austerity politics during the economic crisis, today it is still rather difficult to give concrete evidence of the exact *status quo* of its implementation.

To better understand the rules surrounding the allocation of expenditure responsibilities, we need to take a step back. With the 2001 constitutional reform, all territorial entities have been vested with enhanced financial autonomy. Pursuant to art. 119 ItConst, municipalities, provinces, metropolitan cities, and regions shall have financial autonomy both on the revenue and expenditure side. However, such financial autonomy must be balanced against the principles of solidarity, coordination, and cohesion. As such, it is strongly limited by the actions the central authorities undertake in the field of coordination of public finance. In addition to that, pursuant to constitutional law no. 1/2012, all territorial entities shall respect the principle of a balanced budget and contribute to the enforcement of EU obligations (see details in Ciolli 2014).

One of the major expectations linked with the reform was the constitutional recognition of the autonomy on the revenue side. It was conceived as one of the most interesting innovations in order to make subnational and local levels of government more accountable. However, no revolution of the status quo ante has taken place: under the new scheme territorial entities, especially regions, keep most of the tax revenue they had under the previous system (Muraro 2011). Their taxing powers have been reinforced only to a little extent. The intention of abolishing central transfers to both regions and local entities is, however, noteworthy (with the exception of non-earmarked equalization transfers that will still be in place). Subnational financing shall from now on be based on tax-revenue linked to the fiscal capacity of each territory, not anymore on the principle of historical expenditure. In addition to that, the equalization of resources shall be gradually based on standard costs and needs, which are calculated in relation to each "essential" public service. In other words, a system of predefined and standardized costs shall substitute the principle of historical expenditure. Besides that, the legislative power to tax mainly lingers in the hand of the national legislature and a wide-scope equalization scheme is confirmed, though according to the new "standardized" concept thoroughly described in Sect. 7.

Italy's system of fiscal federalism and financial relations, however, can only be fully understood if one considers the entire block of financial-related constitutional provisions laid down in the 2001 constitutional reform. This means that one has to undertake a combined reading of the art. 119, 117, and 118 of the ItConst. As already explained, art. 117 of the ItConst lists the exclusive legislative powers of the national legislator as well as the concurrent ones, while residual powers lie with the regions. Regulatory powers (art. 117 par. 6 ItConst) are vested with the central authority for issues linked to national exclusive legislative powers (unless they are delegated to the regions). In all other matters, regulatory powers are assigned to the regional level. Local entities have regulatory powers associated with the organization and implementation of the functions attributed to them. At the same time, art. 118 of the ItConst by referring to administrative functions establishes that, as a rule and in compliance with the principles of subsidiarity, differentiation, and proportionality, they are assigned to the municipal level and thus to upper levels of government only in case of necessity.

Conversely, the rules for special regions differ from the above-illustrated principles. Legislative powers of special regions are assigned according to their statutes of autonomy. However, when the 2001 constitutional reform provided ordinary regions with a greater degree of autonomy, this also extended to special regions as long as their statutes were not updated (art. 10 constitutional law no. 3/2001). As to administrative functions, their systems are based on the principle of parallelism. This means that they hold administrative powers in the subject matters they are attributed legislative powers. In practice, they mostly delegate them to municipalities (and other second level local entities).

A close look at the functioning of the constitutional allocation of legislative competences immediately illustrates the Italy's inverted pendulum of fiscal federalism and financial relations. Regional legislation in matters of concurrent legislation is de facto subordinated to national legislation. In theory this means that the national legislature defines fundamental principles, while the regional legislature does legislate on details. In practice, however, this competence type has turned out to be a powerful tool of centralization. The same is valid in case of cross-cutting matters. Emblematic to this regard is the national exclusive legislative power as to the "determination of the basic level of benefits relating to civil and social entitlements to be guaranteed throughout the national territory" [art. 117 par. 2 lit. m) ItConst]. Irrespective of the matter at hand, whenever a regional law provides for benefits related to civil and welfare rights, it must comply with the standards set by the national law regarding those rights. This is not considered a competence title in the classical sense, but it is considered of cross-cutting nature. As such, the national law is allowed to intersect different matters also of regional competence if this is necessary to ensure public functions and services to all citizens within the entire national territory, as the regional law cannot constrain essential rights. This reading has frequently given rise to conflicts in front of the constitutional court, and an extensive interpretation of the central authority powers has mostly prevailed.

Also, even though all residual (not-enumerated) competences lie with the regions (art. 117 par. 4 ItConst), the nature of financial relations essentially is centralistic. This is due to five reasons. First, the national legislature holds the exclusive legislative power over the "major taxes" (see Sect. 6). Second, it does so also regarding the "equalization mechanism" (see Sect. 7). Third, central authorities are the ones being tasked with determining the "essential levels of public services". Fourth, central authorities are also the ones responsible for the "harmonization of budgets of all public entities" and of the enforcement of "the principle of balanced budget". Fifth, the competence on the coordination of both the public finance and the tax system is included in the list of concurrent competences, thus the national legislature ultimately has the upper hand. On this last point, especially as of 2010, the intervention of the national level of government has often gone beyond the determination of the basic principles by introducing detailed regulations. Furthermore, the constitutional court has given an extensive interpretation to what can be considered a "fundamental principle of coordination of public finance". Thus, the scope of national legislation at the expense of both regional financial autonomy and, in general, the political autonomy of territorial entities has been further expanded (among the many, see judgments no. 198/2012, 262/2012, 236/2013, 23/2014, 38/2016, 69/2016, 154/2017). The court's reasoning rests on the fact that this is not to be considered a "competence-title" in the traditional understanding. It is the purpose-oriented nature of coordination that is of relevance. Because of this interpretation, the principle of coordination of public finance is to be understood much more as an exclusive competence rather than a concurrent one. If any, a safeguard to protect subnational autonomy could be found in the principle of loyal cooperation (i.e. the necessity of cooperation and integration between the levels of government). Accordingly, the central authority must make all possible efforts to reach an agreement with subnational entities when decisions affecting their (financial) interests are taken.

5 Discussing the Rules of the Game: Spending Autonomy

The allocation-scheme and its implications also heavily affect the spending autonomy of subnational entities. To understand how this occurs, we must reflect on the scope of legislative and administrative powers. As a rule, the more competences an entity has, the more spending autonomy it enjoys. Considering the spending composition of the regional budgets, data show that ordinary regions are responsible (or co-responsible) for health care, education, environment, social assistance, and economic development. On average, health care spending amounts to more than 50% of the total regional spending, while the administrative apparatus absorbs around 20% of the budget. These are followed by economic affairs (12.8%) that, among others, include local public transport and infrastructure, productive and tourism-related activities. Whereas social assistance and environment are at 3% each, education is only at 2%. The remaining 10% is divided among all other regionally (co-)financed functions (e.g., culture, housing and territorial planning, public safety, water protection and utilities). Palpable discrepancies exist among the regions and mostly reflect the North–South divide. Northern regions' spending is in fact above the national average in all sectors, except for public safety and environment (ISSiRFA 2019).

Special regions present a different picture. As a rule, their spending autonomy is broader than the one enjoyed by ordinary regions, although the ongoing federalizing process aims at reducing the gap. However, in this regard, it is arduous to identify a common pattern, due to the mechanism of bilateral relations they rely on. Each special entity has developed the scope of its self-government in a different way, because of territorial and socio-political peculiarities. This affects the degree of spending autonomy each entity has. For instance, the Aosta Valley and the two autonomous provinces of Trento and Bolzano/Bozen have a broader spending autonomy in the education sector than the other special regions. Their competence-catalogues include both the teaching and the administrative staff (due to the existence of linguistic minorities with special rights; Alber and Trettel 2018). The spending in the health sector offers another example of how special regions differently make use of their scope of autonomy and of how they are different from ordinary regions, too. The special regions in the North do not receive any transfers from the National Health Fund, whereas the ordinary regions do. Indeed, health makes up the biggest part of the transfers from the center in ordinary regions.

Moreover, special regions, unlike ordinary regions, have exclusive legislative and regulatory competence over the system of local government, while respecting the limits set forth by the statutes themselves to their legislative competence (D'Orlando and Grisostolo 2016). In ordinary regions, instead, the system of local government is subject to national legislation (art. 117 par. 2 ItConst reads that the national legislature has exclusive legislative competence on "principles of electoral legislation, governing bodies and fundamental functions of municipalities, provinces and metropolitan cities"). At this stage, it shall be noted that the residual margin of autonomy vested with the regions is very limited and concerns, for example, forms of intermunicipal cooperation. In addition to that, all northern special entities are fully in charge of local finance, whereas in other special regions (i.e. Sicily and Sardinia) this depends on the center.

Regarding spending responsibilities, it is important to stress that each entity can freely decide on how to spend the available resources, including not only own-tax sources, but—as a rule—all resources. As a matter of fact, only a minor part of the regional budget is earmarked (<15%). This basic assumption has to come to terms with the need to ensure on the whole territory public services in the field of education, healthcare, social assistance, and—to a certain extent—also public transport at the essential levels set forth by the national legislature. Regarding these functions and related levels, spending autonomy is somehow guaranteed by the fact that equalization transfers are not earmarked and shall be distributed on the basis of standard costs and needs. Hence, regions are free to spend more or less money, provided that the essential levels of services are safeguarded.

Besides the abovementioned, the ongoing non-implementation of the 2001 constitutional reform adds further complexity when trying to answer the question of how the system works in practice. The central authority is lagging behind. Due to the delayed and desultory implementation of the new rules in fiscal federalism and financial relations, the national legislature has not yet fixed the essential levels of services, with the sole exception of healthcare.

That said, the functioning of the system shows that—in particular, but not exclusively—ordinary regions are bound to respect a couple of additional limitations. First, the austerity measures adopted to cope with the economic crisis have meaningfully reduced transfers to the regions. The legislative decree no. 78/2010, for instance, reduced the transfers from the center to the ordinary regions by 4.5 billions and the ones to the special regions by 1 billion. In 2012, capital expenditure also decreased significantly (−8.4%), especially due to the contraction of investments (−7.1%) (Banca d'Italia 2013). Second, the national level of government has introduced heavy restrictions to regional spending. These links of measures have been used by the national government as privileged tools of spending reviews (Alber 2014: 162–167). The constitutional court in many cases has deemed the constitutionality of these legal acts, even though they contain measures addressing specific sectors the regions would be responsible for (e.g., regional personnel and turnover, number of seats in the regional governing bodies, participated regional enterprises). This was possible because of the extensive interpretation given to the concurrent competence on coordination of public finance, grounded in the need to comply with the obligations stemming from the European Union's economic governance framework and to ensure the enactment of the principle of balanced budget. Accordingly, the measures are justified to the extent that they set an overall and temporary limit, and also because they leave a margin of discretion to the regions when it comes to the allocation of revenue between the different sectors. However, the abovementioned criteria ultimately leave ample room for maneuver to the national legislature.

6 Discussing the Rules of the Game: Taxation Responsibilities

As explained, the ItConst fosters the self-sufficiency of all subnational entities. Pursuant to art. 119 ItConst, regions, municipalities, provinces, and metropolitan cities must fully finance their functions by means of own-tax sources, shared taxes, and non-earmarked equalization transfers. Additional transfers shall be provided only for exceptional cases. In brief, subnational and local entities must ground their financing on "autonomous resources" (Rivosecchi 2010: 121–142). Despite the linkage between territorial financing and tax-revenue generated within the territory, the tax system remains centralized. All major tax-revenue sources are placed under the legislative authority of the center, with minor exceptions (Jorio 2010).

As to ordinary regions, "regional taxes" are classified into three categories. First, "devolved taxes" are set by a national law but devolved to the regions as far as both the revenue and a limited varying power are concerned. Second, "regional surtaxes" that are on top of those national taxes in relation to which regions are allowed to impose an extra charge, within the limits set forth by the center. Third, "autonomous own taxes" that are taxes set by a regional law on a tax-base not preempted by the State. Following this classification, the most relevant revenue sources of ordinary regions include the revenue from a tax on business (so-called IRAP—regional tax on productive activities) and the surtax on the Individual Income Tax (so-called IRPEF). The regional surtax on individual income tax consists of a basic rate of 1.23% (since 2011) as well as an optional rate (up to 2.1% as of 2015) to be applied within certain limits. Regions may also vary the tax rate of the regional tax on the income of the productive activities (so-called IRAP) and eventually reduce it to zero. Autonomous own taxes are very few and the yields are marginal (e.g., the special tax for the landfill of waste).

This scheme results from the stringent limits put in place when it comes to taxing powers of regions with, on the one hand, the prevention of double taxation on the same tax-base, and the constitutional arrangement as to taxing powers on the other hand. The ItConst does not list the own taxes of each governmental level. According to art. 117 par. 2 ItConst e), the center has the exclusive legislative competence over the national tax system, while the regions are granted an exclusive legislative competence over the regional tax system (residual clause, art. 117 par. 4 ItConst). Furthermore, the established doctrine of the constitutional court additionally restrains the scope of autonomy. On the one hand, regional taxes are only those set and regulated by a regional law. This means that they are very few because the fiscal legislation is almost entirely preempted by the national legislature (judgments no. 296/2003, 297/2003; 216/2009; see Nicolini 2010). On the other hand, regions may exert their taxation powers only in compliance with the principles of financial and fiscal coordination set forth by the national authority. As the constitutional court has opted for an extensive interpretation regarding the principle of coordination of the tax system, this de facto nullifies the regional role in tax matters (among the many, see judgments no. 37/2004, 199/2016). Thus, it is mainly the center that sets a tax (e.g., IRAP) and then decides on the powers and shares to be conferred to the regions. On top of that, for several years, the national budget laws have frozen the regional powers to apply surtaxes or vary the rates, with minor exceptions (e.g., the tourism tax).

Notwithstanding all these problems, regional financial autonomy on the revenue side has been somehow consolidated and tax flexibility has been reinforced. At the beginning these powers have remained on paper for long, as several national acts have frozen the powers of the regions to vary tax rates. In 2016, however, regional taxes considered as a whole (i.e. autonomous and devolved) amounted to 45% of the regional budget, while only to 14,8% in 1990 (Istat 2016). Against this picture, tax competition is kept to a minimum from a comparative perspective, although at present the territorial differentiation regarding tax pressure is becoming somewhat sensitive. Still it affects mainly the category of the devolved taxes such as the regional tax on productive activities and the regional surtax on the individual income. As to the latter, the varying power over the tax rate has also translated into diverse solutions. Some regions have introduced a single rate disregarding the income level, while others have opted for a progressive tax rate. However, differences are more significant regarding the regional tax on productive activities, with the option to intervene on the tax rate, the possibility to differentiate it because of the involved sector or taxpayers' category, the obligation to increase the tax rate in case of deficits in the health care sector, and the power to introduce exemptions, deductions, or tax allowances (Court of Auditors 2019). At this stage, it shall also be noted that tax administration, except for regional and local own taxes, is all in all centralized.

Local finance, in the period 2010–2020, also underwent changes due to the implementation of the 2001 constitutional reform. Its structural metamorphosis has been marked by an overall increase in local taxes and a correspondent decrease (−32%) of transfers from the center (IFEL, 2019, with all data on local entities in the chapter referring to the year 2018, if not otherwise specified). At present, the system of financing of local entities within ordinary regions is mostly based on "devolved taxes", that is taxes set and regulated by the national legislature, whose revenues are devolved to local entities. Regarding municipalities, tax-revenue accounts for 46% of the overall revenue. Municipalities are also vested with tax-varying power in some revenue sources. For instance, they can vary the optional tax rate of the surtax on individual income (IRPEF), within the upper limit of + 0.8%. Tax exemptions can also be introduced respecting the restrictions prescribed by the national legislation. In this case, local own-tax sources represent an exception to the general scheme. The tourist tax is one example. The national law entitles municipalities with the full authority to impose this tax, provided that they remain within the upper limit set by the national government (legislative decree no. 23/2011). The financing scheme of provinces and metropolitan cities replicates the same structure. Thus, it rests mainly on devolved and shared taxes, plus equalization transfers. However, the legal framework is complex and uncertain. As to the provinces, this is the result of the national austerity measures that have progressively reduced the transfers, on the one hand. On the other hand, the undergoing process of territorial reorganization regarding the (reductions of) functions allocated to the provincial level also played a role in the same direction. As to metropolitan cities, the situation is even more ambiguous. They were finally established in 2014 (by law no. 56/2014), but their system of financing remains undefined. The result is that the provincial scheme still applies to them and resources to metropolitan cities have generally been reduced, entailing problems of underfunded mandates (Kössler and Kress 2021).

Own taxes are negligible also in the case of special regions. This occurs although the constitutional constraints imposed on their taxation powers are in theory more relaxed. On the other hand, the fiscal room is almost entirely exhausted by State taxes and the political costs for imposing a regional tax are thus well above the expected economic gains. As such, "autonomous own-taxes" are residual also in this case. More interesting are the yields that special regions collect from "devolved taxes". They are entitled to the entire amount that accrues to ordinary regions from the regional tax on productive activities (IRAP) and the surtax on individual income tax. Interestingly in this respect is the fact that special regions are vested with a wider tax-varying power. Within the limit of the maximum tax rate set by the national law, they can introduce whatever alteration of the tax burden on "devolved taxes". The constitutional jurisprudence has accepted an extensive interpretation of the tax-varying power special regions are entitled to by their special statutes, paving the way for more differentiation of fiscal policies (judgments no. 357/2010, 323/2011, 12/2012). Conversely, ordinary regions can only introduce those variations explicitly allowed by the national legislation. However, overall, the margin of discretion as to taxing powers of subnational and local entities is rather limited. This will also be the case in the future. The constitutional court stresses the role of the national legislature in tax-related matters, on the one hand. On the other hand, there is no pressure for change from the subnational level. At present, the taxation system barely guarantees tax harmonization and the respect of the constitutional constraints (i.e. the criteria of progressivity of the tax system and the requirement of a tax effort linked to the fiscal capacity; art. 53 ItConst).

7 Discussing the Rules of the Game: Intergovernmental Fiscal Transfers and Revenue-Sharing

The strong centralization of the tax system together with the significant decentralization of spending responsibilities give rise to a noteworthy vertical fiscal gap (i.e. own taxes do not cover spending needs). This applies to both the local and—above all—the regional levels. Besides own and devolved regional taxes, the national level of government can resort to the following instruments to cover the gap: tax-revenue sharing on a territorial basis and equalization transfers.

To this extent, a share of VAT is in place for ordinary regions (67.07% in 2018), with revenue thereof distributed according to the statistical data of the final consumptions of families, calculated on average on a regional basis. However, the related revenues are not devolved to the single region, but they are used to finance the equalization fund for health care. As such, the amount of revenue calculated on the basis of the derivation principle is then corrected in accordance with the prescribed equalization formula. Depending on the region at stake, the share of VAT covers between 65 and 92% of the regional spending on health care (Bordignon and Ambrosanio 2020). Other than sources linked to a share of tax-revenue generated within the territory, the only constitutionally legitimate intergovernmental grants are non-earmarked equalization transfers from a fund, which has to be established by the national level of government. In fact, the center is vested with the exclusive legislative competence on the equalization system (art. 117 par. 2 ItConst).

Equalization is considered as a crucial component of the Italian system of territorial organization. This is because along with discrepancies in territorial wealth fiscal capacities also oscillate. Taking for instance the net yield of IRPEF the per capita amount of the northern regions is double that of the southern ones (Bordignon and Ambrosanio 2020). The unemployment rate is also particularly telling. While the national average is 10.6%, it reaches 18.4% in the South and only 6.6% in the North. As to variations in human capital, a useful indicator could consist of the results of nation-wide tests (so-called INVALSI) students must take each year. Once again data confirm the North–South divide (with Calabria lagging well behind the group). The quality of decentralized spending significantly varies, too. For instance, inter-regional migrations for health care purposes involve all regions of the South (except Molise). Even though differences can, to a certain extent, be attributed to the morphology or to socio-cultural characteristics of the population inhabiting a region, such huge discrepancies throughout Italy can only be explained by the inefficiency of the public administration.

To this regard, the 2001 constitutional reform has mandated, *inter alia*, the introduction of a new model of equalization that should allow a standardization of territorial financing and foster efficiency and accountability (Antonini 2009; Ferrara and Salerno 2010; Jorio et al. 2009). A twofold mechanism of equalization is envisaged. The first, the "standard approach", refers to guaranteeing "essential levels of services" in the sectors of health, education (for administrative spending only), welfare, and public transport (capital spending only). The services in the essential sectors must be fully guaranteed throughout the country, thus fully supported by the equalization system. Transfers shall, however, in any case be based on standard criteria and not on effective needs. The equalization quota shall be calculated to cover the gap between the standard need and the tax-revenue of the related territory. If the difference is negative, the region will benefit from equalization; otherwise, it will be a net contributor. Tax-revenues to be taken into consideration are the "devolved taxes" (i.e. IRAP), the regional surtax on individual income tax, as well as the regional share of VAT [art. 8 par. 1 d), law no. 42/2009]. Moreover, the standard needs will be calculated on a regional base according to the standard costs as related to the essential levels. The second mechanism shall be in place for all other (residual) regional functions. In this case, the center does not define any common national standard. The single region decides the level of services to be provided and the transfers ensure only a partial equalization. Differences in terms of fiscal capacity per capita will be abridged up to 75%. Even in this case, however, the mechanism is far from being effectively implemented.

At present, the "transfer-based" system of regional financing that has remained untouched for years is, to a great extent, still in force. This is because of the considerable delay of the implementation of the 2001 constitutional reform and its implementing legislation. Neither has the model of standard costs and needs been calculated in full detail yet, nor has the national legislature fully determined the essential levels of services to be guaranteed throughout the country. Moreover, the fiscal capacity per capita has not been calculated yet. The health sector represents a partial exception to this picture. However, having a closer look at the methodology applied, it emerges that the distribution of the Health Care Fund is not based on standards, but it is linked to the demographic parameter (weighted population) as it was the case under the previous system (Bordignon and Ambrosanio 2020).

An analogous equalization mechanism has been foreseen by the 2001 constitutional reform to remedy imbalances among local entities. As in the case of regions (i.e. in relation to the essential levels of services), the center holds the exclusive legislative power over the determination of the fundamental functions of local entities to be ensured in a uniform manner throughout the country. The gradual overcoming of the funding system based on the historical expenditure in favor of a model of standard costs and needs is also envisaged for local government. Based on a twofold classification of decentralized functions, also in this case, two equalization mechanisms shall be established. A first mechanism must ensure the funding of fundamental functions (approximately 80%), while a second one the funding for all other residual and thus non-fundamental functions (approximately 20%). The details as to the mechanisms (methodology and definition of parameters) have been specified in governmental decrees (e.g., law decree no. 216/2010 as later modified), while a public–private company (SOSE) is tasked with the calculation of the standard costs and needs. These must be calculated for each fundamental function and by taking into consideration the peculiarities of the single function and other characteristics of the local entity (e.g., the size). It shall be noted that, within this complex legal framework, the Stability Law 2013 (law no. 228/2012) has set up a Fund of Municipal Solidarity. The Fund is financed through a share of the revenue generated from the local tax on properties—IMU (38.23% in 2015, 24.43% in 2016)—and only a selection of local tax revenues are taken as a benchmark to determine who is entitled to benefit from it. In 2016, the equalization resources distributed on the basis of the new standardized parameters amounted to 30% of the Fund, while the rest was allocated taking into account the principle of historical expenditure. The new system should have fully entered into force by 2021, but de facto as of 2021 additional functions are equalized basing on standard requirements, but the historical expenditure criterion has not yet been completely abandoned.

Regarding the provinces as second level local entities, they receive equalization transfers from the so-called "experimental fund for financial consolidation". This is financed with the provincial share of the individual income tax (0.6%). Although the fund has been in place since 2012, it is meant to be a temporary measure. In fact, an equalization fund like the one illustrated above for municipalities should be established. The financial endowment of the experimental fund is shrinking year after year, in order to ensure that also provinces contribute to the consolidation of national public finance. In addition to that, the austerity measures imposed by the center have progressively reduced to zero the other transfers to provinces. Furthermore, the national level of government has started a process of territorial reorganization regarding in particular the (reductions of) functions allocated to the provincial level. The provincial scheme is temporarily extended to metropolitan cities. Local entities should not receive transfers other than equalization ones. In practice, a few exceptions are in place (e.g., for tiny and increasingly depopulated municipalities).

The financing systems of special regions present a significantly different structure. They are mainly based on a share of well-determined national taxes, calculated in the appliance of the derivation principle. However, significant differences can be detected among them. The list of shared taxes is provided in a specific provision of the special statute and can potentially encompass all State taxes. Although with variations, all entities are thus entitled to a share of the major taxes (e.g., on consumption and on income). The sharing quota is widely diversified, as it varies from a minimum of 25% to a maximum of 90%, while some entities receive the entire amount of certain taxes. As a rule, the share is higher for those special regions vested with major spending responsibilities (e.g., Valle d'Aosta and Trentino-South Tyrol). The same applies to the number and the types of taxes that are shared. Finally, also the sharing criteria are different. In any case, the parameter of apportionment tends to match the allotted amount to the revenue raised within the territory of reference.

In addition to the prominent role vested by shared taxes, the twofold equalization scheme foreseen for ordinary regions does not apply to them. According to law no. 42/2009 (art. 27), special entities should bilaterally agree with the national government upon their contribution to equalization and to the recovery of public finance (including the obligations imposed by the EU). In this case no "one solution fits all" is possible. In practice, it goes along with the economic development. The richer entities contribute proportionally more than the poorer. Several bilateral agreements have been signed in the last years as to the respective contribution to the system of national equalization and to the consolidation of national public finance in the light of the ever more stringent EU obligations. In addition to that, the arrangements have resulted for the northern special regions in an enhancement of their political and financial autonomy. Revenues at disposal have been reduced, on the hand. On the other hand, additional competences have been transferred to them. Although this has been done at the expense of the regional financial endowment, their political autonomy has been reinforced.

As a result of this additional asymmetry, grants tend to be generally less consistent in special regions than in ordinary ones. Nevertheless, even in this case inter-regional discrepancies are profound. In general terms, while the northern special regions tend to rely much more on revenue linked to taxation, the two islands—and Sicily in particular—depend much more from direct transfers from the center (e.g., in the health care sector). To a certain extent, the varying relevance of these different components seems to reflect the existing cleavage in the economic performance.

The asymmetry that characterizes the overall system of the territorial organization also affects local finance. In fact, the above-described system applies to local entities within ordinary regions. For special regions rules are different. First, the general financial rules do not directly apply to them, but they have been asked to reform their systems according to the same basic principles. The specific regulations must be agreed between each special region and the center in a bilateral negotiation. In short, special regions enjoy a higher degree of financial autonomy, but they differ one from the other to a great extent. Second, some special regions run local finance (the northern ones), whereas in others (Sicily and Sardinia) this remains with the center. In this respect, the only exception is represented by the responsibility of all regions (special and ordinary) to ensure the respect of the principle of a balanced budget by taking into account all territorial entities with the regional territory of reference.

As to this last point, all territorial entities shall ensure the equilibrium of their budgets to concur with the compliance of the EU's economic and financial restraints. The new legal framework (law no. 243/2012 as amended by law no. 164/2016) imposes limits to deficits and to the possibility of incurring debts. At the same time, it sets strict limitations to regional overspending. Hence, deviations from the equilibrium could occur, although each region has to ensure the recovery of the deficit through the adoption of a loan repayment plan. Surpluses shall be used either to cover the existing debts or for investment expenditure. To this end, an agreement between the region and the center should be reached, to ensure the balance between revenue and expenditure taking into account all entities within the region (including the region itself).

8 Assessing Recent Trends: The Persistent Lack of Coordination

Unlike a normal pendulum that is stable when hanging downwards, an inverted pendulum is essentially unstable and must be actively balanced in order to remain upright. The task to actively balance the pendulum is, as of early 2020, in the hands of the center—first and foremost because of the Covid-19 emergency (see Section 9), but not exclusively. When it comes to the rules of the game in fiscal matters and financial relations, it was and still is the central authority in Rome that ultimately determines them. As earlier shown, only in some regions, that is in the northern special regions, the subnational governmental level—in the case of the special region Trentino-South Tyrol, the two autonomous provinces of Trento and Bolzano/Bozen—regularly co-decide how financial relations shall look like by means of bilateral negotiations and they do so to a varying degree.

In order words, the inverted pendulum regarding fiscal and financial issues in Italy is, as a rule, balanced by applying a torque at the pivot point that is centrally steered, and not by moving the pivot point horizontally as part of a feedback system in which its multiple territorial actors enter into dialogue on an equal footing. Moreover, the management of fiscal and financial matters is fragmented across multiple bodies in a manner that lacks coordination. For example, and most importantly, this is the case when it comes to tax administration functions. Latter ones are fragmented across multiple bodies to which different rules apply in terms of legal status, objectives, overall performance, and autonomy (the department of finance in the Ministry of Economy and Finance; the revenue agency with decentralized directorates; the customs agency; the Guardia di Finanza responsible for tax fraud investigation; Equitalia in charge of tax debt collection and the national Social Security Institute administering the collection of social security contribution and the payment of social benefits). Roles and responsibilities of this system of multiple bodies overlap and more coordination is needed. As noted by the expert study of the OECD (2016: 8), "all the arrangements in place among actors of the Italian tax administration are heavily focused on the operational level and there are no established processes involving all actors to periodically discuss the overall state of the tax system, identify immediate challenges and priorities, set overall goals and objectives, and/or resolve issues concerning coordination. In other words, there is no top-down strategic oversight involving all key actors and, as a result, no substantive over-arching strategy for improving the effectiveness of tax administration". Beyond the issue of tax administration, from a broader viewpoint, the Italian approach adopted in trying to set up new financial relations is, up to today, characterized by adding complexity rather than avoiding it.

As the previous parts have shown, due to the complexity resulting from the delayed and desultory implementation of the system of fiscal federalism and financial relations, it is very difficult to give concrete evidence as to its actual functioning. A detailed look at the work of the Permanent Conference for the Coordination of Public Finance (hereinafter Permanent Conference) cannot help either. This body is the permanent advisory body tasked with the implementation of the reform. It is composed of representatives of the different institutional levels of government and has functions such as co-defining budget objectives (also with regard to tax pressure and indebtedness), advising on the equalization fund, monitoring the territorial entities' compliance with set objectives and promoting the enforcement of convergence programs as well as managing a reward or sanctions system. The Permanent Conference was essentially set up because of the shortages of the intergovernmental relations' system in Italy.

Coordination and cooperation across and within Italian governmental levels has never been constitutionalized. Subnational entities voice their interests and discuss policy implementation in a consultative Standing Conference for cooperation between the center, the regions, and the autonomous provinces. The Standing Conference is convoked at the request of the central government that also sets the agenda. This cooperation mechanism was established in 1983 and formalized by law no. 400/1988. Over time, this system gained significant political influence. However, it is limited by its inherent diversity, along Italy's North–South divide and along party ideologies. Vertical bilateral coordination between the State and the single region is the preferred channel, even though it is, except in the case of special regions, improperly institutionalized and differently used from one region to another, not least because of the budgetary capacity each region has.

It is obvious that also the recent developments at the European level do significantly hamper the task of effectively balancing the inverted pendulum of the fiscal and financial system. In fact, the start of the implementation of the fiscal federalism reform coincided with the financial-economic crisis in the late 2000s (Ambrosanio et al. 2016). So did national austerity measures severely decrease the overall amount of transfers without providing any form of adequate compensation in terms of own taxes or other tax-revenue sources. Moreover, decentralized spending has been cut to ensure the respect of EU obligations and the regional tax autonomy has been frozen. Consequently, the vertical fiscal gap increased with more significant implications for the richer northern regions. A re-evaluation as to which public services must ultimately be equalized to which extent is work in progress, too. In sum, major equalizing efforts have been concentrated on health care, while other essential functions like education and social assistance have not been considered at all (Bordignon and Ambrosanio 2020).

In addition, the subnational dimension of financial autonomy continues to be vigorously constrained by the concrete functioning of the competence-allocation scheme, in ordinary times and ever more in extraordinary times such as the Covid-19 emergency. Both the delayed implementation of the reform and the extensive interpretation of the national competences have worsened the existing asymmetry between the expenditure and the revenue as far as subnational entities are concerned. This has also further deteriorated the condition of unaccountability. Such a reading of the national jurisdiction has had an impact also on the system of financing of special regions, though in their case the procedural guarantees coming with the principle of bilateralism allow for better, tailor-made negotiated solutions.

Notwithstanding the abovementioned shortcomings and bearing in mind the origins and the development of Italy's territorial organization and socio-political peculiarities, governing Italy by means of coordinated but plural—and thus asymmetric—answers is the only possible way forward. Neither diversity nor asymmetry, within and across governmental levels, are, in the end, issues one can neglect. On the contrary, they are intrinsic to societal and territorial pluralism, in Italy and elsewhere. If managed well, they ultimately can contribute to balancing the effects stemming from an inverted governance pendulum.

As of early 2020, Italy's system of fiscal federalism and financial relations continues to be called into question because of two systemic, long-standing reasons, and one reason linked to the challenges the pandemic bears. The two systemic ones are: First, political instability at the central level. On average, a legislature in Italy lasts 13 months. More than 66 governments have been in office since 1946 (as often, it depends on the counting method: The Draghi government, sworn in on 13 February 2021, is the 67th since the foundation of the Italian Republic, the 64rd since the ItConst came into force and already the 73rd since the end of fascism. Mario Draghi is the sixth head of government who was not elected from parliamentary ranks). Second, the lack of (coordinated) political pressure for change from the subnational level. Regions at last prefer having adequate resources without bearing the political costs associated with tax-raising. Therefore, any real fiscal decentralization that permits the instauration of an effective democratic control over subnational entities is far from being realized. Finally, the management of the Covid-19 pandemic challenges Italy's system of intergovernmental (financial) relations in unprecedented ways.

9 Evaluating the Covid-19 Outbreak Phase: The Ultimate Stress Test

As elsewhere, in Italy in early 2020, Covid-19 was extremely stress-testing both the capacities and the capabilities of all actors of Italian regionalism, within and across governmental levels. The Covid-19 emergency phase officially started end of January 2020 with two Chinese visitors being tested positive in Rome, while its diffusion is linked to a 38-year-old Italian citizen being definitely hospitalized in Codogno, Lombardy, on 21 February 2020. After a very short time, the infections spread beyond all expectations, exceeding the Codogno area and involving not only the whole region of Lombardy but all the northern regions and the two autonomous provinces.

Interestingly, Lombardy, Emilia-Romagna, and Veneto, the three regions that have been among those being most heavily affected by Covid-19, are the ones that since 2017 have been asking for the transfer of additional powers from the center (pursuant to art. 116 par. 3 ItConst). In the proposals, the three regions advocate for assuming a large part of, if not all, the competences listed in art. 117 par. 3 of the ItConst, including, among others, health protection. Against the backdrop of the socio-economic challenges linked to the Covid-19 emergency, the negotiations between the central authority and these regions (but also others) as to the transfer of further powers will inevitably be re-shaped. Resumed negotiations, whenever possible, will call into question the instrument of differentiated regionalism, at least from a political viewpoint. At the national level, demands for re-centralizing the regional competence of health care have been voiced. However, as neatly pointed out by

Bin (2020), the problem is that the public health care service works well in some regions and in others it does not, even though public spending is more or less the same. Better coordination would thus be the solution, not recentralization (Alber et al. 2021). Rather than ignoring the relative success of the regionalized health care sector, one should seriously address deficiencies in intergovernmental coordination (and financial relations). Ultimately, from a federal viewpoint, territorial actors know best the situation on the ground and the center's task would be to efficiently monitor and coordinate the performance and quality of the delivery of public services throughout a country, in both ordinary and extraordinary times.

What Covid-19 teaches us about Italian regionalism is, in essence, that central, regional, and local authorities will have to seriously re-evaluate the question as to their respective governance and coordination capacities, as well as their capabilities, in the field of health care and beyond, not least because up to now procedural aspects in intergovernmental coordination, financial relations and data exchange have not been systematically approached and dealt with. The financial side of the scheme of differentiated regionalism, as well as the implementation of fiscal federalism (on which it should be grounded), are not yet sufficiently developed. For example, none of the preliminary agreements of 28 February 2018 between the regions Veneto, Lombardy, and Emilia-Romagna, and the center properly addresses the quantification of the resources needed to cover the expenses linked to the additional powers (such as health protection). The preliminary agreements, of political relevance only, have a duration of ten years, and they may be modified at any time by mutual agreement between the center and the respective region. Regarding financial resources, the preliminary agreements aim at setting up a State-region joint commission likewise the ones in the special regions. This body should define any details as to the allocation of resources or the revision of current sharing schemes by considering shared taxes and expenditure needs in relation to the exercise of the additional powers, and the criterion of standard costs and needs. From the viewpoint of virtuous regional financial management, the revised system of financial relations would not only have to address all the regional costs linked to the enhanced competence catalogue by making the region accountable for it, but also the costs linked to amply guaranteeing the essential levels of public services in key areas such as health, education, and social assistance. Only by such a virtuous financial management, a region could dispose of a budgetary capacity able to confront challenges also in inauspicious times. It is to be seen to what extent the mentioned regions will continue their negotiations over the transfer of additional powers, and if others will ever aim (and be permitted) to start negotiations (in more detail).

A closer look at how the Covid-19 Italian outbreak phase was handled clearly reveals the (structural) weaknesses inherent to Italy's system of intergovernmental relations, in the health sector and beyond. The ItConst in its art. 32 safeguards "health as a fundamental right of the individual and as a collective interest" and it lists "health protection" as a concurrent legislative competence (art. 117 par. 3 ItConst), with the center determining general principles and the regions adopting detailed rules. As outlined earlier, the ItConst also attributes regulatory powers and administrative functions both to regions, local government, and second level local entities (art. 117 par. 6 and 118 par. 1 ItConst). According to this scheme, regional health services especially at the beginning of the emergency phase reacted differently to the challenges posed by Covid-19. For example, some southern regions imposed the obligation for persons arriving from a heavily affected region to self-isolate for 14 days. At the local level, some mayors ordered the closure of schools and public spaces, and they prohibited persons coming from heavily affected zones access to the municipality. To advert "localist drifts" (Vedaschi and Graziani 2020), the central government deprived measures taken by mayors of "any effect" if not consistent with the provisions laid down at the central level. The center also took legal actions against measures adopted by governors of a region. For example, when the governor of the insisted in closing schools in a period when in the Marches there was no single confirmed Covid-19 infection, the regional administrative court at the request of the council of ministers ultimately suspended the measure (that was adopted on 25 February 2020). However, on the same day of the judicial decision taken by the regional administrative court (27 February 2020), he again signed a regional ordinance to close the schools after having detected Covid-19 cases. He then could legitimately do so because of the occurrence of the factual circumstances and legal requirements envisaged in the decree law no. 6/2020 that provided for the adoption of containment measures in case of infections.

As elsewhere, the central government positioned itself along with its head, the then president of the council of ministers Giuseppe Conte, as the master of the crisis. After the declaration of the public health state of emergency on 31 January 2020 (with a time limit of six months), Conte in the period under examination signed several "Decrees of the President of the Council of Ministers" (hereinafter DPCM; they are of administrative nature) (see Ministero degli Affari Esteri 2020, with some of them available also in English; for the full list of legal responses to Covid-19 see Gazzetta Ufficiale 2020). In a chronological order, the DPCM of 08 March 2020 redefined the areas which were subject to restrictive measures of free movement by including larger areas in the most affected regions. The DPCM of 09 March 2020 extended the lockdown to all the Italian territory until 03 April 2020, while the DPCM of 11 March 2020 ordered the closure of all commercial and retail businesses except those providing essential services. As educational and cultural institutions, public events, and sport manifestations were already suspended nation-wide, both the public and commercial life came to a total halt. Under Italy's quarantine measures, citizens were not allowed to move except from well-grounded work- or health-related reasons, and for getting basic supplies in their own neighborhood (grounds to be stated on a self-certification any person had to bring along). Special rules of self-isolation applied to persons suspected of having Covid-19 and several areas throughout Italy were also subject to even more restrictive measures such as the prohibition to enter or leave a municipality for any ground (except in case of an urgency). The DPCM of 22 March 2020, in addition, ordered the closure of all non-essential businesses and industries. The DPCM of 01 April 2020 extended the general shutdown of Italy's public life and production system until 13 April 2020 and the DPCM of 10 April 2020 further specified the rules as to the lockdown with its extension until 03 May 2020. The DPCM of 26 April 2020 specified the rules for the so-called phase two, the re-opening, starting from 04 May 2020 (without explicitly considering any tailor-made solutions for territories that were barely affected by Covid-19). The closure of educational institutions until autumn 2020 was confirmed, and so were strict physical distancing as well as face mask wearing at work and in the public sphere; a plan as to slowly easing mobility restrictions (within one's own region first, and across regions from 03 June onwards) as well as ideas as to a time-delayed resumption of work was also foreseen or voiced (with the re-opening of non-essential businesses and industries starting first, followed by the re-opening of commercial and retail businesses as well as restaurants and bars in the second half of May 2020). Especially from the end of April onwards, regional unrest as to the top-down management of phase two has been increasingly voiced. Some regions started to take actions by regulating or legislating (only South

Tyrol did so!) on an earlier opening of certain activities, and sectors. A tug of war between the center and the respective region was thereforehas been initiated (Alber 2020).

All in all, the Italian legal response to Covid-19 was (inevitably) enacted in great haste, with some important constitutional issues and safeguards as to the rule of law that have been adjusted only along the way (Beqiraj 2020). Such adjustments concerned the relations between the central and subnational entities, and the role of the central government and its relations with the national parliament. On the one hand, the central government monopolized the emergency management without adequately involving the regions according to the principle of loyal cooperation, and the regions (and municipalities) thus acted on their own. From late February to the beginning of April 2020, regulatory and legal chaos with more than 250 measures made a clear understanding of the relationship between the measures taken at different governmental levels and their effects very difficult (e.g., regarding the right to do sports; see a list of all measures per region in Mallardo 2020; see also Simoncini 2020). On the other hand, the ItConst was of little help as it neither provides any clear procedural guarantees for the exercise of power in an emergency, nor any clear provisions as to the joint management of responsibilities. Indeed, the ItConst does not provide any extraordinary power-relation scenario except in case of a war. In such circumstances, art. 78 of the ItConst, prior to the authorization of the national parliament, enables the government to suspend fundamental rights and freedoms by means of a governmental decree having the same force of law. Within the Italian legal system, other acts that have force of law are the legislative decree (art. 76 ItConst) and the decree law (art. 77 ItConst). The first one, legislative decree, implies that the national parliament delegates the legislative function to the government after having established principles and guiding criteria (such a delegation is limited in time and for specific purposes only; for example, the central government got a "maxi-delegation" as to the implementation of the 2009 fiscal federalism reform). The second one, the decree law, can be used by the central government out of necessity and urgency, without a prior delegation from the national parliament. A decree law must, however, be converted by the national parliament into law within sixty days of its publication as it otherwise becomes void.

In the Covid-19 outbreak phase, in absence of clear constitutional provisions, the central government resorted to the possibility to decree-ruling. It basically seized all power from the regions based on the declaration of the public health state of emergency on 31 January 2020. This declaration is based on a statutory, not a constitutional provision: the Civil Protection Act 2018. This act has empowered the central government to adopt "any necessary measure" within the limits of the "general principles of the legal system and the European Union rules". However, this act does not explicitly empower the central government to limit fundamental rights and freedoms. Therefore, on 23 February 2020 decree law no. 6 was issued (and converted into law on 05 March 2020). The decree law granted the competent authorities with the power to order "any appropriate restrictive measure", and it allowed the central government to resort to several DPCM for the adoption of the lockdown measures. Regional authorities were scarcely consulted. On 25 March 2020, with the adoption of decree law no. 19, the central government clarified the relations and effects between the different measures that were taken at national and subnational level (Beqiraj 2020). It made clear that, in absence of measures taken at national level, subnational authorities may, within well-determined limits, introduce further restrictive measures to cope with specific emergency situations.

From the viewpoint of intergovernmental coordination, consultations with subnational authorities, however, continued to be rather limited. Next to the overall structural deficiencies of Italy's intergovernmental relations (as earlier described in Section. 1 and 8), coordination across (and within) governmental levels was also difficult because of serious flaws in data collection and knowledge exchange. Even though Italy's health information infrastructure is, in theory, considered to be optimal, its different territorial systems were badly interconnected and coordinated as to their preparedness and containment plans (outdated both at the national and the regional levels!) (Carinci 2020). This to varying degrees compromised the effectiveness of the responses to Covid-19, not per se decentralization. Decentralization, as argued in relation to the crisis management of other countries (Gaskell and Stoker 2020; Palermo 2020), would allow for the inclusion of localized capacity, and for the arrangement of multi-level structures into "working governance systems". Rather than re-starting discourses on whether some competences should be recentralized, Italy should address a systematic review of the instruments promoting greater correlation and participation between the different institutional levels. At last, the key to success in solving any problem that transcends borders cannot but be the ability of governmental levels to relate to each other, in ordinary and extraordinary times.

Therefore, a consistent chain of command as to the coordination of actions across levels of government is needed. Likewise, such a chain of command is needed to better understand the functioning of the (envisaged) rules of fiscal federalism and financial relations, not least because they will inevitably be revised against the backdrop of both the policy responses of the national and subnational governments to counteract the impact of Covid-19, and any (framework) conditions related to recovery programs of the EU. In such a scenario, Italy's central authority will continue to play a pivotal role in balancing the ever more unstable inverted pendulum, and the risk of drifting toward further recentralization remains high.

References

Alber, E. 2014, "Italy's Piecemeal Path Towards Fiscal Federalism: One Step Forward, Two Steps Back?" In: Lütgenau, S.A. (ed.), *Fiscal Federalism and Fiscal Decentralization in Europe. Comparative Case Studies on Spain, Austria, the United Kingdom and Italy.*Innsbruck, Wien, Bozen: Studienverlag: 139–171

Alber, E. 2017, "South Tyrol's Negotiated Autonomy." *Journal of Ethnic Studies*, 78: 41–48: https://rig-td.si/en/clanki/south-tyrols-negotiated-autonomy-2/

Alber, E. 2020, "Action and reaction: What Covid-19 Can Teach Us About Italian Regionalism." *UACES Territorial Politics Blog*, 29 May 2020, https://uacesterrpol.wordpress.com/2020/05/29/action-and-reaction-what-Covid-19-can-teach-us-about-italian-regionalism/

Alber, E., and Trettel, M. 2018, "The Italian Education System: Constitutional Design, Organization and Policy Making." In: Wong, K.K. et al. (eds.), *Federalism and Education.* Charlotte NC: IAP Publishing: 131–161

Alber, E., and Valdesalici, A. 2012, "Reforming Fiscal Federalism in Europe: Where Does the Pendulum Swing?" *L'Europe en Formation*, 363, no. 1: 325–365. Available from https://www.cairn.info/revue-l-europe-en-formation-2012-1-page-325.htm

Alber, E., Arban, E., Colasante, P., Dirri, A., and Palermo, F. 2021, "Facing the Pandemic: Italy's functional 'health federalism' and dysfunctional cooperation." In: Steytler, N. (ed.), Comparative Federalism and Covid-19, London: Routledge: 15-32, https://doi.org/10.4324/9781003166771

Albertazzi, D., and Giovannini, A./Seddone, A. 2018, "'No Regionalism Please, We Are Leghisti !' The Transformation of the Italian Lega Nord Under the Leadership of Matteo Salvini." *Regional & Federal Studies*, 28, no. 5: 645–671

Ambrosanio, M.F., and Balduzzi P./Bordignon M. 2016, "Economic crisis and fiscal federalism in Italy." In: Ahmad E., Bordignon M. and Brosio G. (eds.), *Multi-level Finance and the Euro Crisis. Causes and Effects.* Cheltenham: Edward Elgar Publishing: 212–248

Antonini, L. 2009, *La rivincita della responsabilità. A proposito della nuova legge sul federalismo fiscale*, Milano, Fondazione per la sussidiarietà, 7

Arban, E. 2018, "The Referenda for More Autonomy in Veneto and Lombardia: Constitutional and Comparative Perspectives." *Perspectives on Federalism*, 10, no. 1. Available from http://www.on-federalism.eu/index.php

Baldini, G., and Baldi, B. 2014, "Decentralization in Italy and the Troubles of Federalization." *Regional and Federal Studies*, 24, no. 1: 87–108

Banca d'Italia 2013, *Relazione annual. Anno 2012.* https://www.bancaditalia.it/pubblicazioni/relazione-annuale/2012/rel_2012.pdf

Beqiraj, J. 2020 (8 April), "Italy's Coronavirus Legislative Response: Adjusting Along the Way." *VerfBlog*. https://verfassungsblog.de/italys-coronavirus-legislative-response-adjusting-along-the-way

Bin, R. 2020 (3 April), "Caro Orlando, il vero problema della sanità è al centro, non in periferia," *laCostituzione.info*, http://www.lacostituzione.info/index.php/2020/04/03/caro-speranza-il-vero-problema-della-sanita-e-al-centro-non-in-periferia/

Bordignon, M., and Ambrosanio M. F. 2020, "Il nodo (irrisolto?) della perequazione regionale in Italia." In: Palermo, F., Parolari S. and Valdesalici A. (eds.), *Italia e Spagna: costituzioni finanziarie a confronto. Un bilancio a 10 anni dalle riforme.* Napoli: ESI: 151–176

Carinci, F. 2020, "Covid-19: preparedness, decentralisation, and the hunt for patient zero", *BMJ*, p. bmj.m799, available from http://dx.doi.org/https://doi.org/10.1136/bmj.m799.

Ciolli, I. 2014, *The Balanced Budget Rule in the Italian Constitution: It Ain't Necessarily so…Useful?*. Rivista AIC: 1–21

Constitution of the Italian Republic. Available from https://www.senato.it/3801

Court of Auditors 2019, *Rapporto sul coordinamento della finanza pubblica.* https://www.corteconti.it/Home/Documenti/RapportoCoordinamentoFP

D'Orlando, E., and Grisostolo, F.E. 2016, "La disciplina degli enti locali tra uniformità e differenziazione." In: Palermo F. and Parolari S. (eds.), *La variabili della specialità. Evidenze e riscontri tra variabili istituzionali e politiche settoriali.* Napoli: ESI: 99–160

Dunford, M. 2008, "After the Three Italies the (Internally Differentiated North-South Divide: Analysing Regional and Industrial Trajectories." *Annales de géographie*, 664: 85–114. Available from https://www.cairn.info/revue-annales-de-geographie-2008-6-page-85.htm

Eurostat 2019, *Regional GDP per capita ranged from 31% to 626% of the EU average in 2017*. Newsrelease 26 February 2019. Available from https://ec.europa.eu/eurostat/en/web/products-press-releases/-/1-26022019-AP

Felice, E. 2017, "The Roots of a Dual Equilibrium: GDP, Productivity and Structural Change in the Italian Regions in the Long-run (1871–2011), Quaderni di Storia Economica." *Banca d'Italia*, 40. Available from https://www.bancaditalia.it/pubblicazioni/quaderni-storia/index.html

Felice, E. 2018, "The Socio-Institutional Divide: Explaining Italy's Long-Term Regional Differences." *Journal of Interdisciplinary History*, no. 1, 49: 43–70

Ferrara, A., and Salerno, G. M. (eds.) 2010, *Il federalismo fiscale. Commento alla legge n. 42 del 2009*. Napoli: Jovene.

Gaskell, J., and Stoker, G. 2020 (16 April), *Centralised or Multi-Level: Which Governance Systems Are Having a 'Good' Pandemic?*. Available from https://blogs.lse.ac.uk/politicsandpolicy/governance-systemsCovid19/?utm_campaign=Blogs&utm_content=1587715203&utm_medium=social&utm_source=facebook

Gazzetta Ufficiale 2020, *Raccolta degli atti recanti misure urgenti in materia di contenimento e gestione dell'emergenza epidemiologica da COVID-19*. Available from https://www.gazzettaufficiale.it/dettaglioArea/12

Hom, S.M. 2013, "On the Origins of Making Italy: Massimo D'Azeglio and 'Fatta l'Italia, bisogna fare gli italiani'." *Italian Culture*, 31, no. 1: 1–16

IFEL—Dipartimento Finanza Locale 2019, *La finanza comunale in sintesi*, available from https://www.fondazioneifel.it/documenti-e-pubblicazioni/item/download/3410_1784abea3a086d86f6363eaf17c6d78f

ISSiRFA 2019, *La finanza regionale 2015–2016*. Torino: Giappichelli

Istat 2016, *I bilanci consuntivi delle regioni e province autonome*. Available from https://www.istat.it/it/archivio/214338

Istat 2020a, *Population and Households*. available from https://www.istat.it/en/population-and-households

Istat 2020b, *Codici statistici delle unità amministrative territoriali: comuni, città metropolitane, province e regioni – Novità per l'anno 2020*. Available from https://www.istat.it/it/archivio/6789

Istat 2020c, *Conti Economici Territoriali (28 gennaio 2020)*. Available from https://www.istat.it/it/archivio/237813

I.Stat 2020, *Database of Italian Statistics*. Available from http://dati.istat.it/Index.aspx?lang=en&SubSessionId=74ee2340-30c2-4414-b9fe-1da6b6c7c0eb

Jorio, E. 2010, "Federalismo fiscale: lo schema del decreto attuativo sull'autonomia di entrata delle regioni e delle province, sulla perequazione e sulla determinazione dei costi e dei fabbisogni standard nel settore sanitario." *Astrid*. Available from www.astrid.eu

Jorio, E., Gambino S., and D'Ignazio, G. 2009, *Il federalismo fiscale. Commento articolo per articolo alla legge 5 maggio 2009*, 42. Santarcangelo di Romagna: Maggioli

Kössler, K., and Kress, A. 2021, "European Cities between Self-Government and Subordination: Their Role as Policy-Takers and Policy-Makers." In: Hirsch Ballin E./van der Schyff G./Stremler, M. (eds.), *European Yearbook of Constitutional Law 2020: The City in Constitutional Law*. The Hague: T.M.C. Asser Press: 273-302

Mallardo, S. 2020 (4 April) (ed.), *Covid-19. Documentazione regionale*. Available from https://www.federalismi.it/nv14/?sezione=documentazione&sez=1&nrs=411

Ministero degli Affari Esteri 2020, *Normative COVID-19*. Available from https://www.esteri.it/mae/it/ministero/normativaonline/normativa-altre-amministrazioni.htm

Muraro, G. 2011, "Federalismo regionale: la rivoluzione può attendere." *Lavoce.info*. Available from http://www.lavoce.info

Newell, J. L. 2010, *The Politics of Italy: Governance in a Normal Country*. Cambridge: University Press Cambridge

Nicolini, M. 2010, "La disciplina transitoria statale sui tributi propri delle Regioni e la potestà legislativa regionale in materia tributaria. Il caso della regionalizzazione dell'IRAP." *Giurisprudenza Costituzionale*, 1: 911-938

OECD 2016, *Italy's Tax Administration—A Review of Institutional and Governance Aspects*. Available from https://www.oecd.org/tax/administration/oecd-secretariat-reviews-the-functioning-of-the-italian-tax-administration.htm

Palermo, F. 2020, "What Is at Stake? Federalism as Part of Constitutionalism." *Verfassungsblog*, 13 May 2020, https://verfassungsblog.de/is-there-a-space-for-federalism-in-times-of-emergency/

Palermo, F., and Valdesalici, A. 2019, "Irreversibly Different. A Country Study of Constitutional Asymmetry in Italy." In: Popelier, P., and Sahadžić, M. (eds.), *Constitutional Asymmetry in Multinational Federalism -Managing multinationalism in multi-tiered systems*. Basel: Springer International Publishing: 287–315

Pallaver, G., and Brunazzo, M. 2017, "Italy: The Pendulum of "Federal" Regionalism." In: Karlhofer, F., and Pallaver, G. (eds.), *Federal Power-Sharing in Europe*. Nomos: Baden-Baden: 149–180

Rivosecchi, G. 2010, "La legge delega sul federalismo fiscale e il coordinamento della finanza pubblica e del sistema tributario: la difficile quadratura del cerchio." In: De Petris, A. (ed.), *Federalismo fiscale "learning by doing": modelli comparati di raccolta e distribuzione del gettito tra centro e periferia*. Milano: Cedam: 121–142

Simoncini, M. 2020 (9 April), "The Need for Clear Competences in Times of Crisis: Clashes in the Coordination of Emergency Powers in Italy."

VerfBlog, available from https://verfassungsblog.de/the-need-for-clear-competences-in-times-of-crisis/

Valdesalici, A. 2014, "Features and Trajectories of Fiscal Federalism in Italy." In: Lütgenau, S.A. (ed.), *Fiscal Federalism and Fiscal Decentralization in Europe. Comparative Case Studies on Spain, Austria, the United Kingdom and Italy.* Innsbruck, Wien, Bozen: Studienverlag: 73–101

Valdesalici, A. 2018, "Autonomia finanziaria e specialità: un modello per sei sistemi ad alto tasso di differenziazione." In: Palermo, F./Parolari, S. (eds.), *Le variabili della specialità. Evidenze e riscontri tra variabili istituzionali e politiche settoriali.* Napoli: ESI: 161–198

Vassallo, S. 2013, *Il divario incolmabile. Rappresentanza politica e rendimento istituzionale nelle regioni italiane.* Il Mulino: Bologna

Vedaschi, A./Graziani, C. 2020 (6 March), "Coronavirus, Health Emergencies and Public Law Issues." *VerfBlog*. Available from https://verfassungsblog.de/coronavirus-health-emergencies-and-public-law-issues/

Woelk, J. 2013, "South Tyrol Is (not) Italy: A Special Case in a (De)federalizing System." *L'Europe en Formation*, 3/2013, no. 369: 126–137. Available from https://www.cairn.info/revue-l-europe-en-formation-2013-3-page-126.htm

South Africa

Ramos Emmanuel Mabugu and Eddie M. Rakabe

1 Introduction

Towards the end of the twenty-first century, South Africa emerged as one of the latecomers into the prevailing international political order of parliamentary democracy, following decades of authoritarian and oppressive rule by the white minority government under the Apartheid era. The country gained international recognition and reverence in 1994 when it managed to achieve a peaceful transition from white minority rule into a multi-party democracy. The reforms that followed soon thereafter sought to steer the country away from the historical centralist system of government into a modern and constitutionally legislated multi-level

Book Chapter prepared for the Forum of Federations (May 2020).

R. E. Mabugu (✉) · E. M. Rakabe
School of Economic and Management Sciences, Sol Plaatje University, Kimberley, South Africa
e-mail: Emmanuel.mabugu@spu.ac.za; rmabugu@gmail.com

E. M. Rakabe
e-mail: eddie.rakabe@icloud.com

J.-F. Tremblay (ed.), *The Forum of Federations Handbook of Fiscal Federalism*, https://doi.org/10.1007/978-3-030-97258-5_8

government that espouses power sharing between the national and subnational governments. This was a great leap from the apartheid system of governance that was organised along racial lines rather than functional linkages and the fundamental principles of a centralised or decentralised political and fiscal regime. The system created superficial tiers of governments that mainly acted as administrative organs of the apartheid system and instruments of state security control. Arguments continue to rage across the spectrum as to whether multi-level government that South Africa adopted has served the country well.

Readers, unfamiliar with South Africa, can identify the country at the southernmost tip of Africa where the Atlantic and Indian Ocean meet. It has a population of just under 60 million. Black Africans constitute 80% of the population, Whites and Coloured (mixed race) account for 9%, respectively while Indians/Asians comprise 2.5%.[1] The composition of the population, as described herein, has had and continues to have a substantial influence on the shape of modern day intergovernmental fiscal relations (IGFR). Post democratic transition decentralisation reforms sought to inter alia unite historically "race demarcated" jurisdictions and entrench equity in the delivery of basic services and the distribution resources and economic activity. Addressing the historical legacy of racial and spatial inequality remains a central sticking point in the organising of constituent units.

Fundamentally, though, the design and structure of multi-level governance is underpinned by the Constitution, which establishes three distinctive, interdependent and interrelated spheres of government. Furthermore, the Constitution introduces a framework for assignment of powers and functions and sharing of nationally raised revenue across the three spheres. These arrangements resonate with the dominant trend that has emerged worldwide towards decentralised system of governance and fiscal system. In its current form, the South African IGFR system comprises of the national government, nine provinces and three categories or tiers of local government (257 in total), each with specific expenditure and revenue responsibilities. The nature of the fiscal arrangements is such that expenditure responsibilities are highly decentralised while tax powers are centralised. To this end, national government accounts for a lion's share of national revenue and spending while provinces are largely reliant on

[1] South African law classifies Africans, Coloureds and Asians as Blacks.

national transfers for revenue to the tune of over 95% of total revenue. The local government sphere comprises of 257 highly diverse constituent units distinguishable by various characteristics including executive and legislative authority, spatial and socioeconomic conditions, population size and own revenue mobilisation capacity. Municipalities range from those regarded as metropolitan constituencies (with greater national economic significance) to rural local constituencies (with little to zero economic activity).

The size and wealth of provinces or municipality matters little for the influence of national policy and access to resources because the Constitution recognise each sphere and tier of government as an independent constituent unit. All spheres and tiers are overseen by public representative structures elected through "closed party lists" proportional representation system. The system allows every political party which meet registration requirements set by the Electoral Commission to contest for seats or power at every sphere and tier of government thus making government essentially accountable to the legislator and local councils—and ultimately to the electorate. These arrangements are what makes South Africa a rather unique quasi federal state, the so-called administrative federalism, where there is a partial devolution of political, administrative and fiscal powers to the subnational governments. The structure further reflects the dominance of the ruling African National Congress (ANC) party whose traditions are rooted in democratic centralism. This ideological orientation resulted in commentators referring to the South African IGFR system as a "compromise" because of the balance that emerged out of strong arguments for centralisation by the ANC and push back for federalism by small political parties during the pre-1994 negotiations. Haysom (2016), notes that discussions about devolution of powers to subnational government during the democratisation process were polarised along racial lines with those who benefited (Whites) from Apartheid needing to retain formal and informal pre-1994 structures (as federal fiefdoms) while those who were concerned about transforming the institutions and patterns of privilege (Blacks) wanted a unitary state. The government system has remained stable since then, but is constantly challenged to reflect the de facto ANC centralist aspirations.

Beyond, political and citizens accountability, the Constitution provides for a number of levers to promote accountability. The levers include independent institutions supporting democracy such as the Human Rights Commission, the Auditor General, the Public Protector, the Gender

Commission and the Financial and Fiscal Commission, which makes recommendations on key constitutionally defined areas, and report to Parliament and Provincial legislatures. These institutions are particularly created to foster progressive realisation of basic rights (i.e. right to food, water, housing, health care, etc.) to the citizens as enshrined in Chapter 2 of the Constitution (The Bill of Rights). South Africa became one of the few countries in the world to introduce justiciable socioeconomic rights. This means that citizens can turn to the courts as an additional layer of accountability to enforce state provision of basic rights. One of the hallmark successful cases of enforcing state provision of basic rights was recorded in 2000 when the Constitutional court was called upon to rule on the failure of the state to deliver housing to a homeless elderly. Court cases often have far-reaching implications on the design of intergovernmental relations and ignite debates on separation of powers between the executive, legislature and the judiciary.

In terms of economic attributes, South Africa is an upper middle-income country with per capita income of $6,300. While this income level is dwarfed by that of developed countries (e.g. OECD at $40, 300), it is considerably higher than the sub-Saharan Africa average ($1, 500). Unlike many other African countries, the South African economy is relatively diversified and less depended on natural resources. The mining industry has played a crucial role in shaping the South African economy, but its contribution to gross domestic product (GDP) has declined since 1994 (World Bank, 2018). Mineral exports, however, remain the largest earner of foreign exchange reserves, with China having become the largest trading partner, as it continues its crusade for rare earth minerals. A combination of sluggish commodity prices, adverse weather conditions and the aftermath of the 2009 financial crises as well as years of internal fiscal mismanagement have landed the country in a precarious macroeconomic situation. The country is battling deteriorating macroeconomic conditions, with unemployment sitting at 29% and debt to GDP ratio expected to reach 71% by 2022 (National Treasury, 2018). The declining national fiscal position affects the majority of the grant reliant subnational governments, which continue to propagate for a bigger slice of national tax collections rather than taxing powers. To compound the country's problems, South Africa is now saddled with having to deal with the negative ramifications of the COVID-19 pandemic which exerts untoward pressure on the country's intergovernmental system.

The rest of the chapter is organised in the following way: Sect. 2 discusses the structure of government followed by a discussion of taxation powers in Sect. 3. Section 4 outlines fiscal transfers and revenue transfers while Sect. 5 discusses macroeconomic and fiscal policy management. Having acquired a grasp of the working of South Africa's intergovernmental fiscal relations, we offer a preliminary discussion of the ongoing implications of COVID-19 on the country's version of fiscal system including response measures put in place in Sect. 6. Finally, Sect. 7 concludes the chapter by highlighting successes and challenges of fiscal federalism in South Africa.

2 The Structure of Government

South Africa's system of multi-level government derives its structure and shape from Section 40 of the Constitution. Government is constituted as comprising three arms of the state and three spheres of government (national, provincial and local spheres) which are distinctive, interrelated and interdependent. These three rather incompatible elements of the system are most evident in the institutional design for democracy and power sharing, exemplified by (a) the establishment of democratically elected representative institutions in each sphere of government; (b) the division of functions among the spheres of government with many important functions allocated concurrently to the national, provincial and, sometimes, local governments; (c) revenue sharing arrangements prescribed by the Constitution and (d) the constitutional recognition of the importance of intergovernmental arrangements, capped by a second chamber, the National Council of Provinces, which gives provinces a direct say in national decision-making (Murray, 2009). At the advent of democracy in 1994, nine provinces were created alongside three categories of wall-to-wall municipalities, namely:

- Category A or Metropolitan municipalities: A municipality that has exclusive municipal executive and legislative authority in its area (8 in total).
- Category B or Local municipalities: A municipality that shares municipal executive and legislative authority in its area with a category C municipality within whose area it falls (205 in total).

- Category C or District municipalities: A municipality that has municipal executive and legislative authority in an area that includes more than one municipality (44 in total).

Prior to 2000, there were 857 municipalities that included several transitional local councils in former homeland areas (Blacks only localities under the Apartheid system of separate development). In 2000, 284 wall-to-wall municipalities were established. The demarcation process in 2005 and 2016 subsequently resulted in some municipalities being amalgamated as part of the rationalisation agenda. This agenda resulted in the current composition of eight category A (metros), 205 category B (local) and 44 category C (district) municipalities (Financial and Fiscal Commission, 2011).

The establishment of fully-fledged representative institutions in each sphere and the Constitution's recognition of the functional and institutional integrity of all governments ensures that each government at every level has the constitutional status and institutional basis for its legislature and executive to function as coherent bodies. This is in line with the age-old principle of *trias politica*, which advocates that state power should be dispersed among the three existing arms. Hence, the Constitution provides that there should be separation of powers between the legislature, executive and the judiciary, with the necessary checks and balances to ensure accountability, responsiveness and openness (Munzhezdi, 2017). In this way, each organ of the state is able to respond to citizens' needs and exercise the level of discretion necessary to make appropriate decisions on matters under their responsibility. In particular, as distinct political entities, provinces and locals are expected to develop policy, to legislate and to manage their own administrations. However, in doing all these things, they are required to work co-operatively and adhere to national policy imperatives where applicable.

In keeping with the principle of separation of powers, the Constitution establishes three independent arms of government, namely, the legislature, executive and the judiciary. Table 1 gives a schematic representation of the composition of the three arms of government.

The legislature is made up of the National Assembly and the nine provincial legislatures. They are primarily discharged with the responsibility to represent the aspirations of the electorates (decide on matters of national interest) through election of the President, passing of national legislations and overseeing the executive arm in their role as implementers

Table 1 Arms of state and composition

Legislator	*Executive*	*Judiciary*
Parliament (national) • National assembly • National Council of provinces *Provinces* • Provincial legislature	*Cabinet (national)* • President • Deputy president • Ministers *Provinces* • Premier • Members of Executive Council	*Courts* • Constitutional court • Supreme court of appeal • High courts • Magistrate courts

Source Authors compilation

of laws and delivery functions. The cabinet as constituted by President, Deputy President and national minister represent the executive arm and is duly accountable to parliament for the performance and implementation of their functions both as a collective and individually. The judiciary is accorded the ultimate independency and is expected to apply the laws of the republic impartially and monitor the application of separation of powers. Reviews conducted by Siyo and Mubangisi (2015), conclude that South Africa's Constitutional and legislative framework sufficiently insulate the judiciary from improper influence. Notwithstanding, the dejure power sharing arrangements, subsequent section will however illustrate that power relations between the legislature and the executive defy the doctrine of separation of powers. This is a common challenge across many democracies that arises from the skewed distribution of budgeting powers and the party-political hierarchy dynamics between the legislature and the executive.

The principles of separation of powers further emphasise the need to allocate specific powers and functions to each sphere of government and each with clear roles and responsibilities. The Constitution of the country specifically allocates powers and functions to the three spheres, emphasising the obligation to cooperate with one another when undertaking their respective mandates. Some of the powers are exclusive in nature, meaning that only one sphere is responsible for setting policies, funding and implementation, while other functions are concurrent or shared. Function of exclusive national competence includes defence, macroeconomic management, foreign affairs, higher education, criminal justice system (safety and security) and administration and tax collections among others. National exclusive functions typically require strong financial muscle, central coordination and uniformity but also absorb a significant portion of the national budget—which subnational government can barely afford. Provincial functions of exclusive competence include provincial roads, ambulance services and provincial planning.

The bulk of the powers and functions, especially, those concerned with redistribution and transformation are allocated concurrently between national government and provinces and as well as between provinces and local government—as per Schedules 4 and 5 of the Constitution.

Sections 44 and 104 of the Constitution respectively give the national Parliament and provincial legislatures the authority to legislate on matters listed in Schedule 4. Sections 85 and 125, which deal with the executive authority of the national and provincial governments, confer the power on the national and provincial executives to implement such legislation. Local government is not expected to engage in any substantive law making except in cases of passing by-laws to manage their local spaces (Schwella, 2016). Table 2 gives an overview of the current assignment of the key functions across the three spheres (see Table 9 in Annexure A for a detailed outline of concurrent functional assignment). The governance system clearly bears the hallmark of a federation.

As can be deduced from Table 1, national government wields legislative and executive authority over provincial and local government shared area of responsibilities. The established practice in the execution of concurrent responsibility and as prescribed by the Constitution is that national government is responsible for providing leadership, formulating policies, regulations and norms and standards, support subnational governments and monitor implementation. Provinces and local governments are mainly responsible for implementation in line with the nationally determined frameworks. However, in some cases (such as water and electricity) national government is directly responsible for bulk supply while local government takes care of reticulation to households. To a larger extent expenditure assignments follow the principles of benefit spillovers, redistribution, vertical equity and fiscal efficiency. Functions whose benefits are regional in scope (e.g. education and health) are assigned jointly to national and provincial government while local government retains localised services such as electricity and water (Financial and Fiscal Commission, 2012b).

Table 2 Assignment of major exclusive and concurrent functions across the three spheres

Sphere/Functions	National	Provinces (9)	Local (257)
Defence and police	X		
Justice	X		
Higher education	X		
Foreign and domestic affairs	X		
Health	X	X	
Basic education	X	X	
Early childhood development	X	X	X
Water	X		X
Electricity	X		X
Housing	X	X	X
Environment	X	X	X
Roads	X	X	X

Source Adapted from RSA (1996)

De Visser (2008) is of the view that only section 156 (4) of the Constitution may be understood as deriving from the tenet of subsidiarity. The section state that "national and provincial governments must assign to a municipality, by agreement or subject to any conditions, the administration of functions listed in Part A of Schedule 4 and 5, which necessarily relate to local government, if (a) that function would most effectively be administered locally and (b) the municipality has the capacity to administer it". For de Visser (2008), section 156, should be viewed in the context of building a developmental local government rather than a deliberate pursuit for subsidiarity as applied in the European Union (EU) charter. We will illustrate in the subsequent sections that provinces have been reluctant to cede certain powers to local government.

The manner in which concurrent functions are exercised is a cause for ongoing disputes especially because the Constitution confers provinces executive powers to co-legislate on functions listed in Schedule 4 (Murray, 2009). The question that arises is whether provinces exercise executive power when executing concurrent responsibilities in which case they are accountable to their legislatures and electorate or exercise a delegated power, in which case they are answerable to the national government. These disputes persist despite there being a cooperative governance framework laid out in the Constitution and subordinate legislations[2] to foster mutual consultation and decision-making. Much of this quagmire is explained by the skewed distribution of taxation and spending powers—which invariably relegates provinces and majority of local government units to the status of subordinate jurisdictions of national government.

The complex and questionable nature of decentralisation and ambiguities in concurrent power sharing arrangements makes the governance system susceptible to tension and conflicts. Tensions are especially prevalent in the exercise of authority—in its different dimensions, including:

1. Political authority—the authority to establish presence in minds of citizens as a central point of decision-making and initiative. Provinces and local governments run a high risk of losing political credibility due to growing incidents of delivery failures and the consequential assumption of responsibilities by national government either through intervention or through tighter control of the transfers. Simeon and Murray (2008) attributes this risk to the inability of subnational government to establish themselves as autonomous and centres of economic power. This assertion maybe overly simplistic however, in that provinces and local government are more accountable to the political party than to the legislature and councils as prescribed in the Constitution. An ANC discussion document on the role of provinces for its 2007 Policy Conference highlighted deep seated uneasiness to provinces arguing that provinces add little value to the democratic project and are simply too costly to administer (ANC, 2007).

[2] **Intergovernmental Fiscal Relations Act** establishes Budget Council and Budget Forum as statutory bodies in which the provincial and national government consult on any fiscal, budgetary and any financial matter affecting the provincial sphere of government and the **Intergovernmental Relations Framework Act** sets out parameters to facilitate cooperation and coordination between national ministers and their provincial counterparts. The act establishes the President's Coordinating Council and empowers provincial executives and local Mayors to establish similar consultative intergovernmental forums.

2. Legislative authority—authority to formulate policies and legislation responding to specific needs and preferences of the citizens and to hold the executive to account. Although provinces routinely bemoan the lack of autonomy to set policies, many have not initiated legislations speaking to their concurrent mandates. National government actively discourages introduction of complementary legislations through informal "non-binding Agreements" but also exerts inordinate influence on subnational policies through nationally led intergovernmental forums. Tension also arises because of asymmetric assignment of functions between Category B and C municipalities. Certain Category C municipalities are authorised to perform functions on behalf of Category B municipalities while other districts have limited expenditure responsibilities despite receiving considerable amount of transfers.
3. Fiscal authority—the authority to command resources necessary to facilitate execution of assigned responsibilities.
4. Bureaucratic authority—the latitude to actually deliver services to the citizens.
5. Intergovernmental authority—the ability to cooperate and coordinate activities across all levels of government irrespective of hierarchy.

Overall, the framework for the assignment of functions has had serious implications for the functioning of the intergovernmental fiscal system in South Africa, with ambiguities and contradictions (see Box 1 for an illustrative case of the complexity with respect to basic education).

Box 1: Complexities of concurrency in basic education delivery
Basic education is a concurrent function shared between national and provincial governments where the former is responsible for policy and the latter undertakes actual delivery. A supporting Act of parliament (Schools Act) makes provision for delineating roles and responsibilities between the national minister and the member of executive council responsible for basic education. The national minister is charged with the responsibility to determine policy on wide ranging matters including guideline criteria for school admission and norms and standards for school infrastructure, capacity of schools and provision of learning and teaching material (i.e. classroom size,

learner-teacher ratio, school furniture). Members of the provincial executive are expected to "provide public schools" with funds appropriated for this purpose by the provincial legislature.

Provision of public schools is not well defined, but is interpreted as building of schools according to the infrastructure norms, hiring and firing of teachers and purchasing of learner-teacher support material. This delineation seems straight forward enough for all stakeholders to execute yet delivery of basic education, as a concurrent function is fraught with complexities.

First, national government does not always perform its policy duties as legislation prescribe. It was only in 2013 that legally binding norms and standards for infrastructure were published following protracted court battles. Even after publishing, it became clear that such norms and standards were neither costed nor accompanied by a detailed funding plan. For these reasons, provinces find it easier to deviate from national policy citing a lack of funding. Appointment of teachers is another contentious area. Whereas provinces are in principle responsible for teacher appointment, teacher salaries are determined through a national wage bargaining council. Adhering to learner-teacher ratio norms when personnel costs are determined elsewhere causes frictions in the system. Turning to outputs, the national minister of basic education is held responsible for the performance of the system as whole with matriculation pass rate used as a yardstick. The ministry often bemoans shouldering such a responsibility because it lacks the powers to direct allocation of resources by provinces. At the same time, members of the provincial executive are regarded as being accountable to the provincial legislature rather than the national executive. The challenges experienced in concurrency largely reflects weaknesses in upholding cooperative governance as espoused in the Constitution. Even a clear separation of roles and responsibility cannot achieve desired benefits of decentralisation if there is no harmony between the spheres.

This ambiguity causes misalignment between subnational budgets and national priorities and leads to fragmentation (and fluidity) of functional responsibilities and transfers as national government attempts to usurp subnational functions. There is however no shortage of levers to ameliorate intergovernmental disputes. The Constitutional court is the final arbiter on intergovernmental conflicts, but in the interest of cooperative governance, spheres are implored to resolve differences through intergovernmental forums before approaching the courts—a covenant that has been sustained by dominance of ANC in South African body politics. The emergence of stronger opposition parties is likely to agitate for a clearer decentralisation.

Meanwhile the ANC remains steadfast in their disapproval (interpreted as indecisiveness) for a multi-level system of governance. Their own policy statement states that the "three sphere system is a complex system to operate, which results in inefficiency, overlapping roles, long decision-making processes, weak information flows, and the dispersal of public sector skills and experience within the state. To operate the system requires multiple layers of effective political leadership and highly skilled public servants, huge investments of time in coordination, and very strong intergovernmental processes" (ANC, 2007).

3 Taxation Powers at a Glance

Traditional theories of fiscal federalism prescribe limited tax handles for subnational government despite the compelling evidence that greater subnational government powers improve the benefits of decentralisation. Tax sources that are regarded as suitable for subnational governments are only those whose incidence are local residents, can be administered locally and do not cause problems for tax policy harmonisation, intra jurisdiction competition and macroeconomic management difficulties. Admittedly, tax sources that can pass this test are scarce. Over and above, national governments throughout the world are generally reluctant to assign significant tax powers to subnational governments (Bahl and Bird, 2008). South Africa is no exception: Taxation powers in the country are highly centralised for reasons stated above but also related to the country's historical context. The country's troubled history of spatial economic disparities (fiscal capacity) necessitated that government adopts a centralist stance when assigning tax powers in order to drive a national redistribution agenda. Arguably, the *de jure* tax sharing arrangements were a way for the ANC to retain its aspiration for central control having lost the debate on extreme centralisation.

Section 228 and 229 of the Constitution gives provinces and local government the powers to levy taxes as outlined in Table 3. Provinces are allowed to impose a surcharge on any tax except those restricted by the Constitution (i.e. Corporate Income Tax, VAT and custom duties). The Provincial Tax Regulation Process Act of 2001 (for provincial government) and the Municipal Fiscal Powers and Functions Act of 2007 (for municipalities) further regulate the exercise of subnational tax powers.

Table 3 Tax powers by sphere of government

National	*Provinces*	*Local Government*
Not specific excluding rates on property Corporate Income Tax Personal Income Tax Value Added Tax Custom and excise duties Capital Gains Tax Royalty Tax Carbon emission tax Sugar tax Fuel levy	Any tax, levy and duty other than income tax, value added tax, general sales tax, property rates and customs duties Flat rate surcharge on any tax imposed by national government excluding corporate income tax, VAT, property rates and customs duties	Rates on Property Surcharge on fees for municipal services Any other tax, levy and duty authorised by national legislation appropriate to local government

Source Adapted from Republic of South Africa (RSA) (1996)

The two legislations specifically require provinces and municipalities to seek approval for introducing new tax from the Minister of Finance, stating reasons for application, the tax base, desired tax rate and the contemplated collection authority among other things. The absence of locally or regionally suitable new tax sources makes the tax application process superfluous and virtually impossible for subnational government to introduce new taxes. Further, the tax approval requirements reflects signs of mistrust in the capacity of subnationals to handle tax matters responsibly. This is yet another indication of hostility towards multi-level government or federalism. Rao and Khumalo (2000) and Amusa and Mathane (2007) argue that provinces have largely failed to exploit their constitutionally assigned powers. Only two provinces have ever attempted to introduce a Personal Income Tax (PIT) surcharge (Gauteng) and surcharge on fuel levy (Western Cape) since 1994 but the proposals never materialised. Similarly, a proposal to create tax room for provinces made to national government by the Financial and Fiscal Commission[3] was rejected on administration and efficiency grounds.

The Table above reveals further the stark absence of natural resources-based tax in South Africa despite the country boasting among the world's largest mineral reserve, especially the Platinum Group Metals (PGMs). Other mineral endowed federations around the world use resource

[3] The Financial and Fiscal Commission is a permanent Constitutional body advising government with regard to intergovernmental fiscal relations.

receipts as the primary source of discretionary revenue to subnational government allocated on the basis of derivation principle or fixed share (Bird and Smart, 2002). Mining companies are only liable to standard company income tax (same for all industries) and a 5–7% royalty tax on gross sales collectable by the national government. The decentralisation of resources revenue has been criticised as economically and administratively impractical given that mineral deposits are only concentrated in certain regions whereas mining companies declare profits mostly in the major economic hubs.

The tax bases assigned to provinces are generally narrow and as such they collect very little own revenue as a share of total revenue, averaging around 4% since 1994. Table 4 shows the composition of provincial taxes and the size of collection. Overall, the tax source with the largest base or capacity is motor vehicle licences, whose average share has increased from 46 to 77% of total tax receipts between 2005 and 2013. Taxes as a share of total own revenue amount to 65% (between 2010 and 2013), a slight increase from 61% (between 2005 and 2008). This figure buttresses the view that provinces are administrative, implementing and delivery agents of national government as argued in Simeon and Murray (2008).

Municipalities have broader own revenue base derived from utility fees and surcharges on fees for service rendered and the property rates in particular. The power to levy property rates is only granted to Category A and B municipalities. Property rates are regulated through the Property Rates Act No 6 of 2004, which among other things set the limit on annual rate increases for different types of properties, and outline guidelines for

Table 4 Average provincial tax (and other revenues) collection by source

R' million	*2005–2008*		*2010–2013*	
	Amount	*%*	*Amount*	*%*
Tax Receipts	**4,674**	**61**	**7,488**	**65**
Casino Taxes	*624*	*13*	*1,521*	*20*
Horse Racing Taxes	*69*	*1*	*167*	*2*
Motor Vehicle Licences	*2,145*	*46*	*5,800*	*77*
Sale of Goods and Services	**1,439**	**19**	**2,329**	**20**
Interest, Dividends and Rent	**930**	**12**	**817**	**7**
Other receipts	**626**	**8**	**871**	**4**
Total	**7,669**	**100**	**11,505**	**100**

exemption, rebates and reductions. Unlike provinces, this Act provides municipalities some level of flexibility to determine rates in accordance with their respective local circumstances. In addition to property rates, a selected number of municipalities are eligible to a share of the fuel levy as a replacement revenue source for a local business tax (RSC levy) abolished in 2006 for administrative inefficiencies and overlapping with VAT tax base. As can be seen in Fig. 1, taxes constitute approximately 10% of total local government's own revenue. The ability to raise tax revenue and own revenue in general varies markedly across different types and sizes of municipalities. Property rates contribute 17–18% of total revenue for large cities in the urban areas while they account for only 10 per cent of revenue in rural municipalities (Financial and Fiscal Commission, 2019).

The debates about the devolution of taxing powers to subnational governments in South Africa can best be described as enigmatic, hollow and stop-start. There are a number of contributing factors for this. First, national government is indelibly reluctant to create the fiscal space for provinces and municipalities to at least impose taxes granted by the Constitution. This is of course unsurprising given the ruling ANC's affinities to centralist ideals. There are fears of losing political grip from building stronger subnational governments through greater fiscal capacity. This is likely to be reinforced by recent events wherein the ANC lost

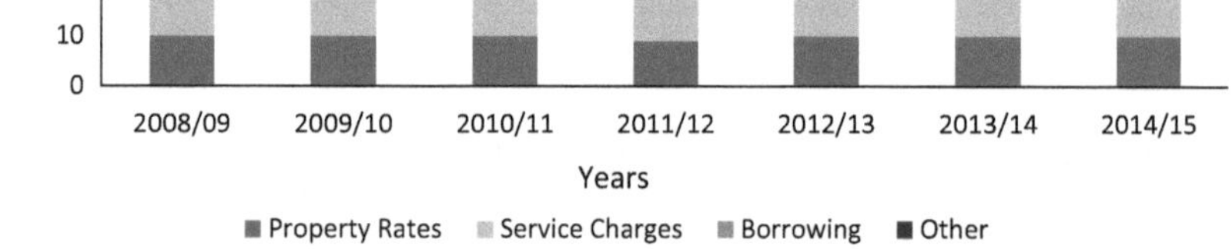

Fig. 1 Local government own revenue composition (*Source* Financial and Fiscal Commission [2019])

control of key metropolitan municipalities in elections.[4] The second reason explaining the unwavering position on tax decentralisation lies in the growing incidents of subnational inefficiencies, governance and delivery failures overlaid by claims of growing corruption or perceptions thereof. Fiscal malfeasance weakens the argument for greater subnational tax power and undermines the legitimacy of sub-central units. The third and perhaps most counterintuitive factor is that subnational governments are unwilling to assume greater tax collection responsibilities because of the guaranteed national transfer entitlements. As an illustration, according to the Financial and Fiscal Commission (2014) rural municipalities are under-collecting their potential property rate base by a factor of 50%. A similar study on provinces revealed mixed results showing that rural provinces have a higher tax effort relative to their urban counterparts while others were found to be over-taxing (Financial and Fiscal Commission, 2012a, b).

4 Anatomy of Fiscal Transfers and Revenue Sharing

The design and structure of South Africa's intergovernmental fiscal transfers and revenue sharing arrangements were shaped in part by economic and political imperatives that prevailed before 1994, key among which was the desire to create conditions for redress and foster equality (racial, gender and space wise). Conscious to the prevailing, historical and deep-rooted economic disparities across the country, the Constitution adopted a socioeconomic reformist approach to the vertical and horizontal revenue sharing model. This was done first by guaranteeing every citizen basic socioeconomic rights, second providing entitlements to the nationally raised revenue and third, obliging each sphere of government to progressively realise delivery of basic rights as per their respective mandates. Sections 214 and 227 of the Constitution specifically state that provinces and local government are entitled to an equitable share of nationally raised revenue. The equitable share is an "unconditional transfer" to ensure delivery of both exclusive and concurrent mandates referred to earlier. Section 214 (1) (c) further provides for additional allocations over

[4] This includes City of Johannesburg, Tshwane (the Capital City) and the City of Cape Town. Together these cities command over three quarter of national output.

and above the equitable share, to the subnational government, to which national government can attach conditions. Conditional transfers in South Africa have been used mainly for two purposes, to aid the implementation of specific national priorities, particularly basic and social services and to address inter-jurisdictional spillovers. The manner in which conditional grants are instituted and implemented is a source of growing tension in the system. These tensions are discussed in subsequent sections.

The vertical and horizontal shares are determined through a criteria outlined in section 214 (a–j) of the Constitution. Factors to be considered include national interest, debt provision, needs of national government and emergencies, the resource allocation for basic services and developmental needs, fiscal capacity and efficiency of the provincial and local spheres, reduction of economic disparities and promotion of stability and predictability. However, the Constitution is not prescriptive on how each of the factors are applied in the division of revenue process across the three spheres. Suffice to point that debt service cost is traditionally treated as a first charge against national revenue. The vertical division of revenue process follows a political process through which the vertical pool is determined by setting national priorities each year. This is part of an elaborate and inclusive budget process which commences with national ministers together with provincial members of executive council (for a particular function) setting spending priorities for the year through consultative forums called MINMECs (Ministers and Members of Executive Council). Adopted decisions from MINMECs are filtered through a number of committees where the finance minister's committee on budget and the Budget Council represents subnational governments until they reach final ratification.[5] There are however concerns that the consultation process with subnational government is superfluous as it tends to overlook provincial policy proposal. To be fair, even the quality of subnational representation during the policy debates is questionable.

It is worth noting that the respective baseline vertical pools of the three spheres results from historical patterns of expenditure and not necessarily estimates of expenditure needs based on responsibilities. Once the vertical share for sphere is determined, it is divided horizontally across the 9 provinces and 257 municipalities through a formula driven process. The principle underlying both the vertical and the horizontal

[5] A legislated consultative forum on fiscal matters constituted by the minister of finance and the nine provincial members of executive council responsible for finance.

allocations in particular is equity and redistribution, expressed through a range of indicators in the respective transfer formulae of provinces and municipalities.

Turning to the vertical allocation, a national legislation called the Division of Revenue Act outlines the amount of funding allocated to each sphere on an annual basis. Throughout the years since adoption of the new system national government has been commanding the largest share of revenue available for sharing across the three spheres. As can be seen from Table 5 the national share of revenue has remained higher than that of provinces and municipalities even though it is declining—to the benefit of local government. Notwithstanding the declining national vertical share subnational governments consistently lament their shares as inadequate insinuating possible existence of vertical fiscal gaps. Arguments for bigger subnational vertical pool are, however, not informed by quantitative estimates of expenditure needs from the de facto assignment of expenditure responsibilities. To be sure, even the roles and responsibilities per concurrent functional areas are not clearly defined.

The absence of an approach to translate expenditure responsibilities into expenditure needs causes constant frictions and misunderstandings between levels of government. Subnational governments consistently bemoan the current level of funding while the national government

Table 5 Vertical shares of available national revenue—%

	2005/2006	*2006/2007*	*2007/2008*	*2015/2016*	*2016/2017*	*2017/2018*
National	**52.5**	**50.2**	**49.8**	**49.0**	**47.9**	**47.8**
Provinces	**42.9**	**43.3**	**42.6**	**42.2**	**43.2**	**43.2**
Equitable share	*86.0*	*82.9*	*82.7*	*82.0*	*82.2*	*82.3*
Conditional grant	*13.4*	*17.1*	*17.3*	*18.0*	*17.8*	*18.1*
Local government	**4.6**	**6.5**	**7.6**	**8.8**	**8.9**	**9.0**
Equitable share	*58.8*	*66.7*	*56.8*	*50.0*	*49.5*	*49.5*
Conditional grant	*41.2*	*29.6*	*45.9*	*38.8*	*39.8*	*39.6*
Fuel levy				11.2	10.7	10.8

Source Authors' computations

argues that the current level of financing is more than adequate. The ongoing rounds of discussions and positions papers from either side on what to do about more financing via additional taxes, tax sharing or other forms of transfers turns out futile because there is no consensus on what expenditure needs of national and subnational governments are. Subnational governments make countless formal and informal submissions to the Financial and Fiscal Commission about the inadequacy of their transfers without quantitative backing of expenditure needs. This is not to say, there are no vertical fiscal imbalances. Until such time, overlapping responsibilities are resolved, this question shall remain a moot point in South Africa.

Disparities are more prominent horizontally, in terms of both fiscal capacity and access to services. Some of these imbalances are historical but have also been perpetuated through a combination of lacklustre spending performance and funding inadequacies. Underspending is a common occurrence across all spheres but is prevalent at subnational governments (see Auditor General [2017]). Figures 2 and 3 illustrate the prevailing economic and fiscal disparities across the nine provinces. Three provinces (Gauteng, Western Cape and KwaZulu-Natal) that host the majority of metropolitan municipalities account for two-thirds of GDP. As can be seen from Fig. 2 both Gauteng and Western Cape Province boast the highest GDP per capita while at other extreme Limpopo and

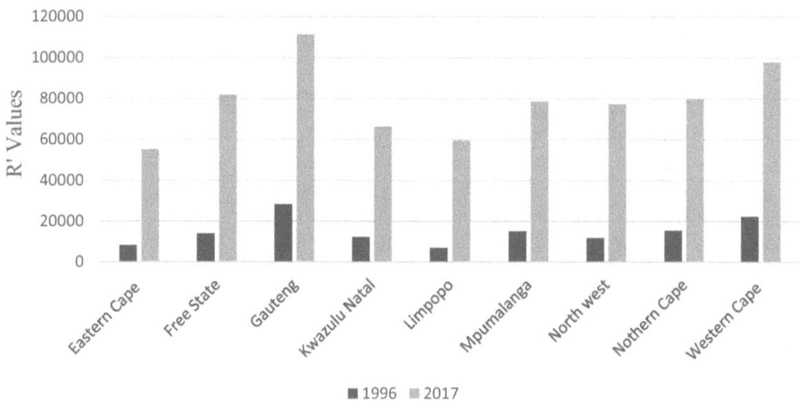

Fig. 2 Gross regional product per capita by province—1996 and 2017 (*Source* Statistics South Africa [1996, 2016])

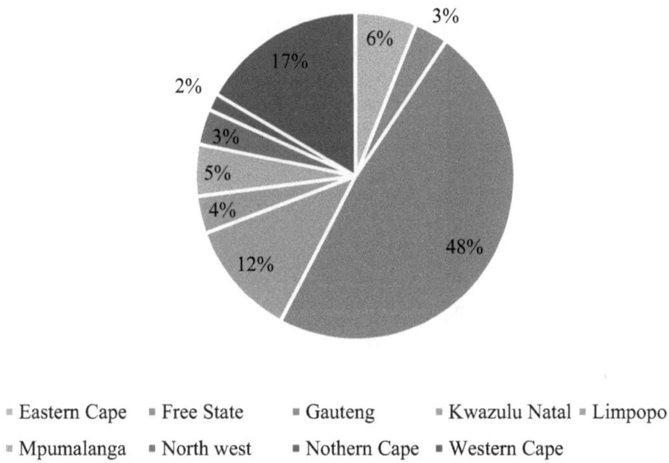

Fig. 3 Personal income tax assessed per province—2015 (*Source* Human Sciences Research Council [2017])

Eastern Cape provinces (homes to the racially segregated territories under Apartheid) have the lowest GDP per capita. By implication, a significant proportion of taxes are collected in the top three provinces. Approximately 48% of Personal Income Tax (PIT) were obtained in Gauteng province. Such acute disparities partly derive from skewed natural resource endowments as well as historical Apartheid spatial planning practices (Human Sciences Research Council, 2017). Post-Apartheid intergovernmental fiscal relations reforms and the ANC's insistence on central control was in part influenced by these disparities. The inherited spatial and racial inequalities called for a stronger national government to effect redistribution through transfers to weaker subnational governments.

Service access and provision disparities are also prevalent across the local government constituent units. Table 6 shows service provision variation in two key functions (water and electricity) assigned to Category A and B municipalities. Category B municipality is further disaggregated into four sub-categories to reflect nuanced spatial characteristics. Metropolitan Municipalities and secondary cities typically have higher service provision levels compared to the small rural town type of municipalities (B3 and B4 in the table). The table further reveals an important implication of asymmetry in the assignment and provision of electricity

Table 6 Household access to basic service by category/type of municipality—2016

Category or type of municipality	*GDP per capita*	*% Households with access to water*	*% Households with access to electricity*
Metro (A)	R110, 236	98.9	88.7
Secondary City (B1)	R85,379	96.2	88.6
Large Town (B2)	R78,902	93.6	86.5
Small Town (B3)	R65,978	54.3	86.0
Rural Town (B4)	R34,112	76.0	85.7
South Africa average	**R74,921**	**0.91**	**87.1**

Source Statistics South Africa (2016)

function. Electricity access is almost identical across all municipalities despite the relative variation in the capacity to deliver. This is explained by active involvement of a national electricity supplier (ESKOM) in the reticulation of electricity in the rural parts and semi-urban areas of different municipalities. Electricity reticulation is an exclusive function of municipalities but ESKOM performs the function in most municipalities that lack the technical capacity to do so. Several years of discussions to devolve the responsibility back to municipalities have been fruitless to date, depriving those municipalities of a potentially important revenue source.

The extent of regional disparities inherited from South Africa's Apartheid past necessitated that fiscal transfer formulae for horizontal allocations are designed with a view to redistribute revenue collected nationally to subnational units with poor socioeconomic attributes and low fiscal capacity. It is for this reason that the Constitution guarantees each sphere an "equitable share" of nationally raised revenue. Government uses the Provincial Equitable Share (PES) and the Local Government Equitable Share (LGES) formulae to determine the respective horizontal allocation for the nine provinces and the 257 municipalities. These formulae were proposed by Financial and Fiscal Commission in 1996 and have been operational since then albeit subjected to periodic reviews. It is worth noting that the PES and LGES are not traditional equalisation grants in the true sense, because of the limited subnational tax powers highlighted earlier. The main thrust underlying these transfers is redistribution and to equalise difference in expenditure needs where the primary need indicator is population rather than an explicit service delivery needs.

The PES and LGES formulae as allocation tools mainly comprises various components as relative indicators of functional responsibilities and need at a given period, across all subnational units. Each component is assigned a weight to express the relative significance of a particular function or need. When combined these components complete the structure of the formula and ultimately determines each province and municipal share of the horizontal pool.

The provincial equitable share formula is made up of six components that resemble constitutional functional assignments. Each component is assigned a weight that is informed by historical expenditure patterns. The components weightings in the formula are neither indicative budgets nor guidelines on how much should be spent on functions assigned to each province or collectively. For every component, each province is allocated its proportional share relative to national total so that the allocation is given as follows:

$$P_a = \sum (E_i^{48} + H_i^{27} + B_i^{16} + P_i^{3} + E_i^{1} + I_i^{5})$$

where P_a is the total provincial equitable share and ${E_i}^{48}$ is the education share of province i (Table 7 describes the full structure of the PES).

The LGES formula on the other hand slightly resembles a traditional equalisation grant because it attempts to capture local expenditure needs and fiscal capacity. The formula takes the asymmetric functional assignment, explained earlier, as an inbuilt constraint and allocates resources to fund delivery of basic municipal services through the basic, institutional and community services components. The LGES formula is given as follows:

$$\text{LES} = \text{BS} + (\text{I} + \text{CS})^{*}\text{RA} \pm \text{C}$$

Table 8 gives a detailed description of each component.

A key question that arise with every transfer formulae is whether they are able to achieve the desired objective. As mentioned earlier, subnational governments in South Africa are consistently questioning the redistributive powers of the horizontal transfers. In particular, rural subnational units claim that the formula ignores historical social and economic disparities and infrastructure backlogs, which result in uneven service standards between provinces. Figure 4 suggests that the PES formula makes

Table 7 Structure of the PES formula

Component	*Weight (%)*	*Description and need indicator*
E = Education	48	Targets primary and secondary schooling and based on the size of the school-age population (ages 5–17) and the number of learners (Grade R to 12) enrolled in public ordinary schools
H = Health	27	Provides for delivery of primary health care and is based on the health risk profile and health system case load of each province
B = Basic	16	Derived from each province's share of the national population
I = Institutional	5	Divided equally between provinces for funding costs of administration
P = Poverty	3	Is derived from each province's share of the poor population (Bottom 40%). Component is intended to reinforce redistribution
E = Economic activity	1	Derived from each province contribution to national GDP It is a proxy for provincial tax capacity

Source National Treasury (2018)

no discernible variation in allocations to provinces commensurate with provincial patterns of disparities. Per-capita allocations are almost even across all provinces. Attempts to enhance the redistributive capacity of the PES by incorporating the poverty component have yielded insignificant results not only because the weighting attached to the component is small but also because poverty is increasingly urbanising (poor people are migrating to urban provinces in search of opportunities). This is a function of over-reliance on demographic variables as need indicators. Up to 90% of PES allocations are driven by the proportion of each province's share of various population groupings such as school-age population, proportion of poor people and people without medical insurance. Similarly, the economic activity component fails to capture the essence of equalisation principles in that each province's share of this component is progressively determined rather than regressively as is done in traditional equalisation grants. In other words, the higher a province's contribution to economic activity is the higher the allocation. Thus the economic activity component constitutes a revenue sharing mechanism, albeit, poorly designed.

Table 8 Structure of the LES formula[6]

Component	*% share*	
BS = Basic services	80.7	Provides for the operational and maintenance costs of delivering free basic services (water, electricity, sanitation and refuse removal) to poor households. It is derived by allocating each household R335 per month for a package of free basic services for 59% of SA households with an income of less than 2 old age pensions per month
I = Institutional	7.7	Provides for the costs of administering local government. Component is made of a base allocation of R5.9 million per municipality and additional amount based on the number of council seats
CS = Community services	11.6	Provides for funding of other municipal services other than basic services
RA = Revenue adjustment	–	Ensures that funds from this part of the formula are only provided to municipalities with limited potential to raise their own revenue. Municipalities that are least able to fund costs of basic services from their own revenues receive the most funding
C = correction	–	Ensures predictability and stability of the formula. The component ensures that municipalities are guaranteed 90% of their published forward allocations to cushion the impact of annual data updates—though phasing-in of the impact over a five year period

Source National Treasury (2018)

The design of the provincial equitable share formula and its outcomes (invariable per capita allocations) is partly a direct reflection of the centralised nature of taxation which obviate the need to factor in fiscal disparities when determining PES allocations. However, those with opposing views suggest the disregard of expenditure needs disparities in the PES formulation prejudice rural and poor provinces, whose developmental needs are lagging and perhaps the cost of delivering services are relatively higher. Little effort has been made in this regard to measure expenditure needs or obligation of provinces. A 2001 proposal by the

[6] The current structure of the LGES resulted from a review conducted in 2011 that sought to update the formula with latest census data and improve its redistributive ability.

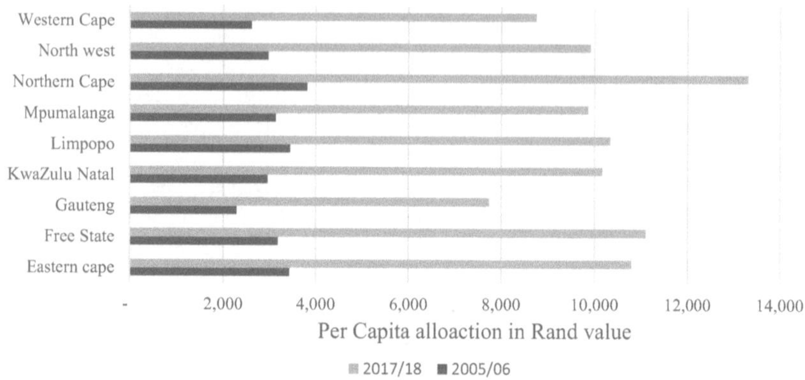

Fig. 4 Per capita PES allocation (*Source* Authors' calculations)

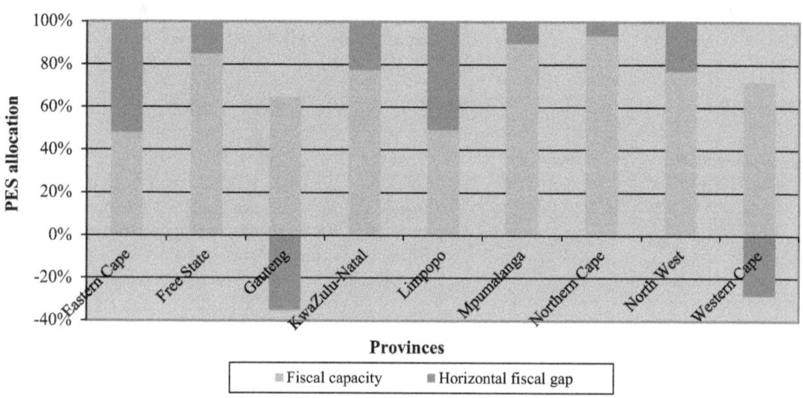

Fig. 5 Hypothetical horizontal fiscal gap—(2013) (*Source* Financial and Fiscal Commission [2013])

FFC to determine allocations on the basis of a set of costed norms was met with resistance and rejected as discussed earlier.

Contrary to the popular perception, the Financial and Fiscal Commission (2013) suggests that the PES formula is horizontally redistributive. Figure 5 shows this by estimating the average amount of revenue provincial government can potentially generate given the respective size of their economies[7] and the amount by which the revenue should be adjusted to meet current PES funding levels. All provinces with the exception of Gauteng and Western Cape (two of the richest provinces) are unable to meet their funding unless redistribution takes place. In contrast to the PES, the LGES is generally regarded as redistributive. A 2011 review resulted in a significant shift in allocation from the urban to the rural municipalities by increasing the poverty threshold and changing the structure of the formula. The LGES share of rural towns increased from 20 to 23% in one go with some municipalities failing to absorb the sudden increase in spending allocations.

Seemingly, horizontal equity is not an overwhelming area of contention in South Africa's quasi federal system. In the main the equitable share transfers suffers from flaws in the design of other basic pillars of South Africa's decentralisation system. This relates to the perceived lack of discretion by provinces in budget allocations and misalignment between national policies and provincial budgets within the context of concurrent functions. Provinces perceive the earmarking of PES funds for national priorities and the subsequent expenditure benchmarking exercises, which prescribe guidelines on what to allocate to policy priorities, as an erosion of their authority over expenditure and budgets. Intrinsic in this view, is the recognition that provinces have an executive and legislative authority to take decision independently through qualified institutions and by extension the prerogative to allocate their unconditional share of nationally raised revenue. However, the extent of this discretion is a matter that continue to be uncertain given the understanding that the equitable share may not be used by the national government as a means to force provinces to fulfil their functions (Murray, 2009).

As mentioned earlier, the Constitution of South Africa provides for additional subnational transfers which can be dispersed with conditions. Conditional grants were introduced in the early 2000s following rising concerns about the ability of subnational governments to deal with historical infrastructure backlogs. A backlog component was removed from the PES formula and replaced with a package of conditional grants.

The Division of Revenue Act (DoRA) provides four types of conditional grants listed below:

[7] Potential revenue is calculated by assuming a standard tax rate on the F.

- Schedule 4 conditional grants are allocations to provinces and municipalities made to supplement the funding of programmes or functions funded from provincial and municipal equitable shares.
- Schedule 5 type grants are allocations made for specific purposes of national interest, without a requirement for additional funds from provincial and municipal own budgets.
- Schedule 6 type grants are also specific purpose in-kind allocations to provinces and municipalities for designated special programmes.
- Part A of Schedule 7 type grants are specific allocations that may be released to provinces and municipalities to fund disaster response, in terms of the Disaster Management Act, 2002 (Act No. 57 of 2002).

Between 2005 and 2017, conditional grants transferred to provinces increased considerably in number and value (FFC, 2014). The number and value of provincial conditional grants increased from 15 (R25 billion) in 2006 to 24 (R100 billion) in 2018, respectively. Local government conditional grants grew even stronger (at an average rate of 122%) from R7 billion in 2006 to R50 billion in 2018. Figure 6 below shows that the share of conditional grants as share of total transfers to provinces has remained steady at 20% level while the growth rate of both unconditional and conational transfers is seemingly uniform at 8% per annum in nominal

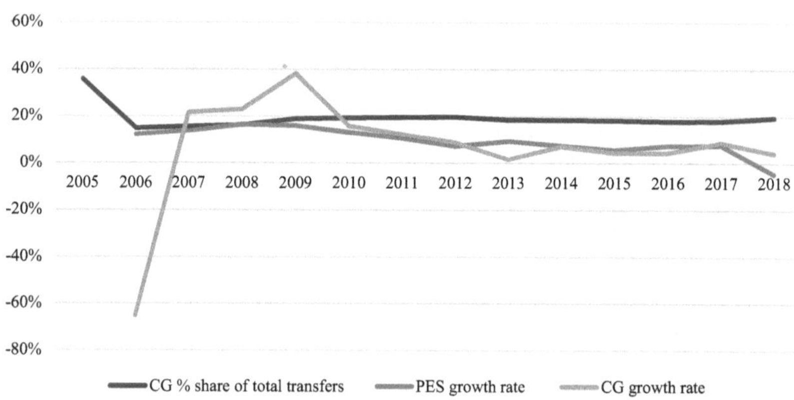

Fig. 6 Conditional grants share of total transfers and growth rate (*Source* Authors' computations)

terms. There is general perception that conditional allocations for infrastructure are not appropriately synchronised with unconditional transfers to fund attendant operational costs.

The lack of clear expenditure responsibilities as well as perceptions of subnational poor delivery performance in recent times has resulted in a proliferation of the so-called indirect conditional grants where national government gets directly involved in the implementation of projects on behalf of subnational governments. The reality with conditional grants is to limit the attendant discretion or spending authority of recipient subnational governments. In the final analysis, the fiscal Constitution inherently entrenches through the asymmetric expenditure assignment a "centralised system" within the fiscally decentralised government through constrained decision-making spaces for subnational government in areas of concurrency and to an extent, exclusive responsibility.

5 Macroeconomic and Fiscal Policy Management

The South African fiscal Constitution vests economic and fiscal policy powers in the Minister of Finance when it comes to intergovernmental financial and fiscal matters and an independent Reserve Bank when it comes to monetary policy. The Minister has the sole discretion to determine national debt and expenditure levels, unconstrained, after taking into account the country's macroeconomic conditions and service delivery requirements. The mandate of the Reserve Bank on the other hand is expressly stated in the Constitution as being to protect the value of the currency. Inflation targeting has been chosen as the primary instrument for managing price stability. In the 25 years that the system has been in place, debt levels and price stability have been managed prudently.

A package of post constitutional fiscal legislation was enacted to facilitate the management and control of intergovernmental fiscal affairs to promote good financial management, accountability and prevent profligacy. These pieces of legislation derive directly from Chapter 13 of the Constitution and require the Minister of Finance and Parliament to put in place national legislation to enable the powers of the different spheres of government in terms of finance to be exercised. Key among these pieces of legislation are the Public Finance Management Act of 1999 (PFMA) and the Municipal Finance Management Act (MFMA). These pieces of legislation mainly deal with, national treasury norms and standards, budget and expenditure related controls and are often further expressed in the form of Treasury Regulations, Circulars, Instructions and Practice Notes. They define roles of Accounting Officers and Executive authorities and seek to decentralise decision-making to Accounting Officers of institutions with Executive Authorities exercising oversight on the organs of state. Because these are national pieces of legislation, subnational Governments often regard the accompanying regulations and instructions as infringements of discretion over their budgets. It has been argued that through the excessive use of secondary legislation such as Treasury Regulations, Circulars and Instructions imposes undue interference with the decision-making space of Accounting Officers and Executive Authorities in the provincial and local government sphere and further on other organs of state, and thus creating an all too powerful National Treasury at the centre. Recently municipalities in particular have raised concerns around this particular tendency of running their finances through Circulars. Noticeably this has a negative impact on the fiscal decentralisation process.

In addition, the Provincial Tax Regulation Processes Act of 2001 and the Municipal Fiscal Powers and Function Act of 2007 set controls and consultation requirements for managing the conduct of subnational governments when setting the tax rates. In all instances, the approval of the Minister of Finance and consideration of the recommendations of the Financial and Fiscal Commission must happen before power is exercised. This again means the legislation is designed in such a way as to leave all discretion to the central government.

Sections 100 and 139 of the Constitution and by extension, provisions 6 and 136 of the PFMA and MFMA, respectively provide for a continuum of national interventions in cases where subnational governments fail to fulfil their executive obligations or fall into financial distress. This is done through monitoring, support and supervision, issuing directives to take remedial steps and actual take-over of powers and functions. Failure to fulfil obligations entails among other things inability to deliver services, failure to approve a budget, default on financial obligations, inability to pay suppliers, unbalanced budget outcomes, operating deficit in excess of five per cent of revenue, inability to submit annual financial statements and sustained adverse audit opinions.

As already indicated, Section 220 of the Constitution and the Financial and Fiscal Commission Act of 1996 establish an independent Financial and Fiscal Commission responsible for making recommendations on the equitable division of revenue between the three spheres of government. The Commission's recommendations are addressed to Parliament and the Minister of Finance responds to such recommendations on behalf of government. The Minister of Finance is obliged to respond to them as part of the documents that must be tabled with the Division of Revenue Bill. Parliament has the responsibility to ensure that recommendations that have been accepted by government are implemented. Further, in terms of legislation the Minister of Finance is also required to consult with the Financial and Fiscal Commission at least two weeks before tabling the budget. Feedback on how the Minister has considered the recommendations is exchanged through this process.

Section 230 of the Constitution grants provinces and municipalities the right to borrow. However, this right is granted under specific conditions. Borrowing to finance current expenditure is only permitted for bridging purposes within a fiscal year. Long-term borrowing is strictly restricted to funding of capital expenditure (RSA, 1996) and should only be denominated in local currency. Provincial borrowing is regulated by the Borrowing Powers of Provincial Government Act (BPPGA) of 1996 while Municipal Finance Management Act of 2003 regulates municipal borrowing. The BPPGA establishes the Loans Coordinating Committee, constituted by the Minister of Finance and his/her provincial counterparts, to coordinate the borrowing requirements of national governments, assess contingent liabilities, risks and ability to service the debt and consult the Financial and Fiscal Commission for its recommendations. Section 5 of the BPPGA further prohibits national government from providing guarantees on or underwriting any loan granted to provinces to prevent moral hazard problems associated with contingent liabilities in order to foster hard budget constraints. The MFMA makes similar provisions with regard to municipal debt.

With respect to provinces, there is standing moratorium on provincial borrowing agreed to at the Budget Council, in response to the potential macroeconomic risk that ensued when certain provinces fell into financial problems prior to 1998. Recently, national government borrowed on behalf of Gauteng province to fund the rapid rail transport system and Gauteng used proceeds from its own revenue sources to pay back the national government. In local government, the situation is different with Metros and the large cities very active in the market, including the issuing of bonds by some of the bigger Metros. A significant number of relatively well-off local municipalities borrow mainly from a state owned DFI namely Development Bank of Southern Africa (DBSA) because their loans are accompanied by technical assistance.

South Africa has no specific solvency framework but legislation such as the MFMA and the PFMA to protect subnational government against prospects of insolvency. For example, sections 152 and 153 of the MFMA empower municipalities to apply through the judiciary for stay of legal proceedings by creditors and suspension and termination of municipal financial obligations to creditors for a period not exceeding 90 days. There are, however, stringent conditions under which such application can be granted. For instance, the municipality must have demonstrated inability to meet financial obligation to creditors in the foreseeable future, all assets not reasonably required to deliver minimum basic services must have been liquidated and all employees discharged. In the period the MFMA (2003) has been in existence, no such application has ever been made. This is attributable to the active monitoring of municipal debt by the National Treasury. Stricter loan approval process, the explicit no-bailout rule and a combination of market discipline mechanisms have had a discipline enhancing effect on subnational governments. Provinces are systemically disallowed from borrowing and municipalities can only access the capital market subject to meeting strict credit rating requirements. Only a handful of municipalities from a total of 257 has been assessed for credit rating. Cases of soft budget constraints largely arise from expenditure mismanagement rather than borrowing.

6 Intergovernmental Response to COVID-19 in South Africa

Just before concluding this chapter, South Africa was overwhelmed by the most severe and deadly health crises which has morphed into a global economic catastrophe. It took 3 months for the Coronavirus Disease 2019 (COVID-19) since first being reported to the World Health Organization (WHO) on 31 December 2019 following a pneumonia of unknown cause was detected in Wuhan, China to reach South Africa. South Africa recorded its first case of the coronavirus on March 5, 2020 in KwaZulu-Natal province. Since the confirmed index case, the number of confirmed COVID-19 cases has risen steadily reaching 5000 within a two months period, well below the infection rate experienced in the key pandemic epicentres such as China, Spain and the US.

South Africa's Constitution governs states of emergency; inter alia to prevent the abuses of earlier times. The main legislation around which South Africa's response to the virus has been organised is in terms of the Disaster Management Act 57 of 2002.[8] Two weeks from the first reported case for the country, the President announced a national disaster (March 15) in terms of Section 27 of the Disaster Management Act, followed on 25 March 2020 with amendments made to the legislation to cater for the outbreak, with the main intervention being an initially 21-day national lockdown commencing from midnight of March 26 which was then extended for another two weeks to end of April 2020. The amendments outlined contain measures pertaining to (a) restrictions on the movement of persons and goods, (b) prohibition of public transport and (c) resources by the state during lockdown. On the economic policy front, because of the high budget deficit, there is limited room available to the government for direct expenditure increases. Instead, government effort initially focused on mobilising off-budget funding (Unemployment Insurance Fund (for workers)) and Industrial Development Corporation (for businesses), special loan schemes, tax relief for those affected as well as exemption of banks from the Competition Act to allow them to provide relief for affected customers. The Central Bank has reduced the repo rate twice in the space of a month by 200 basis points to pump liquidity in the economy. Government has recently announced a sizable fiscal support package of R500 billion or 10% of GDP. These interventions will have implications on the effectiveness of these type of response relative to direct expenditure.

Given the exceptional circumstances around the COVID-19 pandemic, we have designed in Box 2 an outline of how government's responses to the crisis have taken shape in the context of the country's quasi federal system. There are other non-fiscal responses led by the country's central bank as well as the private sector that are not covered here given the focus of the chapter.

Box 2: Intergovernmental response to disasters—The case of COVID-19

This chapter was written at the time when the world was overwhelmed by a health crises which has morphed into a global economic catastrophe. It has taken approximately 3 months for South Africa to record its first case of COVID-19 on March 1, 2020 when there were already nearly 150,000

[8] Amended by the *Disaster Management Amendment Act* 16 of 2015.

existing cases worldwide. The rapid spread of the disease has forced governments throughout the world to institute unprecedented disaster responses and economic relief measures in an effort to contain the virus, save lives and prevent economic meltdown. Governments have reacted with varying approaches, speeds and intensity, but generally settled on a set of similar measures including imposing varying degrees of lockdowns, social (physical) distancing, voluntary and obligatory isolation, providing different types of economic relief and importantly directing additional resources to the health care system for personal protective equipment (PPE) for health workers, testing kits, ventilators, field hospitals, etc. These measures recognise that the COVID-19 pandemic is a human tragedy that is both a health and economic crises.

Response to disasters in South Africa are governed in terms of the Disaster Management Act which primarily facilitate integrated and coordinated preventative and mitigation measures for risk of disaster, rapid and effective response to disaster and post-recovery measures. The Act further provides for the President to establish an Intergovernmental Committee on Disaster Management made up of the relevant Cabinet ministers and provincial heads of executive as well as the national, provincial and municipal disaster management centres whose role is to promote integrated and coordinated disaster prevention, mitigation and recovery approach across the three spheres of government.

By law disaster management is a shared function between national and provincial government whereas the health function is spread across the three spheres to the extent that local government provides environmental health. Guided by this legislative framework, South Africa responded to the COVID-19 pandemic through a Presidential declaration of a national disaster (not to be confused with a state of emergency) thus paving the way for the various functional authorities to develop enabling regulations. Such regulations relates to the release of resources, restrictions on movement of people, goods and services and dissemination of information among other things.

Since declaration of the national disaster, South Africa has arguably followed the international best practices in responding to the COVID-19 pandemic. That is, setting up a national nerve centre for coordination, planning and monitoring; focusing on surveillance, rapid response teams and case investigation; increasing the capacity of the national laboratories; improving case management (hospital care and home care); infection prevention and control; investing in early investigation protocols; risk communication and community engagement and suspending points of entry and mass gatherings.

The National Command Council made up of the President, Cabinet ministers, Premiers of provinces and Organised local government is responsible for monitoring the situation and making strategic decisions informed by a national joint operational and intelligence structure and COVID-19 Data Management Centre. Some of these interventions include deployment of the police and military to enforce lockdown and traffic restrictions, 10,000 fieldworkers to screen, test, trace and help with medical management of COVID-19 cases, designating certain public hospitals to deal with COVID-19 cases, 24 hour hotline and procurement of test kits and PPEs for medical personnel. Provinces and municipalities have also introduced interventions of their own focusing on social relief for homeless and the vulnerable, distribution of sanitizers to those without access to running water and disinfecting public spaces. They have also deployed provincial police to enforce lockdown procedures within their jurisdictions. To date, the COVID-19 intervention has been well coordinated unlike other areas of concurrent responsibility as discussed in the chapter.

Much of the initial COVID-19 interventions in South Africa had occurred without additional budget allocation to the most affected functional sector(s) and subnational governments despite the crises being declared a national crisis and there being a legislative leeway (through section 16 of the PFMA) for the Minister of Finance to use the National Revenue Fund to defray expenditure of exceptional nature which has not been provided for or cannot be postponed to the future. Section 25 of the PFMA also states that provinces can use up to 2% of the provincial revenue fund to deal with unforeseen expenditure. Both these provisions require authorisation from the relevant legislative structure (In other words, a Special Appropriation is required to ratify the s16 PFMA expenditure and extend it further to meet the necessary funding requirements.). A study by the FFC (2012) found that funding for disasters in South Africa is generally characterised by lengthy bureaucratic processes and prone to focus on relief rather than mitigation. On 21 April 2020, Government finally announced a sizeable **fiscal support package** for the economy of R500 billion, or approximately 10% of GDP. This intervention has been made within a context of very restricted and fragile state for government finances.

The low COVID-19 hospitalisation cases or disease burden due to low incidence rates and decisive Government interventions that have slowed viral spread, mean that the country has bought some time. Paradoxically, this may partly explain the timid approach adopted by government in appropriating emergency funding for the disaster and enunciate the reason why provinces in particular are unperturbed by the potential budget crises.[9] The country is yet to reach the devastating COVID-19 hospitalisation rates of 15–20% seen in China or the calamitous 40% observed in Italy (WHO, 2020). In fact, as of 13 April 2020, whereas the country has reacted swiftly to contain the virus, there remain concerns about the capacity of the healthcare system, subnational governments and the overall budget to handle the abnormal pressure that will be impacted on the various budgets (should a doomsday pessimistic scenario of the pandemic spread materialise).

Source Authors' compilation.

7 Successes and Challenges of Fiscal Federalism in South Africa

With a focus on South Africa's evolving unitary federal system, this chapter has examined the range of fiscal institutions used as well as their rationale and effectiveness. Issues covered included the structure of Government and allocation of expenditure responsibilities, taxation responsibilities, intergovernmental fiscal transfers and revenue transfers, macroeconomic management and challenges to fiscal federalism. The story of multi-level government reforms and the associated democratisation process in South Africa is one of success and a marvel to a number of countries undergoing transition. Coming from a catastrophic Apartheid past, the new dispensation was able to install and operationalise a new system of multi-level governance within 5 years of adopting the Constitution. An important part of the success story commences with a constitutionally recognised framework for distinctive, interrelated and

[9] It, however, must be pointed out that at the time this chapter was being concluded, Government had not yet invoked section 16 formally yet. Departments were given until 10 March to submit their emergency budget bids and National Treasury was still processing that requirement. Also, a number of measures have already been announced e.g. 446 million rands for PPE, etc.

interdependent spheres of government, each with its own constituency who elect their preferred public representatives through a democratic process. The current structure of subnational governments result from a complex process of integrating a myriad of white and black only regional and local authorities into a single union made up of nine provinces and 257 municipalities. The government system is supported by a myriad of enabling legislations and institutions to harness accountability and fiscal management as well as the intergovernmental transfers to facilitate delivery of basic services. Since establishment of the provinces in 1994 and the new local government structure in 2000, the system has enjoyed relative stability, having undergone six and four elections, respectively. More recently, the system appears to have weathered two severe external shocks, namely the Great Recession of 2008/2009 and the ongoing COVID-19 pandemic. Provinces and local authorities are accountable to their own legislatures, local councils, subnational executives can make spending decisions with relative autonomy, and the national government has sufficient powers to intervene where subnationals deviate from standard practice.

Whereas the legislative and institutional framework for multi-level government are firmly in place, challenges persist as the system evolves in search of an identity. The first challenge is linked to the absence of political commitment to a clear model of federal decentralisation, especially on the part of the ruling party. Policy makers and politicians continue to debate the desirability of subnational structures (provinces and district municipalities in particular) which in turn contributes to disorderly intergovernmental fiscal and political arrangements. There is no firm decision about the future of provinces currently, but ongoing reforms points to a gradual "hollowing out" exemplified by the following (Ajam, 2014):

1. Shifting certain functions to national level: The new National Health Insurance Bill seeks to centralise funding and provision of healthcare leaving provinces as mere administrators of residual responsibilities.
2. Devolving other provincial functions to cities and other municipalities: These would include accreditation of housing functions, public transport and land use planning.

3. Restrictions on the input side of the budget: Centralised procurement at national level of large tenders such as school books have been introduced to overcome supply chain management weaknesses and corruption within the provincial sphere
4. Allocating transfers via indirect (in-kind) grants: National government builds schools on behalf of provinces to overcome weakness in capacity to deliver.

The lack of a clear vision for multi-level governance serves to reinforce long standing challenges in the execution of concurrent functions i.e. clarity on the nature of decentralised expenditure assignment, tax powers and revenue autonomy as well as vertical fiscal gap. An important factor affecting the working of IGFR relations is that a clear decision is yet to be made on the definition of "own" responsibilities of the provincial governments for which they can make decisions with complete autonomy and on the definition of "delegated" responsibilities, for which provincial governments have to comply with standards of provision provided by national government. Currently, for example, there is no clarity regarding whether general education and health services constitute "own responsibilities" or "delegated responsibilities". It seems like the system continues to debate the desirability of both. There is a high degree of disquiet on the part of the national departments with what happens to funding priorities agreed nationally and the subsequent allocations at provincial level. These issues clearly affect the definition/quantification of expenditure needs in the provincial equitable share transfer and how provincial governments are to spend (some of) the funds they receive from national government. Lacking vision, reforms are carried out from a narrow perspective where the national government champions initiatives to improve the administrative and technical capacity of subnational governments while usurping a great part of the responsibilities.

Annexure A

(Table 9).

Table 9 Constitutional assignment of powers and functions

Schedule 4		*Schedule 5*	
Part A (functional areas of concurrent national and provincial competence)	*Part B (local government functions with national and provincial competence*	*Part A (functional areas of exclusive provincial competence)*	*Part B (Local government functions with provincial competence)*
Agriculture	Water and sanitation	Ambulance services	Street trading
Education	Electricity and gas reticulation	Liquor licensing	Traffic and parking
Health services	Storm water	Provincial planning	Refuse removal
Welfare services	Municipal planning	Provincial roads and traffic	Markets
Public transport	Building regulation	Provincial sport	Local amenities
Tourism	Municipal health	Veterinary services	Public places
Administration of indigenous forests	Air pollution	Abattoirs	Beaches and amusement facilities
Airports other international and national airports	Municipal public transport	Libraries excluding national	Billboards & advertising in public places
Animal control and diseases	Child care facilities	Museums excluding national	Cemeteries
Casinos	Fire fighting	Provincial cultural matters	Control of public nuisance
Consumer protection	Local tourism	Provincial recreation and amenities	Fencing
Cultural matters	Municipal public works		Municipal abattoirs
Disaster management	Municipal airport		Local sport facilities
Environment	Pontoons, ferries and harbours		Municipal parks and recreation
Housing	Storm water management		Municipal roads

(continued)

Table 9 (continued)

Schedule 4		*Schedule 5*	
Part A (functional areas of concurrent national and provincial competence)	*Part B (local government functions with national and provincial competence*	*Part A (functional areas of exclusive provincial competence)*	*Part B (Local government functions with provincial competence)*
Police	Trading regulations		Refuse removal and solid waste
Language policy			Local sport facilities
Media services			Licensing and control of food trading
Nature conservation			
Pollution control			
Population development			
Property transfer			
Public works			
Road traffic regulation			
Soil conservation			
Tran rude			
Traditional leadership			
Urban and rural development			
Vehicle licensing			

Source Adopted from Republic of South Africa (1996)

References

Ajam, T. 2014. The Financial and Fiscal Commission: Two Decades of Institutional Evolution, Paper presented at the Financial and Fiscal Commission 20th Year Anniversary Conference, Cape Town, South Africa.

Amusa, H. and Mathane, P. 2007. "South Africa's Intergovernmental Fiscal Relations: An Evolving System", *South African Journal of Economics*, 75 (2): 265–292.

ANC. 2007. Legislature and Governance – Discussion document, 5th National Policy Conference, 30th June–05 July 2017, Gallagher Convention Centre, Midrand, South Africa.

Auditor General. 2017. Consolidate General Report on National and Provincial Audit Outcomes: MFMA 2016/17. Auditor General, South Africa.

Bahl, R. W. and Bird, R. M. 2008. Subnational Taxes in Developing Countries: The Way Forward (September 25 2008). Institute for International Business Working Paper No. 16, Available at SSRN: https://ssrn.com/abstract=1273753.

Bird, R. M. and Smart, M. 2002. "Intergovernmental Fiscal Transfers: International Lessons for Developing Countries", *World Development*, 30 (6): 899–912.

De Visser, J. 2008. "Institutional Subsidiarity in the South African Constitution", *Stellenbosch Law Review*, 21 (1): 90–115.

Financial and Fiscal Commission, 2011. Local Government Fiscal Framework Review, Financial and Fiscal Commission, Midrand, South Africa.

Financial and Fiscal Commission, 2012a. Debating National Intervention in Financially Distressed Provincial Government in South Africa, Financial and Fiscal Commission, Midrand, South Africa.

Financial and Fiscal Commission, 2012b. Submission to the Division of Revenue, Financial and Fiscal Commission, Midrand, South Africa

Financial and Fiscal Commission, 2013. Submission for the Division of Revenue, Financial and Financial Commission, Midrand, South Africa.

Financial and Fiscal Commission, 2014. Submission to the Division of Revenue, Financial and Fiscal Commission, Midrand, South Africa

Financial and Fiscal Commission, 2019. Submission to the Division of Revenue, Financial and Fiscal Commission, Midrand, South Africa

Haysom, N. 2016. The Federalism Debate in the South African Constitution Making Process, Available at http://biblio.juridicas.unam.mx/libros/4/1640/23.pdf.

Human Sciences Research Council, 2017. Reducing Spatial Inequality Through Better Regulation, Report to the High Level Panel on the Assessment of Key Legislation and the Acceleration of Fundamental Change, Available at https://www.parliament.gov.za/storage/app/media/Pages/2017/october/High_Level_Panel/Commissioned_reports_for_triple_challenges_of_poverty_unemployment_and_inequality/Diagnostic_Report_on_Spatial_Inequality.pdf.

Munzhezdi 2017. The Role of Separation of Powers in Ensuring Public Accountability in SA, Article Published for the 2nd Annual International Conference on Public Administration and Development Alternatives 26– 28 July 2017, Tlotlo Hotel, Gaborone, Botswana, Available at http://ulspace.ul.ac.za/bitstream/handle/10386/1882/munzhedzi_role_2017.pdf.

Murray, C. 2009. Constitutional Issues for PES Review, Unpublished.

National Treasury. 2018. Budget Review. National Treasury, Pretoria, South Africa.

Rao, G. and Khumalo, B. 2000. Sharing the Cake: A Review of the Provincial Equitable Share Formula in South Africa. National Institute of Public Finance and Policy, India and Financial Fiscal Commission, Midrand, South Africa.

RSA. 1996. The Constitution of the Republic of South Africa, Republic of South Africa, Pretoria, South Africa.

Republic of South Africa. 1996. The Constitution of the Republic of South Africa, Pretoria, South Africa.

Schwella, E. 2016. Federalism in South Africa, A Complex Context and a Continued Challenge, Available at https://www.hss.de/download/publications/Federalism_2016_06.pdf.

Simeon, R. and Murray, C. 2008. Reforming Multi-Level Government in South Africa, 2008, Available at www.publiclaw.uct.ac.za/usr/public_law/staff/Simeon%20Murray.

Siyo, L. and Mubangisi, J.C. 2015. "The Independence of South African Judges: A Constitutional and Legislative Perspective", PER, 18 (4): 816–846.

Statistics South Africa, 2016. The State of Basic Service Delivery in South Africa. Statistics South Africa, Pretoria, South Africa.

World Bank. 2018. Republic of South Africa Systematic Country Diagnostic, An Incomplete Transition—Overcoming the Legacy of Exclusion in South Africa, World Bank Group.

WHO (World Health Organisation). 2020. Strenghtening Health Systems Response to Covid-19, Recommendations for the WHO European Region. Policy Brief (1 April 2020), Available at http://www.euro.who.int/__data/assets/pdf_file/0003/436350/strengthening-health-system-response-COVID-19.pdf?ua=1.

Spain

Julio López-Laborda, Jorge Martínez-Vázquez, and Carlos Monasterio-Escudero

1 Introductory Overview of the Country

The Kingdom of Spain, defined in the 1978 Constitution as a parliamentary monarchy, is an "Autonomic State" with essentially, de facto if not de jure, most of the features of a federation. The legal system is based on the Civil Law and the system of government is a stable full democracy.

Currently Spain has a population of 46,7 million, with a territory of 505,989 square kilometres, which incorporates the mainland in the Iberian Peninsula, plus the Balearic and Canary Islands and the North African city-enclaves of Ceuta and Melilla. The official language is

J. López-Laborda (✉)
University of Zaragoza, Zaragoza, Spain
e-mail: julio.lopez@unizar.es

J. Martínez-Vázquez
Georgia State University, Atlanta, GA, USA
e-mail: jorgemartinez@gsu.edu

C. Monasterio-Escudero
University of Oviedo, Oviedo, Spain
e-mail: monaster@uniovi.es

J.-F. Tremblay (ed.), *The Forum of Federations Handbook of Fiscal Federalism*, https://doi.org/10.1007/978-3-030-97258-5_9

Castilian (Spanish), which is co-official with Catalan, Euskera and Galician in the respective Communities where those other languages originate.[1]

Historically, the country-state was the result of a process of unification of different kingdoms and territories, which culminated in the later part of the fifteenth century. These constituent units, often identified with significant geographical differences, had and continue to have in many cases strong cultural identities, including different languages. This historical legacy is critically important in understanding the strong demands for self-government and fiscal decentralization, which in the last quarter of the twentieth century have transformed Spain from one of the most centralized countries in the world at the time of General Francisco Franco's death in 1975 into one of the most decentralized currently. The historical legacy is also fundamentally the reason for the adoption in the Spanish Constitution of an asymmetric system of intergovernmental finance where, as we will see below, two regions (the Basque Country and Navarre) operate with a fiscal framework completely different from that of the rest of the regions. The fast pace of reform and adaptation that Spain's fiscal federalism continues to experience is influenced in many ways by these historical-political issues.

The current vertical organization of government includes, besides the central government, 17 Autonomous Communities (as the regional governments are called) and 2 Autonomous Cities at the intermediate level, and at the local level, 50 provinces and 8,131 municipalities.[2] The Constitution recognizes explicitly the existence and right to self-governance of local governments and the Autonomous Communities. Although the Autonomous Communities have some regulatory powers over the local governments, essentially the structure of government and

[1] Catalan (official in Catalonia, the Balearic Islands, and the Valencian Community, where it is known as Valencian) is spoken by 17% of the population, Galician by 7%, and Basque (official in the Basque Country and in the Basque speaking area of Navarre) by 2%. By ethnic origin, 86.4% of the population is Spanish, 1.8% Moroccan, 1.3% Romanian and 10.5% other. By religious affiliation, 70.2% of the population is Roman Catholic and 25% atheist or non-believer.

[2] The Autonomous Communities are highly diverse in terms of size, population, per capita income and other factors. The largest is Andalusia with a population of 8,405,300 inhabitants, 87,599 square kilometres and a per capita income of 19,132 euros (in 2018). The smallest is La Rioja with a population of 312,700, an area of 5,045 square kilometres, and a per capita income of 26,833 euros. There are also large variations in size among municipalities; these range from large modern cities to very small municipalities in rural areas.

the fiscal system are not hierarchical.[3] Local governments have their own sources of revenues and receive transfers directly from the central government in what we can call a bifurcated system of finance, where the central government deals directly with the intermediate level and the local level governments and there are minimal fiscal relations between intermediate and local level governments.[4]

Overall, the very significant decentralization thrust of the past 40 years has benefited the intermediate level of government, the Autonomous Communities, that have gone from not existing to representing 32% of the consolidated public sector in 2016 (see Table 4). Over the last several decades the Autonomous Communities have emerged as the fastest growing level of government, with these expenditures mainly focused on health and the education, the two largest components of the total public expenditures after pensions.

Meanwhile, local government budgets represent 11% of total expenditures in 2016, very close to what they represented at the start of the decentralization process nearly forty years ago.[5] The fact that the decentralization process has been dominated by the devolution of competences and revenues to the Autonomous Communities has led many observers and political forces in Spain to continue to talk about the need for a "second decentralization" focused on local governments.[6]

The level of political accountability is relatively high as all government representatives are democratically elected and responsible to their respective constituencies at the same time there is a significant presence of civil

[3] "The Constitution guarantees the autonomy of municipalities. These shall enjoy full legal personality. Their government and administration shall be vested in their Town Councils, consisting of Mayors and councillors. Councillors shall be elected by residents of the municipality by universal, equal, free, direct and secret suffrage, in the manner provided for by the law. The Mayors shall be elected by the councillors or by the residents. The law shall lay down the terms under which an open council of all residents may proceed" (Article 140 Constitution).

[4] There is an exception to this general principle in the case of the two Autonomous Communities with the "special regime" (Navarre and the Basque Country), in which municipalities—and, in the Basque Country, the own regional government—are financially dependent on the first tier of local government, the provinces.

[5] In a different dimension, the Autonomous Communities represent more than 50% of general government employment, and local governments, more than 20%.

[6] See Pedraja et al. (2007).

society[7]; however, there are no important elements of direct democracy.[8] The Constitutional Court handles disputes between different levels of government. At the national level, the dominant role of the two political parties positioned at the centre-right and the centre-left has eroded, with the introduction of three other new national parties to the left and right as well as centre of the two traditional parties, prompting the need for parliamentary coalitions in order to govern; regional parties, especially in Catalonia and the Basque Country, continue to play key roles in their regions and as coalition members in the National Parliament.

Over the initial 30 years, when rapid decentralization took place, Spain enjoyed high rates of economic growth and prosperity, spotted with unusually high rates of unemployment associated with rigidities in labour market institutions. In 2008, GDP per capita was 24,275 euros. Over the same, Spain underwent a considerable increase in tax burden. In 1975 total tax revenues as a percent of GDP stood at less than 20%. By comparison, at that time, the average tax collection in the OECD was 31% of GDP. By 2002, Spain had converged to the OECD average with total tax revenues representing over 35% of GDP. The increases in real GDP and the considerably higher presence of the public service in the economy also allowed over that period a significant jump in the provision of public services at all levels of government. The Great Recession starting in 2008 hit the Spanish economy with significant virulence leading to significant increases in unemployment and the overall level of the national debt. Only in the most recent years has the level of economic activity recovered with rates of economic growth among the highest in OECD countries (in 2017, GDP per capita was 25,064 euros, above the level reached in 2008), but unemployment has only been reduced to about 14%. Most

[7] Provincial deputies, at the first tier of local government, are not directly elected, but designated by the municipal councils. The provincial deputies select one of their own as president of the Provincial Council.

[8] Spanish Constitution allows for some elements of direct democracy: "All Spaniards shall have the right to individual and collective petition, in writing, in the manner and subject to the consequences to be laid down by law" (Article 29); "The Houses may receive individual and collective petitions, always in writing" (Article 77); and "Political decisions of special importance may be submitted to all citizens in a consultative referendum. The referendum shall be called by the King on the President of the Government's proposal after previous authorization by the Congress" (Article 92).

recently, the tax burden has risen to almost 40% of GDP, while the overall level of national debt stands at 95% of GDP.

2 The Allocation of Expenditure Responsibilities

The Constitution addresses the fundamental division of responsibilities across different levels of government. Table 1 shows the current assignment of responsibilities that, in general, follows conventional fiscal federalism principles, including subsidiarity. The responsibilities assigned to the central government concern stabilization and redistribution functions and the delivery of services with benefits extending to the entire national territory, such as international relations, defence, customs, financial system regulation, basic Social Security legislation and funding, national infrastructure and transport and so on. The central level is also responsible for ultimately guaranteeing the functioning of the internal common market, using its competence on the bases and coordination of the general planning of economic activity (Article 149.1.13 Constitution), as well as for guaranteeing the basic equality of all Spaniards in the exercise of rights and in the fulfilment of constitutional duties (Article 149.1.1).

With regard to the Autonomous Communities, the actual responsibilities assignment evolved over the years, ending with the Autonomous Communities taking on responsibility for the provision of a wide range of public services of a regional-local nature, such as health and education services, agriculture, industry, environment or regional infrastructures.

An interesting aspect of the devolution of responsibilities in Spain is that it has been asymmetrical. Originally, and mostly for historical-political reasons, only a small group of Autonomous Communities were devolved responsibilities in education and health matters. This led to a distinction between "high level Communities" (i.e. those with a high level of devolved responsibilities) and "low level Communities". With time all Autonomous Communities came to have substantially the same responsibilities,[9] although some minor asymmetries persist (e.g. only some Communities have powers for administration of the prison system and the police).

[9] For example, the full devolution of healthcare responsibilities to regional governments took place only in 2002.

Table 1 The assignment of responsibilities at different levels of government in Spain

1. Central Government
Regulation of the basic conditions that guarantee the equality of all Spaniards
Defence
International representation
Justice
National Police
Civil, criminal, labour and commercial legislation
Customs, foreign trade
Financial system regulation
General planning of the economic activity
General Public Finance
Basic Social Security legislation and economic regime (pensions, unemployment benefits, etc.)
National infrastructure: highways, railroads and hydraulic river works across more than one Autonomous Community; commercial ports and airports
2. Autonomous Communities
Education, at all levels (primary, high school and colleges)
Health
Agriculture
Industry, energy and mines
Environment
Tourism and domestic trade
Social services
Historical and artistic patrimonial protection and own region's language protection
Housing and territorial arrangement
Regional infrastructures: highways and railroads within the Autonomous Community, sport ports and sport airports
3. Local Governments
3.1 Municipalities
All municipalities: public lighting, cemeteries, waste collection, public cleaning, drinking water supply, sewer system, access to urban areas, food surfacing, and food and drink control
Municipalities with more than 5,000 inhabitants: public parks, public libraries, market and waste management
Municipalities with more than 20,000 inhabitants: civil defence, social work, fire safety and sport facilities for public use
Municipalities with more than 50,000 inhabitants: urban passenger transport and environment protection
3.2 Provinces

(continued)

Table 1 (continued)

Coordination of municipal services
Legal assistance and managerial support to small size municipalities
Provision of specific services in smaller municipalities
Provision of services of a supra-municipal nature

Source Authors' elaboration

A more permanent manifestation of asymmetrical assignments is at the local level, where the minimum services to be provided by municipalities depend on their size (see Table 1). Local governments are assigned services with typically local benefit areas, such as water and sewerage, parks, street lighting and so on. It is notable that none of the education services (e.g., basic education) or health services (e.g., primary health) are assigned at the local level. Although there has been and continues to be considerable discussion about the devolution of more expenditure responsibilities from the intermediate to the local level of government, and most in particular basic education, in the context of the "second decentralization", the assignment of responsibilities has remained stable for many years now. At the local level, a cooperative approach among local governments with insufficient scale for the provision of a variety of services is well developed. The cooperative arrangements are known as *mancomunidades*, or associations of local governments, and they operate as special districts across several local governments in the provision of water services, garbage collection, tourism and social services.

The responsibility assignments in Table 1 need to be qualified further. While the Autonomous Communities exercise their powers within a framework of complete freedom in the case of some functions (such as regional public works, infrastructure and transport), in some other cases their autonomy is restricted with differing intensity by upper-level governments. The most significant limitations are present in the area of social services for healthcare and education. These are truly co-shared responsibilities (*competencias concurrentes*). Although the Autonomous Communities have responsibility for delivery and implementation of those services, the central government has significant regulatory powers for several service dimensions, such as establishing the basic conditions for the provision of the service or the rules governing access by users, among others. These rules typically provide minimum standards nationwide and cannot be altered by the regional governments. However, the

Table 2 Non-financial expenditures by function and level of government in 2016 (Percent)

Function	*Central*[a]	*Regional*	*Local*	*ALL*
General public services	64.40	18.21	17.39	100
Defence	100	0.00	0.00	100
Public order and safety	53.15	22.38	24.47	100
Economic affairs	45.42	31.80	22.78	100
Environmental protection	6.52	21.89	71.59	100
Housing and communal services	1.03	34.97	64.00	100
Health	6.49	92.31	1.20	100
Recreation, culture and religion	17.13	22.81	60.06	100
Education	3.66	91.21	5.13	100
Social protection	90.79	5.80	3.41	100

Note [a]Including the social security system
Source Authors' elaboration, based on Ministry of Finance

Autonomous Communities have the power to enact specific regional laws applicable within their territory with the purpose of improving service provision and so on.

Table 2 presents the most recent available data (2016) on the functional distribution of expenditures at different government levels. As can be seen, the central level is specialized in defence, social protection, general public services and public order and security; the Autonomous Communities, in education and health services[10]; and local governments, in environmental protection, housing and communal services, and recreation, culture and religion.

3 Taxation Responsibilities

The system of revenue assignments—taxes and grants—in Spain is rather complex by international standards. This complexity arises from two sources. First, there are significant differences in the bifurcated revenue assignments at the intermediate and local levels of government and those two systems need to be discussed separately. Second, the system of

[10] Note that both types of services are also privately provided. For example, in the case of health services, around 70% of the costs are financed publically and 30% privately.

revenue assignments at the intermediate level of government is complicated by a very marked asymmetry between two groups of Autonomous Communities. Thus, it is useful to separate in the discussion the financing of regional governments and their two types, and the financing of local governments.

3.1 Revenue Assignments of the Autonomous Communities: The Common Regime[11]

The Spanish Constitution establishes two basic different systems for financing the regional governments. The "common" regime applies to all Autonomous Communities with the exception of two: The Basque Country and Navarre. These two Autonomous Communities operate under the "special" or "charter" (in Spanish *foral*) regime.[12] The two systems introduce a fundamental asymmetry in the financing of regional governments that fundamentally benefits the two Autonomous Communities under the special regime.

The revenue assignment in the common regime was originally established by the "Autonomous Communities Financing Act" of 1980 (*Ley Orgánica de Financiación de las Comunidades Autónomas—LOFCA*); this law was comprehensively refurbished in 2001 and 2009. For this reason, the revenue assignments in the common regime are typically known as the "LOFCA system". While LOFCA establishes the basic principles of the system, specific implementation issues as well as disputes are settled within the "Fiscal and Financial Policy Council" (*Consejo de Política Fiscal y Financiera -CPFF*), a consultative intergovernmental body, composed of the ministers of finance and public administrations of the central government and the finance ministers of the Autonomous Communities. The representatives of the central government have the same weight

[11] See Monasterio (2010), López-Laborda and Zabalza (2011), and Lago-Peñas and Martinez-Vazquez, coord. (2009, 2015) for general discussions of the autonomous financing.

[12] Actually, there are some other minor deviations from the common regime in the case of the Autonomous Community of the Canary Islands which due to its geographical location receives certain special treatment. However, the Canary Islands are typically treated as part of the "common" regime. The two North African cities of Ceuta and Melilla also have a special status, which is halfway between the position of a municipality and an Autonomous Community.

as the sum of the autonomic representatives. One of the most important responsibilities of the CPFF has been to assess the evolution of the regional finance system on a regular basis and to recommend any necessary changes. The recommendations made by the CPFF are embodied in a Financial Act passed by the National Parliament. Significant reviews of the LOFCA system took place in 1986, 1992, 1996, 2001 and 2009.

Initially (end of the 1970s and early 1980s), the financing system of the regions in the common regime was based on lump-sum general grants. These grants were calculated to cover the expenditure needs arising from the devolved expenditure responsibilities using the "net effective cost" method. In essence, this method attempts to establish the monetary value (cost) of each devolved competence in each Autonomous Community, identifying all costs (direct, indirect, new and replacement investment) incurred by the central level to provide that competence in each region in the year prior to its devolution, and subtracting, where appropriate, the fees charged to users of the service, since those fees are also transferred to the Autonomous Community.[13] Although this methodology suffers from some well-known problems, it must also be recognized that the effective cost method did provide an effective bridge in the process of devolution and avoided excessive budgetary tensions. The problem lies in the fact that, as explained below, this methodology is to certain extent still in use for the computation of equalization grants.

This approach had two very clear weaknesses. First, it tended to perpetuate whatever differences existed across regions under the centralized provision of services before their devolution to the regional governments. Thus, the approach did not guarantee an equal provision of public services. Second, the complete reliance on grants, as opposed to own taxes, meant that regional governments had practically no revenue autonomy. This blunted the greater efficiency and accountability benefits typically associated with fiscal decentralization.

Both central and regional government authorities commonly agreed to these flaws. The subsequent evolution of revenue assignments to regional governments can be seen as a continued process of gradual corrections to these problems, starting with the tools offered by the LOFCA's initial version in 1980.

[13] See López-Laborda and Monasterio (2007) for a discussion of this methodology.

On the one hand, the method for calculating expenditure needs was modified. In 1986, there was an agreement to replace the net effective cost method with a quantification of regional spending needs based on indicators that would more accurately reflect the expenditure needs of each Autonomous Community. The concept of expenditure needs was identified as the costs each regional government would need to incur in order to provide the same level of public goods and services as other regional governments. In the following section we will explain in more detail how regional expenditure needs are currently calculated.

On the other hand, the revenue assignment to the Autonomous Communities was also reformed. Funding of regional governments exclusively on the basis of general purpose grants was abandoned after an initial period and replaced from 1982 to 1984 with a system consisting of a set of devolved or "ceded taxes" (*tributos cedidos*) and the following general equalization transfers: until 2001, the "Sharing in Central Government Revenues" (*Participación en Ingresos del Estado*); between 2002 and 2008, the "Sufficiency Fund" (*Fondo de Suficiencia*); and since 2009, the "Transfer from the Guarantee Fund for Fundamental Public Services" (*Transferencia del Fondo de Garantía de Servicios Públicos Fundamentales*) and the "Global Sufficiency Fund" (*Fondo de Suficiencia Global*). These tools provided regional governments with revenue sources much in line with standard practices in other decentralized countries. Next, we will describe the taxes ceded. Equalization transfers will be dealt with in the next section.

Ceded taxes are taxes established and regulated by the central level, whose revenues are totally or partially assigned to the Autonomous Communities. Until 1997, regional governments were granted no discretion vis-à-vis the structure of the ceded taxes, although in some cases they were put in charge of their administration and collection. Thus, in the initial period through 1997, ceded taxes should be considered an extension of the tax sharing system instead of own taxes providing regional governments with meaningful tax autonomy. Starting in 1997, several degrees of discretion were granted to the regional governments vis-à-vis some of the ceded taxes, allowing the Autonomous Communities to set the tax rate and establish tax credits and allowances. Thus, progressively, some ceded taxes became own taxes for the regional governments.[14]

[14] The standard assumption in the fiscal federalism literature is that some minimum degree of discretion over the structure of the tax is required (e.g., ability to change the

Table 3 provides the current status of the ceded taxes regarding the arrangements for the distribution of revenue collections, the level of government in charge of administration and collection and the discretionary powers granted to the regional governments over that particular tax. Table 3 shows that, at present, almost all direct taxes over which the Spanish government has full regulatory capacity (as these taxes are not affected by the harmonizing rules of the European Union (EU)) have been ceded (in different shares) to the Autonomous Communities accompanied by autonomous regulatory powers. The only significant direct taxes that have not been ceded to the Autonomous Communities are the Corporate Income Tax and Social Security Contributions; the central government retains exclusive authority over the collection, administration and regulation of these taxes. However, the restrictions imposed by the harmonization of indirect taxes (VAT and excises) in the EU means that with respect to these taxes the formula of tax sharing is maintained, and therefore the Autonomous Communities share in their revenues but have no regulatory powers over their structure.

The arrangements for the personal income tax deserve special mention because they are not those found in a typical piggyback scheme in other decentralized countries. The law divides the tax schedule for the personal income tax into a central government schedule and a regional government schedule. The revenues from the central government schedule, which is equal to 50% of the total tax, are allocated at the central level, while those from the regional schedule, equal to also 50%, are allocated to each Autonomous Community. Central and regional governments may maintain this tax schedule, in which case they will receive 50% of the total tax take, or they may increase or reduce the rates and, in that case, the impact on tax revenues will be separately confined to the government that has undertaken that measure. Regional governments share 50% of general tax credits and may also establish their own tax credits, which would only affect regional tax liabilities.

Overall, regional autonomy in the personal income tax is exercised in a coordinated and harmonized fashion with the central government in order to minimize taxpayer compliance costs. The definition of taxable income is common for both central and regional taxes. Taxpayers need to fill out only one tax return that incorporates the central and regional

tax rate) before we can consider the tax as an own sub-national government tax. See, for example, Bird (1993), or Blöchliger and Nettley (2015).

Table 3 Taxes assigned to Autonomous Communities

Tax	*Sharing of Collection [Initial % of assignment]*		*Administration by regional governments*		*Discretion by regional governments*	
	Common regime	Charter regime	Common regime	Charter regime	Common regime	Charter regime
Personal income tax	[50%]	100%	No	Yes	Tax schedule and tax credits	Full
Tax on net wealth	100%	100%	Yes	Yes	Threshold, tax schedule and tax credits	Full
Inheritance and gift tax	100%	100%	Yes	Yes	Allowances, tax schedule, tax credits, administration	Full
Corporate income tax	–	100%	–	Yes	–	Full
Non-Resident income tax	–	100%	–	Yes	–	Full for permanent establishments
Capital transfer tax, taxes on the raising of capital and stamp duties	100%	100%	Yes	Yes	Tax rates and tax credits (with some exceptions), administration	Full (with some exceptions)
Gaming taxes	100%	100%	Yes	Yes	Allowances, taxable base, tax rates, administration	Full (with some exceptions)
Vehicle excise (registration)	100%	100%	Yes	Yes	Tax rates (subject to limitations)	Tax rates (subject to limitations), declaration and payment forms and payment periods

(continued)

Table 3 (continued)

Tax	*Sharing of Collection [Initial % of assignment]*		*Administration by regional governments*		*Discretion by regional governments*	
	Common regime	Charter regime	Common regime	Charter regime	Common regime	Charter regime
Value-added tax	[50%]	100%	No	Yes	No	Only on declaration and payment forms and payment periods
Excise duties: alcoholic beverages, tobacco and hydrocarbons	[58%] (100% of the special rate of the Tax on Hydrocarbons)	100%	No	Yes	No	Only on declaration and payment forms and payment periods
Electricity tax	100%	100%	No	Yes	No	Only on declaration and payment forms and payment periods
Tax on insurance premiums	–	100%	-	Yes	–	Only on declaration and payment forms and payment periods

Tax	*Sharing of Collection [Initial % of assignment]*		*Administration by regional governments*		*Discretion by regional governments*	
	Common regime	Charter regime	Common regime	Charter regime	Common regime	Charter regime
Tax on gaming activities[a]	100% electronic, computer or telematic games 100% revenue from increase in tax rate	100%	No	Yes	Tax rates (subject to limitations), when the organizers reside in the Community, applicable only to players residing in the Community	Tax rates (subject to limitations), when the organizers reside in the Community, applicable only to players residing in the Community Declaration and payment forms and payment periods
Environmental taxes: electricity, nuclear fuel, gas, oil and condensate, fluorinated gases	–	100%	-	Yes	–	Only on declaration and payment forms and payment periods
Tax on deposits with credit Institutions[a]	100%	100%	–	Yes	No	Only on declaration and payment forms and payment periods
Special tax on coal	–	100%	–	Yes	–	Only on declaration and payment forms and payment periods

Note [a]Although the Communities under the common regime have a share in this tax, it does not have (yet) the legal status of ceded tax
Source Authors' elaboration

income taxes. In the case of the regions under the common regime, the State Tax Administration Agency (*Agencia Estatal de Administración Tributaria—AEAT*) collects and distributes the revenues between the central and the regional governments.

The Autonomous Communities have made use of their regulatory powers on ceded taxes, albeit in different ways according to different regions and tax instruments. In general, the Autonomous Communities have reduced their fiscal effort for direct taxes (in particular, wealth tax and inheritance and gift tax) and have increased it for indirect taxes (capital transfer tax, stamp duties). With regard to the personal income tax, the Autonomous Communities have habitually established their own tax credits, but until 2007, no Community had modified the regional tax rates. During the Great Recession, all the Autonomous Communities have legislated changes on their tax schedules, in general, to increase the tax burden of their residents.

There is some evidence that taxpayers have reacted to differences in taxation between Autonomous Communities by moving to another region to purchase some goods (such as fuel: see Leal et al. 2009) or to change their residence, in response to regional differences in direct tax burdens (Agrawal and Foremny, 2019; López-Laborda and Rodrigo, 2022). For years there has been a genuine race to the bottom in the case of the inheritance and gift tax, which could ultimately lead to its disappearance, as has already happened in other federal countries.

Besides the ceded taxes, regional governments may introduce their own regional taxes and surtaxes, as well as fees, charges and public prices. For these taxes, the Autonomous Communities have full powers of collection, administration and regulation. However, the LOFCA imposes strict bounds on the type of taxes regional governments can introduce on their own. Most importantly, this law prohibits regional governments from levying taxes on taxable activities that are already subject to levies by the central level or by municipalities. However, the central level can levy taxes on taxable activities already taxed by the Autonomous Communities. If this results in a decrease in the revenues of the Autonomous Communities, the central level must implement the appropriate compensation or coordination measures in favour of the regions.

The above limitations have led the Autonomous Communities to specialize, above all, in environmental taxes. Although there are currently more than seventy "genuine" autonomic taxes, their collection is very limited. Politicians and business people are often concerned about how the proliferation of regional taxes may affect the internal market and the overall economic union of the country.

3.2 *Revenue Assignments of the Autonomous Communities. The Charter System*

The charter (foral) system applies to two Autonomous Communities: Navarre and the Basque Country. The financing arrangements for these two regions are called the *Convenio* in Navarre and the *Concierto* in the Basque Country, with both terms referring to the asymmetric conditions incorporated into the two special laws for the two regions: the "Economic Agreement between the State and Foral Community of Navarre Act", (*Ley del Convenio Económico entre el Estado y la Comunidad Foral de Navarra)* and the "Economic Agreement with the Autonomous Community of the Basque Country Act", (*Ley del Concierto Económico con la Comunidad Autónoma del País Vasco).*

In contrast to the financing system for the Autonomous Communities under the common regime, the charter system is not based on the assignment of specific revenues to fund a given level of spending. The chief feature of the charter system is that it provides the two regions concerned with a very high level of fiscal autonomy. Both the *Convenio* and the *Concierto* basically recognize the capacity of the charter regions to establish and regulate their own tax systems,[15] provided that the solidarity principle and a common economic space is guaranteed together with all other Autonomous Communities in the country[16]; this means that the freedom of movement and residence of people and the freedom of movement of goods, services, and capital are all ensured.

[15] However, the Spanish Constitutional Court has specified that the foral territories "must establish taxes in which the image of those who make up the national tax system can be identified" (ruling 110/2014, 26 June).

[16] In the Spanish Constitution, the principle of solidarity has two objectives. The first objective is projected on individuals, and this is the guarantee of a minimum level of provision of fundamental public services throughout the Spanish territory; this objective is fulfilled by the equalization transfers. The second objective is projected directly on the territories, and is the correction of the differences of income and wealth between jurisdictions; this objective is fulfilled with the regional development transfers. As we will see below, the charter regions contribute to financing these second type of transfers (not very important in quantitative terms), but not the first.

In essence, the charter regions are financed exclusively through tax revenues called "agreed taxes" (*tributos convenidos* in Navarre and *tributos concertados* in the Basque Country). The two charter regions have wide powers over these taxes, which are, in general, considerably greater than the powers that have been granted to the Autonomous Regions under the common regime in the case of the ceded taxes.[17]

Table 3 lists the "agreed taxes" and the powers granted to the charter regional governments over them, which in most cases are full powers. Social Security Contributions are the only relevant tax that is currently outside the charter regime list of agreed taxes.

In contrast to the tax assignments for regional governments under the common regime, the charter regions have full powers over personal and corporate income taxes. The finance departments of the charter regions also have control over the administration of the main indirect taxes, the VAT and excise duties.[18] However, for the indirect taxes the charter regions have no regulatory powers, for the reasons explained above.

The Autonomous Communities under the charter regime have lower effective tax rates than the rest of the country but, given that they have higher relative income per capita, the tax burden is similar and the tax collection per capita is clearly higher than for the average of Autonomous Communities under the common regime (Zubiri, 2015).

The high degree of tax decentralization in the charter Autonomous Communities and the relatively high income levels of these two regions guarantee full financing of their expenditure needs without any transfers from the central government. In fact, the regimes for the Basque Country and Navarre call for negative transfers to be remitted from those two regional governments to the central government. These negative transfers

[17] In the case of the Basque Country, actually the tax autonomy is granted to the three provinces or "Historical Territories" of Álava, Guipúzcoa and Vizcaya. The "agreed taxes" in the Basque Country are regulated, administered and collected at the provincial level, with the regional government playing only a coordinating role. In this manner, the Autonomous Community is basically financed by transfers from the provincial governments. Note that this is not the case for Navarre, because there the provincial and regional levels perfectly overlap.

[18] The case of VAT and excise duties is quite complex. For example, in the case of VAT, the tax collected by the foral governments, according to regional value added, has to be adjusted to obtain the final yield that corresponds to those governments, according to consumption by the residents of the Autonomous Community. See Zubiri (2000) for a complete explanation of these steps.

are called the "quota" (*cupo*) in the case of the Basque Country and the "contribution" (*aportación*) in the case of Navarre. The rationale for these negative transfers is for the two regions to contribute to the financing of the cost of public goods and services provided by the central government in the entirety of the national territory. In contrast to this single payment, or quota for short, by the charter regions, all other regions under the common regime can be seen as "contributing" to the financing of central government services in several ways. The most important of these are the non-ceded taxes collected in their territories (50% in the personal income tax, 100% in the corporate income tax, 50% in the VAT, 42% in excises and so on).

The amount of the negative transfer or quota for the charter regions is based on a fairly complex formula. In short, the share in the cost of central government goods and services (the so-called "non-assumed expenditures", *cargas no asumidas*) attributable to each charter region is based on an "imputation index", which is basically a relative income function (vis-à-vis the entire national economy). The imputation index is 1.6% for Navarre and 6.24% for the Basque Country.[19]

The quota is calculated for a base year, and the calculation methodology should be reviewed every five years. For any year after the base year, the quota is calculated by applying to its value in the base year the rate of growth of central government taxes equivalent to the foral "agreed taxes".

The discussion above provides a description of the "basic financing model" for the charter regions. But as in the case of the common regime regions, the Basque Country and Navarre may establish their own taxes and surtaxes, fees, charges and public prices.

In 2016, own taxes amounted to 4.1% of non-financial revenues for Navarra, and 3.4% for the Basque Country; agreed taxes represented 93.9% of non-financial revenues for Navarra, and 94.3% for the Basque Country; and grants represented 2.0% for Navarra and 2.3 for the Basque Country. It should be borne in mind that, in the Basque Country, agreed taxes are provincial in nature and no autonomic (see note 16).

An evaluation of the charter system produces a mixed scorecard. This system scores high from the standpoint of financial autonomy and accountability of sub-national governments. In contrast to the common

[19] For a more detailed description and analysis, see Zabalza and López-Laborda (2017).

regime regions, the charter regions finance all their expenditure out of their own revenues. But, there is more. In fact, the degree of fiscal autonomy provided by the charter system to the regional government is quite unique in the international experience. A similarity can be found in the "single channel" scheme that some Russian regions practiced in the early 1990s against the wishes of the federal government in Moscow, whereby the regions collected on their own all taxes, including those that were supposed to be federal taxes and negotiated with Moscow a single payment or remittance (Wallich, 1994).

It would be misleading to confuse the degree of autonomy granted to the charter regions in Spain with that existing in the world's most fiscally decentralized countries, such as the United States, Switzerland or Canada. In those countries, some of the federal taxes may be administered by the sub-national governments and then remitted, as in the case of Canada and Switzerland, and sub-national governments have their distinct separate taxes, as in the United States and Canada, but in none of those countries are sub-national governments assigned most or all the taxes and then agree with the centre on a single payment transfer as a contribution to the cost of providing federal services.

The important drawbacks of the charter system emanate from the asymmetric nature of the arrangement vis-à-vis the common regime applied in the rest of the Spanish regions. In the first place, the greater financial autonomy provided by the charter regime provides the means and incentives for asymmetric tax competition between these regions and the regions under the common regime. For example, if a charter region decides to implement tax measures to attract firms from other regions, for the most part the regions under the common regime are unable to react, because, for example, they do not have regulatory powers over corporate income tax. Although there is much concern about this issue, especially among regions neighbouring the foral ones, evidence of the existence of tax competition is only anecdotal to date. Moreover, it is also true that this asymmetry has been reduced as the common regime Autonomous Communities have been expanding their regulatory powers on the ceded taxes.

Secondly, the charter regime may be seen as unfair to the rest of the regions under the common regime. A comparison of the structure of the common and charter financing systems shows that an equal level of tax effort will provide the charter regime regions with higher revenues while both types of regions have the same expenditure obligations: depending on the estimates, between a minimum of 30% more per capita revenues, and a maximum of more than 100% (Zubiri, 2015; Zabalza and López-Laborda, 2017). In other words, the regions under the common regime would need to levy higher tax rates on their constituents to provide the same standard of regional public services. An explanation for this difference is that the charter system is so designed that citizens residing in the charter regions finance out of their taxes the cost of regional public goods and -with the quota remittance- the respective share of national public goods and services, but do not contribute to financing interregional equalization transfers. However, the citizens of the regions of common regime finance with their taxes the respective regional public goods and services and their part in the national public goods and services, but they also finance transfers to allow equalization among Autonomous Communities under this regime. The literature also points to other deficiencies in the application of the charter regime such as the calculation of the non-assumed expenditures[20] or the adjustment for VAT and excise duties (explained in note 17).

3.3 Revenue Assignments of Local Governments

Municipal governments have their own revenue assignments separately from those of the regional governments. Local revenues are regulated by the "Law on Local Finance" (*Ley Reguladora de las Haciendas Locales*) of 1988, updated in 2004 and frequently amended since then.[21] As in the case of the charter regions, and in contrast to what is practiced vis-à-vis the common regime regions, the financing system of local governments is not based on the computation of expenditure needs that then have to be financed with a particular set of revenues.

Five taxes are currently assigned to municipal governments. Three are mandatory in all the municipalities: the property tax (*Impuesto sobre Bienes Inmuebles—IBI*: the most important in terms of revenue), the local

[20] The literature has shown that the cost of the competences devolved to the Autonomous Communities is overestimated, which leads to an underestimation of the non-assumed expenditures (*cargas no asumidas*), and which are still provided by the central government, and, therefore, it also leads to an underestimation of the quota remitted by the foral regions to the central level. See Zubiri (2015).

[21] Revenue assignment to the municipalities in the foral Autonomous Communities is regulated by the laws of the respective foral territories. As far as taxes are concerned, there are no significant differences with the municipalities in the common system.

business tax and the vehicles tax. The other two taxes, a tax on land value increases and a tax on constructions, facilities and infrastructure, are optional taxes; it is up to the municipal council whether these two taxes are to be introduced or not.[22] In practice, most municipalities have decided to apply these two optional taxes. In general, municipal governments enjoy a high level of autonomy in setting tax rates, allowances and tax credits for local taxes within the framework of the (centrally issued) law, and make wide use of these powers. Therefore, it is fair to say that local taxes are truly own municipal taxes.

In the case of the property tax, the Ministry of Finance, through the Office of the Cadastre (*Dirección General del Catastro*), centrally manages the most significant aspect of this municipal tax, the assessment of property values. This is an unsatisfactory situation for many municipalities, especially in the case of large cities, which feel they would be better able to manage the assessment of property values within their borders. Large local governments have at different times requested from the central government the ability to do their own property assessments. In periods of fast increases in property values, as was the case between 2000 and 2007 throughout Spain, the delay in assessed values catching up with real market values made this problem more acute. This situation has led to expensive emergency revisions of cadastral values in order to increase revenue collections from the property tax. Nevertheless, the typical municipality had proceeded to lower the property tax rates after a revised increase in cadastral values. Property tax burdens have become a particularly sensitive issue and the overall equity of the tax has been increasingly questioned, especially in the light of the fact that housings expenditures are proportionally higher for the lower income population and the lack of circuit-breakers for pensioners whose property values have increased quite considerably but their incomes have not.

With some exceptions (such as property assessments or the census of economic activities), local taxes are administered by the municipal governments themselves. However, in the case of small municipalities lacking administrative capacity and skilled personnel, it is often the case that tax

[22] The plenary session of the municipal council must decide in its "Fiscal Regulations" (*Ordenanzas Fiscales*) before the start of the fiscal year, which taxes are approved for implementation and within which margins as specified by the law. There is a third optional municipal tax on luxury expenditures that falls on the use of hunting and fishing grounds. This tax has little revenue significance.

administration is delegated upward to the tax agency of the province or the regional government.

Despite the significant degree of local tax autonomy, there has not been any considerable degree of tax competition, perhaps with the exception of the anecdotal case of the vehicle tax, where some small municipalities have bet on the minimum tax rates allowed in order to attract the rental vehicles market.[23]

Large cities (those with a population larger than 75,000 inhabitants, and also the capital cities of all provinces and of the Autonomous Communities, regardless of their population size) also have a share on three central government taxes: the personal income tax (with a sharing rate of 2.1336%), the VAT (with a sharing rate of 2.3266%) and excise taxes (with a sharing rate of 2.9220%). The municipalities have no powers over the regulation or administration of these tax shares.

Another important financing source for municipalities are charges based on the straight application of the benefit principle, such as user fees for local services for water, access to municipal sports facilities and local transport.

The only tax assigned to the provincial governments is a surtax on the local business tax raised by the municipalities in the provincial territory. Metropolitan areas can establish a surtax on the taxable base of the property tax of properties located in their territory. No other local entity may levy taxes or surtaxes. Like large cities, provinces have a share on the personal income tax (at a rate of 1.2561%), VAT (with a sharing rate of 1.3699%) and excise taxes (with a sharing rate of 1.7206%).

To conclude this section, Table 4 shows the changes in non-financial expenditures and revenues by level of government since 1995. We can see that, while the share of the local level in general revenues and expenditures has hardly changed throughout the period being considered, the share of the autonomic level has increased quite significantly. Table 4 also shows that the recent economic crisis slowed down the process of decentralization of expenditures, especially to the Autonomous Communities.

[23] Bosch and Solé-Ollé (2007) and Delgado et al. (2015) find evidence in favour of yardstick competition with local taxes. Jofre-Monseny and Solé-Ollé (2010) find that differences in property and business taxes affect the intraregional location of new manufacturing plants.

Table 4 Composition of non-financial public expenditures and revenues by level of government, 1995–2016 (Percent)[a]

Year	Central Government[b]		Autonomous Governments		Local Governments	
	Expenditures	Revenues[c]	Expenditures	Revenues[c]	Expenditures	Revenues[c]
1995	67.34	82.95	21.54	7.09	11.11	9.96
2002	54.86	76.43	32.36	13.69	12.78	9.87
2009	50.65	71.77	35.82	17.87	13.53	10.36
2012	59.29	69.74	30.48	19.49	10.22	10.77
2016	56.59	72.19	32.11	16.74	11.30	11.08

Notes [a]Non-financial expenditures exclude interest and repayment of public sector debt, and acquisition of financial assets. Non-financial revenues exclude revenues from public sector debt and from the sale of financial assets

[b]Including the Social Security system

[c]Taxes are allocated to the level of government that has discretion to set the tax rate

Source OECD Fiscal Decentralization Database

In 2016, the Autonomous Communities accounted for almost one-third of the country's non-financial expenditure and one-sixth of non-financial revenues.

4 Intergovernmental Fiscal Transfers and Revenue-Sharing

Because Spain's decentralization system works in a bifurcated fashion without any significant hierarchical relationship between regional and local governments, it is necessary to discuss the system of central transfers to the regions and that to local governments separately.

4.1 *Transfers to Regional Governments*

Autonomous Communities under the common regime receive unconditional equalization grants and also conditional grants.[24] The following

[24] As we have seen above, the two regions under the charter regime receive no equalization grants. Actually, in their case there is a negative transfer from these two regions to the central treasury. These Communities do receive other transfers from the central government and the European Union, as do the common regime Communities. See Lago-Peñas and Martinez-Vazquez, eds. (2011) for general discussions of the transfer system.

paragraphs describe the most salient features of the methodology used to determine the equalization transfers under the regional financing model applied since 2009. According to the Spanish Constitution, the degree of equalization must be established between two limits, neither of which must be exceeded. The upper limit is that of full equalization. The lower limit corresponds to the equalization of fundamental public services (the exact services to be identified by the central government), and which in any case must be satisfied in order to comply with the principle of equality of all Spaniards.

The first stage consists of calculating the expenditure needs of each Autonomous Community. To this end, regional services are divided into two categories: "fundamental public services", made up of education, health and essential social services, which represent around 70% of all regional expenditure, and the remaining autonomic services, which we will identify as "non-fundamental public services".

For fundamental public services, the expenditure needs of each Autonomous Community are calculated year by year through the use of a set of agreed indicators that reflect the demand and cost factors related to the provision of these services. The indicators used are: population (with a weighting of 30%), population protected by the public health system according to age groups (38%), population over 65 (8.5%), population between 0 and 16 (20.5%), surface area (1.8%), population dispersion (0.6%) and insularity (0.6%). The population of an Autonomous Community corrected by these indicators is called the "adjusted population".

For non-fundamental public services, a less precise procedure is applied, which does not quantify expenditure needs by means of indicators. The financing needs for non-fundamental services are calculated for each region simply as the difference between the total expenditure guaranteed to that Community by the previous financing model in the base year established by the intergovernmental body CPFF (with some corrections due to the contribution of additional revenues by the central government) and its expenditure needs for fundamental public services. In short, the model restricts itself to ensuring that no Autonomous Community receives less revenue to finance its services than it has historically received, which constitutes the much-discussed "hold harmless" or "status quo clause" which, to a certain extent, continues to link regional revenues to the effective cost calculated decades ago.

The second stage consists of calculating the fiscal capacity of each Autonomous Community, which is the potential revenue collections that it could obtain from its ceded taxes if it required its citizens to make the same level of fiscal effort as the other Communities.

Finally, the third stage consists of calculating the transfers, which constitute the closing element of the financing model. For fundamental public services, a transfer is applied which is called the "Transfer from the Guarantee Fund for Fundamental Public Services". It is calculated each year as the difference between the expenditure needs of each Community in these services, quantified as explained above, and 75% of the fiscal capacity derived from the ceded taxes plus some fees and charges. This transfer, which may be positive or negative, is therefore a genuine equalization grant, which guarantees, year after year, that if an Autonomous Community requires its citizens to make the same tax effort on its ceded taxes as the other Communities, it will also be able to provide, if it so wishes, the same level of educational, health and social services.

As for non-fundamental public services, there is also a transfer, known as the "Global Sufficiency Fund", which is calculated as the difference between the financial needs of each Community, quantified as described above, and 25% of the fiscal capacity derived from the ceded taxes plus some fees and charges. This transfer can also be positive or negative and its objective is not equalization but sufficiency, for two reasons. On the one hand, as has been pointed out above, the system does not accurately calculate the Autonomous Communities' expenditure needs on these services. On the other hand, the transfer of the Global Sufficiency Fund is not recalculated every year, as is the case for the transfer of the Guarantee Fund: the value of the Global Sufficiency Fund in the base year evolves for all the Autonomous Communities at the same rate as the taxes at the central level (the so-called National Tax Revenues, *Ingresos Tributarios del Estado—ITE*). Both the Transfer from the Guarantee Fund for Fundamental Public Services and the Global Sufficiency Fund are negative for Madrid and the Balearic Islands, the two regions with the greatest tax capacity.

There are still two other transfers, quantitatively less important than the previous ones, which are known as "Convergence Funds" (*Fondos de Convergencia*). The "Competitiveness Fund" (*Fondo de Competitividad*) seeks to avoid, first, that the revenues that the model provides to the richest Autonomous Communities are excessively less than what they could obtain if their revenues depended solely on their fiscal capacity, and second, that there are large differences in the total "per adjusted inhabitant" financing between Autonomous Communities. The "Cooperation

Fund" (*Fondo de Cooperación*) aims to stimulate regional convergence. It is therefore more of a regional development instrument than an autonomic financing instrument in the strict sense.

All these transfers are unconditional, so the Autonomous Communities can freely decide how to use these revenues.

Figure 1 summarizes the operation of the financing system in 2016 by comparing, for each Autonomous Community, its "per adjusted inhabitant fiscal capacity" with its "per adjusted inhabitant total financing", i.e. once all the transfers explained above have been applied. This Figure reflects at least two results that may attract attention. The first is that, after operating the various transfers, there is still certain dispersion in the per adjusted inhabitant financing of the Autonomous Communities. The second is that these differences are not related to the tax capacity of the Autonomous Communities. It is observed that the ranking of the Communities according to their tax capacity is reversed after the transfers, so that, for example, the three richest Communities end up having fewer revenues per adjusted inhabitant than almost all the others; in other words, the so-called "principle of ordinality" is not respected in the current system of transfers. This is true, and it has caused the complaints of some Autonomous Communities, like Catalonia, which has introduced

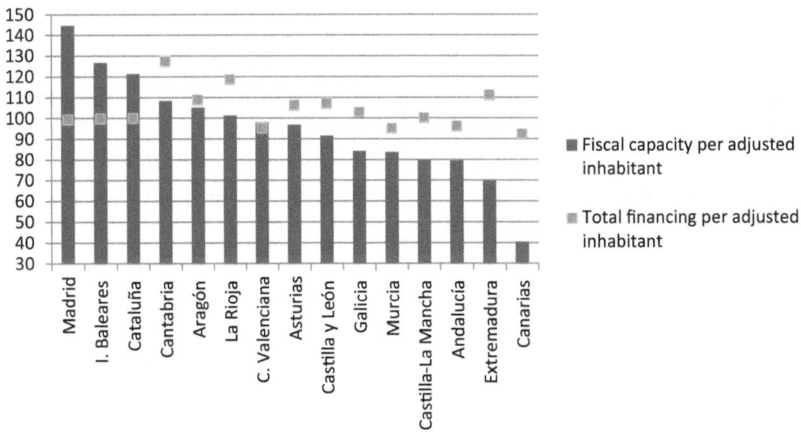

Fig. 1 Fiscal capacity and total financing of the Autonomous Communities per adjusted inhabitant, 2016 (Average = 100) (*Source* Authors' elaboration, based on De la Fuente [2018])

into its Autonomy Statute the guarantee of the fulfilment of this principle (with some qualifications). But it should not be ignored that, as has been explained, the objective of the current financing system is not to make possible equality in the levels of provision of all autonomic services, for the same fiscal effort, but only for public services that have been classified as fundamental. In addition, although Fig. 1 provides a representation of the autonomic financing that is usually carried out, it must be interpreted with caution, because it is evaluating the revenues available to the Autonomous Communities to finance all their services with an indicator—the adjusted population—that the autonomic financing model only uses to quantify the expenditure needs of the fundamental services, as also explained above.

In addition to the transfers described so far, the regions receive conditional transfers from the central government to finance certain regional policies, for example, in the area of unemployment or dependency (known as "Managed Grants", *Subvenciones Gestionadas*), or to finance collaborative projects between the central government and the Autonomous Communities, for example, in the area of scientific and technical research (known as "Agreements and Contracts-Programme", *Convenios y Contratos-Programa*). Some regions also receive conditional grants intended to foster regional development, under the overall objective of reducing regional disparities in income and wealth. Examples of this type of grant are the "Inter-Territorial Compensation Funds" (*Fondos de Compensación Interterritorial—FCI*) and several grants from the European Union budget, such as the "European Regional Development Fund".

In 2016, own taxes amounted to 6.2% of non-financial revenues for all the Autonomous Communities under the common regime, and ceded taxes, 74.8%. On the other hand, equalization grants represented 12.9%, and other grants, 6.1%, respectively, of non-financial revenues.

4.2 *Transfers to Local Governments*

The current transfer system for local governments was last updated in 2004.[25] It provides municipalities primarily with unconditional grants directly from the central government. Although the system of unconditional grants is ultimately enacted in a law from the National Parliament,

[25] In this sub-section, we will refer only to the local governments of the Autonomous Communities under the common regime.

the substance of the law is elaborated in a process of negotiation between the Ministry of Finance at the central level and the Spanish Federation of Municipalities and Provinces (*Federación Española de Municipios y Provincias—FEMP*), representing all local governments.

The funds are distributed according to different formulas that differentiate between large cities and medium and small municipalities.[26] Large cities receive the "Complementary Fund" (*Fondo Complementario*), which is calculated for the base year as the difference between the transfers received by each municipality with the financing model prior to 2004,[27] and the tax sharing calculated as explained in the previous section. For any year after the base year, the Supplementary Fund is calculated by applying to its value in the base year a growth rate equal to the increase in central government taxes, ITE.

For all other municipalities, medium and small, the amount of a transfer fund, called "Sharing in Central Government Revenues" (*Participación en Ingresos del Estado*), is distributed among them every year according to an index formula with three variables: population, with an assigned weight of 75%, the inverse of the tax capacity, with a weight of 12.5% and fiscal effort, with also a weight of 12.5%.[28] The pool of funds is adjusted every year by the rate of growth in central government taxes, ITE.[29]

The system of local transfers has been criticized from several angles.[30] For example, the distinction between the large and the rest of the municipalities lacks a clear rationale and transparency. In addition, the formula lacks flexibility vis-à-vis the new problems faced by the country, such as the massive increase in the number of immigrants in certain parts of the national territory which has resulted in considerable increases in municipal

[26] See Pedraja et al. (2007).

[27] This transfer used to be computed in a similar manner to the transfer system now in use since 2004 for the small and medium municipalities.

[28] Tax capacity is calculated by the relationship between the taxable base of the property tax in each municipality and the average taxable base of municipalities in the same population stratum. The measurement of tax effort is much more elaborate, and differs by tax. For the property tax, tax effort is determined according to tax capacity, measured as explained above, and the relationship between the tax rate set by the municipality and the minimum and maximum tax rates allowed by the tax law

[29] The system of transfers for tourist municipalities with populations over 20,000 is in between the two systems just described.

[30] See, for example, Pedraja and Suárez-Pandiello (2004).

(and regional) expenditures for social protection.[31] Several equity issues have also arisen because of the out migration from rural and mountain areas and the maintained support to facilities and services in those areas vis-à-vis urban areas with much higher population densities. In addition, it is only very indirect that the transfers to the local governments pursue an equalization objective.

Provincial governments also benefit from the "Complementary Fund", which is calculated and evolves as explained above for large cities.

In addition to transfers from the central level, local governments also receive transfers from the Autonomous Communities and provinces, although of lesser importance.

In 2016, own and shared taxes represented 64.5% of non-financial revenues for all municipalities, and transfers, the remaining 35.5%. This means that there is a significant level of autonomy and accountability at the municipal level, although there are significant variations in tax effort (and expenditure levels) across municipalities.

5 Macroeconomic Management

Macroeconomic coordination and control of the subcentral deficit and indebtedness has gone through several phases in Spain. In a first stage, from the Constitution of 1978 until the end of the eighties of the last century, it was based on compliance with classic rules: for instance, regional debt burdens could not exceed 25% of current public revenues, the debt with a term longer than one year could only be issued to finance investments and central government authorization was required to issue Public Debt titles or to borrow in foreign currency (Article 14 LOFCA).

Subsequently, the process of Economic and Monetary Union in the framework of the EU and the integration into the Euro area since 2002 meant a far-reaching change, given the European restrictions to the deficit (which must be less than 3% of GDP, except in exceptional cases), to the debt (with a reference limit of 60% of GDP) and, especially, by the commitment to subject national macroeconomic policy to EU scrutiny, through the Stability Programmes, which contain the national budgetary policy in the medium term (the current year and the three following years).

[31] See Joumard and Giorno (2005: 8, 20).

Given that the central government is responsible to the EU for complying with those limits, and given the degree of fiscal decentralization reached in Spain, this made it necessary to strengthen internal budgetary coordination mechanisms within the European framework. The tool used has been the successive Budgetary Stability Laws, initially formulated in 2002 and with a 2012 version currently in force, the "Budgetary Stability and Financial Sustainability Law" (*Ley Orgánica 2/2012, de 27 de abril, de Estabilidad Presupuestaria y Sostenibilidad Financiera—LOEPSF*). This latest version of the budgetary stability law is motivated by the reform of article 135 of the Spanish Constitution, carried out in September 2011 to formulate at the constitutional level the obligation of all public administrations to maintain structural budget balances, except in the exceptional cases provided for in the LOEPSF itself.[32] These cases allow separation from the budgetary balance only in situations of serious economic recession or emergency situations, due to natural disasters or any other cause beyond the control of the public administrations. Apart from the obligation to respect budgetary stability, understood as structural budget balances or budgets close to balance, and control of the Public Debt/GDP ratio, the LOEPSF establishes a spending rule, in the sense that the growth of expenditure in all public administrations must not exceed the medium-term GDP growth rate. As we will see later, this rule has been important, especially for local governments.

The process of setting budgetary policy begins with the Stability Programme presented by Spain to the EU, which contains the maximum projected deficit for the Spanish Public Sector as a whole, disaggregated by levels of government. The medium-term budgetary policy proposal is presented to National Parliament by the central government, which must previously request the report from the CPFF (which proposes the deficit and debt path of the Autonomous Communities) and from the "National Commission of Local Administration" (*Comisión Nacional de Administración Local—CNAL*), which proposes the path corresponding to local governments. In all cases, the recommendations and opinions of the supervisory bodies of the EU must also be taken into account. It is the National Parliament that finally approves the medium-term budgetary path for the Spanish Public Sector as a whole.

[32] Only for the central government and the Autonomous Communities. Local governments must present balanced budgets at all times.

The central government formulates a proposal for the distribution of the regional deficit objectives among the different Autonomous Communities and the CPFF must give its opinion on this proposal. Although the CPFF must obligatorily issue its report on it, it is the central government that finally sets the debt and deficit objectives for each Autonomous Community. In practice, except for one year, the objective set for the Autonomous Communities as a whole has been the one established for each of them.

Any public administration that fails to meet its deficit or debt objectives or the spending rule must formulate an "Economic and Financial Plan" (*Plan Económico-Financiero—PEF*), explaining the reasons for non-compliance, specifying the measures to be applied to return to the path of stability and the timetable for its implementation. If the central government is the noncompliant one, its PEF will be presented to the National Parliament for its approval. If the noncompliant is an Autonomous Community, its PEF will be submitted to the CPFF for approval and subsequent follow-up. Non-compliance by a local government means submitting a PEF of the same characteristics indicated above to its Autonomous Community, if this latter has assumed the powers of local financial supervision in its Autonomy Statute, or to the Ministry of Finance, in the other case. In either case, the CNAL is informed. Sanctions are contemplated in the event that any public administration fails to comply with its obligations to submit a PEF or fails to comply with the provisions thereof, which may amount to a fine of 0.2% of its GDP.

As can be seen in Table 5, for the period 2007–2017, except for the surplus of 2.2% of GDP recorded in 2007, there has been a deficit in the remaining years due to the effects of the 2008 crisis, to which we will refer later.

In the most recent period, starting in 2012, with the entry into force of the current version of the LOEPSF, the most striking fact is the change of sign of the budgetary policy of local governments, which since 2012 have been in surplus, with an average annual value of 0.5% of GDP. Three factors contribute to explain this result. First, the fact that local governments largely base their revenues on a property tax (IBI) levied on cadastral values, which have maintained their value in the period. Second, and to a large extent, the application of the spending rule to these governments. And third, the fact that, as we have explained above, there are no exceptional circumstances that allow local governments to evade the obligation of budgetary equilibrium.

Table 5 Deficit as a percent of GDP, 2007–2017

	2007	*2008*	*2009*	*2010*	*2011*	*2012*	*2013*	*2014*	*2015*	*2016*	*2017*
Central Government	1.3	−2.8	−9.3	−5.0	−5.1	−4.26	−4.52	−3.55	−2.71	−2.48	−1.86
Autonomous Communities	−0.2	−1.6	−2.0	−3.5	−2.9	−1.87	−1.58	−1.78	−1.73	−0.84	−0.32
Local Governments	−0.2	−0.5	−0.6	−0.6	−0.4	0.32	0.55	0.53	0.42	0.61	0.59
Social Security	1.3	0.8	0.8	−0.2	−0.1	−0.98	−1.13	−1.04	−1.21	−1.59	−1.48
Total Public Sector	2.2	−4.1	−11.1	−9.3	−8.5	−6.79	−6.67	−5.84	−5.23	−4.29	−3.07

Source Ministry of Finance

The deficit of the Autonomous Communities has been gradually reduced, greatly influenced by the behaviour of some Autonomous Communities of great economic and demographic weight, which have registered deficits (Catalonia and Valencian Community, in particular). Also since 2014, the central government deficit has been significantly reduced, due to the combined effect of the LOEPSF rules and the effects of the economic recovery.

When analyzing the constitutional reform of September 2011, enshrining budgetary stability, it must be realized that it began to be applied in a context of significant economic difficulties. The crisis starting in 2008 had deep effects on the subcentral deficit and debt in Spain. The fall in revenues associated with the crisis caused significant delays in payments to suppliers, deteriorating the situation of the private sector. At the same time, the locking of the financial markets made it practically impossible to finance the deficit through debt issues or bank loans. The lesson of that period was that market discipline does not act gradually, making the credit of the most indebted Autonomous Communities more expensive, but rather abruptly cuts off credit flows to all subcentral governments, without discriminating as to their level of indebtedness.

In order to reconcile the new stability framework with the financial problems of that moment, two extraordinary financing mechanisms were issued by the central government in 2012, with the purpose of allowing a gradual adjustment of the subcentral indebtedness. The first of them provided credit to meet payments to suppliers of the autonomic and local governments pending before 2012. The second mechanism, the "Autonomic Liquidity Fund" (*Fondo de Liquidez Autonómico—FLA*), was aimed at financing the autonomic deficit, in view of the locking of the financial markets.

However, these instruments, initially conceived as extraordinary mechanisms, which made sense as a practical solution for gradually approaching budgetary stability, were modified in 2014, creating the so-called "Fund for Financing Autonomous Communities" (*Fondo de Financiación a Comunidades Autónomas—FFCCAA*) mainly to set up the FLA as a permanent financing instrument, intended both to finance the current deficit, and deviations from the deficit of previous years. Bearing in mind, moreover, that in several years the interest rate on these loans has been set at 0% and the repayment term has been extended, the result is that a "soft budget constraint" has been created with this mechanism. A "Local Entities Financing Fund" was also created in the same reform.[33]

A recent report by the Spanish Court of Auditors (*Tribunal de Cuentas*) shows that 37% of the total resources of the FFCCAA were used in 2015 to finance deficit deviations from previous years and that in 2016 this percentage was 19.3% (Court of Auditors, 2019: 27). Although the regions that obtain funding from the FFCCAA are subject to conditionality requirements and must present a PEF, describing the adjustment measures to be adopted and the deadline for returning to the situation of budgetary equilibrium, experience shows that the PEFs of the noncompliant Autonomous Communities are repeatedly altered and new PEFs are formulated, which place the goal of budgetary equilibrium on a longer time horizon.

From a critical perspective, it is somewhat paradoxical that the setting of the objective of budgetary sustainability at the constitutional level in 2011, when accompanied by financial facility instruments, initially designed to operate temporarily—so that the most indebted Autonomous Communities would gradually re-establish their budgetary situation—has resulted in the creation of incentives for a, seemingly permanent, soft budget constraint.

As the most noncompliant Autonomous Communities have absorbed the majority of the FFCCAA (out of a total of 148,597 million € provided to the fifteen Autonomous Communities under the common regime between 2012 and 2016, the two most indebted represent more than 50% of the total: Catalonia, with 50,037 million € and Valencian Community, with 34,225 million €) and have replaced loans from financial institutions with loans from the FLA, market discipline has ceased to function at the regional level. There is also the anomalous situation that the central government is the main and almost the only lender of the most

[33] According to Royal Decree-Law 17/2014, which created the FFCCAA, the supplier payment fund has remained a mechanism to be extinguished and the FFCCAA is divided into three "compartments": the "Financial Facility" (*Facilidad Financiera*), for regions that meet their deficit and debt objectives and the period of payment to suppliers; the new FLA, for noncompliant regions and the "Social Fund" (*Fondo Social*), which finances the payment of the outstanding obligations of the autonomous governments to local governments, in the area of social spending. The Local Entities Financing Fund is divided into two compartiments: The "Ordination Fund" (*Fondo de Ordenación*), for local governments at financial risk, and the "Economic Impulse Fund" (*Fondo de Impulso Económico*), for compliant local governments.

indebted autonomous governments, with the added problem of making intergovernmental political relations more intricate.

In 2018, Spain exited the EU's Excessive Deficit Procedure (EDP), as its deficit was below the European reference value of 3% of GDP. However, several regional governments are still excessively dependent on the FLA and should reduce their high level of indebtedness, due to the high interest rate risk they will face when the ECB proceeds to normalize interest rates, with the consequent effect on the cost of debt.

Finally, it should be noted that investments by subcentral governments have been the main budgetary adjustment tool following the economic crisis of 2008. Subsequently, when the effects of the economic recovery have been felt, from 2013 onwards, the spending rule has meant that the growth in current expenditure (salaries and supplies) has left no room for investment by local treasuries, despite the fact that, as seen above, these have been in a continuous surplus position since 2012.

6 Challenges to Fiscal Federalism

Spain has undergone a fast and deep process of decentralization since the late 1970s. Over this period, what was a rigidly centralized country has emerged as one of the most decentralized in the world, in which sub-national governments play a fundamental role in the provision of the public goods and services that are closest to the lives of citizens and are most likely to affect their welfare. A growing body of evidence confirms that decentralization is contributing to improve the provision of goods and services such as education, health or infrastructure (Solé-Ollé, 2009), although its effects on inequality are less clear.

The Great Recession has had a harsh impact on the intergovernmental relations in Spain, calling into question the assignment of responsibilities and revenues between levels of government. For some observers, central government intervention in many areas of responsibility of Autonomous Communities remains too high and has increased during the recent economic crisis, effectively reducing sub-national autonomy (Viver and Martín, 2012). Consequently, there have been demands for the further clarification of the division of responsibilities between levels of government and increased recognition and respect for subcentral competences.

On the revenue side, there are widespread demands for a new revision of the revenue assignments at the regional and local levels. In 2017, two commissions of experts were appointed—one for regional financing and the other for local financing—which produced reports that same year offering a diagnostic of the main problems and offering reform proposals (Ministerio de Hacienda, 2018). Although no progress has been made since then, it is very likely that a new reform of regional and local financing will be tackled in the short-medium term. This reform will have to address the problems that have been on the table for a long time, some of which are briefly discussed below. For reasons of space, we will limit ourselves to those at the regional level.

As we have seen in the previous sections, although the decentralization of tax sources has lagged behind expenditure responsibilities, progress in this area has been very significant. However, there are still some avenues open for deepening tax decentralization. In the first place, it is possible to further increase the allocated share in some ceded taxes (e.g., excises). Secondly, since European Union regulations prevent the existence of regional differentiated VAT rates, the Autonomous Communities can be allocated the power to collectively decide the common regional VAT rate as is done, with different qualifications, in countries such as Australia or Canada. In this way, the Autonomous Communities could face symmetrical economic shocks, enacting policy changes in both direct and indirect taxes.

The third way forward is more ambitious. As we have seen, ceded taxes are characterized by having a common regulation imposed by the central level, although in some cases the Autonomous Communities have the power to establish the tax rate and tax credits and allowances. This formula does not differ substantially from that followed in other federal countries, in which, although regional governments have more powers over their taxes, in practice they seek to harmonize their basic elements. The fundamental difference is that in these countries tax harmonization is voluntary, while in the case of ceded taxes it is imposed by the central level. Within this framework, a possible reform would consist of extending the powers of the Autonomous Communities in the ceded taxes, favouring harmonization between regions, but not imposing it.

Finally, there is also a broad consensus on the need to ensure greater participation of the Autonomous Communities under the common regime in tax administration, participation which is currently very limited, as shown in Table 3.

The above measures may contribute to further reducing the dependence of the Autonomous Communities under the common regime on central transfers, to make possible the existence of greater asymmetries between regions in tax regulations and management (as some Communities claim) and to reduce the enormous differences that still exist between the common regime and foral regime Communities.

Vertical fiscal imbalances remain an issue of debate. Regional (and local) governments have continued to complain about the lack of sufficient funding and have demanded (and frequently have received) additional funding from the central government, being less important whether these funds came as transfers or as an increase in tax decentralization. Beyond the issues of whether regional governments have been assigned adequate autonomous tax sources and how much they have been predisposed to use these sources, we note two things here that are clearly quite decisive in resolving any issue of vertical imbalances. First, that all regional expenditure responsibilities have been devolved by mutual agreement between the regional and central governments, after using the "effective cost method" as a way to derive expenditure needs. Second, it remains a disputed issue and in no case has it been conclusively demonstrated that the evolution of central and regional revenues has resulted in any vertical fiscal imbalance to the detriment of the Autonomous Communities.

The incentives and behaviour of the regional and central governments further contribute to muddle the issue of vertical imbalances. Regional governments in Spain have been operating under a soft budget constraint. Concerning expenditure responsibilities, citizens see the central government as ultimately responsible for the delivery of certain regional services, such as health and education. As far as revenue is concerned, as we discussed in the previous section, the extraordinary funding mechanisms introduced from 2012 onwards, and especially the Fund for Financing Autonomous Communities, have also contributed to the softening of the Autonomous Communities budget constraint. On the other hand, the central government sometimes has taken decisions de facto involving unfunded expenditure mandates for the Autonomous Communities in certain expenditure programmes. In other occasions, the central government has undertaken tax reforms which have had a significant impact on the revenues of regional governments, for example reducing the yield of various (ceded) regional taxes, without compensation or counterbalancing measures.

With regard to the correction of horizontal fiscal imbalances, the current system of intergovernmental financing provides a strong level of equalization between regions under the common system, but only for the so-called fundamental public services. It would be desirable to extend the equalization system to the other services of the Autonomous Communities, and to reduce the numerous transfers that now exist to a single one, in order to gain in simplicity and transparency.

Determining the degree of regional equalization is the issue of greatest conflict between Autonomous Communities. This is ultimately a political decision with positions naturally taken according to who benefits and who pays. Beneficiary regions support full equalization on the grounds of solidarity, while those regions with the highest fiscal capacity point to the disincentive and efficiency effects of high levels of equalization and support, at most, a partial level of equalization that guarantees, in any case, the fulfilment of the "principle of ordinality".

The asymmetric treatment of common regime and charter regions continues to be a thorny issue. The Spanish Constitution permits the existence of two financing systems with very different structures. However, the Constitution does not allow the results of the two systems to differ; that is, for Autonomous Communities with the same expenditure responsibilities to provide different levels of public services depending on whether they receive funding under the common or charter regime. As we have already explained, the literature has clearly identified the shortcomings of the charter system and how to resolve them. An obvious measure, among others, would be to involve the charter regions, probably gradually, in the system of equalization with the rest of the Autonomous Communities.

From the point of view of macroeconomic management, the Fund for Financing Autonomous Communities should be reformed so as to stop financing deficit deviations. It would also be necessary to call for greater compliance with the Economic and Financial Plans, in order to prevent its repeated modification (and prolongation). To reinforce this last aspect, it could be interesting to study the possible application of bankruptcy mechanisms to subcentral governments, in exceptional cases, as they currently exist in some other countries (Harold, 2018).

Finally, and from an institutional point of view, a reform of the Fiscal and Financial Policy Council (CPFF), whose recommendations always depend on the agreement of the central government, also seems necessary. The position of the Autonomous Communities should be strengthened in those issues that are of their preferential or exclusive interest, such as the distribution of the overall deficit objective of the Autonomous Communities among the different regions.

Acknowledgements The authors would like to thank Jean-François Tremblay for his comments and suggestions, which have helped to improve the chapter. Julio López-Laborda acknowledges the financial support of the Regional Government of Aragón (Public Economics Research Group).

References

Agrawal, D. R. and D. Foremny (2019). "Relocation of the Rich: Migration in Response to Top Tax Rate Changes from Spanish Reforms". *Review of Economics and Statistics*, 101 (2): 214–232.

Bird, R. (1993). "Threading the Fiscal Labyrinth: Some Issues in Fiscal Decentralization". *National Tax Journal*, 46: 207–227.

Blöchliger, H. and M. Nettley (2015). "Sub-central Tax Autonomy: 2011 Update". *OECD Working Papers on Fiscal Federalism*, 20, Paris: OECD Publishing.

Bosch, N. and A. Solé-Ollé (2007). "Yardstick Competition and the Political Costs of Raising Taxes: An Empirical Analysis of Spanish Municipalities". *International Tax and Public Finance*, 14 (1): 71–92.

De la Fuente, Á. (2018). "La liquidación de 2016 del sistema de financiación de las comunidades autónomas de régimen común". *Estudios sobre la Economía Española*, 2018/19, Madrid: FEDEA.

Delgado, F. J., S. Lago-Peñas and M. Mayor (2015). "On the Determinants of Local Tax Rates: New Evidence from Spain". *Contemporary Economic Policy*, 33 (2): 351–368.

Harold, K. (2018). "Insolvency Frameworks for Sub-national Governments". *OECD Working Papers on Fiscal Federalism,* 23, Paris: OECD Publishing. https://doi.org/10.1787/f9874122-en.

Jofre-Monseny, J. and A. Solé-Ollé (2010). "Tax Differentials in Intraregional Firm Location: Evidence from New Manufacturing Establishments in Spanish Municipalities". *Regional Studies*, 44 (6): 663–677.

Joumard, I. and C. Giorno (2005). "Getting the Most Out of Public Sector Decentralisation in Spain". *OECD Economics Department Working Paper*, 436, Paris: OECD Publishing.

Lago-Peñas, S. and J. Martinez-Vazquez, coord. (2009). *La asignación de impuestos a las Comunidades Autónomas: desafíos y oportunidades*. Madrid: Instituto de Estudios Fiscales.

Lago-Peñas, S. and J. Martinez-Vazquez, eds. (2011). *Las transferencias intergubernamentales en España: análisis y propuestas de reforma*. Madrid: Instituto de Estudios Fiscales.

Lago-Peñas, S. and J. Martinez-Vazquez, coord. (2015). *La nueva reforma de la financiación autonómica: análisis y propuestas. Papeles de Economia Española*, 143.

Leal, A., J. López-Laborda and F. Rodrigo (2009). "Prices, Taxes and Automotive Fuel Cross-border Shopping". *Energy Economics*, 31 (2): 225–234.

López-Laborda, J. and C. Monasterio (2007). "Regional Governments: Vertical Imbalances and Revenue Assignments". In J. Martínez-Vázquez and J.F. Sanz (eds.), *Fiscal Reform in Spain*, pp. 422–452, Cheltenham, UK: Edward Elgar.

López-Laborda, J. and F. Rodrigo (2022). "Mobility of Top Income Taxpayers in Response to Regional Differences in Personal Taxes: Evidence from Spain" *Economics*, 16 (1): 152–169.

Ministerio de Hacienda (2018). *Reforma de la financiación territorial: informes de las comisiones de expertos de 2017*, Madrid: Instituto de Estudios Fiscales. https://www.ief.es/docs/destacados/publicaciones/libros/lb/2018_ReformaFinanciacionTerritorial.pdf.

Monasterio, C. (2010). *El laberinto de la Hacienda Autonómica*, Cizur Menor: Thomson Reuters.

Pedraja, F., J. Salinas and J. Suárez-Pandiello (2007). "Financing Local Governments: The Spanish Experience". In J. Martínez-Vázquez and J.F. Sanz (eds.), *Fiscal Reform in* Spain, pp. 453–483, Cheltenham: Edward Elgar.

Pedraja, F and J. Suárez-Pandiello (2004). "La última reforma de la participación municipal en los tributos del estado. Un análisis cualitativo". *Papeles de Economía Española*, 100: 77–92.

Solé-Ollé, A. (2009). "Decentralization and Service Delivery: The Spanish Case". In G. Brosio and E. Ahamad (eds.), *Does Decentralization Enhance Service Delivery and Poverty Reduction?* pp. 257–284, Cheltenham, UK: Edward Elgar.

Tribunal de Cuentas (2019). *Informe de fiscalización del Fondo de financiación a Comunidades Autónomas. Ejercicios 2015 y 2016*. https://www.tcu.es/repositorio/074d5101-3e05-4c73-8b08-a41e583b8dc9/I1301.pdf.

Viver, C. and G. Martín (2012). "The Recentralisation Proces of the State of Autonomies". *IEB's Report on Fiscal Federalism,* 12: 46–59.

Wallich, C., ed. (1994). *Russia and the Challenge of Fiscal Federalism*. Washington D.C.: The World Bank.

Zabalza, A. and J. López-Laborda (2011). "The New Spanish system of Intergovernmental Transfers". *International Tax and Public Finance*, 18: 750–786.

Zabalza, A. and J. López-Laborda (2017). "The Uneasy Coexistence of the Spanish Foral and Common Regional Finance Systems". *Investigaciones Regionales—Journal of Regional Research*, 37: 119–152.

Zubiri, I. (2000). *El Sistema de Concierto Económico en el contexto de la Unión Europea*. Bilbao: Círculo de Empresarios Vascos.

Zubiri, I. (2015). "Un análisis del sistema foral de la Comunidad Autónoma del País Vasco y sus ventajas durante la crisis". *Papeles de Economía Española*, 143: 205–224.

Switzerland

Christoph A. Schaltegger and Lukas A. Schmid

1 Introduction

Despite its comparatively small territory, Switzerland has an extensive federal structure.[1] Its subnational jurisdictions, the cantons, enjoy wide-ranging political and fiscal freedom. The high degree of autonomy is extended to the local level and based on the principle of subsidiarity—the idea that tasks should only be centralized if local or subnational authorities cannot perform them effectively. In addition, the Swiss political system grants the most extensive political rights to its citizens worldwide. Initiatives and referenda are institutionalized in all three tiers of government: local, cantonal, and federal.

Comparatively, the fiscal autonomy of lower-tier governments is particularly extensive on the revenue side of the budget. Apart from subnational jurisdictions in Canada, Swiss cantons and municipalities are granted the

[1] See Federal Chancellery (2019) or Linder (2010) for detailed accounts of the Swiss political system.

C. A. Schaltegger (✉)
University of Lucerne, Lucerne, Switzerland
e-mail: christoph.schaltegger@unilu.ch

L. A. Schmid
Avenir Suisse, Zürich, Switzerland

J.-F. Tremblay (ed.), *The Forum of Federations Handbook of Fiscal Federalism*, https://doi.org/10.1007/978-3-030-97258-5_10

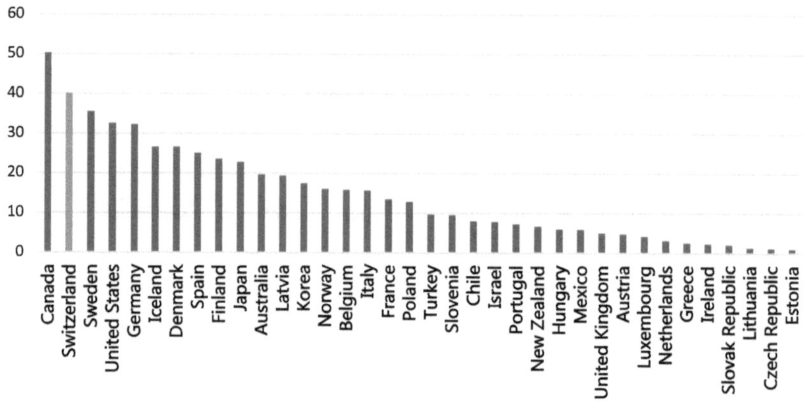

Fig. 1 Tax decentralization OECD countries (2017): subnational tax revenue in % of general government tax revenue (incl. social security revenue) (*Source* OECD revenue statistics)

most autonomy with respect to tax policy (see Fig. 1). However, given the semi-direct-democratic system, tax changes by cantonal governments and parliaments are usually subject to public approval. In addition to participatory institutions, Switzerland has an internationally unmatched degree of administrative (jurisdictional) fragmentation (see Fig. 2).

This unique combination has several implications: Fiscal responsibility, referenda, and budget rules induce efficiency in expenditure, high-tax compliance, and satisfaction of regional preferences. Tax competition restricts excess supply of public goods and services. A comprehensive redistributive framework at the federal level sets boundaries to ensure that tax competition is not at the expense of fiscally weaker cantons. This chapter emphasizes the distinctive features of the Swiss fiscal federal system and discusses empirical evidence on its implications as well as recent policy developments.

2 Switzerland: Facts and Figures[2]

Although Switzerland is small, with a land area of 41,285 km^2 (15,940 sq. miles) and a population of 8.5 million people, its constituent parts,

[2] This second part of our chapter largely relies on Kirchgässner (2007).

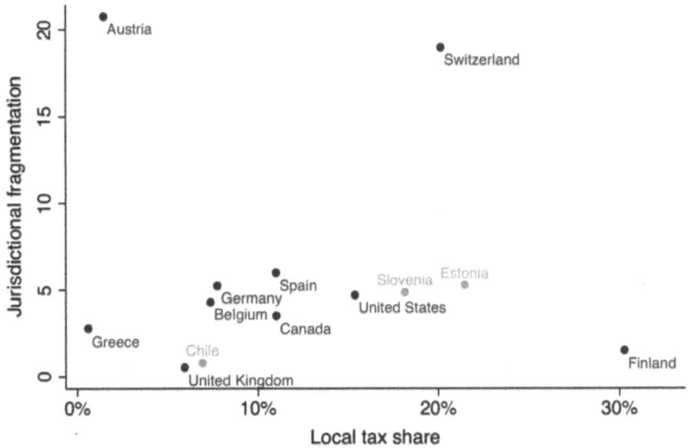

Fig. 2 Tax shares at local level and jurisdictional fragmentation (*Source* Brülhart et al. [2015, Fig. 17.8]. Jurisdictional fragmentation: average number of municipalities per 100,000 inhabitants. ALTS: local tax revenue with real tax autonomy; LTS: all local tax revenuee)

the 26 cantons, are remarkably different (see Fig. 3).[3] It has four official national languages along with the corresponding cultures: 63% speak (Swiss) German; 23%, French; 8%, Italian; and 0.5%, Romansh. English, Portuguese and Albanian are the predominant foreign languages.

With respect to religion, more than two-thirds of the Swiss population claim affiliation to Christianity with a relative majority of Roman Catholics (37% of the population) over Protestants (25%) and other Christian denominations (6%). The residents who are not members of any religion have been on the rise for several years and now amount to a quarter of the population. Islamic denominations make up for about 5% of the population.

Almost 25% of the population are foreigners. This is a higher percentage than in any other country in Europe (apart from some microstates such as Monaco or Liechtenstein). Given the linguistic,

[3] If not indicated otherwise, statistics in the introduction are drawn from Federal Chancellery (2019).

Swiss Confederation

Constitution	Republic, founded in 1848, current constitution in effect since 2000
Status of local governments	Autonomy guaranteed by cantonal constitutions
Official languages	German, French, Italian, Romansh
Population (2018)	8.5 Million
Area	41'285 km2
p.c. GDP (2016)	78'900 CHF

Cantons (26)	Population (2018)	Area (km2)	p.c. GDP CHF (2016)	Languages
Zurich (ZH)	1'520'968	1729	93'742	German
Berne (BE)	1'031'126	5959	76'210	G, French
Lucerne (LU)	406'506	1493	66'611	G
Uri (UR)	36'299	1077	52'827	G
Schwyz (SZ)	157'301	908	59'925	G
Obwalden (OW)	37'575	491	66'878	G
Nidwalden (NW)	42'969	276	69'048	G
Zug (ZG)	125'421	685	67'852	G
Glarus (GL)	40'349	239	153'895	G
Fribourg (FR)	315'074	1671	59'391	F, G
Solothum (SO)	271'432	791	65'396	G
Basel-Stadt (BS)	193'908	37	173'185	G
Basel-Land (BL)	287'023	518	68'811	G
Schaffhausen (SH)	81'351	298	87'083	G
Appenzell-Ausserrhoden (AR)	55'178	243	56'237	G
Appenzell-Innerrhoden (AI)	16'105	173	62'128	G
St. Gallen (SG)	504'686	2026	72'884	G
Grisons (GR)	197'888	7105	71'914	G, Romansh, I
Aargau (AG)	670'988	1404	61'867	G
Thurgau (TG)	273'801	991	60'834	G
Ticino (TI)	353'709	2812	83'416	Italian
Vaud (VD)	793'129	3212	72'232	F
Valais (VS)	341'463	5224	53'276	F, G
Neuchatel (NE)	177'964	803	85'276	F
Geneva (GE)	495'249	282	98'350	F
Jura (JUR)	73'290	838	62'341	F

Fig. 3 Switzerland and its cantons (*Source* Federal Statistics Office [2018])

cultural, and religious heterogeneity, Switzerland is a nation shaped by the resolve of its citizens and is well aware of its many diversities.[4]

The federal roots trace back to the thirteenth century when the three primary cantons—Uri, Schwyz, and Unterwalden—entered into a treaty. In 1848 the modern Swiss Confederation was founded and the current federal structure was institutionalized after a short civil war between the Protestants and Catholic separatists (known as the *Sonderbundkrieg*). The fact that Switzerland did not split up along its linguistic divisions in the second half of the nineteenth century (when its neighbors, Italy and Germany, created their national states) is presumably owed to its rather decentralized federal structure. The other key ingredients that constitute the Swiss nation are its direct democracy and its political neutrality in international affairs.

The cantons vary greatly in size and in population density (see Fig. 3). The average canton has about 325,000 people, but population sizes range from 16,100 in Appenzell Innerrhoden to 1.5 million in Zurich. The average population density is 205 people per km^2. Compared with some other European countries such as Belgium or the Netherlands this might not seem low. However, Switzerland's territory is diverse with

[4] In German, there is a specific term that refers to the kind of state Switzerland is: a "nation of will" (Willensnation).

some densely populated area such as the "Mittelland", a narrow tract that stretches from Lake Geneva to the Lake of Constance and includes most of the medium-sized cities as well as Zurich and its suburbs. North and west of the Mittelland bordering France are the Jura Mountains, to the south and east are the Alps. Large parts of these mountainous areas are unproductive and, as a result, quite sparsely populated.

Given the volatile economic environment in Europe, recent economic activity in Switzerland has recorded solid growth rates of GDP between 1 and 3%. With the exception of 2009 when owing to the financial crisis, growth was negative, GDP has grown since the end of 1990s with foreign trade playing a key role (FSO 2018). Based on purchasing power, international comparisons show that Switzerland is the fourth richest country in the world with GDP per capita amounting to 68,105 US-Dollars (PPP) lagging behind Luxembourg, Singapore and Ireland only (OECD 2019).

Within Switzerland, however, there are substantial economic discrepancies. In 2016, the average per capita GDP was 78,869 Swiss Francs (median per capita GDP was 68,332 Francs) with the canton Basel-Stadt being 120% above and the canton of Uri being 33% below the national average (FSO 2018). Although the discrepancies used to be larger, they remain a source of public and political controversy.

3 The Structure of Government and the Division of Fiscal Power

The Swiss federal system is characterized by the widespread autonomy of its subfederal jurisdictions, the 26 cantons, guaranteed by several articles in the federal constitution (namely Art. 3, 5a, 43, 47 and 48). The latter grants great freedom with respect to the cantons' political systems. Their constitutions are merely required to be democratic, not contradict federal law and allow for revisions if a majority of the electorate demands. In order to finance expenditure for those tasks, the cantons can levy their own income and property taxes (see *V. Public revenue*). They are free to decide not only on the tax rates but also on the tax schedule as well as on how progressive these taxes are. The Confederation has authority only in those areas in which it is empowered by the federal Constitution (e.g., foreign affairs, defense, customs, and monetary policy) meaning that tasks that do not explicitly fall within the scope of the Confederation are handled by the cantons. Table 1 provides an overview of the distribution of responsibilities between the respective levels of government.

Table 1 Distribution of responsibilities between the three levels of government

Federal responsibilities Based on federal constitution	*Cantonal responsibilities Based on cantonal constitutions*	*Municipal responsibilities depending on cantonal legislation*
Organization of federal authorities	Organization of cantonal auth	Waste management
Foreign affairs	Cross-border cooperation	Municipal roads
Army and civil protection	Police	Local infrastructure
National roads (highways)	Relations betw. state and religion	Local police
Nuclear energy	Culture	Zoning
Postal services and telecommun.	Public health	Citizenship
Monetary policy	Cantonal roads	Municipal taxes
Education: technical universities	Education: secondary school, universities	Education: kindergarten, primary school
Social security	Forests, water, natural resources	
Civil law, criminal law	Cantonal taxes	
Customs	Citizenship	
Principles for zoning and environmental protection	Protection of environment, nature, and heritage	
Principles for citizenship		
Energy policy		
Federal taxes		

Source Linder (2010)

Each canton has its own constitution, parliament, government, and courts. The cantonal parliaments have between 50 and 180 members who are elected based on the system of proportional representation. The cantonal governments have five or seven members. They are directly elected in majority systems by the people at the ballot box except for the government in the canton Appenzell Innerrhoden, where the annual general assembly (Landsgemeinde) elects the government in April.[5] In all other cantons elections take place every four or five years.

Despite multiple shared responsibilities with the federal government—usually assigned by the federal Constitution—cantons act independently in many policy fields to a large extent. Among other fields, high degree of autonomy is guaranteed in education, health, police, law and courts as

[5] The only other canton holding an annual general assembly is Glarus. However, in contrast to AI, the government is elected by secret ballot.

well as transport, cultural service, social assistance, energy supply, or waste (water) management. Many of those fields are shaped by local policies on the municipal level. As of 2019, there were 2,212 municipalities. In recent years, a decreasing trend has emerged due to mergers that often are encouraged by financial incentives set by cantonal governments or parliaments. Around one-fifth of municipalities have their own parliament; in the other four-fifths, decisions are taken by direct democracy in a local assembly.

The scope of local autonomy is determined by the respective canton and, therefore, varies considerably. However, given the autonomy for local government provided in the cantonal constitutions, neither the cantons nor the federal authorities have the right to interfere with local decisions. The only exception occurs when the financial situation of a local commune deteriorates seriously. In such a case, the local budget has to be approved by the cantonal government.

3.1 Federal Scope of Responsibilities and Its Evolution

After the foundation of the modern Swiss state in 1848, the federal government's scope of powers was extended in three waves (e.g. Blöchlinger and Frey 1992). In an early phase, common foreign and military policy were developed and the foundations for a common market were laid. Social policy was enshrined into federal law in several steps during the interwar period and shortly after World War II (Sommer 1978). In a third step, the federal level was endowed with public responsibilities emerging in 1960s and 1970s such as energy, highway, environmental policy and regional development planning.

As a result, the once distinctive division of responsibilities has subsequently been overruled by the mechanisms of intensive cooperation between the three levels of the federal system creating a broad array of shared responsibilities (Linder 2010). In primary education, for example, many cantons grant their municipalities wide-ranging autonomy. At the same time, the federation sets standards for the duration of compulsory school attendance, school entrance age, or the duration of and objectives for different levels of education. While secondary education largely remains a cantonal responsibility, there is a strong federal impact on tertiary education with two federal universities (Swiss Federal Institutes of Technology in Zurich and Lausanne) and research funding being a federal task. In addition, the federal government subsidizes the cantonal universities depending on the number of students enrolled.

Similarly, the federal government has a large impact on health policy that is formally in the domain of the cantons by setting the legal framework for the (private) health insurance (Feld et al., 2017b). Yet the provision of health services such as hospitals is ensured by the cantons and municipalities. Responsibilities for social welfare are split, too. Despite consistent political pressure to harmonize social assistance, it has remained a cantonal and local task. Social insurance such as the pension system or unemployment insurance, however, essentially is a federal task except for the supplementary benefits to old age and disability pensions, which is shared with the cantons. Hence, most cantonal responsibilities are in the provision of public consumption and investment goods rather than social protection or the transfer system although this «principle» is violated in various ways. The federation is more involved in the redistribution of income given its responsibilities with regard to social protection and regional or agricultural policy.

Figure 4 shows the governmental division of expenditure by various functions. Although insightful for public spending analysis, it ignores the

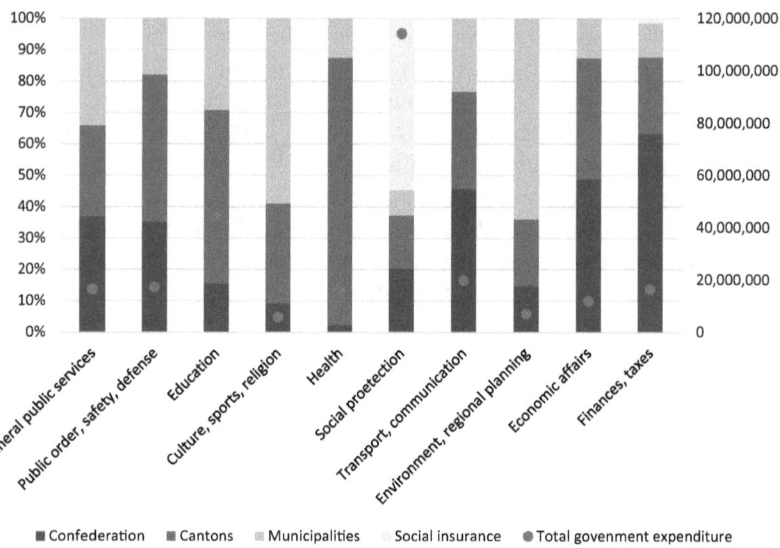

Fig. 4 Expenditure share by level of government (left axis) and total government expenditure in 1,000 CHF (right axis) by function in 2017. Data: Federal Finance Administration

high degree of integration between the three levels of government in different policy fields. As mentioned above already, this is particularly striking for health. The federal government's impact on health policy is significantly larger than its share of expenditure suggests. This is an example of where the central government exhausts or even exceeds its legislative powers at the expense of the subnational jurisdictions that are reduced to executing superior legislation. In order to strengthen their position toward the federal government, the cantons have formed the conference of cantonal governments as well as policy-specific conferences of ministers (e.g. finance, health, education) often resulting in expenditure and revenue sharing agreements with the federal government.

3.2 Issues with Centralization

While the conferences of cantonal governments and ministers are a legitimate measure to represent interests[6] and co-ordinate cantonal arrangements in policy fields in which they have significant responsibility, increasing revenue and expenditure sharing (further) undermine fiscal equivalence and direct democracy. As the conferences grow more important, they establish an intermediate level of government between the Confederation and cantons resulting in a power shift from cantonal legislature to executives (Rother and Rühli 2017). In a direct-democratic system, this development is problematic because it restricts parliamentary responsibilities and undermines the fact that there is little room for direct statutory interference between the different levels of government.[7] In addition, their decisions have centralizing character because they imply a national consensus from which it is more difficult to deviate, likely changing the odds of winning a referendum. Similarly, increasingly powerful conferences impair the principle of fiscal equivalence that establishes a multi-level government setting by "perfect mapping" uniting

[6] Until mid-twentieth century most members of the Council of States, the Swiss equivalent to the US Senate, were appointed or elected by cantonal governments or assemblies, respectively. As actual representatives of the cantonal governments they directly vouched for their canton's interest.

[7] For example, the federal government cannot take repercussions (e.g. in the form of withholding grants) against cantons that do not implement federal provisions. The Federal Supreme Court in Lausanne, only, has the power to declare cantonal legislation unconstitutional. However, on the federal level, it cannot investigate into the constitutionality of legislation.

those who fund, benefit from, and determine policy. Although "inequivalence" is prevalent in practice, additional deviation from the principle could threaten accountability or bureaucracy benefits of decentralization.

The tendency of more sharing agreements has two implications: First, the politically painful process of disentangling responsibilities between federal and cantonal level can be postponed further. Second, the procedural provisions that protect the centralization of taxes and tasks such as popular initiative and the referendum are partially impaired.[8] In particular, the latter is commonly considered a safeguard against centralization.[9] On the federal level, the signatures of 50,000 citizens are sufficient to call for a petition or veto referendum on any new national legislation. Constitutional changes are subject to a mandatory referendum vote.[10] The Swiss electorate votes on the resulting policy proposals that appear on the ballot for approval or disapproval three to four times per year.

Despite these institutional barriers and efforts to disentangle responsibilities in a large reform in 2008 the trend to centralize persists. Out of 159 changes in jurisdictional responsibilities between 2000 and 2016 none—apart from the reform itself—constituted a decentralization (Fässler et al. 2017). While 25% of changes devolved formerly cantonal responsibilities to the federal level, 75% concerned changes from formerly cantonal to shared tasks. The reform whose purpose was to strengthen the subsidiary structure of the Swiss system revealed how difficult the process of disentanglement is. Although a number of responsibilities were allocated to a new, single level of government, many tasks remained integrated due to political compromise.

Centralization is the longer the more accepted as the inevitable outcome of the increasingly globalized and independent world (Rother and Rühli 2017). To many, Switzerland's high degree of fragmentation seems incompatible with the associated challenges. Yet, centralization and

[8] Matsusaka (2018) defines the initiative to be a process by which citizens vote on a policy proposed by the citizens themselves and the referendum to be a process by which citizens vote on a policy proposed by government officials.

[9] In recent years popular initiatives attempting to centralize responsibilities have increased. A successful example is the approved provision that limits the share of secondary homes in every municipality at 20%.

[10] In addition, eight cantons can launch a referendum against federal legislation if they consider their interests violated. Since 1874 the cantons have (successfully) made use of this instrument once (2003).

sharing agreements are driven by the mutual interests by many (political) actors. For example, in a more transparent world, acceptance for the trial and error approach of federalism has diminished. If the public perceives the provision of cantonal public goods insufficient, calls for a federal framework follow suit. Furthermore, the erosion of local, traditional media has emphasized the significance of national politics. Therefore, politicians have an incentive to add subnational and local policy issues to the national agenda. Importantly, the cantons are also to blame for this development given their tendency to cede autonomy in return for financial reimbursements by the federal government.

4 Fiscal Federalism and Macroeconomic Management

Monetary policy is a strictly federal issue, although, in practice, the responsibility for this is delegated to the Swiss National Bank. Its independence is embodied as a principle in the Constitution. According to the National Bank Act, the SNB's main objective is to ensure price stability. In doing so, it is bound to take into account business cycle developments. After the breakdown of the Bretton Woods system in the 1970s, SNB policy focused on the quantity of money until 1999. However, as this was considered one of the factors contributing to the low growth of the Swiss economy in the second half of the 1990s it changed course. Ever since the SNB's strategy has been to attempt to keep the rate of inflation between 0 and 2%.

It is generally accepted that the SNB has been effective at achieving its main goal given that Switzerland has one of the most stable currencies in the world. From 1980 (2002) to 2018, the average inflation rate was 1.7 (0.4) percent, compared with 3.1 (2.1) percent in the United States (and percent 1.7 in the Euro area). This is also reflected in the development of the exchange rate. Since 1974, when the Swiss franc began floating against all other currencies, it has appreciated significantly against all major currencies constantly challenging the strongly export-oriented economy.

In the aftermath of the financial and European sovereign debt crisis, the SNB implemented unconventional monetary policy by ceiling the exchange rate to the Euro at 1.20 CHF as a measure against the Franc's overvaluation. The cap was introduced in September 2011 and, to the surprise of markets, scraped in January 2015. The present monetary policy environment remains challenging. Switzerland continues to be a credible safe haven forcing the SNB to keep interest rates at a record low if it wants to protect the Franc from appreciation. At the same time, high growth rates, continuously increasing investment activity and demand (particularly in parts of the real inheritance market), and the yield requirements in the pension system call for an increase in interest rates.

According to the federal constitution, stabilization policy is a federal responsibility. However, as a small open economy, the scope for fiscal policy in Switzerland is limited. Even large federal deficits, as seen in the 1990s, hardly provide an impulse to the Swiss economy (Schaltegger and Weder 2010). Automatic stabilizers such as the unemployment insurance, "short-time work" compensation, the progressive tax system or the federal debt brake have proven more successful. In addition, cantonal impulses have often been pro-cyclical and tended to cancel out each other.

In order to strengthen the cantons' fiscal discipline, the conference of the cantonal finance ministers agreed on a model law for cantonal budgeting in 1981 (Burret and Feld 2018). For the current budget the law requires a balanced budget in the medium term and a depreciation of balance sheet deficits by at least 20% p.a. For the investment budget, the law requires the self-financing ratio for net investments to be at least 80% if cantonal net debt exceeds revenue by more than 100%. The two rules are directly linked as depreciation of investments and of balance sheet deficits need to be included in the current budget. Anti-cyclicality is implicitly ensured by the provision to balance the budget in the medium term.

However, the provisions did not prevent cantonal debt from increasing considerably during the 1990s. Low economic growth rates and canton-specific fiscal shocks (e.g. bailouts of public-owned cantonal banks) undermined many cantons' fiscal position. Consequently, cantonal gross debt increased by 43% (in real terms) from 1990 to 2004, but the development varied depending on the specific canton (FFA 2018). For example, among the six cantons that recorded a real decrease in gross debt, four introduced a debt break during that period or had done so previously. At the other end of the scale, debt in Vaud and Geneva increased twofold or more. While Geneva remains the most indebted canton in per capita terms (36,400 Swiss Francs or 260% above the national average in 2017), Vaud's debt level has decreased by almost 50% both overall and per capita. Overall, cantonal gross debt is slightly lower than 15 years ago.

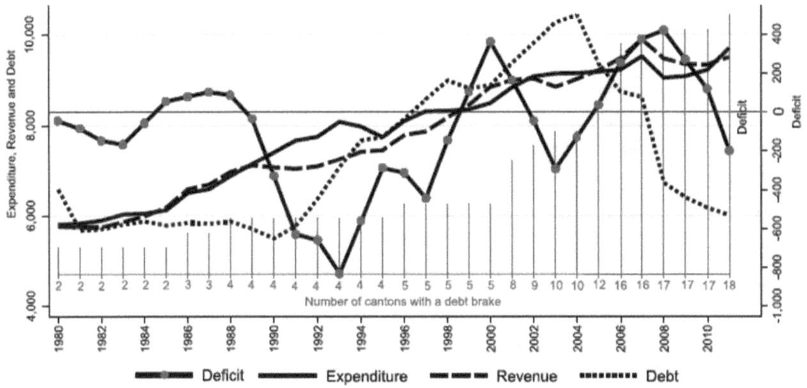

Fig. 5 Cantonal finances in real Swiss Francs per capita and the number of cantonal debt brakes 1980–2011 (*Source* Burret and Feld (2018), Fig. 1)

5 Fiscal Rules and Referenda

Although economic aggregates developed much more favorably in the 2000s, easing many cantons' debt levels, empirical evidence suggests that fiscal institutions matter (e.g. Burret and Feld 2018). Considerable decreases in debt were primarily observed subsequent to the introduction of debt breaks. Today fiscal constraints can be found in nearly all cantonal constitutions and corresponding budget laws. The fact that per capita debt remains the lowest in the only canton without any fiscal rule (AI) is most likely due to its strong direct-democratic institutions and not an indicator of the lack of effectiveness of fiscal rules.

The effectiveness of fiscal rules largely depends on their credibility. For a rule to be credible one of the following criteria needs to be fulfilled (e.g. Feld and Kirchgässner 2008; Feld et al. 2017a): (a) a link between budget planning and final accounting, or (b) a numeric deficit limit or (c) non-discretionary sanctions in the form of tax or expenditure adjustments. At present, a total of 18 cantons have adopted one or more of these requirements.

St. Gallen, for example, with its historically stringent budget rule that was introduced in 1929 fulfills all three requirements. Requirement (a) is satisfied by the provision that a current deficit in the final accounting that cannot be covered by savings is transferred into the budget plan of the year after the next year. The budget law also stipulates a deficit ceiling of 3% of the "simple tax revenue"[11] satisfying requirement (b). Lastly, in order to fulfill requirement (c), if a deficit is expected, the tax multiplier has to be increased up to a level such that the deficit ceiling is not violated. The latest instance when cantonal finances in St. Gallen were constrained by the budget rules was in 2013, forcing the government to adopt spending cuts, liquidating savings worth 110 million Francs, and increase the multiplier by ten percentage points.

5.1 *Favorable Evidence on Budget Rules…*

The most recent econometric assessment of the effect of cantonal debt breaks on cantonal finances provides conclusive evidence that the fiscal rules are associated with sound cantonal and local finances. Burret and Feld (2018) not only show that cantonal fiscal rules reduce public deficits. As most debt breaks constrain current budget variables, there is an implicit risk of evasion into unconstrained accounts. While there is no evidence of evasion into funds and special financing, debt breaks are partly associated with increased spending in the investment budget. Moreover, the authors reject the common concerns that debt breaks undermine public investments or restrict fiscal measures in response to fiscal shocks. With respect to the third tier of government, the evidence demonstrates that the introduction of cantonal debt breaks improves local finances. A possible explanation, supported by Burret and Feld (2017), lies in the statutory cantonal responsibility for municipal finances that may be taken more seriously subsequent to the introduction of a cantonal debt brake.

The deterioration of federal finances in 1990s—gross debt increased by 160% in real terms between 1990 and 2002—prompted the Confederation to propose a federal debt break. The subsequent vote on the constitutional change was approved by over 85% of the electorate. The basic rule of the debt brake constrains the federal government to balance the financial accounts in the medium term.[12] Effectively, the level of

[11] The "simple tax revenue" is the basis for the income and property tax revenue and amounts to around 30 million Swiss Francs. Actual revenue is given by the simple tax revenue times a multiplier in the sense of a tax surcharge, which currently amounts to 115%.

[12] Like most cantonal budget rules the rule is applied to the budget (as well as supplementary credits) and the closing accounts.

expenditure is restricted by the cyclically adjusted revenues ensuring anti-cyclical fiscal policy. Deficits and surplus are credited to the compensation account and, by construction, treated asymmetrically. Deficits, that is the expenditure ceiling is violated, need to be compensated in the subsequent years. Surplus, that is expenditure fall short of revenues, are used to reduce debt.

The federal debt brake has been evaluated favorably. Counterfactual analysis shows that the introduction of the debt brake lead to an annual debt reduction of around 2% until 2010 (Salvi et al. 2020). The positive impact is associated with its precise and cyclically adjusted target, the comprehensive scope to prevent loopholes in the budget, and the strict political enforcement mechanism. In addition, there is no evidence supporting the claim that the debt brake has a negative impact on federal investment spending. The investment share in the federal budget has fluctuated around 12% since the 1990s.

5.2 *...and Fiscal Referenda*

Besides fiscal rules, Switzerland also has extensive institutional barriers of direct democracy. The major difference in this respect between the federal and cantonal level is the cantonal fiscal referendum.[13] As Table 1 shows, except for Vaud, mandatory and/or petition referendums exist in all cantons.[14] In the majority of cantons (16), outlays above a certain expenditure threshold require popular approval. In nine cantons, voters can launch a petition for spending programs above a certain expenditure threshold. Twelve cantons have two different thresholds for mandatory and petition referendums (Table 2).

Absolute thresholds vary significantly owing to large differences in populations and, subsequently, budgets. Thus, the threshold relative to total cantonal revenues constitutes a more meaningful measure. Thresholds for petition referendums generally are lower than for mandatory requirements (Leuzinger and Kuster 2017). The former range between

[13] Although efforts to introduce a voluntary fiscal referendum at the federal level have not been successful, fiscal loss of control is constrained by the debt brake as well as the constitutionally guaranteed maximum rates of the federal income tax and the value-added tax. Moreover, the federal taxing power and maximum rates are subject to a sunset clause that usually is extended every 15 year by popular approval.

[14] Fiscal referendums are also common on the local level.

Table 2 Direct democracy in Swiss Cantons. Based on Matsusaka (2018)

Canton	*Mandatory ref.*	*Petition ref.*	*Canton*	*Mandatory ref.*	*Petition ref.*
ZH	Yes	Yes	SH	Yes	Yes
BE	–	Yes	AR	–	Yes
LU	Yes	Yes	AI[a]	Yes	Yes
UR	Yes	Yes	SG	Yes	Yes
SZ	Yes	–	AG	–	Yes
OW	Yes	–	GR	Yes	Yes
NW	Yes	Yes	TG	Yes	Yes
ZG	–	Yes	TI	–	Yes
GL[a]	Yes	–	VD[b]		
FR	Yes	–	VS	–	Yes
SO	Yes	Yes	NE	Yes	Yes
BS	–	Yes	GE	–	Yes
BL	–	Yes	JU	Yes	Yes

[a]In cantons with a town assembly, citizens can directly intervene at the meeting
[b]Formally, Vaud constitutes a special case as it does not have a fiscal referendum. Bills inducing expenditure are subject to the regular petition referendum with no binding expenditure threshold

0 and 0.5 (0.25) percent of revenues for nonrecurring (reoccurring) spending programs. In Vaud, Neuchatel, and Geneva there is no lower bound for starting a referendum meaning any parliamentary budget decision to be contested. The latter range between 0.1 (0.01) and 5 (1.0) percent of revenue for nonrecurring (reoccurring) spending. Referenda rights are most extensive in Aargau where nonrecurring expenditure amounting to one-tenth or one-hundredth of a percent of total revenue (5 million francs opposite a total median expenditure of 5 billion francs in 2014–2016) can be disputed.

Several studies provide empirical evidence on the constraining impact of the fiscal referendums on cantonal finances (Feld and Matsusaka 2003; Funk and Gathmann 2011, 2013). Depending on the time period studied and the research design, the mandatory referendum is found to reduce both cantonal expenditure and revenue by 12–19%. According to Galletta and Jametti (2015) cantonal fiscal referendum increases local spending for municipalities without fiscal referenda indicating the importance of direct-democratic control on all levels of government. With respect to the effect on debt, evidence is scarce. Feld and Kirchgässner (2001) find an increasing, yet statistically insignificant effect on public debt. Feld et al.

(2008) demonstrate that fiscal referenda induce less centralization from the local to the cantonal level working as a safeguard for the interests of municipalities.

6 Public Revenue

A special feature of the Swiss fiscal constitution is the substantial autonomy of the cantons not only on the expenditure side but also on the revenue side of the budget. Cantonal tax revenue is mainly financed by personal, corporate income, wealth, and inheritance taxes. The federal government mainly relies on a value-added tax (VAT) and other (indirect) consumption taxes, a highly progressive income tax, and a proportional tax on the profit of legal entities. In addition, it levies a withholding tax on capital income (so-called *Verrechnungssteuer*), which has a rate of 35%. When capital incomes are declared, the tax is reimbursed. Capital income on private assets (as opposed to business assets) is tax-free. Capital income on real inheritance, however, is taxed by all cantons. Inheritance and wealth taxes are exclusively charged by the cantons as well. While there is no deductibility of personal income taxes, corporate income taxes are partly credited with different tiers of government. Most federal taxes are based on explicit constitutional provisions. The subsequent restricted access to some tax bases is relevant only to a limited extent as other tax receipts are governed either by the respective political area in the Constitution (e.g. motorway tax, heavy vehicle charge) or at statutory level (e.g. CO2 tax, casino tax). Prohibiting cantons to levy a specific tax requires an excluding provision in the federal Constitution such as article 134 that restricts the VAT, other excise taxes, the withholding and stamp tax to the federal level.

Figure 6 shows how tax revenue is split between three levels of government. The subnational (cantonal) ratio of total tax revenue amounts to a high value of 53 (33) percent. Income and wealth tax revenue amounts to 84 (51) percent of subnational (cantonal) tax revenue illustrating how the federal government is much less dependent on income tax revenue. For 2017, 82% of the federal tax revenue can be allocated to excise taxes (with two thirds of revenue from VAT) and income taxes (with equal shares from personal and corporate income), respectively. An institutional idiosyncrasy is the fact that income taxes are levied by the cantons. The federal government compensates this effort by reimbursing

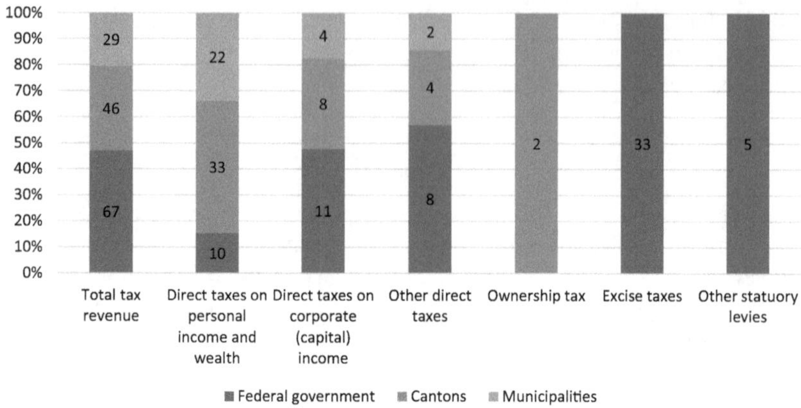

Fig. 6 Tax revenue by level of government 2017 in billion Swiss Francs and in % of combined government revenue (*Source* Federal Finance Administration [2019][15])

21% of its income tax revenue to the cantons based on the cantonal tax base. The federal personal income tax is piecewise linear with constant marginal tax rates by brackets. Marginal tax rates range from roughly 1 to 11.5%. Owing to a basic tax exemption, the highest 5% of income taxpayers (taxable income above CHF 150,000) pay about two-thirds of the revenue of the federal income tax (figures based on 2016 federal tax statistics).

6.1 *Cantons Exploit Tax Autonomy*

The federal constitution guarantees cantons the autonomy to determine their tax rates, tax surcharges (multiplier), and exemptions (Feld et al. 2017b).[16] Until the adoption of the federal tax harmonization law in the 1990s, cantons enjoyed wide-ranging flexibility in tax design matters.

[15] As Fig. 5 does not include social security revenue the numbers in Figs. 1 and 5 deviate.

[16] In almost all cantons the parishes of the three national churches (roman-catholic, protestant and christian-catholic) levy a church tax (multiplier in addition to cantonal tax rate) on their members as well as on the legal entities.

Today restrictions apply with respect to tax liability, tax base, tax calculation, and procedural provisions. Although those provisions are of formal nature, court rulings on constitutional tax principles have limited cantonal flexibility. Particularly, the federal supreme court's decision to rule the regressive tax schedule in Obwalden unconstitutional in 2007 can be considered an interference with cantonal tax autonomy as there are no statutory restrictions with respect to tax rates. The court ruled against Obwalden's tax reform because the tax schedule was in violation of the constitutional rule to tax households according to their economic capacity.

Municipalities' fiscal autonomy depends on the extent to which they are explicitly authorized to levy taxes by the respective canton. In practice, they determine their level of taxation by adding multipliers to the canton-specific tax rates. Tax competition among municipalities differs substantially to tax competition among cantons because the former is limited to the scope of taxation that is needed to finance public expenditure, whereas cantons are free to determine their tax burden to a large extent as well as the design of their tax legislation.

A comprehensive cantonal comparison of tax burdens is shown in Fig. 7. Tax exhaustion quantifies the share of a canton's economic capacity

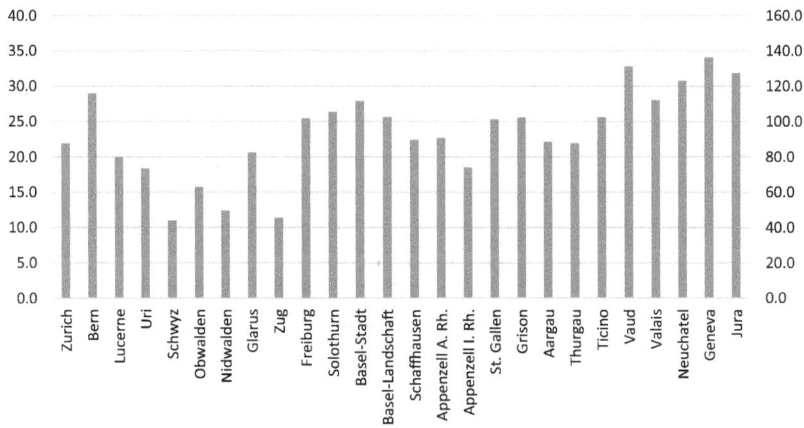

Fig. 7 Tax exhaustion as a percentage of economic capacity (left axis) and as an index (right axis). *Data* Federal Finance Administration

that, on average, can be fiscally absorbed.[17] The countrywide average fiscal burden is 25% (or 100 on the tax exhaustion index) with substantial differences among cantons. While taxpayers in Geneva cannot resort to 34% of their income, profits, or accretion, Schwyz and Zug absorb 11% of their taxpayers' resources. From an international perspective, the Swiss tax burden is low compared with most other locations in Europe and the United States. This holds even for the higher-tax Swiss cantons. However, this perspective fails to include other compulsory charges such as for mandatory health or accident insurance or the occupational pension scheme.[18]

These differences imply that cantons take advantage of their autonomy in tax matters which can lead to large differences in liabilities. Let's consider, for example, the 2018 tax burden for two identical taxpayers in the city of Zurich and the municipality Wollerau in the canton of Schwyz, which is about a 30-min drive or train ride from the city. Taxes due for a single person with a gross income of CHF 50,000 amount to 6.5% in Zurich and 4% in Wollerau, respectively (FFA 2019). For a married couple with a gross income of CHF 500,000, two kids and a workload split of 70–30%, Zurich charges 17.4%, whereas the cantonal tax burden Wollerau is 7.3%. Note that both couples pay an additional 7.7% to the federal government. As mentioned, the federal income tax is highly progressive meaning, in this specific case, the cantonal tax burden of the individuals with a gross income of CHF 50,000 increases by merely 0.4%.

The progressivity of the tax system is further put into perspective if the fact is accounted for that there is spatial sorting of taxpayers one effect being that high-income households are more likely to live in low-tax jurisdictions. Quantifying the effective level and progressivity of income taxation in Switzerland, Schmidheiny, and Roller (2016) show that high-income households face significantly lower average and marginal tax rates. Very high-income households without children even face regressive taxes. Half of the reduction in the tax burden on top incomes between 1975 and 2009 is due to reductions in statutory tax rates and about half to stronger income sorting of the population.

[17] The measure captures all tax bases cantons and municipalities can exploit, i.e., mostly income.

[18] The so-called 2nd pillar of the Swiss social insurance system is fully funded. Contributions by employer and employees are credited to a personal account.

6.2 Largely Benevolent Tax Competition

In recent years, there has been an increasing number of scientific contributions providing robust evidence on fiscal interdependencies among cantons and municipalities. They confirm both the presence of strong tax competition as well as subsequent behavioral responses to differences in tax burdens. Investigations confirm the intuitive conjecture that location (canton or municipality) choices are tax-induced. The proportion of high-income earners in a canton is significantly influenced by the canton's tax rate (e.g. Schmidheiny 2006). Among local communities, the effects of tax competition are also prevalent. This can be shown by exploiting an institutional feature that keeps foreign nationals with an annual income below CHF 120,000 subject to a special tax scheme (Quellenbesteuerung) for at least the first five years of residency (Schmidheiny and Slotwinsky [2018]). The authors observe two behavioral effects: First, foreign households located in a high-tax municipality are likely to move away once they are no longer subject to the scheme. Second, the same households systematically seek to keep their income below the threshold, whereas foreign household in low-tax municipality attempt to exceed the threshold. In a different attempt to detect the presence of tax competition, Eugster and Parchet (2019) provide evidence that the decentralization of fiscal responsibilities limits local governments from setting their culturally preferred tax rates. This finding is based on the empirically established fact that differences in municipal tax rates narrow as proximity to a (intra-cantonal) language border increases despite differences in preferences for public expenditures between French and German-speaking municipalities (with the former exhibiting preferences for more public expenditure).

An inherent issue of public policy debates is whether tax competition is in the interest of society. One recent study tries to answer this question in the setting of Swiss municipalities (Brülhart and Jametti 2019). The authors find that tax (multiplier) competition is beneficial when the intensity of direct-democratic control in local tax matters is low. The likelihood of an excessive tax burden is significantly higher without fiscal competition and insufficient control by direct-democratic institutions such as town-hall meetings or compulsory referendum. In this case, policymakers are less constrained to increase taxes for the purpose of preferred projects. In addition, the findings are valid outside of the Swiss case as the scope of vertical fiscal externalities and revenue maximization is likely larger in other federations. The former can be explained by Swiss municipalities' high fiscal share in international comparison which indicates increased scope as the prevalence of vertical externalities is inversely related to the size of local fiscal shares. And the latter is based on the fact that direct-democratic rights additionally constraining revenue maximization are less extensive in other nations.

The emphasis on tax-induced location choices may also be overstated in the political process as indicated by an investigation that studied the mobility of elderly taxpayers in response to a continuous decrease in cantonal inheritance taxes that—with a few exceptions—have been significantly reduced (Brülhart and Parchet 2014). The authors provide evidence that there was no systematic effect of cantonal inheritance taxes on the tax base from retired taxpayers and that the widespread exemptions had a negative effect on cantonal inheritance tax revenue after a tax cut.

Switzerland, relative to the size of its public sector, has the highest level of annual wealth taxation in the developed world. Revenue amounts to around 9% of total subnational tax revenue. The tax is raised on all types of wealth, e.g., cash, financial assets, real inheritance, and luxury durable goods. Exemptions apply for standard durable household goods, compulsory pension assets, and a limited amount of voluntary pension. Exemption levels and tax rates vary by canton with current top marginal wealth tax rates between 0.13 and 1.01%. An investigation into the elasticity of taxable wealth shows strong behavioral responses (Brülhart et al. 2019): A 1 percentage point decrease in the wealth tax rate increases reported wealth by 43% after six years owing to taxpayer migration, capitalization into housing prices, and changes in taxable financial assets of taxpayers suggesting changes in evasion behavior. In contrast to popular belief, the results suggest that the extent of tax avoidance is remarkably constant along with the wealth distribution.

6.3 *Corporate Tax System Under Change*

Corporate income taxes in Switzerland also vary considerably among cantons. The lowest tax rates can be found in central Switzerland where rates are 40–50% lower than in the higher-tax cantons.[19] While two out

[19] Like the confederation (8.5%), most cantons apply a flat rate tax to corporate income. In a few cantons rates (e.g. BE, VS) change discretely at certain profit levels.

of three companies subject to corporate income taxation did not pay any taxes in 2015, almost 90% of federal revenue was born by 2.8% of liable companies (KPMG 2019).

Due to peculiarities of the corporate income tax system, statutory and effective tax rates can differ. Half of the Swiss cantons have an effective average tax rate below 15%. Economic centers such as Zurich, Basel, or Geneva position themselves favorably in international tax competition although differences between cantons and international economic hubs have declined in recent years.[20] As Table 3 shows, low effective tax rates are predominantly located in central and eastern Switzerland. The figures refer to maximum effective tax rate that a company located in a cantonal capital faces and that does not enjoy any tax exemptions, that is it includes federal, cantonal, and local corporate tax liabilities.

In the past decade there has been a downward trend in cantonal corporate tax rates. On average the statutory tax rate has decreased by 3.7% since 2007. Cantons with a reduction of more than five percentage points (GR, BS, VD, SH, LU, NE and AR) can be found throughout the country. This trend is likely to continue with further changes announced (subject to parliamentary and/or voter approval) in the wake of recent federal and cantonal tax policy reforms.

The most recent changes in federal corporate tax legislation were approved by voters in May 2019 and brought Switzerland into line with internationally accepted tax rules. The reform has come a long way and was rooted in strong opposition by the EU and OECD against Switzerland's treatment of so-called holding, mixed, and domiciliary companies. It was mostly multinationals that benefited from preferential rates on foreign revenue opposite domestic income. As a result of the abolishment of the privileged tax regimes, affected companies would have faced a significant increase in their tax burden. In order to prevent an erosion of the tax base, the reform introduced new, internationally accepted tax instruments (e.g. patent box or discounts for R&D spending) and most cantons cut corporate tax rates. Table 3 offers an overview of cantonal changes in corporate tax rates and the respective allowances for different tax instruments.

[20] While at the beginning of the 2000s only Ireland had an effective tax rate as low as Zug, three countries in (South-)Eastern Europe tax corporate income at an effective rate of 9–10%.

Table 3 Key parameters of cantonal corporate tax reforms

Canton	*Tax rate*$_{corp}$[a]		*Tax rate*$_{pers}$[b]	*Tax reform parameters*[c]	*Canton*	*Tax rate*$_{corp}$[a]		*Tax rate*$_{pers}$[b]	*Reform parameters*[c]
	2019	*Post-reform*				*2019*	*Post-reform*		
ZH	21.1	19.7	40.0	90/50/70	**SH**	15.8	12.0	31.6	90/–/70
BE[d]	21.6	21.0	41.4	NA	**AR**	13.0	13.0	30.7	50/50/50
LU	12.3	12.3	31.2	10/–/20	**AI**	14.2	12.7	24.7	30/–/50
UR	14.9	12.5	25.3	30/–/50	**SG**	17.4	14.5	33.3	50/40/40
SZ	15.0	14.1	27.5	90/50/70	**GR**	16.1	14.0	32.2	70/–/70
OW	12.7	12.7	24.8	90/50/70	**AG**	18.6	18.6	34.5	90/50/70
NW[d]	12.7	12.0	25.6	90/–/70	**TG**	16.4	13.4	32.5	40/–/50
GL	15.7	12.4	31.5	10/–/10	**TI**	20.6	15.9	40.6	90/50/30
ZG	14.3	11.9	22.4	90/50/70	**VD**	14.0	14.0	41.5	NA
FR	19.9	13.9	36.0	90/50/20	**VS**[d,e]	21.7	11.9/17	36.5	90/50/34
SO	21.4	15.4	34	90/50/50	**NE**	15.6	13.4	38.1	20/50/40
BS	13.0	13.0	37.5	90/–/40	**GE**	24.2	14.0	45.0	10/50/90
BL	20.7	13.45	42.2	90/20/50	**JU**	20.5	15.0	40.3	90/50/70

[a]Effective maximum tax rate on corporate income in % (federal, cantonal and canton's capital municipality)
[b]Maximum marginal tax rate in % of taxable income for a single individual with no children in 2019 (federal, cantonal and canton's capital municipality)
[c]Reform implementation plans: Maximum allowance for patent box/R&D discount/overall discount threshold
[d]Corporate tax rate legislation subject to parliamentary and/or voter approval as of May 2020
[e]Bill puts forward a corporate tax rate of 11.9% for profits below CHF 250,000 and 17% for profits above this threshold
Source Leisibach und Schaltegger (2019)

With increased mobility of many firms in the wake of globalization and the subsequent effects on (international) tax competition, the interest in tax sensitivity of corporate income and its mobility across jurisdictions has increased too. The only study assessing the tax elasticity of corporate income in Switzerland finds a semi-elasticity of −2.2, i.e., an increase in the local corporate tax rate by 1 percentage point leads to a decrease in reported corporate income by 2.2% (Staubli 2018). In addition, tax sensitivity depends on the level of the corporate tax rate: The semi-elasticity is higher for municipalities with relatively low and relatively high-tax rates, whereas municipalities with medium tax rates record lower semi-elasticities.

7 Redistribution Framework

Fiscal equalization constitutes another essential element of Swiss fiscal federalism. Given the profound differences in tax burdens and fiscal capacity, the institutional framework can be seen as the counterpart to tax competition ensuring redistribution through various features. The highly progressive federal income tax and the withholding tax on capital incomes have been mentioned previously in this article.

In addition, there is substantial redistribution through the (first) pay-as-you-go pillar of the pension system. Contributions are proportional to labor income and of pure tax character above CHF 85,000 (i.e. there is no upper limit in contrast to many other countries) as this is the threshold that defines the maximum insurance which, as of now, is set CHF 2,370 (3,525) for a single individual (couple) per month. The minimum insurance is CHF 1,185 per month. Almost 60% of recipients receive the maximum pension. The fourth element in the framework is the fiscal equalization system aimed at reducing regional disparities.

The current equalization scheme redistributes around 5.2 billion Swiss francs or 0.75% of Swiss GDP (2018) between the Confederation, high-income cantons, and low-income cantons. The endowment is determined by parliament every four years. The mechanism's primary objective is to ensure that every (low-income) canton reaches 85% of the country's average tax potential (the threshold has been increased to 86.5% starting in 2020).

7.1 *The Widely Successful Reform of the Equalization Scheme*

It has been in force since 2008 when it replaced an older system that was widely criticized for its poor incentive structure and small equalization effect relative to the overall transfer volume. In addition to restructuring the scope and volume of transfers, the reform also included the disentanglement of tasks that had been carried out by both the federal and cantonal governments often reducing cantons to pure enforcers of federal regulation. With respect to transfers, the reform included the following elements (Bessard 2013):

- The main redistribution mechanism, fiscal capacity or resources equalization, is now based on cantonal tax potential, defined as standardized (opposed to effective) tax revenues over a six-year period from income, wealth, and profits in relation to taxable income and wealth. The barely straightforward indicator was introduced because, under the old system, cantons could directly manipulate their fiscal capacity through tax policy, for example. Resources equalization amounts to about 80% of total transfers. Within the pot, the federal government transfers about 2.5 billion francs to financially "weak" cantons (19) to increase their fiscal capacity, whereas the seven financially "strong" cantons contribute about 1.7 billion francs (2019 figures).
- Charges equalization, which was not separated from resources equalization prior to the reform, considers financing needs for various specific factors that can be pooled in three categories: equalization for (1) geographic factors such as mountainous, unproductive areas, socio-economic factors faced by (2) urban agglomeration or (3) large city centers (by Swiss criteria). The division of funds between geographic-topographic and socio-economic categories (1:1) is the result of political bargaining. Given the comfortable majority of cantons benefiting from transfers equalizing geographic factors, this is unlikely to change despite a study indicating that socio-economic factors constitute burden cantonal and local expenditure significantly higher (Ecoplan 2013). Charges equalization is entirely financed by the Confederation and amounts to about 14% of total transfers.
- In contrast to the old equalization scheme, the federal government can no longer earmark transfers meaning cantons are free with respect to the disposition of transfers. Before 2008, about three

quarters of transfers were matching grants. As a result, grants were often independent of cantons' fiscal performance.

- For political reasons, the reform included a "hardship" fund that reimburses cantons that were adversely affected by the introduction of the new mechanisms. As of 2019, six cantons remain recipients of this fund which will be terminated no later than 2035. It is financed by the other cantons (1/3) and the Confederation (2/3).

Figure 8 shows the average per capita equalization payments for each canton over the last five years. The wealthy and lower-tax cantons of Schwyz, Nidwalden, and Zug as well as the economic centers Zurich, Basel, and Geneva have the highest per capita contribution. The highest net recipients (Uri, Valais, Jura) are all situated in the periphery (by Swiss standards) and receive more than 2000 Swiss francs per capita. Considering the disparities in fiscal capacity, it is no surprise, that there are large differences in the recipient cantons' dependency on equalization transfers too. The highest net recipients receive around 20% of their

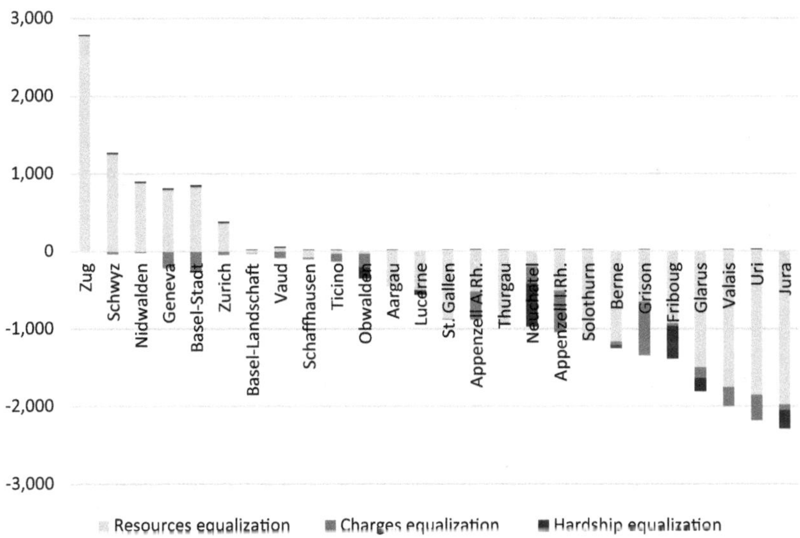

Fig. 8 Per capita equalization payments by fund 2015–2019 (*Source* Federal Finance Administration [2019])

revenue directly from the equalization grants, whereas up to 45% of the contributing cantons' revenue is redistributed.

There is little doubt whether the reform improved the fiscal equalization scheme. Thanks to the elimination of matching grants and the new tax potential indicator, redistribution of resources work leading to a reduction in disparities. Since 2012 all cantons have reached 85 or more points on the tax potential index thus exceeding the mechanism's main objective. The main beneficiaries of the redistribution effects were those 11 cantons whose tax potential was below the key threshold. The mechanism additionally redistributes funds to seven more cantons although their potential was higher than the threshold. This is due to the progressive allocation of funds at the lower end of the resource index as can be observed by the significant leveling at the lower end of the resource index in Fig. 9—in contrast to the linear absorption of resources from the contributing cantons at the top (Leisibach und Schaltegger 2019). As a result, contributing cantons have faced increasing liabilities to the system for years. In order to address this source of increasing tension the tax potential threshold (86.5) is now a statutory variable and no longer subject to parliamentary bargaining.

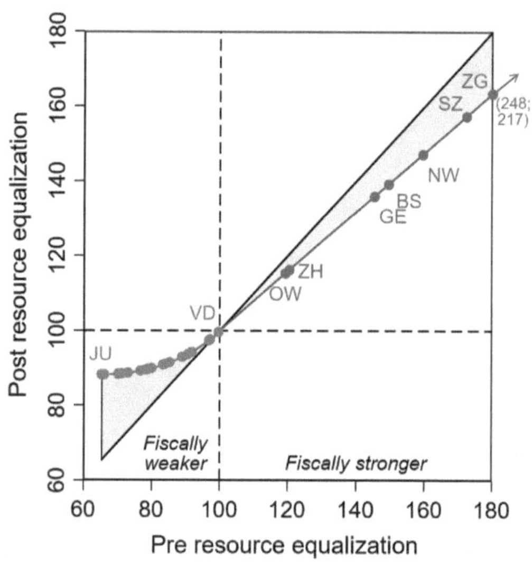

Fig. 9 Resource equalization 2019 (*Source* Leisibach and Schaltegger (2019), Fig. 4)

7.2 *Disincentives and Flaws of Redistribution Mechanism*

The construction of the redistribution mechanisms has a direct impact on cantons' and (municipalities') incentives in determining their tax policy (Brülhart and Schmidheiny 2015). It substantially restricts cantons' fiscal benefits from attracting additional tax revenue. One way to quantify those restrictions is by calculating so-called marginal absorption rates, that is how much transfer payments change as a result of changes in fiscal capacity (e.g. as a result of changes in tax revenue). For fiscally weaker (stronger) cantons it is defined as the share by which transfers decrease (increase) for additional tax revenue.[21]

Figure 10 shows the marginal absorption rates for each canton in 2019 (Leisibach und Schaltegger 2019). For example, an increase in resource potential by 100 francs in the canton of Schwyz, increases its contribution by 5 francs regardless of whether or how much the canton exploits the newly gained potential. Most fiscally weak cantons face higher absorption rates owing to the progressivity of the mechanism explained above. On average, the (weighted) average absorption rates for those cantons amount to (13,4) 16%. With the exception of Obwalden, that adopted a bold tax reform in 2008 introducing a flat-rate tax on personal incomes and reducing corporate tax rates by half, marginal absorption rates have remained stable since the introduction of the new fiscal equalization scheme over a decade ago.

The debate on these disincentives is ongoing. They certainly have not undermined tax competition which has been relatively intense since the last reform. There is also good economic reasoning why high marginal absorption rates are justified—namely if cantons attract corporate profits from other cantons instead of from abroad. And while under the current mechanism disincentives could only be avoided if corporate profits would be excluded from resource potential, the implicit tax rates on new resources do reduce the incentives to maintain revenue growth considerably with unknown long-term consequences. The fact that fiscally weak cantons are affected stronger relative to fiscally strong cantons may increase disparities in the future and indirectly strengthen support for uniform corporate taxes. This problem is amplified by a recent decrease in

[21] Marginal absorption rates differ for (new) income or profit depending on whether the individual or company moved within Switzerland or to Switzerland from abroad (Leisibach and Schaltegger 2019).

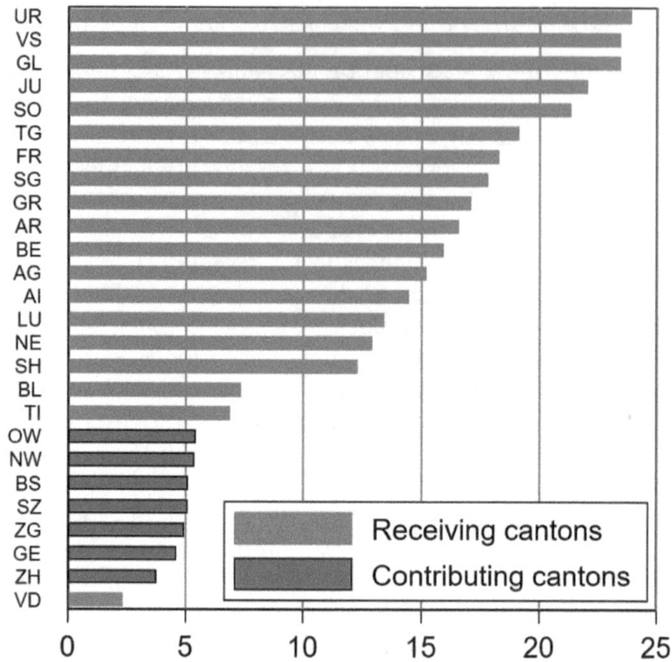

Fig. 10 Marginal absorption rates for new resources in 2019 in percent for contributing (red) and receiving (blue) cantons (*Source* Leisibach and Schaltegger [2019], Fig. 5)

taxes on corporate profits in almost all cantons as a reaction to the recent abolition of privileged tax regimes (see *V. Public revenue*). A fundamental reform of the resource equalization and its mechanism could address disincentives in the interest of the entire federal system.

7.3 The Effect of Direct Democracy and Fiscal Federalism on Income Inequality

Spatial sorting is often said not only to affect regional disparities but also the distribution of income among citizens. The fact that in a federal system tax bases are mobile lead exponents of the traditional theory of federalism to favor the assignment of distributional responsibilities at the federal level (e.g. Musgrave 1959; Oates 1972, etc.). This ideal, however, is a long way from the reality of fiscal structures—in Switzerland and elsewhere. Many responsibilities on the cantonal level have redistributive character.

It seems that this has not been to Switzerland's disadvantage as an international comparison of inequality outcomes show. Inequality in market incomes is low compared to most other industrialized countries reducing the need to redistribute and the associated efficiency losses (Frey et al. 2019). Inequality in disposable incomes after redistribution is equivalent to the OECD median.[22] A similar pattern is observable for poverty rates.

Recent evidence shows that fiscal federalism and direct democracy play a systematic role in those favorable outcomes as they largely determine how fundamental economic trends translate into income inequality. Fiscal federalism actually reduces income concentration conditional on jurisdictional fragmentation, i.e., the inequality decreasing effect of decentralization becomes weaker the smaller municipalities are (Feld et al. 2021). Similarly, the voter initiative is associated with a significant decrease in top incomes to the benefit of the upper middle class, whereas referendums seem to have an opposing effect (Frey and Schaltegger 2019). These effects are observed in market outcomes already meaning the results are not driven by shifts in redistribution via income taxes.

The public health and economic response to COVID-19 in Switzerland

Switzerland's first COVID-19 case was discovered on February 25, 2020 in Ticino, the Swiss canton closest to some of the Italian regions that were most significantly affected by the virus. By May 15, Switzerland had confirmed more than 30,400 positive cases and 1879 deaths due to COVID-19 (see www.corona-data.ch for the latest figures). There are striking spatial differences with more than 600 positive cases per 100,000 residents in Ticino, Vaud, or Genera opposite 150 to 300 positive cases in most German-speaking cantons.

[22] Furthermore, Switzerland's top income shares have been strikingly stable since decades (Alvaredo et al. 2018).

The Swiss public health response has largely been based on the Law on Epidemics adopted in 2012 that grants the federal government—in consultation with the cantons—the authority for the interference into public life in case of an unusual or extraordinary epidemiological situation. A few cantons made use of the statutory provision that allows them to extend federal measures, most notably Ticino that declared a state of emergency five days prior to the federal response on March 16. The Swiss Federal Council adopted measures similar to those in other countries including the ban of all private and public events and gatherings of more than five people. With the exception of grocery stores, banks, pharmacies and post offices, stores were closed for six weeks. By mid-April, a three-step exit strategy was announced to be employed until the beginning of June. Ticino was the only canton to extend the state of emergency until the beginning of May.

To tackle what is likely to develop into the worst economic crisis since World War II, the federal government has implemented a variety of measures concerning liquidity bottlenecks, monetary and macro-financial stability, employment, compensation for self-employed as well as the culture or sports sector. In total, it has set aside around 65 billion Swiss francs in support of the economy, an amount almost equivalent to its annual budget. Many cantons have adopted additional stabilization measures in favor of areas not covered by federal efforts. In light of the many uncertainties regarding the virus It is unclear to what extent the commitments will exert pressure on the existing landscape of fiscal institutions on different levels of government.

8 Conclusion

Fiscal federalism and direct democracy are key parts of the Swiss political DNA that have contributed to political stability and economic success. They are associated with several fiscal benefits such as lower debt levels, lower government expenditure, or the prevention of an excess supply of government services. The widespread autonomy of subnational jurisdictions with respect to fiscal power as well as participatory institutions creates a framework that has proved conducive to increased citizen impact on political outcomes.

Recent empirical evidence has significantly advanced the understanding of the effects of decentralized tax autonomy and its interdependencies. These largely favorable outcomes place Switzerland at top positions by international comparison and provide a universal economic rationale for a fiscal hierarchy and subsequent tax competition. Yet the underlying equilibrium between competitive and cooperative elements of Swiss fiscal federalism is more fragile than it seems.

This is exemplified by the recent corporate income tax reform and subsequent cantonal changes in tax rates. The current mechanism of the fiscal equalization scheme partly impedes a level playing field for cantonal tax competition as fiscally weaker cantons are disproportionally affected by disincentives rooted in the mechanism design. While not all disincentives are unjustified from an economic point of view, their long-term effects on the system are uncertain. Specifically, they could undermine the public's trust in the system if disparities increase and lead contributing cantons to question the scheme's solidarity as the funds to redistribute continue growing. For now, a bold reform is politically unrealistic given the receiving cantons solid majority in both councils in the federal assembly. In the medium term, however, this moral hazard is likely to weaken the effectiveness of the equalization scheme at best.

There is also increasing pressure on the system with respect to the division of responsibilities between different levels of government. Some call for another, more profound disentanglement to correct for what was missed by the 2008 reform. Others see most policy solutions at the federal level, possibly because the federal system's potential benefits are of dynamic nature (e.g. the taming effect on the Leviathan state, the competition of ideas), whereas its potential drawbacks (e.g. coordination costs, economies of scale not fully exploited) are static and therefore more easily observable (Rother and Rühli 2017).

In order to preserve the principle of subsidiarity and not adopt a system in which cantons are reduced to executing federal regulation, advocating another reform is necessary. Importantly, such an institutional revision should prevent the cantons from exchanging responsibilities for reimbursements or grants. Instead, a decentral shift in responsibilities should be combined with a decentral shift in tax autonomy ensuring that cantons have enough revenue to finance their expenditure.

Integrated tasks will exist beyond a reform reflecting the complex reality of fiscal structures. Ideally, federal legislation sets a regulating framework without interfering with specific cantonal autonomy. For example, health insurance providers need to be regulated on the federal market to guarantee access to the domestic market but standardizing the financing of hospitals leads to competition for subsidies instead of innovative financing solutions. Furthermore, cantonal conferences should refrain from legislative action in order to uphold the principle of fiscal equivalence and direct democracy and ensure the proper working of procedural provisions. Instead, they could adopt an "IMF"-like role: support cantons in the provision of public goods and services by assisting them with knowledge and developing benchmarks.

References

Alvaredo, F., Chancel, L., Piketty, T., Saez, E., & Zucman, G. (2018). World Inequality Report. In *World Inequality Lab*. https://wir2018.wid.world/files/download/wir2018-full-report-english.pdf. Retrieved June 17, 2018.

Bessard, P. (2013). Switzerland's reformed fiscal equalization system. In J. Clemens, & N. Veldhuis, *Federalism and Fiscal Transfers: Essays on Australia, Germany, Switzerland and the United States* (pp. 43–54). Fraser Institute.

Blöchliger, H., & Frey, R. L. (1992). Der schweizerische Föderalismus: Ein Modell für den institutionellen Aufbau der Europäischen Union? *Aussenwirtschaft*.

Brülhart, M., & Jametti, M. (2019). Does tax competition tame the Leviathan? *Journal of Public Economics, 96*, pp. 1063–1078.

Brülhart, M., & Parchet, R. (2014). Alleged tax competition: The mysterious death of bequest taxes in Switzerland. *Journal of Public Economics, 111*.

Brülhart, M., & Schmidheiny, K. (2015). *Steuerförderalismus in der Schweiz: Erfolgsmodell dank Leitplanken*. FGN-HSG: WPZ Politikanalyse Nr. 6.

Brülhart, M., Gruber, J., Krapf, M., & Schmidheiny, K. (n.d.). Behavioral Responses to Wealth Taxation: Evidence from Switzerland. *Working paper: University of Lausanne*.

Brülhart, M., Schmidheiny, K., & Bucovetsky, S. (2015). Taxes in cities. In Duranton, Henderson, & Strange, *Handbook of Regional and Urban Economics* (pp. 1123–1196).

Burret, H. T., & Feld, L. P. (2018). (Un-)intended effects of fiscal rules. *European Journal of Political Economy*(52), pp. 166–191.

Burret, H., & Feld, L. (2017). Vertical effects of fiscal rules—The Swiss experience. *International Tax and Public Finance*(25(3)), pp. 673–721.

Ecoplan. (2013). *Kostenrelevanz und Gewichtung von Indikatoren im Lastenausgleich*. Bern: Federal Finance Administration.

Eugster, B., & Parchet, R. (2019). Culture and taxes. *Journal of Political Economy*(127), pp. 296–337.

Fässler, L., Schaltegger, C. A., & Winistörfer, M. M. (2017, 10). Verflechtungen bedrohen den Föderalismus. *Die Volkswirtschaft*.

Federal Finance Administration. (2018). *Swiss Fiscal Data*. https://www.efv.admin.ch/efv/de/home/themen/finanzstatistik/daten.html.

Federal Chancellery. (2019). *The Swiss Confederation: A Brief Guide*. Bern: Swiss Confederation.

Federal Office of Statistics (2018). *Gross Domestic Product*. https://www.bfs.admin.ch/bfs/de/home/statistiken/volkswirtschaft/volkswirtschaftliche-gesamtrechnung/bruttoinlandprodukt.html.

Feld, L. P. & Kirchgässner, G. (2001). The political economy of direct legistlation: Direct democracy and local decision-making. *Economic Policy*, pp. 329–367.

Feld, L. P., & Kirchgässner, G. (2008). On the effectiveness of debt brakes: The Swiss experience. In R. Neck, & J.-E. Sturm, *Sustainability of Public Debt*. Cambridge and London: MIT Press.

Feld, L. P., & Matsusaka, J. (2003). Budget referendums and government spending: New evidence from Switzerland. *Journal of Public Economics*(87), pp. 2703–2724.

Feld, L. P., Frey, C., Schaltegger, C., & Schmid, L. A. (2021). Fiscal federalism and income inequality: An empirical analysis for Switzerland. *Journal of Economic Behavior and Organisation* (185), pp. 463–494.

Feld, L. P., Kalb, A., Moessinger, M.-D., & Osterloh, S. (2017a). Sovereign bond market reactions to fiscal rules and no-bailout clauses: The Swiss experience. *Journal of International Money and Finance*(70), pp. 319–343.

Feld, L. P., Schaltegger, C. A., & Schmid, L. A. (2017b). Schweizerische Finanzordnung. In L. P. Feld, & C. A. Schaltegger, *Föderalismus und Wettbewerbsfähigkeit in der Schweiz - Staatsstrukturen für eine erfolgreiche Schweiz im 21. Jahrhundert* (pp. 25–46). Zürich: NZZ Libro.

Feld, L. P., Schaltegger, C. A., & Schnellenbach, J. (2008). On government centralization and fiscal referendums. *European Economic Review*(52), pp. 611–645.

Frey, C., & Schaltegger, C. A. (2019). The Initative, the Referendum and the Distribution of Income: An Empirical Analysis for Swiss Cantons. *Working Paper University of Lucerne*.

Frey, C., Schaltegger, C. A., & Schmid, L. A. (2019). Inequality and institutions: The case of Switzerland. In P. Grünenfelder, N. Rother, S. Rutz, & M. Salvi, *Inequality - An International Think Tank Report on Inequality and Equality*. Zurich: Avenir Suisse.

Funk, P., & Gathmann, C. (2011). Does direct democracy reduce the size of government? New evidence from historical data, 1890–2000. *The Economic Journal*(121).

Funk, P., & Gathmann, C. (2013). Voter preferences, direct democracy and government spending. *European Journal of Political Economy*(32), pp. 300–319.

Galletta, S., & Jametti, M. (2015). How to tame two Leviathans? Revisiting the effect of direct democracy on local public expenditure in a federation. *European Journal of Political Economy*(39), pp. 82–93.

Kirchgässner, G. (2007). Swiss Confederation. In A. Shah, & J. Kincaid, *The Practice of Fiscal Federalism: Comparative Perspectives* (pp. 318–343). McGill-Queen's University Press.

KPMG. (2019). *Clarity on Swiss Taxes.*

Leisibach, P., & Schaltegger, C. A. (2019). Zielkonflikte und Fehlanreize: Eine Analyse der Anreizwirkungen im Schweizer Finanzausgleich. *Perspektiven der Wirtschaftspolitik.* https://doi.org/10.1515/pwp-2018-0012.

Leuzinger, L., & Kuster, C. (2017). Wo man gegen eine Ausgabe von 1 Franken das Finanzreferendum ergreifen kann. Retrieved from https://napoleonsnightmare.ch/2017/10/12/wo-man-gegen-eine-ausgabe-von-1-franken-das-finanzreferendum-ergreifen-kann-und-wo-erst-ab-9-millionen/.

Linder, W. (2010). *Swiss Political System.* Retrieved from https://www.wolf-linder.ch/.

Matsusaka, J. (2018). Public policy and the initiative and referendum: A survey with some new evidence. *Public Choice*(174), pp. 107–143.

Musgrave, R. (1959). *The Theory of Public Finance.* New York: McGraw-Hill.

Oates, W. E. (1972). *Fiscal federalism.* New York: Harcourt Brace Jovanovich.

OECD. (2019). *Gross Domestic Product.* https://data.oecd.org/gdp/gross-domestic-product-gdp.htm.

Rother, N., & Rühli, L. (2017). *NFA 2 - Für die Revitalisierung des Schweizer Föderalismus.* Zürich: Avenir Suisse.

Salvi, M., Schaltegger, C. A., & Schmid, L. D. (2020). Do fiscal rules cause lower debt? A case study for Switzerland. *Kyklos (forthcoming).*

Schaltegger, C. A., & Weder, M. (2010). Fiskalpolitik als antizyklisches Instrument? Eine Betrachtung der Schweiz. *Perspektiven der Wirtschaftspolitik*(11), pp. 146–177.

Schmidheiny, K. (2006). Income segregation and local progressive taxation: Empirical evidence from Switzerland. *Journal of Public Economics*(90), pp. 429–458.

Schmidheiny, K., & Roller, M. (n.d.). Effective Tax Rates and Effective Progressivity in a Fiscally Decentralized Country. *CEPR Discussion Paper 11152.*

Schmidheiny, K., & Slotwinsky, M. (2018). Tax-induced mobility: Evidence from a foreigners' tax scheme in Switzerland. *Journal of Public Economics*, pp. 293–324.

Sommer, J. (1978). *Das Ringen um soziale Sicherheit in der Schweiz: Eine politisch-ökonomische Analyse der Ursprünge, Entwicklungen und Perspektiven sozialer Sicherung im Widerstreit zwischen Gruppeninteressen und volkswirtschaftlicher Tragbarkeit*. Diessenhofen: Rüegger.

Staubli, D. (2018). The Elasticity of Corporate Income: Panel Data Evidence from Switzerland. *Working Paper*.

United States

Teresa Garcia-Milà and Therese J. McGuire

1 Introduction

The United States has a long history of fiscal federalism. It began as a collection of independent states in the late eighteenth Century and evolved over the course of the years, including the major upheavals of the Revolutionary War, the Civil War, and the Great Depression into being one of the foremost examples of a federation, both economically and politically. Unlike other federations, where the central government has devolved expenditures and revenue responsibilities to states or regions, the power to impose and collect taxes by the federal government was agreed upon by the founding states when the US Constitution was ratified in 1789. The Constitution (and subsequent amendments) allowed broad taxing powers for the federal and state governments, while also limiting access to certain types of taxes for one level of government or another,

T. Garcia-Milà (✉)
Universitat Pompeu Fabra and Barcelona School of Economics, Barcelona, Spain
e-mail: teresa.garcia-mila@upf.edu

T. J. McGuire
Northwestern University, Evanston, IL, USA
e-mail: therese-mcguire@northwestern.edu

J.-F. Tremblay (ed.), *The Forum of Federations Handbook of Fiscal Federalism*, https://doi.org/10.1007/978-3-030-97258-5_11

for example, states cannot impose tariffs and the federal government cannot impose property taxes. Over the years, the federal government has expanded significantly, but the independence of the states and their fiscal autonomy have persisted.[1]

There are three layers of government, one central (the federal government), 50 regional governments (the states), and thousands of local governments. The federal government has three branches: the executive branch (headed by a directly elected president), the legislative branch (the senate with two senators per state and the congress with 435 representatives distributed according to population), and the judicial branch (with the US Supreme Court being the highest court in the country). The term of the president is four years, the term of a senator is six years, and the term of a representative is two years. The governor is the elected executive of a state and, except for Nebraska, which has a unicameral, each state has both a senate and a house. Local governments have elected executives and boards or councils. There are general-purpose local governments, e.g., cities and counties, and special purpose local governments, e.g., school districts and library districts.

The federal government puts few restrictions on state taxes, preserving the states' revenue-raising authority and discretion, which is evident in the large diversity across the states in sources of revenue. This diversity is also present on the expenditure side, as states spend significantly different amounts per capita on education, healthcare, transportation, and other categories. This diversity across the states, documented in detail below, is a distinct characteristic of the fiscal federalism system in the US, not found in most other federations.

Local governments are creatures of the states and the states have exercised their powers in defining and restricting local taxes. A primary example is state limits on local government access to the property tax.

In 2018, total (federal, state, and local) spending as a share of GDP was 33.0%. The federal government was responsible for over half of this amount (19.1% of GDP) with the states and localities having responsibility for the remainder (13.9% of GDP). Total revenues as a share of GDP was 26.9%, with the federal government at 17.0% of GDP and the share for states and localities at 9.9% of GDP. The difference in shares between expenditures and revenues at the federal level reflects

[1] See Dilger (2018) and Wallis (2000) for interesting accounts of the historical evolution of the US fiscal federal system.

borrowing, and at the state and local level, it reflects both borrowing and intergovernmental transfers from the federal government to subnational governments. These transfers, which account for significant amounts of total state and local revenues, do not generally aim to equalize resources across states, a characteristic common in other federations, for example, in Canada and Germany (see Garcia-Milà and McGuire 2019). The limited amount of equalization across regions is another distinctive characteristic of the federal system of the US.

The federal, state, and local governments dedicate a significant share of their budgets to healthcare provision (in 2016, 18.4, 29.0 and 9.2%, respectively), mainly through the Medicare and Medicaid programs. However, the US does not provide universal healthcare coverage, a widespread practice in developed counties, and particularly generous in some European countries.

The US is a large and prosperous nation. The population of the US was 326.5 million in 2018, making it the third-largest country in the world by population (far behind China and India; slightly ahead of Indonesia). The largest state by far in 2018 was California, with a population of 30.6 million; the smallest state was Wyoming with 578,000 residents. The US is one of the wealthiest countries in the world, with a GDP per capita in 2018 of $62,795, compared with $47,603 in Germany and $39,290 in Japan (source: the World Bank online data). There is large variation across the 50 states in personal income per capita; in 2018, Connecticut and Massachusetts had income per capita of $76,481 and $71,886, respectively, while West Virginia and Mississippi had income per capita of $40,907 and $37,904, respectively (source: the US Bureau of Economic Analysis online data).

In the remainder of the chapter, we explore in more detail the revenues, expenditures, and intergovernmental relations of the three levels of government in the US. We highlight the dimensions of the US system that make it distinctive compared to systems in other countries.

2 Revenues and Expenditures

In Table 1, we display aggregate revenues and expenditures of each of the three levels of government in 2016. The federal government relied most heavily on the individual income tax and payroll taxes (dedicated to Social Security and Medicare) for revenues (47.3 and 34.1% of total revenues, respectively), while state governments, in terms of own-source

Table 1 Revenues and expenditures by functional category and level of government, 2016 (thousands of dollars)

	Revenues					
	Federal		*State*		*Local*	
	Amount	*% of Total*	*Amount*	*% of Total*	*Amount*	*% of Total*
Total Revenue	3,267,961,000	100	2,136,454,470	100	1,805,682,720	100
Individual Income Tax	1,546,075,000	47.3	343,620,739	16.1	32,676,759	1.8
General Sales Tax	0	0.0	291,472,708	13.6	85,507,726	4.7
Property Tax	0	0.0	15,945,411	0.7	487,316,738	27.0
Selective Sales Tax	95,026,000	2.9	149,651,791	7.0	32,239,223	1.8
Corporate Income Tax	299,571,000	9.2	46,201,841	2.2	8,057,481	0.4
Intergovernmental Grants	0	0.0	637,167,820	29.8	593,490,699	32.9
Charges and User Fees	0	0.0	208,904,262	9.8	289,244,596	16.0
Payroll Taxes & Investment Income	1,115,065,000	34.1	134,985,193	6.3	14,400,403	0.8
Other Revenues	212,224,000	6.5	308,504,705	14.4	262,749,095	14.6
	Expenditures					
	Federal		*State*		*Local*	
	Amount	*% of Total*	*Amount*	*% of Total*	*Amount*	*% of Total*
Total	3,852,612,000	100	2,225,106,823	100	1,838,514,959	100
K-12 Education	16,649,540	0.4	7,561,943	0.3	683,504,771	37.2
Higher Education	1,026,460	0.0	274,999,016	12.4	47,000,015	2.6
Healthcare	709,187,000	18.4	646,090,942	29.0	168,986,614	9.2
Defense	593,372,000	15.4	0	0.0	0	0.0
Public Welfare	260,836,000	6.8	62,712,561	2.8	48,558,391	2.6
Public Safety	52,232,000	1.4	74,928,728	3.4	177,500,861	9.7
Transportation	28,690,000	0.7	179,040,307	8.0	124,601,942	6.8
Retirement Benefit Payments	1,064,601,000	27.6	237,133,153	10.7	52,340,598	2.8
Intergovernmental Grants	660,833,000	17.2	532,698,646	23.9	16,339,742	0.9

(continued)

Table 1 (continued)

	Expenditures					
	Federal		*State*		*Local*	
	Amount	*% of Total*	*Amount*	*% of Total*	*Amount*	*% of Total*
Other Expenditures	465,185,000	12.1	209,941,527	9.4	519,682,025	28.3

Note State and local government expenditures from the Census Survey of State and Local Government Finances. Federal expenditures by functional category from OMB Historical Table 3.2, adjusted to remove grant spending from the functional categories using data from OMB table 12.2. K-12 grants were calculated as 38% of total education grants based on the Department of Education budget statistics: https://www.usaspending.gov/#/agency/1068

revenues, relied most heavily on individual income and general sales taxes (at 16.1 and 13.6% of total revenues, respectively). Local governments relied most heavily on property taxes for own-source revenues (27.0% of total revenues). The different levels of government focused their spending in distinct areas. Of the federal government's total expenditures, 27.6% was on retirement benefits (Social Security), 18.4% was on healthcare, and 15.4% was on defense spending. For state governments, the largest spending categories were for healthcare (largely expenditures for Medicaid recipients) at 29.0%, intergovernmental grants to local governments (the most important in terms of dollars being grants to school districts) at 23.9%, and higher education at 12.4%. The largest spending share for local governments was for K-12 education (primary and secondary education) at 37.2%. Public safety at 9.7% was a distant second (and nearly tied with healthcare) for local governments.

Intergovernmental grants from the federal government to state and local governments represented 17.2% of federal spending, with the largest grant being to support Medicaid. As a source of revenue, intergovernmental grants contributed the largest share of revenues for state and local governments, 29.8% of total state revenues and 32.9% of total local revenues.

All levels of government rely on individual and corporate income taxes, although they are minor sources of revenue for local governments. The corporate income tax presents issues with defining the tax base and in terms of competitive pressures, as many corporations are not only multistate but also multinational. The individual income tax tends to be the engine for progressivity in the tax systems of the federal government and the states, although many states have flat-rate or effectively flat-rate tax structures. State governments have complete autonomy to administer and collect income taxes, and while the state measure of income for tax purposes begins with a federal measure, most state income base definitions deviate from the federal definition through the use of state-specific deductions and exemptions.

No governments employ value-added taxes in the US. Instead, state and local governments rely on general sales taxes, which are ad valorem taxes on purchases, and all three levels of government rely on selective (or excise) taxes, which can be ad valorem or per-unit taxes. Prominent selective sales taxes include taxes on gasoline, alcohol and tobacco products, and hotel stays. General sales taxes were created early in the twentieth century and in many states were imposed on purchases of tangible goods at brick-and-mortar stores. As the economy has shifted away from goods to services and toward purchases on the internet, the general sales tax base in many states has withered.[2]

The property tax is a tax on land and improvements to land (and in some instances, on other types of property such as machinery) and is a meaningful source of revenue for local governments only. Even though it is a local revenue source, state governments have the authority to define and constrain the tax. Many states impose limits on the property tax rate or growth rate of property tax revenues, and they define different classes of property for assessment purposes.

The federal government collects royalty payments on oil, natural gas, and coal extracted from federal lands and offshore waters. It also imposes a reclamation fee on coal mining operations, with the receipts dedicated to the Department of the Interior's Abandoned Mine Reclamation Fund. Thirty-four states impose a severance tax or fee on the extraction of oil and natural gas; typically, the severance tax is on the value or volume of oil and natural gas extracted. Some states allocate a portion of their oil and natural gas revenues to local governments; however, as a rule, revenues are deposited in the state general fund (Kolesnikoff and Brown 2018).

[2] A 2018 ruling by the US Supreme Court (South Dakota v. Wayfair) opened the door for states to impose sales taxes on internet sales even when the firms do not have a physical presence in the state.

In a study of 13 coal-producing states, the authors describe an array of state and local taxes imposed on coal companies and the extraction of coal. All but four of the 13 states impose a severance tax on the extraction of coal (either a fixed amount per ton or a percentage of the gross value of the coal) and all but two states impose a separate reclamation fee, with the revenues being dedicated to the cleanup of abandoned mine sites (Kent and Eastham 2011).

Severance taxes on non-renewable natural resources (oil, natural gas, coal and other natural resources) make up an important share of total own-source revenues for some states. In 2016, Alaska, New Mexico, North Dakota, and Wyoming obtained between seven and 24% of their total own-source revenues from severance taxes on natural resource extraction.

The two largest public health insurance programs are Medicaid and Medicare. Medicare is a program of the federal government that makes payments to healthcare organizations and medical professionals for providing medical care to individuals aged 65 and older. Medicaid (and its associated program CHIP, the Children's Health Insurance Program) is a program delivered by state governments and jointly funded by the federal government and the states. It is the single largest source of healthcare coverage in the country. The program provides payments to healthcare organizations and medical professionals for delivering medical care to low-income individuals and families and to individuals with disabilities. Expenditures on Medicaid and Medicare have grown rapidly in recent decades in part because of the rising cost of healthcare and the aging of the population.

K-12 education is provided by local school districts free of charge to families and is largely jointly funded via local property taxes and equalizing grants from state governments. Postsecondary or higher education is provided by state governments and largely funded by direct state expenditures and tuition fees paid by students. In both the K-12 and higher education sectors, there are many private providers. In the public sphere, publicly funded but privately run K-12 charter schools are growing in importance, particularly in urban areas.

Even though the federal government provides a small share of the funding for K-12 education (on average, less than ten percent of total K-12 revenues), it has played an important role in shaping policy in an attempt to hold states and school districts accountable for improving student achievement. In 2002, the George W. Bush administration passed the No Child Left Behind (NCLB) Act, which required states to show yearly adequate progress in students' reading and mathematics test scores. NCLB represented a marked increase in the federal role in setting K-12 education policy. Thirteen years later, in 2015, after finding that virtually no state was meeting the goals of NCLB, the administration of Barak Obama passed the Every Student Succeeds Act, which largely turned back to state governments the task of setting and monitoring achievement standards for students in the states' schools.

Through the Social Security program, the federal government provides monthly cash benefits to retired individuals, surviving spouses, and disabled individuals. The size of the cash benefit depends on years of work and level of wages; however, there is a cap on the cash-benefit level, and it applies in a large share of cases. Many state and local governments have pension systems that provide annuities for their retired employees. In recent years, at all levels of government, retirement benefits have become a financial strain as the ratio of workers to retirees has declined with the aging of the population.

3 Intergovernmental Grants

Unlike in many other countries, federal grants in the US are not a concern in terms of vertical fiscal imbalances. States have full autonomy to raise their own revenues, with authority to impose taxes on the major tax bases. Thus, discussions of the appropriateness of federal transfers are not, as in other federations, about the sufficiency of the transfers' amount to cover states' expenditures, but rather on the purpose and design of the grants.

There are several grants from the federal government to state and local governments. The largest in terms of dollars is the grant to states for Medicaid. Medicaid, a program that provides healthcare insurance for low-income families and disabled persons, is administered at the state level. Its funding is joint between the states and the federal government. The funding from the federal government is through a matching grant, with a matching rate that varies across states according to their income per capita. All states receive at least a 50% matching grant so that for each dollar a state spends on Medicaid, the federal government funds another dollar. However, poorer states can receive much more, with matching rates that can be as high as 75.65%, as is the case of Mississippi for FY 2018. The 2010 Affordable Care Act (ACA) expanded the coverage of Medicaid. For expenditures on newly covered individuals, the federal government increased the matching rate to 100% for three years, and to 90% thereafter. States, according to a ruling of the Supreme Court, could decide whether to implement the Medicaid expansion. As of 2019, all but 14 states participated in the ACA Medicaid expansion program. Federal grants have increased significantly for those states that participate in the expansion program.

Other significant grants from the federal government to subnational governments include grants for education, transportation, and income security. As can be seen in Table 1, in FY 2016, total estimated federal grants to state and local governments were $661 billion. From Dilger (2018) we observe that almost 60% of the total went toward supporting healthcare expenditures (largely Medicaid), more than 15% of the total for income security programs (largely cash assistance), nearly nine percent each for education and transportation (highways and public transit), and the remainder for a variety of other purposes.

The main income security program for over sixty years, Aid to Families with Dependent Children (AFDC), was replaced in 1996 with the establishment of the Temporary Assistance for Needy Families (TANF) program. Federal funding support for the cash-assistance program was converted from a matching rate grant to a block grant for a total amount of $16.6 billion for the 50 states. The amount of the block grant has remained constant in nominal dollars since the program started in 1997 (with a slight decrease in 2017 to a total of $16.5 billion). Over time, the inflation adjusted value of the block grant has decreased by one third. The distribution among states is based on the federal contributions to each state to the AFDC program in 1994. States are required to spend own funds on an amount equal to at least 75% of their expenditures on AFDC in FY 1994 under the maintenance of effort requirement. While the federal government designed the overall requirements and guidelines for the TANF program, states were empowered to determine the eligibility for benefits and administer the program. The welfare reform that established TANF emphasized promoting job preparation and moving welfare recipients into employment. To achieve these goals the states are required to promote work so that 50% of all families, and 90% of two-parent families, participate in work activities. (For more information, see Congressional Research Service 2019.)

Transportation grants are important sources of revenue for spending on highways and transit. The federal government grants to state and local governments for highways and transit are in the form of both formula grants and competitive grants. Federal grants to state governments amount to more than thirty percent of state revenues for highway and transit spending. About ten percent of local government revenues for highways and transit are funded by federal grants. More than twenty percent of transportation expenditures of local governments are funded by state grants.

One of the more important federal grants for K-12 education is Title I, an aid program to support schools serving children from low-income families. Title I funds are distributed to school districts based on the concentration of low-income families in a district as determined by Census data. Additionally, the federal government has grant programs in support of special education for children ages three through 21. Overall, federal support for K-12 education amounts to less than ten percent of total K-12 revenues.[3]

State grants to school districts are large, accounting for almost half of school districts' revenues for K-12 education. The most common form of state aid to local school districts is a foundation aid program, which aims to ensure an adequate level of education spending for all students, irrespective of the school district they attend.

In many countries, the explicit goal of the federal grant system is to reduce the variance across jurisdictions in revenues per capita. This is not an explicit goal of the US grant system. Instead, some grants are targeted to address underlying poverty, as is the case of the Medicaid program, which provides a larger percentage match in its matching rate grant to poorer states, and the federal transfers for K-12 education, which are larger for school districts with greater percentages of poor students (but which are quite small in amounts).

We examine the redistributive result of federal grants to state and local governments in Fig. 1. The top part of Fig. 1 shows the income per capita of the 50 states ordered from largest to smallest. The bottom part displays the corresponding federal grants to state and local governments per capita. Comparing the two parts of the graph we observe that there is no pattern that would indicate that federal grants are redistributive in nature. Some rich states receive large per capita federal grants, while relatively poor states receive amounts similar to those of rich states.

[3] For a detailed description of federal grants to state and local governments, see Congressional Budget Office (2013).

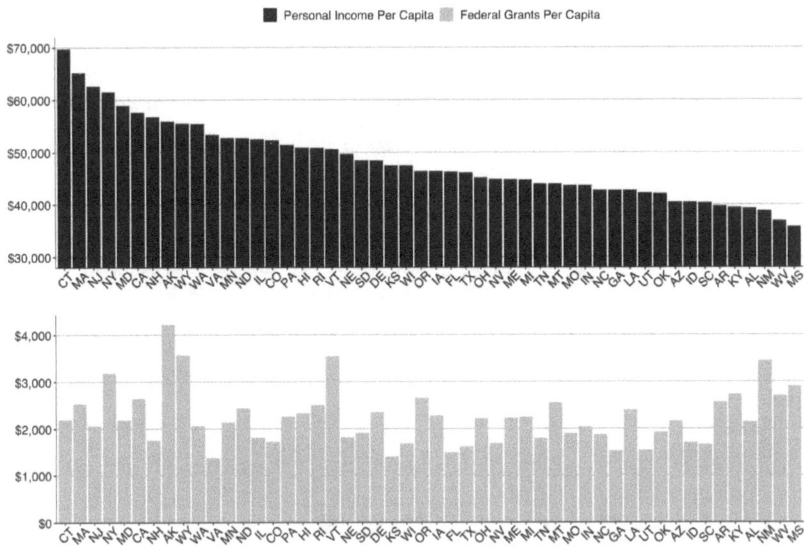

Fig. 1 Personal income and federal grants per capita to state and local governments: By state, 2016 (*Source* Annual Survey of State and Local Public Finances; Bureau of Economic Analysis)

State grants to local governments are a large source of revenue for many local governments. In Table 2, we display revenue sources for each of three types of local governments: counties, cities, and school districts. For both counties and school districts, state grants are the largest source of their revenues, respectively, 26.3 and 52.4%. For cities, their reliance on state grants is 12.8%, after property tax and charges and fees. The relevance of federal grants to local government revenues is much smaller, ranging from 3.7% for the cities to 0.9% for the school districts.[4]

4 Trends

In Table 3, as a measure of the size of government, we display total expenditures and total revenues as a share of GDP over time for the federal

[4] The percentage for school districts is larger than the data indicate. See the note to Table 2.

Table 2 Local government sources of revenue by type of local government, 2017 (thousands of dollars)

	County		*City*		*School district*	
	Amount	*% of Total*	*Amount*	*% of Total*	*Amount*	*% of Total*
Total Revenue	452,731,442	100	656,617,943	100	575,610,755	100
Property Tax	120,325,503	26.6	120,995,052	18.4	212,105,355	36.8
Sales Tax	37,101,092	8.2	69,269,772	10.5	5,364,211	0.9
Income Tax	5,530,379	1.2	32,204,359	4.9	2,352,183	0.4
State Grants	119,188,159	26.3	84,018,705	12.8	301,592,518	52.4
Federal Grants	12,428,579	2.7	24,148,742	3.7	4,975,727	0.9
Charges & Fees	87,905,896	19.4	105,588,929	16.1	20,235,386	3.5
Utility Revenue	6,523,684	1.4	93,393,642	14.2	0	0
Other	63,728,150	14.1	126,998,742	19.3	28,985,375	5

Note The figures for state grants and federal grants for school districts are misleading in that the vast majority of federal grant monies for school districts pass through the states. Accounting for this fact, as a rough approximation, we estimate the state grants share is 45% and the federal grants share is 10% for school districts

Source U.S. Census Bureau, 2017 Census of Governments

Table 3 Current expenditures and own source revenues as a share of GDP by level of government

	Expenditures			*Revenues*		
Year	*Total*	*Federal*	*State + Local*	*Total*	*Federal*	*State + Local*
1950	0.213	0.148	0.065	0.220	0.163	0.058
1960	0.242	0.165	0.077	0.247	0.172	0.074
1970	0.297	0.188	0.110	0.266	0.172	0.094
1980	0.313	0.193	0.120	0.280	0.187	0.093
1990	0.327	0.199	0.129	0.287	0.182	0.105
2000	0.295	0.164	0.131	0.306	0.202	0.104
2005	0.314	0.174	0.140	0.282	0.177	0.105
2010	0.371	0.218	0.154	0.262	0.163	0.099
2015	0.334	0.191	0.142	0.290	0.189	0.101
2018	0.330	0.191	0.139	0.269	0.170	0.099

Source National Income and Product Accounts, Tables 3.1, 3.2, 3.3

government, state and local governments combined, and the total across all levels of government. From 1950 until 2018, government spending in the US grew from 21.3% of GDP to 33.0%. Over that period, the percentage of GDP spent by state and local governments more than doubled from 6.5 to 13.9%, whereas federal spending grew more slowly, from 14.8 to 19.1%. The growth spurts for state and local government spending were from 1960 to 1970, a period which encompasses the creation of the Medicaid program in 1965 and the expansion of other social-safety-net programs, and from 2005 to 2010, which includes the roll out of the American Recovery and Reinvestment Act (ARRA), the Obama administration stimulus program enacted in the wake of the Great Recession. Federal spending also increased dramatically from 2005 to 2010 due to ARRA.

Revenues displayed similar although slower growth trends. Note that state and local revenues are in every year lower than state and local expenditures, reflecting the fact that state and local governments rely to a significant extent on grants from the federal government (which are counted as revenues of the federal government). For the federal government, its spending is greater than or virtually equal to its revenues in every year except 2000, when it ran a surplus. In some years, the deficit implied by the numbers is quite large, for example, in 2010, the year that reflects the stimulus spending of ARRA.

Table 4 displays federal grants to state and local governments measured in real 2012 dollars per capita in total and for four large categories of

Table 4 Federal intergovernmental grants by functional category, 2012 dollars per capita

Year	*Total*	*Healthcare*	*Education*	*Transportation*	*Income Security*
1950	113	6	8	23	67
1960	233	7	17	100	88
1970	541	87	144	103	130
1980	949	164	227	135	192
1990	850	276	137	120	232
2000	1297	566	166	146	311
2005	1654	765	221	168	351
2010	2043	975	328	205	387
2015	1857	1095	180	181	301
2018	1927	1165	168	179	306

Source Office of Management and Budget Historical Table 12.2; categories not exhaustive

Table 5 Share of tax revenues across all levels of government by category

Year	*Income*	*Sales*	*Property*	*Other*
1950	0.603	0.210	0.120	0.067
1960	0.588	0.215	0.144	0.053
1970	0.579	0.209	0.162	0.050
1980	0.638	0.190	0.120	0.052
1990	0.613	0.191	0.142	0.054
2000	0.663	0.175	0.117	0.045
2005	0.614	0.186	0.138	0.062
2010	0.571	0.200	0.170	0.058
2015	0.632	0.181	0.135	0.051
2018	0.599	0.193	0.150	0.059

Source National Income and Product Account Tables 3.2, 3.3

spending. There has been a rapid rise in the level of federal grants and a marked shift in the relative levels across categories. In 1950, grants for income security dwarfed the level of grants for other purposes. By 2018, grants for healthcare dwarfed grants for other purposes. Grants for healthcare took a large leap from 1960 to 1970 due to the creation of Medicaid in 1965, a state-run program for low-income and disabled families; Medicaid is jointly funded by matching grants from the federal government and state own-source revenues. After the Medicaid program was adopted, grants for healthcare continued to grow at a fast pace throughout the period. Grants for transportation grew dramatically between 1950 and 1960 when states started building out the interstate highway system, an initiative largely funded by federal grants.

In Table 5, we examine major categories of tax revenues, aggregated across all levels of government. Income taxes (individual and corporate combined) as a share of total tax revenues bounced around a bit over the decades, a reflection of the relative volatility and responsiveness of the taxes to the underlying economy and also a reflection of major federal tax changes enacted by different administrations. Sales taxes remained steady as a share of total taxes, hovering around 20%.

Property taxes as a share of taxes fell between 1970 and 1980 reflecting the impact of the property tax revolt, which began with the passage of Proposition 13 in California in 1978. As property tax values increased rapidly in California in the 1970s and local governments failed to adjust

Table 6 Share of total expenditures across all levels of government by major category

Year	*Education*	*Healthcare*	*Defense*
1960	11.3	4.2	33.8
1970	13.8	7.5	26.5
1980	13.4	10.2	16.1
1990	13.2	12.5	15.2
2000	14.9	16.6	10.2
2005	14.1	18.8	11.7
2010	13.3	19.7	11.7
2015	13.4	23.2	9.7
2017	13.3	23.7	9.2

Source National Income and Product Account Tables 3.1, 3.16; categories not exhaustive

their property tax rates, property tax revenues and property tax liabilities soared. There was a tax revolt that culminated in the passage by voter referendum of Proposition 13, an amendment to the California constitution. Proposition 13 limited the overall property tax rate to 1% and limited the growth rate of assessed valuation to 2% per year unless the property was sold, at which time its assessed value reflected its sale price. Over the next few years, the tax limitation movement swept across the country and various limitation measures were approved by the voters or enacted by state legislatures.[5]

Over the course of the past nearly 60 years, the share of total government expenditures devoted to healthcare increased dramatically, from 4.2% in 1960 to 23.7% in 2017 (see Table 6). This large increase reflects the passage of major new government healthcare programs over the period (both Medicaid and Medicare were signed into law in 1965), the rising costs of healthcare provision, and the aging of the population. Defense spending as a share of total government expenditures declined significantly, from 33.8% in 1960 to 9.2% in 2017, reflecting the decline in US involvement in warfare after the 1960s and 1970s. The share of spending devoted to education (K-12 education combined with higher education) was relatively stable over the period.

[5] See O'Sullivan et al. (1995) for a detailed treatment of Proposition 13.

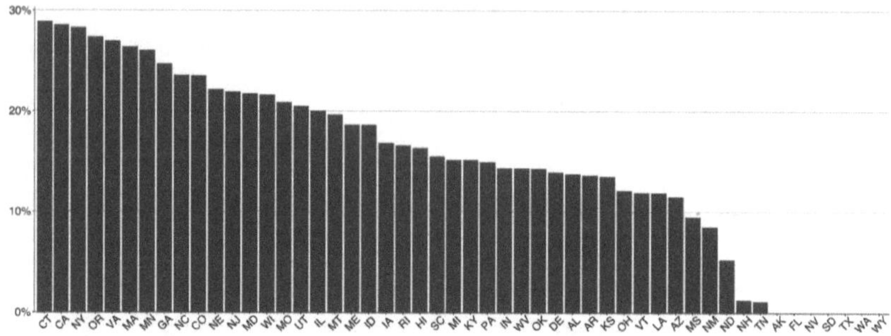

Fig. 2 State reliance on the income tax, 2016: Individual income tax as a percentage of total state general revenues (*Source* Annual Survey of State and Local Public Finances)

5 Diversity

States and local governments in the US have significant revenue-raising autonomy and spending responsibility. As noted above, in 2018, state and local government own-source revenue was 9.9% of GDP compared to 17.0% for the federal government; state and local government spending was 13.9% of GDP compared to 19.1% for the federal government.

An important distinction of the US system is that there is great variety across the states in how they raise revenues and set spending priorities.[6] Because the individual income tax and general sales tax are by far the two largest sources of revenue for states other than intergovernmental grants from the federal government, we focus our examination on these two taxes. In Fig. 2, we portray states' reliance on the individual income tax in 2016, calculated as the percentage of total state general revenue raised through the individual income tax. We observe large differences across states, with seven states without an individual income tax, while for other states revenues from the individual income tax amount to almost 30% of their revenues. In Fig. 3, we portray states' reliance on the general sales tax in 2016. We identify five states without a general sales tax, while at the other extreme we find states that raise more than 30% of their total general revenues through the general sales tax.

[6] For a detailed study of diversity across states in the US see Garcia-Milà et al. (2018).

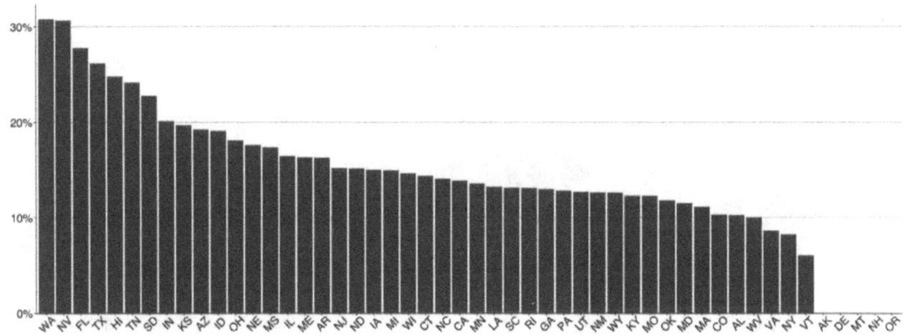

Fig. 3 State reliance on the general sales tax, 2016: General sales tax as a percentage of total state general revenues (*Source* Annual Survey of State and Local Public Finances)

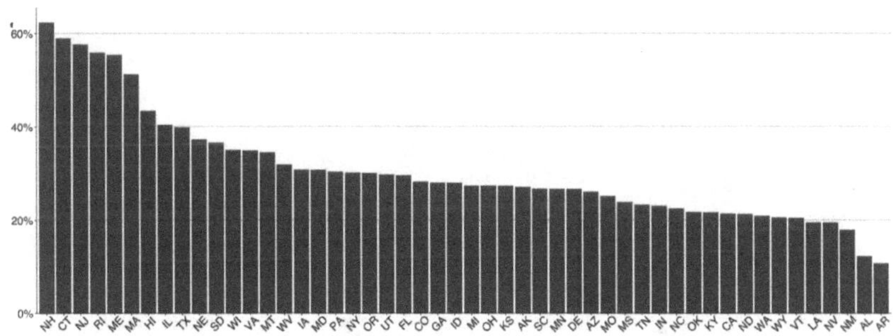

Fig. 4 Local government reliance on property taxes, 2016: Property tax as a percentage of total local general revenues (*Source* Annual Survey of State and Local Public Finances)

Because local governments raise the vast majority of property tax revenues (97% in 2016), we examine local government reliance on the property tax, which is the largest source of revenues for local governments after intergovernmental grants. In Fig. 4, we display the percentage of total local general revenues raised through property taxes. We observe that local governments rely on the property tax in all states, although there is a large diversity, from a reliance of ten percent to above 60%.

On the spending side, we also see wide discretion for state and local governments. For all 50 states, for 2016, we examine in current dollars per capita, combined state and local spending on several categories of

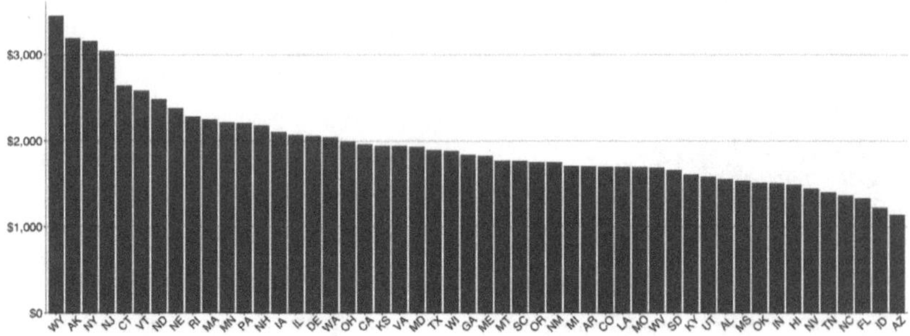

Fig. 5 State and local direct expenditures on K-12 education, 2016 (dollars per capita) (*Source* Annual Survey of State and Local Government Finances)

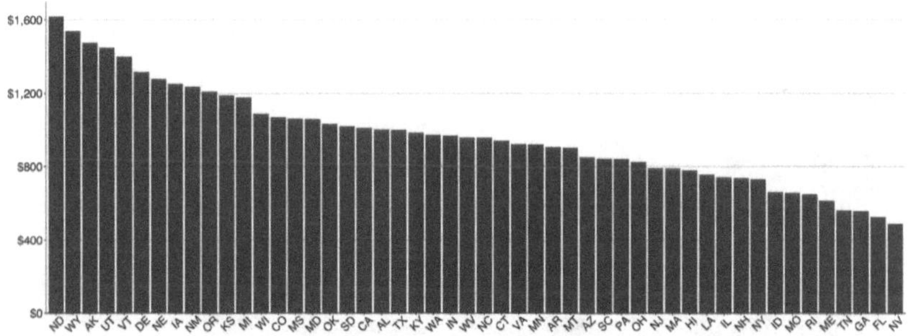

Fig. 6 State and local direct expenditures on higher education, 2016 (dollars per capita) (*Source* Annual Survey of State and Local Government Finances)

spending that account for the largest components of the state and local budget (see Table 1). In Fig. 5, we observe the diversity of spending on K-12 education, which ranges from $3,449 per capita in Wyoming to $1,136 per capita in Arizona. For higher education, the differences are proportionally even larger, with Nevada, the state at the bottom of the distribution, spending $486 per capita, less than one third of the spending in North Dakota at $1,617 per capita (see Fig. 6). Expenditures on Medicaid, displayed in Fig. 7, also reveal large diversity across the states, not dissimilar to the differences observed in education spending. Figure 8 displays values for expenditures on transportation, with the values for Alaska and North Dakota being far above the values of any other state.

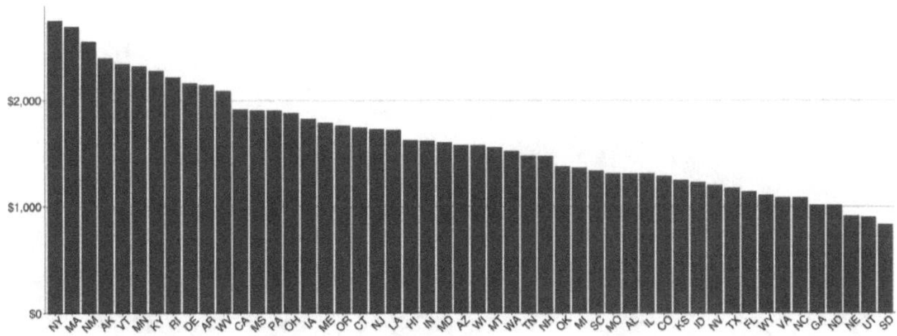

Fig. 7 State and local direct expenditures on Medicaid, 2016 (dollars per capita) (*Source* Annual Survey of State and Local Government Finances)

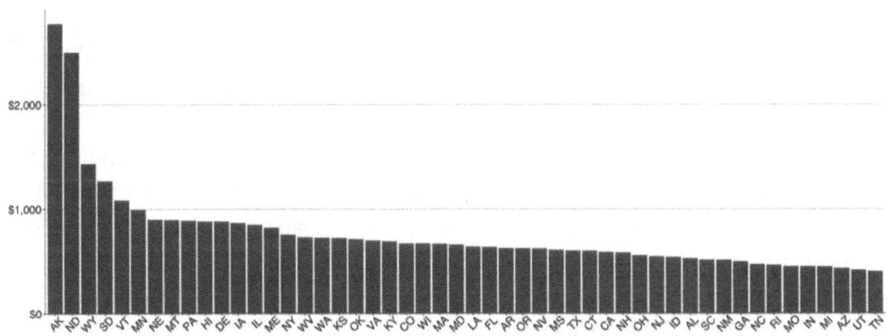

Fig. 8 State and local direct expenditures on Transportation, 2016 (dollars per capita) (*Source* Annual Survey of State and Local Government Finances)

Even abstracting from these two outliers, diversity is clearly present, with Tennessee spending 28% of what Wyoming spends.

Another area of significant diversity in the fiscal federal system in the US is how the states fund K-12 education. The provision of K-12 education is under the responsibility of local school districts and on average funding for K-12 is split approximately 50% state and 40% local, with the remaining 10% funded by the federal government. There is, however, great variance across the states in the share funded by the state. In Fig. 9 we display the share of total revenues for K-12 education that come from the state. The diversity across states is quite remarkable, ranging from a

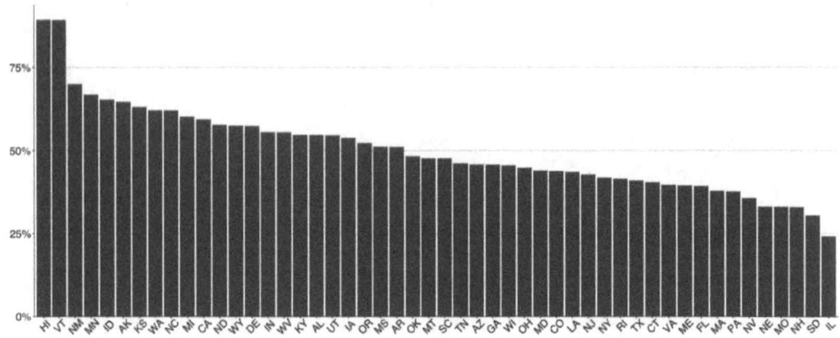

Fig. 9 State intergovernmental grants as a percentage of total education revenues, 2016 (*Source* Nation Center for Education Statistics)

low of 24% in Illinois, up to nearly 90% in Hawaii and Vermont, indicating that there are important differences across states in approaching education funding.

States have wide discretion and have chosen different paths in the rules, regulations, and practices surrounding budgets and funds. Most states have balanced budget requirements (BBRs) that apply to their general fund (which funds the operating budget), but the stringency of the requirement varies from state to state.[7] In some states, all that is required is that the governor propose a balanced budget whereas in other states the legislature must pass (and the governor sign) a balanced budget and any unexpected deficit cannot be carried into the next fiscal year nor covered by short-term borrowing. All states have rainy day funds (RDFs), also known as budget stabilization funds, which provide reserves that can be tapped during economic downturns. However, the conditions and requirements for deposits into and withdrawals from the funds differ across the states. For example, in some states, RDFs can be accessed when an unanticipated budget gap arises, whereas withdrawals in other states can be triggered by revenue volatility. The authority for withdrawal can rest with the governor, the legislature, a state agency or, as is the case in California, all three. Once depleted, the rules for replenishing the

[7] It is difficult to agree upon an exact count of states with BBRs because the laws and practices are open to interpretation. For example, the National Association of State Budget Officers identifies 49 of 50 states (see National Conference of State Legislators 2010) whereas Rueben and Randall (2017) identify 46 states.

RDF also vary across states, with some states being required to replenish the funds in the next fiscal year (Rhode Island and Wyoming) and other states allowing several years for replenishment (Alabama allows ten years, for example). See Walczak and Cammenga (2020).

6 Challenges and Future Directions

The US fiscal federal system has been remarkably stable for several decades. However, the aging population and rising healthcare costs are presenting challenges for all three levels of government. Income support for retirees and support for healthcare are two of the fastest-growing components of public budgets. We saw in Table 6 that healthcare spending as a share of total expenditures (across all levels of government) increased from 4.2% in 1960 to 23.7% in 2017, far outstripping the share for education, the second-largest category. Most state and local governments provide publicly funded pensions to their retired employees. In Fig. 10, we see that from 1993 to 2018, aggregate state and local pension benefit payments for retired public-sector employees grew much faster than GDP (benefits grew more than six times while GDP growth was just shy of doubling). The rapid growth in expenditures for healthcare and for income support for retirees is making it more challenging for state and local governments to deliver desired levels of other government services.

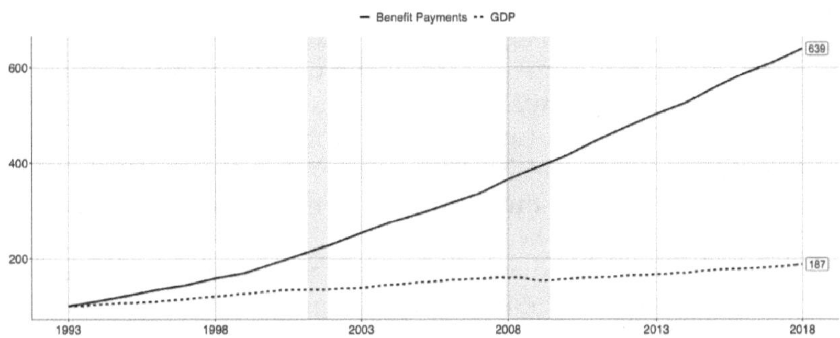

Fig. 10 Pension funding dynamics—growth in state and local pension benefit payments compared to growth in GDP: Series indexed to 100 in 1993 (*Source* Annual Survey of Public Pension)

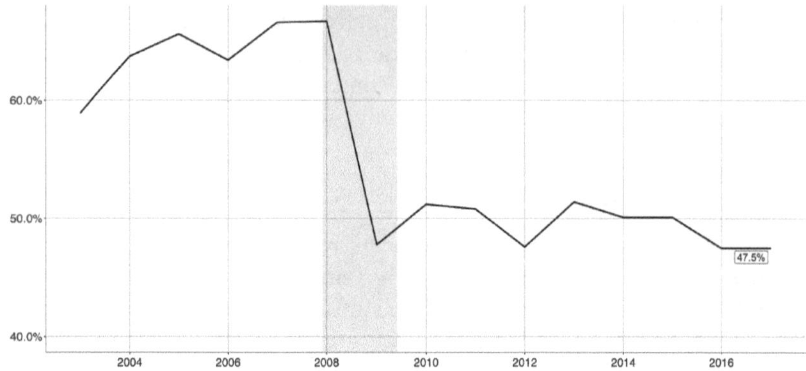

Fig. 11 State and local pension fund assets as a percentage of liabilities (*Source* Federal Reserve Board of Governors, Financial Accounts of the United States)

Many state and local government pension systems are underfunded, in some cases, severely so.[8] In Fig. 11, we display the ratio of aggregate state and local pension fund assets to liabilities over the period 2002 to 2016. After peaking at 66.7% in 2007 before the start of the financial crisis, the ratio declined to 47.5% in 2016. The aging of the population and the generosity of defined benefit pension plans, the most common form of the pension plan for state and local governments, contributed to the growth in liabilities. Underfunded pensions have played a role in budget difficulties for several state and local governments, most notably in the bankruptcy proceedings of the city of Detroit, Michigan in 2013–2014. The city's inability to meet its pension obligations brought the city to bankruptcy. The city exited bankruptcy after 16 months when parties agreed to the "Grand Bargain": financial contributions by philanthropic organizations, grants in aid from the state government, financial contributions by the Detroit Institute of Arts, and retirees agreeing to a cut in the generosity of retirees' benefits.

Disregarding intergovernmental expenditures, spending on healthcare has become the single largest category of expenditures for state governments (at 29.0% in 2016), the second-largest category of expenditures for the federal government (at 18.4%, behind only retirement benefit

[8] For a discussion of the funding status of state pension funds, see Pew Charitable Trusts (2019).

payments at 27.6%), and the third-largest category of expenditures for local governments (behind spending on K-12 education and public safety). (See Table 1.) The Affordable Care Act of 2010 resulted in an expansion of healthcare coverage to additional families. For states that agreed to cover more families under the program, the federal government increased the matching rate to 100% on state Medicaid expenditures for the newly covered families.[9] All but 19 states initially and, as of 2019, all but 14 states agreed to expand coverage. Still, 8.5% of the population in the US is not covered by either public or private health insurance.

The two primary issues with public K-12 education are inequities in resources across school districts and low student achievement. In recent decades, state supreme courts have ruled that their state's school funding systems are in violation of the state constitution.[10] Murray et al. (1998) examined the impact of court challenges and found that court-ordered education finance reform reduced within-state inequality in spending per pupil across school districts. The reduction in inequality resulted largely through increases in spending per pupil at the bottom of the distribution; spending per pupil at the top of the distribution remained unchanged.

Another recent development in public K-12 education is the growth of charter schools. Charter schools are publicly funded but privately operated elementary and secondary schools. They are prevalent in cities with large public school systems, particularly in areas where student achievement levels in traditional public schools are low. The evidence on the effectiveness of charter schools is voluminous and mixed (for two examples see Angrist et al. 2013 and Center for Research on Education Outcomes 2013).

The US has one of the world's most highly regarded public higher education systems. However, there are concerns that public universities are becoming unaffordable for many families. The concerns center around

[9] After the first three years, the 100% match phased down and by 2020 the match was 90%.

[10] There is no authoritative list of state supreme court decisions regarding the constitutionality of state school funding systems, but the courts in at least two-thirds of states have delivered rulings since the early 1970s. In several states, notably New Hampshire and New Jersey, the state supreme court has ruled in multiple cases over the years. In a recent ruling in 2018, the Connecticut Supreme Court overruled a lower court's decision and upheld the existing school funding system.

the level of tuition fees and the level of student debt, which has become cripplingly high for many students.[11]

There is a two-pronged challenge with transportation: declining revenues dedicated to transportation and the deteriorating condition of the infrastructure. Federal funds to support state and local spending on transportation infrastructure have been declining in recent years due to the inability to raise the federal tax on gasoline (at 18.4 cents per gallon since 1993) and the rise of more fuel-efficient cars.[12] States have been stepping into the breach to address the nation's crumbling infrastructure, but they have uneven financial capabilities and political willingness. In addition, many transportation systems cross state lines, making state provision inefficient.

Many of the challenges that the US fiscal federal system faces, in particular, the challenges of an aging population and rising healthcare costs, are common to fiscal federal systems around the world. The challenges in education and transportation are distinctive to the US situation; they exist in part because of the specific approaches the US has taken to funding education and transportation at different levels of government. These approaches are not commonly employed in other countries. Overall, however, the fiscal federal system in the US is viewed in a favorable light. It has been both stable, withstanding the test of time, and flexible, adjusting over time as changing conditions warranted. A distinctive characteristic of the US system is the uncommon degree of revenue-raising authority of its subnational governments. It is a clear strength of the US system and a model for other countries.

Acknowledgements We wish to thank Michael Fogarty for superb research assistance. Garcia-Milà acknowledges financial support from the Spanish Ministry of Science, Innovation and Universities, through SEV-2015-0563 and HAR2017-ECO2017-82696-P.

Afterword

While we were writing this chapter, the coronavirus pandemic crisis was putting a strain on the country's fiscal federal system. States, which are

[11] For a discussion of the policy issues related to student debt see Dynarski (2014).

[12] See Transportation Research Board (2006).

responsible for providing healthcare to low-income families, the disabled, and low-income residents of nursing homes, were experiencing increased demand for these services. States and cities were also addressing the complicated logistics of organizing an adequate supply of emergency services, addressing an overflow of hospital capacity, and designing and implementing confinement measures for the population to reduce the spread of the pandemic.

The revenues of state and local governments were being heavily affected by the economic consequences of the measures taken to address the Covid-19 health crisis. Income tax revenues are highly volatile and tend to drop precipitously during economic downturns; this time will not be any different. Many states and localities rely on sales taxes that tend to be more stable over the cycle. This economic crisis, though, is different, as social distancing and mandatory closures have had a large negative impact on consumer spending, which will result in a larger than typical drop in sales tax revenues. Revenues from excise taxes, for example, on motor fuel consumption, and from special taxes on hotels, bars, and casinos, will drop dramatically.

The federal government approved on March 27, 2020, the Coronavirus Aid, Relief and Economic Security Act (CARES Act), consisting of a federal stimulus package of $2 trillion. Within this program, $150 billion has been assigned to support state and local governments through the Coronavirus Relief Fund. This fund, for states, tribal areas, and local governments serving a population larger than 500,000, is dedicated to expenditures related to the Covid-19 emergency through the period March 1 to December 30, 2020. The allocation of these funds is roughly proportional to the population, with a minimum per state of $1.5 billion. Additionally, through the CARES Act, the federal government will cover half of the unemployment benefit payments through the end of 2020, and the full unemployment benefit payments for the 13 weeks extension that can be applied for when the state unemployment benefit coverage ends. There is an allocation in the Act of $25 billion for transportation grants to cover operating expenses of transit agencies during the emergency. In addition, funds up to $6.3 billion will be distributed by the Administration for Children and Families through grants to state and local programs that support children and needy families. The Act also includes $30 billion in funds to state agencies for K-12 education and to institutions of higher education (both public and private).

References

Angrist, J., P. Pathak and C. Walters. 2013. "Explaining Charter School Effectiveness." *American Economic Journal: Applied Economics*, 5(4): 1–27.

Congressional Budget Office. 2013. *Federal Grants to State and Local Governments*. Washington, DC: CBO Publishing.

Congressional Research Service. 2019. *The Temporary Assistance for Needy Families (TANF) Block Grant: Responses to Frequently Asked Questions*. Washington, DC: CRS Publishing.

Center for Research on Education Outcomes. 2013. *National Charter School Study*. Stanford, CA: CREDO Publishing.

Dilger, R. 2018. *Federal Grants to State and Local Governments: A Historical Perspective on Contemporary Issues*. Washington, DC: CRS Publishing.

Dynarski, S. 2014. "An Economist's Perspective on Student Loans in the United States." Brookings Institution, ES working paper.

Garcia-Milà, T. and T. McGuire. 2019. "When Theory Meets Practice: Can We Implement the Optimal Fiscal Federal Structure?" Mimeo.

Garcia-Milà, T., T. McGuire and W. Oates. 2018. "Strength in Diversity? Fiscal Federalism Among the Fifty US States," *International Tax and Public Finance*, 25–4: 1071–1091.

Kent, C. and E. Eastham. 2011. *Taxation of Coal: A Comparative Analysis*. Huntington, WV: Marshall University Center for Business and Economic Research Publishing.

Kolesnikoff, A. and C. Brown. 2018. *State Oil and Gas Severance Taxes*. Denver, CO: National Conference of State Legislatures Publishing.

Murray, S., W. Evans and R. Schwab. 1998. "Education-Finance Reform and the Distribution of Education Resources." *The American Economic Review*, 88–4: 789–812.

National Conference of State Legislatures. 2010. *NCSL Fiscal Brief: State Balanced Budget Provisions*. Denver, CO: NCSL Publishing.

O'Sullivan, A, T. Sexton and S. Sheffrin. 1995. *Property Taxes and Tax Revolts: The Legacy of Proposition* 13. Cambridge: Cambridge University Press.

Pew Charitable Trusts. 2019. *The State Pension Funding Gap: 2017*. Philadelphia: Pew Charitable Trusts publishing.

Rueben, K. and M. Randall. 2017. *Balanced Budget Requirements: How States Limit Deficit Spending*. Washington, DC: Urban Institute Publishing.

Transportation Research Board. 2006. *The Fuel Tax and Alternatives for Transportation Funding*. Washington, DC: Transportation Research Board of the National Academies Publishing.

Walczak, J. and J. Cammenga. 2020. *State Rainy Day Funds and the COVID-19 Crisis*. Washington, DC: Tax Foundation Publishing.

Wallis, J. 2000. "American government finance in the long run: 1790 to 1990." *Journal of Economic Perspectives*, 14–1: 61–82.

Comparative Perspectives on Fiscal Federalism Systems

Jean-François Tremblay

There is great diversity across federal systems in how fiscal arrangements are designed. This applies to the allocation of spending responsibilities and taxation powers among orders of governments, regulatory functions, fiscal transfer systems, fiscal rules, and policy harmonization mechanisms. Central elements of fiscal arrangements generally reflect the character and specificities of each federation. At the same time, fiscal arrangements are critically important for many defining features of federal countries including the effective autonomy of subnational governments, accountability and fiscal discipline, economic efficiency, fiscal disparities across subnational units, and so on.

The eleven fiscal federalism systems reviewed in previous chapters highlight such diversity. Some of them are relatively centralized including those of Australia, India, Italy, and Spain. In these countries, the central government plays a relatively dominant role in the taxation system and in the provision of public services, sometimes through influence on subnational government programs. Other countries, such as Canada, Switzerland, the United States and to some extent Brazil, are more decentralized

J.-F. Tremblay (✉)
Department of Economics, University of Ottawa, Ottawa, ON, Canada
e-mail: jtrembl2@uottawa.ca

J.-F. Tremblay (ed.), *The Forum of Federations Handbook of Fiscal Federalism*, https://doi.org/10.1007/978-3-030-97258-5_12

with subnational governments having substantially more autonomy in formulating public services programs and in raising revenues. Some federations are characterized by cooperative decision-making and interdependency. That is the case, to varying degrees, for Germany, Ethiopia, and South Africa. In some countries, there are asymmetries in the extent of fiscal decentralization with some subnational units having more autonomy and responsibilities than others (e.g. Spain, India, Italy).

This chapter provides a comparative overview of fiscal federalism arrangements in these eleven countries highlighting both the diversity of fiscal arrangements and some common features. Section 1 discusses the assignment of expenditure responsibilities among orders of government. The allocation of taxation powers is reviewed in Sect. 2 with a particular focus on how the structure of tax systems determines the effective revenue-raising autonomy of subnational governments. Section 3 looks at fiscal transfer systems with some emphasis on how different systems pursue equalization objectives. Section 4 discusses macroeconomic management focusing particularly on tax harmonization, fiscal rules, and restrictions on government borrowing. Finally, common challenges to fiscal federalism systems are briefly outlined in the last section.

1 Expenditure Responsibilities

There are many common features in the assignment of expenditure responsibilities. Central governments are typically responsible for functions that have an important national dimension, that involve interregional spillovers and for which policy harmonization across subnational units is especially important (Anderson, 2008; Boadway and Shah, 2009). This includes foreign affairs, international trade, national defense, monetary policy, the regulation of rail and air transportation and usually financial markets regulation, telecommunications, as well as competition and industrial policy. State governments are generally involved, to varying degrees, in the areas of education, health care, social welfare services, natural resources, and environmental management, sometimes through exclusive responsibilities and sometimes through concurrent or shared responsibilities. Local governments are usually responsible for public services for which benefits are largely local in nature and for which delivery is more effectively managed at the local level. This includes policing, water supply and sewer services, local roads and transit, housing, recreation and culture, fire protection, among others.

The eleven fiscal federalism systems reviewed in this book are generally in line with the standard allocation of responsibilities although the central government is much more influential in the core areas of education, health care, and social welfare services in some cases while state and local governments enjoy more powers and autonomy in others (see Table 1).

1.1 Decentralization, Concurrent Responsibilities, and Central Government Influence

In some countries, state governments hold most responsibilities and legislative authority with respect to education, health care, and social services, and enjoy high autonomy in fulfilling these responsibilities. That is the case in Australia, Canada, Switzerland, and the United States. Canadian provinces have exclusive legislative powers in health care and education. The role of the federal government is essentially limited to providing some of the funding and establishing broad conditions in the case of health care. In the US, the federal government has had some influence on state education policies by imposing student achievement standards, but states otherwise have high autonomy in legislating and managing the education system. In both Canada and the United States, while provincial and state governments hold legislative powers in education, the education systems are partly managed by special-purpose local governments (i.e. school boards in some Canadian provinces, school districts in the US). The extensive responsibilities and legislative authority held by Australian and Canadian provinces, Swiss cantons, and US states have resulted in considerable diversity in programs and levels of expenditures across subnational units in these countries.

In most of the eleven federations surveyed, however, central governments are more actively involved in the provision of core public services. In India, Union and state governments have concurrent responsibilities in education, health care, social security, environmental management, and economic and social planning. In Germany, there are several areas of concurrent legislation of the federal government and the Laender, with federal paramountcy in general. In practice, the federal government exerts considerable influence on subnational policies through legislation that affects the administrative functions of Laender or municipalities, even though such legislation requires the approval of the Bundersrat in which Laender are represented. In Spain, education and health care are, in effect, shared responsibilities of the Autonomous Communities and the central

Table 1 Decentralization of expenditure responsibilities

	Decentralization of responsibilities to states	*Decentralization of responsibilities to local governments*	*Constitutional status for local governments*	*Central government influence on state programs and policies*	*State government influence on local programs and policies*
Australia	Extensive	Limited	No	Moderate	Strong
Brazil	Limited	Extensive	Yes	Moderate	Weak
Canada	Extensive	Extensive	No	Weak	Moderate
Ethiopia	Moderate	Moderate	No	Strong	Strong
Germany	Extensive	Limited	No	Moderate	Strong
India	Extensive	Limited	Yes	Moderate	Strong
Italy	Moderate	Moderate	Yes	Strong	Weak
South Africa	Extensive	Moderate	Yes	Strong	Moderate
Spain	Extensive	Moderate	No	Moderate	Moderate
Switzerland	Extensive	Extensive	Yes	Weak	Moderate
United States	Extensive	Extensive	No	Weak	Moderate

government. Autonomous Communities are responsible for delivering services in these areas while the central government sets regulations over various dimensions of service provision including minimum standards of services, conditions for access to services, etc.

In these three countries, despite the existence of concurrent or shared responsibilities in many areas, state governments hold substantial autonomy and legislative authority, although to varying degrees. Subnational autonomy in the provision of core public services is much more limited in other countries such as Ethiopia, South Africa, and Italy despite the existence of concurrent or shared responsibilities.

In Ethiopia, states are responsible, or share responsibilities with the federal government, for delivering many public services such as health care, education, public safety, and for managing the natural resource sector and labor markets. However, the federal government has considerable influence on how states fulfill their responsibilities through the establishment of national standards and policies. As a result, the effective autonomy of state governments is quite limited. In South Africa, provincial governments have considerable responsibilities but little effective autonomy. In most cases, provincial governments have concurrent responsibilities with either the federal government (e.g. health, education, welfare services, public transportation) or with both the federal government and local governments (e.g. housing, environment, roads). Generally, subnational governments are responsible for delivering services subject to the policies, regulations, and standards set by the federal government. In Italy, regional governments have responsibilities in many areas including education, health care, social assistance, and environmental management. However, regional government responsibilities are essentially concurrent responsibilities over which the central government exercises high influence by defining principles, levels of services, standards, etc. In effect, the autonomy of regional governments in areas of concurrent responsibilities is extremely constrained.

In Brazil, the role of local governments is particularly important, especially in health care and education. The Brazilian Constitution recognizes local governments and assigns them considerable spending and taxation responsibilities. Despite constraints imposed by federal legislation, local governments enjoy significant autonomy, more so than state governments. Education, health care, social assistance, and public safety are concurrent responsibilities, although in practice the federal government is largely responsible for social assistance while local governments are more heavily involved in education and health care and state governments play a more important role with respect to public safety. Local governments also have constitutional recognition in Switzerland, India, and South Africa, but do not enjoy as much autonomy as in Brazil, especially in the case of India.

1.2 Distribution of Expenditures

Diversity in the allocation of responsibilities and in the effective roles played by each order of government in providing public services leads to wide variations in the share of expenditures by each order of government. As depicted in Fig. 1, the expenditures of state and local governments combined in total government expenditures (excluding intergovernmental transfers) are above 65% in Canada and over 50% in India, South Africa, Switzerland, and the United States, while it is below 30% in Italy. The relative role of local governments in subnational expenditures is

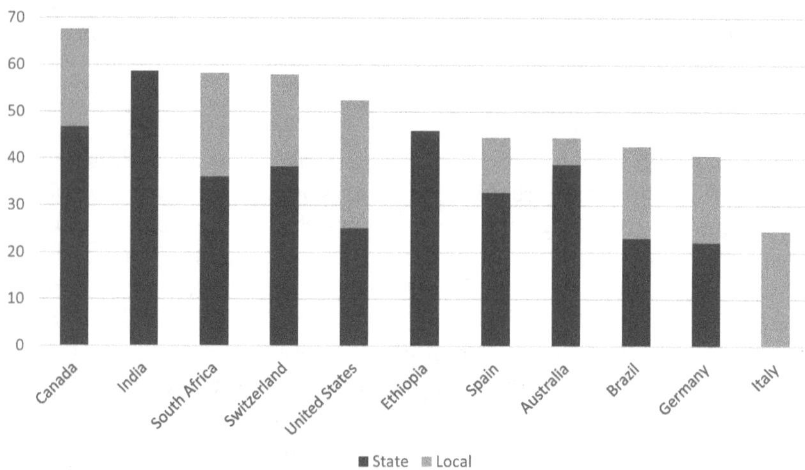

Fig. 1 Share of expenditures, excluding grants paid to other governments, in total government expenditures (%) (*Sources* IMF Government Finance Statistics and various chapters from this book. Data is for 2019 for all countries except Ethiopia [2017], India [2017], and South Africa [2018]. Data not available for local governments in Ethiopia and in India. Data for local governments in Italy includes all subnational governments)

particularly important in the United States, Brazil, and Germany, and very limited in Australia.

1.3 *Asymmetry in the Allocation of Responsibilities*

In some countries, there are asymmetries across subnational units in the allocation of responsibilities. That is the case in Italy, where asymmetries exist between the fifteen ordinary regions and the five special regions. Special regions have bilateral relations with the central government and hold a wider range of responsibilities and higher effective autonomy than ordinary regions. Some autonomous communities in Spain also hold more responsibilities than others, in the area of policing for example, although such asymmetries have become more limited over time. Asymmetric arrangements also exist in India where some states have special status. These states are mainly located in mountainous areas and tend to be disadvantaged economically. Special status provides these states with some advantages such as exemptions from some union taxes and more generous grants from the Union government, some intended to promote economic development. In Canada, there are three northern and sparsely populated territories with fiscal arrangements with the federal government that are different than those applying to the ten provinces. A different system of federal transfers applies to these territories and the federal government plays a more extensive role in the provision of some public services such as health care.

2 Taxation Powers and Revenue Decentralization

Generally speaking, personal incomes taxes, corporate income taxes, and taxes on international trade tend to be more centralized while subnational governments generally have more access to sales and value-added taxes, property taxes, and several narrow-based taxes and use fees such as real estate transfer taxes, alcohol and fuel taxes, motor vehicle taxes and parking fees (Anderson, 2010). That is generally the case in the eleven countries surveyed here, with a few notable departures from the standard assignment.

2.1 *Tax Decentralization* and *Revenue-Raising Autonomy*

State level governments have access to the personal and corporate income taxes in some of the more decentralized federations such as Canada, the United States, and Switzerland. This is a key distinguishing feature of tax systems in these countries. In Canada, the federal and provincial governments have unrestricted access to almost all main broad-based taxes with the exception of taxes on natural resources which are reserved for provincial governments and taxes on international trade which are available only to the federal government. The personal and corporate income tax bases are jointly occupied by the federal and provincial governments. Although there exist tax collection agreements between federal and provincial governments, provinces enjoy full autonomy and set their own income tax policies independently of the federal government.

As in Canada, the United States constitution gives full access to most major tax bases to the federal and state governments. States have high revenue-raising autonomy, which has led to considerable diversity in relative reliance on different taxes across states, even more so than in Canada. In Switzerland, the autonomy of cantons over tax policy is also guaranteed by the constitution. Cantons have access to personal income taxes, corporate income taxes, wealth and inheritance taxes, among others, and the constitution provides them freedom to set tax rates, as well as defining the tax bases and special provisions.

State level governments in all other federations have less access to broad-based taxes and enjoy less revenue-raising autonomy (see Table 2). In Australia, all main broad-based taxes are levied by the federal government. That includes personal income taxes, corporate income taxes, the value-added tax, customs duties, and various excise taxes. Subnational governments levy less than 20% of total government tax revenues. In South Africa, the constitution gives provinces the power to impose surcharges on all taxes, except the corporate income tax, the VAT, and custom duties, subject to the approval of the federal government. In practice, however, provincial governments collect very little own-source tax revenues. In fact, local governments have more flexibility than provincial governments with respect to their own tax sources, in particular the property tax.

Table 2 Taxation powers and revenue decentralization

	Taxation powers/autonomy of states	*Taxation powers/autonomy of local governments*	*Shared taxes and formula-based revenue-sharing*	*Size of vertical fiscal gap*	*Size of horizontal fiscal imbalances (before equalization)*
Australia	Low	Low	No	Large	Moderate
Brazil	Low	Moderate	Yes	Moderate	Large
Canada	High	High	No	Moderate	Small
Ethiopia	Moderate	Low	Yes	Large	Large
Germany	Low	Moderate	Yes	Moderate	Moderate
India	Moderate	Low	Yes	Large	Large
Italy	Low	Low	Yes	Large	Moderate
South Africa	Low	Low	Yes	Large	Large
Spain	Moderate	Moderate	Yes	Moderate	Moderate
Switzerland	High	High	No	Small	Small
United States	High	High	No	Small	Small

2.2 Asymmetries in Taxation Powers

There are asymmetries across subnational units in the allocation of tax powers in Spain and Italy, although taxation remains relatively centralized in both countries. In Spain, Autonomous Communities under the common regime have a fair degree of autonomy in setting tax rates, credits, and other special provisions for some of the main revenue-raising taxes including the personal income tax, and taxes on wealth, and inheritances. In the case of the Autonomous Communities operating under the charter regime (Navarre and Basque Country), these taxes, among a few others, are fully decentralized. This is an important element of asymmetry in the Spanish fiscal federalism system. In Italy, ordinary regions have very little taxation autonomy. Most of their tax revenues come from devolved taxes, which are largely set and controlled by the central government with limited regional flexibility, regional surtaxes imposed on central government taxes, and a few own taxes which raise relatively little revenues. Overall, in ordinary regions, tax revenues account for less than half of total regional government revenues, the rest coming from transfers. The constitution provides more taxation autonomy to special regions. For example, they have more flexibility in setting tax rates on devolved taxes. However, given that all the main revenue-raising taxes are largely occupied by the central government, in practice the effective taxation autonomy is relatively limited even in the case of special regions.

2.3 Shared Taxes and Formula-Based Revenue-Sharing

In some federations, there are constitutionally based shared taxes and revenue-sharing systems. In Germany, for example, the main broad-based taxes are shared taxes. The revenues from the personal income tax, the VAT, and the withholding tax are shared between all three levels of government in predetermined proportions while revenues from the corporate income tax are shared equally between the federal government and the Laender. Through representation in the Bundersrat, Laender determine, jointly and cooperatively with federal government representatives, the definition of tax bases and tax rates for these shared taxes. Hence, both levels of government have limited exclusive autonomy in terms of taxation.

There is an extensive constitutionally established revenue-sharing system in Brazil that also applies to the main broad-based taxes. Revenues from the federal income tax and tax on manufactured goods are shared in fixed proportions among the three levels of government while revenues from state value-added taxes, motor vehicle taxes, rural property, and other minor taxes are shared with local governments. The federal government has little discretion over the size of the revenue-sharing transfers and these transfers are largely unconditional. Hence, despite having relatively limited taxation autonomy, subnational governments have high revenue autonomy given that their shares of revenues collected on several tax bases are constitutionally guaranteed.

In India, revenue-sharing with state governments applies for all Union government taxes which includes all the main broad-based taxes. The percentage of revenues transferred to states and the allocation among states is determined by the Union government based on recommendations from an independent expert commission. The distribution of revenues among states is formula-based. It takes into account several criteria and is intended to act as an equalization mechanism based on interstate disparities in both fiscal capacities and expenditure needs.

2.4 Own-Source Revenues of Subnational Governments

The own-source revenues of subnational governments combined is above 50% of total government revenues in Canada, and above 40% in Switzerland and the United States (see Fig. 2). At the other end of the spectrum, that proportion is below 20% in South Africa and Italy. Subnational governments in India, Germany, and Brazil have substantial own-source revenues, although much of these revenues come from shared taxes over which subnational governments have little discretion. At the same time, their share of revenues from shared taxes is determined by formula-based revenue-sharing systems. Hence, subnational governments in these countries enjoy strong revenue autonomy but little tax policymaking authority.

2.5 Natural Resource Taxation

In all federations that are well endowed in natural resources, the assignment of tax powers and the allocation of resource revenues are sources of tension. Natural resources are often highly concentrated geographically implying that subnational ownership and taxation of resources generate fiscal disparities among subnational units. At the same time, centralized

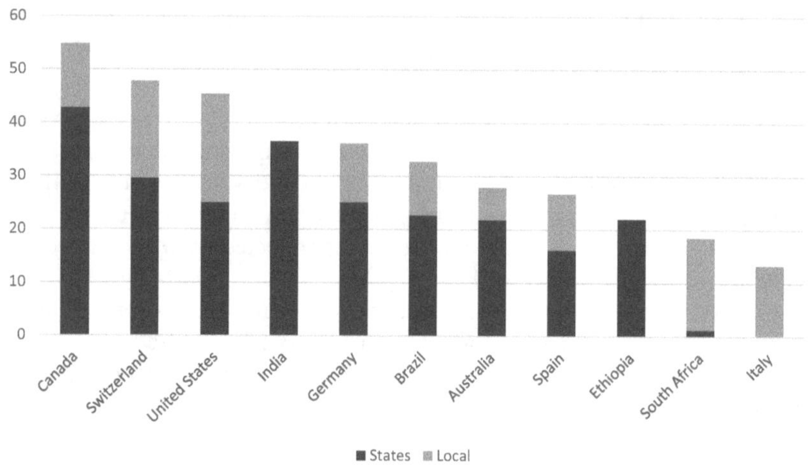

Fig. 2 Share of revenues, excluding grants received from other governments, in total government revenues (%) (*Sources* IMF Government Finance Statistics and various chapters from this book. Data is for 2019 for all countries except Ethiopia [2017], India [2017], and South Africa [2018]. Data not available for local governments in Ethiopia and in India. Data for local governments in Italy includes all subnational governments)

management and taxation of natural resources is often perceived as unwarranted, especially when extraction activity imposes local environmental costs (e.g. Boadway and Shah, 2009; Anderson, 2010).

In some federations, subnational ownership of resources is established by the constitution. That is the case in Canada. The Canadian Constitution gives exclusive jurisdiction over natural resource management to provincial governments as well as the exclusive right to impose taxes on renewable and non-renewable resources. This is an important source of horizontal disparities and tensions. In the United States, the federal government can impose royalties on resources extracted offshore or from federal lands. States have the power to levy taxes on fossil fuels and the majority of them do so. In Australia, state governments own natural resources and impose various resource royalties. In Brazil, royalties on natural resources are shared between all three levels of government, on a derivation basis, with local governments being the main beneficiaries. As in Canada and Australia, resources generate substantial government revenues in resource-rich areas and are sources of horizontal fiscal disparities.

2.6 Vertical Fiscal Gaps

In all federations, there is greater decentralization in terms of expenditures than in terms of taxation. This implies that subnational governments' own-source revenues fall short of their expenditures. In other words, it gives rise to vertical fiscal gaps that are filled by intergovernmental transfers. The size of vertical fiscal gaps varies widely across countries, as reported in Table 3 where vertical fiscal gaps are measured by the difference between the revenue share and the expenditure share for each level of government.

Vertical fiscal gaps at the state level are largest in South Africa, where the own-source revenues of provincial governments represent less than two percent of total public sector revenues. Vertical fiscal gaps are also sizeable in Ethiopia, India, Australia, and Spain. In some countries, vertical fiscal gaps are larger at the local government level than at the state level. That is the case when local governments rely more heavily on transfers to finance their expenditures. This holds in Brazil, Canada, Germany, and the United States. Based on vertical fiscal gaps, the relative fiscal autonomy of local governments is greater than that of state level governments in Australia, South Africa, Spain, and Switzerland.

3 Fiscal Transfer Systems

The intergovernmental transfer system is a critical pillar of any fiscal federalism system. In addition to filling the vertical fiscal gap, and therefore accommodating greater decentralization of expenditures than taxation, it serves several other purposes (Boadway, 2007). Most importantly, it contributes to horizontal equity by equalizing fiscal capacities across subnational units. Intergovernmental grants are also used to pursue various national objectives such as achieving standards in the provision of public services, inducing policy harmonization across subnational units, and promoting economic efficiency and development. Transfers also play a risk-sharing function among subnational governments (von Hagen, 2007).

Table 3 Vertical fiscal gaps

		Share of revenues			*Fiscal gap*	
		Before transfer	*After transfer*	*Share of expenditures*	*Before transfer*	*After transfer*
Australia	Central	72.14	60.74	55.54	16.60	5.20
	State	21.83	33.45	38.78	−16.95	−5.33
	Local	6.03	5.81	5.68	0.35	0.13
Brazil	Central	67.27	55.29	57.33	9.94	−2.04
	State	22.68	25.65	23.12	−0.44	2.53
	Local	10.05	19.06	19.55	−9.50	−0.49
Canada	Central	45.27	37.89	32.45	12.82	5.44
	State	42.83	44.41	46.84	−4.01	−2.43
	Local	11.90	17.70	20.71	−8.81	−3.01
Ethiopia	Central	78.00	NA	54.00	24.00	NA
	State	22.00	NA	46.00	−24.00	NA
Germany	Central	63.84	57.46	59.32	4.52	−1.86
	State	25.12	26.29	22.22	2.90	4.07
	Local	11.04	16.25	18.46	−7.42	−2.21
India	Central	63.50	46.82	41.44	22.06	5.38
	State	36.50	53.18	58.56	−22.06	−5.38
Italy	Central	86.70	75.01	75.45	11.24	−0.44
	Local	13.30	24.99	24.55	−11.24	0.44
South Africa	Central	81.49	57.06	41.81	39.69	15.26
	State	1.25	25.43	36.17	−34.92	−10.74
	Local	17.26	17.51	22.02	−4.77	−4.52
Spain	Central	73.34	58.56	55.44	17.90	3.12
	State	16.19	28.94	32.88	−16.68	−3.93
	Local	10.47	12.50	11.68	−1.22	0.82
Switzerland	Central	52.25	46.80	42.12	10.13	4.68
	State	29.54	35.16	38.35	−8.81	−3.19
	Local	18.21	18.05	19.53	−1.32	−1.49
United States	Central	54.65	45.32	47.59	7.06	−2.27
	State	25.07	29.63	25.24	−0.16	4.40
	Local	20.27	25.04	27.17	−6.90	−2.13

Sources Computed using data from IMF Government Finance Statistics and various chapters from this book

Data is for 2019 for all countries except Ethiopia (2017), India (2017) and South Africa (2018)

Data not available for local governments in Ethiopia and in India

Data for local governments in Italy includes all subnational governments

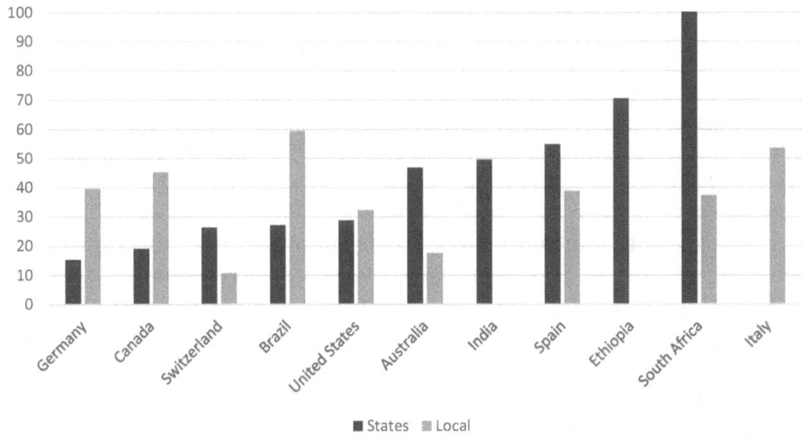

Fig. 3 Transfers received by state and local governments as a percentage of their expenditures (%) (*Sources* IMF Government Finance Statistics and various chapters from this book. Data is for 2019 for all countries except Ethiopia [2017], India [2017], and South Africa [2018]. Data not available for local governments in Ethiopia and in India. Data for local governments in Italy includes all subnational governments)

3.1 Subnational Governments' Reliance on Transfers

State level governments finance most of their expenditures with their own revenues in some countries while they are heavily dependent on transfers in others, as shown in Fig. 3. Transfers received by states represent less than 20% of state governments' expenditures in Germany and Canada, and less than 30% in Switzerland, Brazil, and the United States. In contrast, that proportion is around 70% in Ethiopia and close to 100% in South Africa. In some countries, local governments rely much more heavily on transfers than state level governments. That is the case in Germany, Canada, and Brazil. The opposite holds in Switzerland, Australia, and South Africa.

3.2 Equalization

The key objective of equalization is pursued, to varying degrees, in the transfer systems of all eleven countries surveyed in previous chapters. However, there is a variety of ways in which transfer systems are designed to do so. In some countries, equalization transfers are based on estimates of both fiscal capacities and expenditure needs and transfer systems aim for a high equalization standard (see Table 4). That is the case in Australia where equalization transfers are financed from the federal goods and services tax (GST). The allocation of transfers is based on fiscal capacities and expenditure needs, estimated from three-year averages of revenues collected across states and levels of services provided. The system is designed to ensure that each state has the capacity to provide the same level of services assuming equal revenue-raising effort and equal efficiency. Canada's equalization system has a similar objective, i.e., ensuring that all provinces have the capacity to provide comparable public services at comparable tax rates. However, transfers are determined only by disparities in fiscal capacities, not expenditure needs.

Germany's equalization program is mainly implemented through VAT revenue redistribution. This is part of the revenue-sharing system among the three levels of governments but the allocation of VAT revenues across Laender involves an equalization component. There are also additional transfers from the federal government to Laender intended to further close fiscal disparities and to address specific fiscal needs of some Laender. Overall, the standard of equalization is very high, leaving little post-transfer fiscal disparities across Laender.

In South Africa, equalization transfers are mandated by the constitution to provide subnational governments with an equitable share of national revenues. The allocation formula takes into account different indicators of expenditure needs, such as population in various age-groups and poverty rates, as well as provincial GDP as a proxy for fiscal capacity. However, given the extremely centralized nature of the tax system, the weight of provincial fiscal disparities in determining the allocation of transfers is small. Transfers are largely determined by provincial expenditure needs. The federal government also provides unconditional transfers to local governments which are largely based on expenditure needs but also take into account revenue-raising capacity. Despite this, the equalization impact of transfers in practice, both at the provincial and local levels, is relatively limited.

Some equalization systems involve horizontal transfers, although that is quite uncommon. It is the case in Switzerland where two types of equalization transfers to cantons are in place, one type targeting differences in cantonal tax capacities and the other intended to compensate for differences in expenditure needs. The first type is a horizontal transfer system

Table 4 Intergovernmental transfer systems

	Size of central-state transfers	*Extent of fiscal equalization*	*Equalization of state fiscal capacities*	*Equalization of state fiscal needs*	*Conditionality of central-state transfers*	*Advisory fiscal commission*
Australia	Large	High	Yes	Yes	Moderate	Yes
Brazil	Moderate	Low	No	Yes	Moderate	No
Canada	Moderate	Moderate	Yes	No	Weak	No
Ethiopia	Large	High	Yes	Yes	Weak	No
Germany	Moderate	High	Yes	No	Weak	No
India	Large	Moderate	Yes	Yes	Moderate	Yes
Italy	Large	Moderate	Yes	Yes	Weak	Yes
South Africa	Large	Moderate	No	Yes	Moderate	Yes
Spain	Moderate	High	No	Yes	Strong	Yes
Switzerland	Moderate	Moderate	Yes	Yes	Weak	No
United States	Small	Low	No	No	Moderate	No

in which cantons with above-average tax capacities contribute to the pool of funds while cantons with below-average capacities receive an equalization payment intended to bring their tax capacity to 85% of the national average. Tax capacities are based on income, profits, and wealth taxes. The second type of equalization involves transfers from the federal government to cantons with relatively high expenditure needs. Measures of expenditure needs are based on geographic and topographic factors (e.g. mountainous area) and socio-economic factors (e.g. population density).

In some countries, there are asymmetries in how the transfer system applies to different groups of regions. That is the case in Spain and Italy. In Spain, equalization transfers are provided to Autonomous Communities that are under the common regime (all but two). Transfers are calculated based on expenditure needs and fiscal capacities. For fundamental public services, expenditure needs calculations take into account the total population, as well as the proportion of elderly and of school-age children, the size of the geographic area and population dispersion, among others. Autonomous Communities under the charter system (Navarre and Basque Country) are not part of the equalization system. In fact, because tax decentralization is much more pronounced in Navarre and Basque Country than in the rest of the country, and given their relatively high fiscal capacities, these two Autonomous Communities are making net transfers to the central government which are intended as their contributions to financing some public services provided by the central government. Hence, these two Autonomous Communities are financing all of their expenditures out of their own revenues.

Italy is slowly transitioning to an equalization system involving fiscal capacity and expenditure needs equalization among regions. Fiscal capacity calculation will take into account regional devolved taxes, regional surtaxes on personal income taxes, and the regional share of the VAT. The equalization system applies only to ordinary regions. In the case of special regions, regional government funding is largely based on revenue-sharing of national taxes. The regional share of revenues is transferred on a derivation basis and the regional share of revenues varies across regions. Therefore, ordinary regions and special regions are subject to completely different transfer systems.

Some countries do not have intergovernmental transfers explicitly designed as equalization transfers, although transfers may still have implicit equalizing effects. For example, there is no explicit system of federal-state equalization transfers in the United States. There is, however, an implicit equalizing element in federal-state transfers for Medicaid to the extent that these are matching grants (so involves some implicit needs equalization) with matching rates being higher for relatively poorer states. Federal grants to school districts are based on low-income concentration so are also implicitly equalizing. There is no system of equalization transfers in Brazil either. There is an extensive constitutionally established revenue-sharing system and sizeable conditional grants, but with relatively limited redistributive effects.

3.3 Decision-making Process for Transfer Systems and Advisory Fiscal Commissions

In some countries, the size and allocation of transfers are largely determined by the central government. This is essentially the case in Switzerland, for example. Centralized decision-making results in transfer systems that are generally more flexible and responsive to fiscal shocks or to changing circumstances. However, it also tends to provide the central government with more power to influence subnational programs, sometimes excessively (Spahn, 2007). At times, there is also a tendency for central governments to reduce transfers to subnational governments in response to their own fiscal pressures resulting in distortions to the optimal allocation of public funds.

In other countries, transfers are determined, at least to some extent, through intergovernmental consultations and negotiations (Shah, 2007). In Canada, for example, federal-provincial meetings sometimes lead to negotiated changes to the transfer system. This provides opportunities for provinces to participate in the decision-making process, although achieving consensus is always difficult given competing provincial interests. In other countries, subnational influence on the transfer system is achieved through subnational representation in national institutions. In Germany, Laender has some impact through representation in the Bundersrat, the upper house of parliament. The House of Federation in Ethiopia, which is the upper house of Parliament and is composed of members elected by state councils, has the power to review and approve budgetary measures of the national governments that impact states including intergovernmental transfers. In fact, the total pool of funds available for equalization is determined by the federal government but the House of Federation determines the formula for allocating transfers across states.

Transfers are, in other countries, determined on the basis of recommendations from advisory commissions. In India, the Finance Commission provides recommendations about the vertical and horizontal distribution of revenues from Union taxes as well as about the size and allocation of specific-purpose grants to states. The commission is appointed by the President and is renewed every five-year. The commission is independent from the union and state governments, it is composed of experts on intergovernmental fiscal issues, and its recommendations are usually adopted by the government. In Australia, the Commonwealth Grants Commission is an independent expert body responsible for assessing the fiscal capacities and spending needs of states that are used to determine equalization payments. The Commission is appointed by the federal government, partly based on consultations with the states. Once appointed, the commission is largely independent. The commission has an advisory role only, but its recommendations are usually adopted by the government.

In contrast to the cases of India and Australia, advisory commissions are not always as influential. In South Africa, the Financial and Fiscal Commission is responsible for making recommendations about the size and allocation of federal transfers to provincial and local governments. The constitution, which establishes the commission, requires that the recommendations be taken into account by the government. However, there is no obligation for the government to adopt them, and in practice, recommendations are not always adopted. The Financial and Fiscal Commission is also consulted on matters of government borrowing and debt.

Fiscal commissions sometimes play various roles with respect to fiscal monitoring and dispute resolution. In Spain, implementation issues and disputes about the revenue assignment system are referred to the Fiscal and Financial Policy Council, which is an intergovernmental body with members from the central government and from the Autonomous Communities. It is responsible for assessing the revenue assignment system and submitting reform recommendations to the National Parliament. In Italy, the Permanent Conference for the Coordination of Public Finance is an advisory body that provides advice regarding the equalization system and budgetary objectives and monitors the public finances of subnational governments to ensure compliance with budgetary objectives.

4 Macroeconomic Management

Rules and mechanisms to induce good macroeconomic governance are crucial in federal systems, especially when fiscal decentralization is relatively pronounced. Harmonization of tax policies is important for the efficiency of internal economic unions. Fiscal rules and coordination mechanisms are central in maintaining fiscal discipline and achieving sound public finance management.

4.1 Tax Policy Harmonization

Some federal systems have been more successful than others at inducing tax policy harmonization and mitigating harmful tax competition (see Table 5). Canada, for instance, has done well in this area despite very pronounced tax decentralization. While Canadian provinces have substantial autonomy in setting tax policy, tax collection agreements between the federal and provincial governments have succeeded in maintaining a relatively harmonized system, both vertically and horizontally. In the case of the corporate income tax, for example, tax collection agreements preclude provincial governments from adopting measures that would discriminate against corporate taxpayers from other provinces. Tax collection agreements also include a formula-apportionment system that serves to allocate the taxable income of firms that operate in multiple provinces. This

Table 5 Macroeconomic management

	Tax harmonization across states	*Restrictions on subnational borrowing*	*Fiscal rules/ fiscal policy coordination*	*Fiscal discipline at subnational level*
Australia	Moderate	Strong	Strong	Strong
Brazil	Low	Moderate	Moderate	Weak
Canada	High	Weak	Weak	Strong
Ethiopia	High	Strong	Strong	Weak
Germany	High	Moderate	Strong	Moderate
India	High	Strong	Moderate	Weak
Italy	High	Moderate	Moderate	Weak
South Africa	High	Moderate	Moderate	Strong
Spain	Moderate	Moderate	Strong	Weak
Switzerland	Low	Moderate	Weak	Strong
United States	Low	Weak	Weak	Strong

mitigates tax avoidance practices by firms as well as tax competition incentives of provincial governments. Likewise, in Spain, while Autonomous Communities operating under the common regime have considerable autonomy in setting tax rates and tax credits for most direct taxes, they generally use essentially the same centrally defined tax bases, so the tax system remains relatively well harmonized. However, there is much less harmonization between the Autonomous Communities under the common regime and those under the charter regime where policymaking over direct taxes is almost fully decentralized. In Ethiopia, harmonization of state and federal tax systems is required by the Federal Financial Administration Law and coordinated by the federal ministry of finance. Harmonization is certainly facilitated by the high degree of tax centralization relative to most other federal systems, but the mechanisms in place have nonetheless been relatively successful.

Other countries have not had as much success at inducing tax policy harmonization. In the US, there are wide variations in income tax rates across states, as well as in the definition of taxable income because of state-specific provisions. As a result, there is limited harmonization of income tax systems across states. In Switzerland, harmonization of cantonal tax policies is relatively limited. Moreover, the high level of autonomy of cantons and tax policy flexibility has apparently led to considerable tax competition. There is little harmonization of state value-added taxes in Brazil where substantial variations exist in rates applying on different types of goods or according to the origin or destination of interstate sales. This lack of harmonization is an important source of economic inefficiency given that the state value-added tax is the tax instrument that raises the most revenues in the Brazilian federation.

4.2 *Restrictions on Borrowing at Subnational Level*

Various types of restrictions on subnational borrowing, especially at the local level, apply in all countries. For example, long-term borrowing by municipalities is only allowed for the financing of capital expenditures in Australia, Canada, Germany, and South Africa. In Ethiopia, the federal government sets conditions under which states can borrow and all state borrowing must be approved by the federal ministry of finance. In Switzerland, cantons are required by law to maintain budget balance in the medium term and most cantons have debt brake laws intended to limit the growth of public debt, in most cases with reasonable success. In

South Africa, the right to borrow from states and municipalities is guaranteed by the constitution but subject to various conditions and controls. In Australia, some local governments must borrow directly from state governments, and state budgetary deficits and borrowing are coordinated by the Australian Loan Council.

4.3 *Fiscal Rules, Coordination,* and *Fiscal Discipline*

Some fiscal coordination is ensured in Germany through the Stability Council, which is composed of federal and Laender ministers of finance. The Council monitors compliance with fiscal rules regarding budgetary balance and recommends adjustment measures when the federal government or state governments do not comply. In Spain, the Budgetary Stability and Financial Sustainability Law requires all governments to achieve structural budget balance, with exceptions allowed during emergencies or serious economic crises. The law also imposes a ceiling on the growth rate of government expenditures, which cannot exceed the medium-term growth rate of GDP. At the same time, central government funds (Fund for Financing Autonomous Communities) have been used to provide liquidities to subnational governments running deficits. While the Budgetary Stability and Financial Sustainability Law has had some success, the mechanisms put in place to provide liquidities in response to subnational fiscal imbalances have arguably led to a soft-budget constraint problem. In Brazil, the Fiscal Responsibility Law was put in place in 2000 to achieve more fiscal discipline at all three levels of government. The law imposes limits on debt and debt service payments as a share of current revenues, as well as constraints on the establishment of new recurrent spending. In Switzerland, the strong direct democracy tradition has contributed to fiscal discipline at the cantonal level. In most cantons, significant increases in government expenditures require public approval by referendum as long as a successful petition is launched to request it.

5 Challenges to Fiscal Federalism Systems

There are many common challenges to fiscal federalism systems. Most importantly perhaps, achieving and maintaining fiscal balance, both vertically and horizontally, is a constant concern in most of the countries surveyed. For many of them, the vertical fiscal balance is currently threatened by the fiscal implications of demographic trends. Government functions that are most heavily impacted by population aging, including health care, public services targeted at the elderly such as long-term care, as well as pensions and income support programs for retirees are often largely performed by subnational governments. In countries where that is the case, demographic trends are imposing great fiscal stress on subnational governments and tend to produce vertical fiscal imbalances. This generates pressure for more revenue decentralization. That is the case in Canada, for example, where the expenditures of provincial governments on health care are growing much more rapidly than other public spending and than public sector revenues. It is also the case in the United States where, in addition to rapidly rising public health care costs, underfunded pension systems are imposing severe fiscal pressure on many state and local governments. Several other countries are facing similar issues, to varying degrees.

Subnational governments in all countries surveyed are calling for greater revenue decentralization and subnational revenue autonomy, some with more success than others. At the same time, revenue decentralization tends to exacerbate the potential for horizontal fiscal imbalances. The capacity of transfer systems to maintain horizontal fiscal balance is challenged in several countries. This has been a concern in Brazil, Ethiopia, India, South Africa, and Spain, for example. In some countries, especially Australia, Brazil, and Canada, horizontal imbalances tend to be aggravated by the unequal distribution of natural resource revenues.

In several of the countries surveyed, there are strong pressures for disentangling some of the functions and tasks of different orders of government to improve effectiveness in the delivery of public services and promote accountability. Such pressures tend to emerge in countries where central government influence in areas of concurrent or shared responsibilities is perceived to be excessive. In recent times, this has been the case in Germany, Spain, Switzerland, South Africa, and Italy, for example. Clarifying roles and responsibilities is crucial to safeguarding effective subnational autonomy. It is also critical for government responsiveness to shocks or to changing circumstances, as was highlighted in many countries following the start of the Covid-19 pandemic. Some lack of clarity about the powers and responsibilities of different orders of government with respect to public safety and public health in emergency situations has been problematic in some countries, at least in the early stages of the pandemic. At the same time, the pandemic also highlighted the need for intergovernmental coordination and cooperation in the areas of public health and public safety.

Fiscal arrangements, especially the tax system, are important to the efficiency of internal economic spaces in federations. In some countries, tax policy harmonization is a key concern. The lack of effective harmonization mechanisms can lead to tax competition, which has arguably been the case in Switzerland where cantons enjoy high autonomy in setting tax policies. Limited harmonization of tax policies can also impede interregional trade patterns. This has been an issue with respect to value-added taxes in Brazil. There are also concerns about variations in the structures and rates of income taxes in the United States, Spain, and Canada.

Finally, maintaining fiscal discipline is a difficult challenge in all federal systems. Designing fiscal arrangements leads to tensions between, on the one hand, sharing fiscal risks across subnational governments and promoting horizontal fiscal balance, and on the one hand, maintaining strong incentives for fiscal discipline. The dramatic impacts of the Covid-19 pandemic on budgetary balances will only make this challenge more difficult.

References

Anderson, G. (2008), *Federalism: An Introduction*, Oxford University Press, 85 pages.

Anderson, G. (2010), *Fiscal Federalism: A Comparative Introduction*, Oxford University Press, 96 pages.

Boadway, R. (2007), 'Grants in a Federal Economy: A Conceptual Perspective', in *Intergovernmental Fiscal Transfers: Principles and Practice*, in R. Boadway and A. Shah (eds), The World Bank, Washington, DC.

Boadway, R. and A. Shah (2009), *Fiscal Federalism: Principles and Practice of Multiorder Governance*, Cambridge University Press, 620 pages.

Shah, A. (2007), 'Institutional Arrangements for Intergovernmental Fiscal Transfers and a Framework for Evaluation', in *Intergovernmental Fiscal Transfers: Principles and Practice*, in R. Boadway and A. Shah (eds), The World Bank, Washington, DC.

Spahn, P. B. (2007), 'Resolving Fiscal Conflicts', in *Unity in Diversity: Learning from each Other*, Proceedings of the 4th International Conference on Federalism, Forum of Federations.

Von Hagen, Jurgen (2007), 'Achieving Economic Stabilization by Sharing Risk within Countries', in *Intergovernmental Fiscal Transfers: Principles and Practice*, in R. Boadway and A. Shah (eds), The World Bank, Washington, DC.

Index

J.-F. Tremblay (ed.), *The Forum of Federations Handbook of Fiscal Federalism*, https://doi.org/10.1007/978-3-030-97258-5

FSC
www.fsc.org
MIX
Papier | Fördert gute Waldnutzung
FSC® C083411

Kolibri 360 GmbH
Ferdinand-Jühlke-Straße 7
99095 Erfurt, Deutschland
produktsicherheit@kolibri360.de